Representations of Justice

P.I.E. Peter Lang

Bruxelles · Bern · Berlin · Frankfurt am Main · New York · Oxford · Wien

Antoine MASSON & Kevin O'CONNOR (eds.)

Representations of Justice

Book supported by the Fonds National de la Recherche
(Luxembourg)

Cover Picture © "Au Palais" by H. Daumier, published in Paris
Guide, Lacroix and Verboeckhoven, 1867, Vol. 2, p. 1826.
www.daumier-register.org.

© P.I.E. PETER LANG S.A.
Éditions scientifiques internationales
Brussels, 2007
1 avenue Maurice, B-1050 Bruxelles, Belgium
www.peterlang.com; info@peterlang.com

Printed in Germany

ISBN 978-90-5201-349-7
D/2007/5678/44

Bibliographic information published by "Die Deutsche Bibliothek"

"Die Deutsche Bibliothek" lists this publication in the "Deutsche Nationalbibliografie";
detailed bibliographic data is available on the Internet at <http://dnb.ddb.de>.

CIP available from the British Library, GB
and the Library of Congress, USA.

We are extremely thankful to Alberte, Yvonne, Jacques, Anne and especially to Claire and Julien who married this year.

Preface

Kevin O'CONNOR

The law, as represented on television and cinema is always dramatic. Ask a law student as to why he or she decided to do law and some will answer that they were influenced by a television series or a cinema production and the portrayal of justice and the legal system in that media. They see the lawyer as a champion of the oppressed, introducing dramatic evidence which results in an acquittal or an unexpected win, when all the evidence appears to go against the accused. They see the lawyer as extracting the truth from a witness who, up to a certain point, had adhered to a particular version of the story which was prejudicial to the lawyer's client. Through skilful cross-examination they see the lawyer 'breaking the witness down' leading to an acquittal.

Thus, in choosing a profession, television and cinema have probably influenced young people at the outset as to what career they may choose. The same cannot be said for accountancy, dentistry (but not medicine), or some of the other less public professions. Thus television and cinema appear to play a large role in creating a first impression of the law and the role of the lawyer in the court system; a fact borne out in the articles of this book.

But, of course, to obtain good television ratings or to make the film a marketable commodity or even a box office hit, the courtroom drama has to be dramatic. As all lawyers know however, dramatic cases are few and far between. Evidence is produced long before a hearing and trials are generally predictable affairs, more so now that trial 'by ambush' is generally frowned upon by the judiciary. Most of a lawyer's time is taken up with mundane matters where lawyers have to earn their 'bread and butter'. Such unexciting issues as the transfer of property, dealing in succession matters or road traffic offences would be typical of their day to day work. Barristers spend their time waiting in courts for their cases to be called, adjourning cases, applying for discovery orders or making intoxicating liquor licence applications – all quite undramatic in content and form.

In the courtroom drama, the administration of justice always seems to be speedy and efficient; cases do not appear to go to courts of appeal or to a Supreme Court or Constitutional Court. Such matters would not be of interest to the viewer. The viewer is not interested in the internal workings of the administration of justice. The viewer just wants the decision and for justice to be done. This 'feel good' factor makes such series popular.

However the media can sometimes act as an objective critic of the administration of justice and indeed of members of the judiciary. It can question decisions of judges, criticise the inordinate delays which appear to be a feature of most judicial systems, mock the judiciary where the judiciary appear to be out of touch or elitist (the example of the High Court judge who, after hearing Counsel's description of a Defendant's attire, asks "What is a 't-shirt'?" comes to mind).

The television lawyer is a figment of a writer's imagination and the role thus depicted can be far removed from reality. The articles produced in this collection develop that theme in depth by looking at various aspects of the representations of the Courts and the administration of justice generally. They look at such representations in different countries and not only in the present era but also in the late 19th and 20th Centuries.

It is fundamental to the proper administration of justice that justice is not only done but must be seen to be done. The articles in this book show that the various media, when representing justice, go some considerable way to portraying the means by which justice is seen to be done albeit at times for reasons of commerciality rather than the common good.

Contents

Preface 9
Kevin O'Connor

List of Figures and Tables 13

Introduction to the Interactions between Law
and Representation of Justice 15
Antoine Masson

PART I
LAW, POPULAR CULTURE AND REPRESENTATION OF JUSTICE

Allegory of Justice and Representation of Punishment
in Crime Fiction. A Franco-Irish Comparison 23
Dominique Jeannerod

The Administration of Justice as Portrayed in *Le Charivari*
and *Le Journal Amusant* at the End of the 19th Century.
Scepticism and Derision 39
Solange Vernois

Decoding Justice. Intellectual Discourse
and the Trial of the Malagasy Deputies 59
Mairéad Ni Bhriain

Developments in Law and Popular Culture.
The Case of the TV Lawyer 75
Peter Robson

The Portrayal of the Judicial Process
in the French and Irish Media 95
Pascale Duparc Portier and Laurent Pech

Portrayal of Justice on German Television 115
Ruth Herz

A History of Representations of Justice.
Coincident Preoccupations of Law and Film 131
Jessica Silbey

PART II
JUSTICE IN ACTION: REPRESENTATION AND REFLECTION

Representation of the Legal Profession on Television.
Professional Ethics and Client Expectations 155
  Barbara Villez

Talk of Law. Contested and Conventional Legality 173
  Susan S. Silbey

From 'Rites' to 'Rights' of Audience. The Utilities and
Contingencies of the Public's Role in Court-Based Processes 195
  Judith Resnik and Dennis E. Curtis

Representation of the European Court of Justice. Conscience
of the People of Europe or Political Juggernaut? 237
  Claire Micheau and Alexander Conrad Culley

Deconstructing 'Justice' and Reconstructing 'Fairness'
in a Convergent European Justice System. An Aristotelian
Approach to the Question of Representation of Justice
in Europe 249
  Theo Gavrielides

PART III
ECONOMICS PERSPECTIVES OF REPRESENTATION OF JUSTICE

Representation of Justice in Law and Economics 271
  Bruno Deffains and Samuel Ferey

Representation of Justice and Companies Judicial
Strategies in France 289
  Didier Danet

Representations of Justice in Economic Comparisons
of Legal Systems 307
  Thierry Kirat

Cross Representations of Law and Economics
in Corporate Governance Approach 325
  Tristan Boyer

Index 335

Personalia 341

List of Figures and Tables

Baric, 'Nos Paysans', *Le Journal Amusant,*
3 février 1894, No. 1953, p. 2 43

Léonnec, 'Ruraux', *Le Journal Amusant,*
8 avril 1893, No. 1910, p. 6 48

Henriot, 'Gens de Justice', *Les Maîtres Humoristes,*
2ᵉ série, No. 8, 1909 54

'L'Arrivée d'un Train en Gare',
Auguste et Louis Lumière, 1895 135

'Trip to the Moon', Georges Méliès, 1902 136

'The Great Train Robbery', Edwin S. Porter, 1903 138

'The Cabinet of Doctor Caligari', Robert Wiene, 1920 138

'M', Fritz Lang's, 1931 144

'The Vierschaar' in the Town Hall of Amsterdam 199

'The Judgment of Brutus' 201

'The Blinding of Zaleucus' 202

A Comparison of Court-based and Administrative
Judiciaries in the US Federal System (as of 2002) 218

A Comparison of the Numbers of Evidentiary
Proceedings in US Federal Courts and
in Four Federal Agencies (2001) 218

Introduction to the Interactions between Law and Representation of Justice

Antoine MASSON

University of Luxembourg

Justice is a system of representation: Representation of truth by litigating parties in their arguments and embodiment by legal system themselves of their own powers. However the image given is not always the one perceived. The public understanding of law is gleaned from cultural representations of Justice which reflects in fact, popular culture. Movies, caricatures, portrayal of trials by media or crime fiction shape the image of justice.

The result of this is that various systems for the representation of justice merge into one concept based on individual expectation, collective phantasms and historical myths meet. These systems of popular representations have certainly a distorting effect, but they also contribute to make law more familiar for the citizens, though not fully understood. Indeed, as Pierre Bourdieux noted: the Law certainly makes Society, but no one must forget that Society also makes the Law. Some anecdotes provoke a smile, like the one concerning a criminal who tried to physically attack his lawyer because he hadn't use enough lawyer' tricks as in certain TV shows, but we observe that analyzing Law without a reference to its cognitive environment does not allow us to fully understand legal practice and judicial behaviour. For example, the symbolic force attached to the concept of 'Human rights' is used in many speeches of political justification (i.e. Guantanamo), that exploit the various meanings of this term and the different legal realities to which it can refer.

However, there is always a gap between Law and Justice. Each system is based on the accepted notion of Justice by Society which entrusts its application and enforcement to lawyers and judges. But the application of legal principles doesn't always mean the application of the principles of equity and fair play. Firstly, 'Justice' can be an ambiguous notion, and secondly application of the legal rules supposes a simplification of social relations. Facing this dichotomy, an increased importance was given in the popular culture to the trial which only implements rights and gives consistency to Law ('Law in action'). Indeed, traditionally, in order to perpetuate this difference between law and Justice, legal systems seek to reconcile the judicial decision or ruling with the concept of Justice in such way that the visibility of Justice in Court will enhance the legitimacy of Justice and facilitate the enforcement of the Law. Thus the adage that Justice must not only be done but it must be seen to be done. Therefore, legal systems were victims of the image which they have contributed themselves to create. Indeed, the increasing mobilization of Law illustrates the rising importance played by the Representations of the Law in everyday life. Whereas a certain number of collective conflicts, for example related to labour, were formerly settled in a non legal way such as strikes or negotiations, they are now adjudicated in court rooms. The case of legal activism is interesting in that it is emblematic of the interactions between Law and Justice.

Firstly, the militant lawyer is himself an iconographic object. He enjoys a particular notoriety in public opinion. He incarnates the ideal of Justice. Standing up, its index finger pointed accusingly; his words are pronounced with force in order to be engraved in everyone's memory! Selfless, he is ready to sacrifice everything for his clients.

Secondly, the practice of a political lawyer, unlike that of a general practitioner, is determined by a perception of Law as a political weapon. Law is subordinated to Politics; it is the instrument of the representation of the notion of fairness, despite the fact that this representation of fairness is far from being uniform. A symptomatic example is the difference between the French 'avocat politique' and the US political lawyer. If both show political engagement in the case in which they are acting, the first acts in the collective interest of a society, whereas the second primarily acts in the interest of a client who is a member of a specific and disadvantaged minority group. This difference within each approach is far from being neutral and expresses, it seems, a particular conception of social relations inherent in each legal culture.

Thirdly, the militant mobilization of the law is indicative of a dichotomy between a legal reality concerned mainly by its coherence, and collective expectations arising from a system of representation. To some extent, the militant lawyers are good indicators of the representations of Justice taking place in Society since they express social aspirations perceived as realizable within the existing legal system, without which it would be necessary to resort to the legislative procedure.

Fourthly, the militant lawyer plays on the legal imagery of judges and of juries, to serve his own cause. Being an expert in the representation of law, he tries to bring the perception of the law close to the representation of fairness by citizens.

However, the political lawyer is not the only phenomenon to exploit these four forms of interaction between representation of justice and Law. Indeed it seems that they are characteristic of all legal systems.

Law as a Source of Representations of Justice

The representations of the law are connected with those of Justice, which is considered as a philosophical ideal. The legal systems thus generate various forms of popular representations such as caricatures, films, TV series, etc. which will be largely analyzed further in this book. I will just give one of the more surprising examples of the economic re-use of these representations. Indeed, whereas Law is often perceived as something inexpressible, a legal tourism is emerging based on the cultural representations of places where Justice is dispensed. For a few years, certain states or metropolises try to seduce a new form of customer, by praising the benefits of their political and legal scene. A case in point is Luxembourg which uses the lure of the European Court of Justice to attract groups of tourists. It curiously seems to have received the support of the Commission. This one publishes on the website of its representation in Luxembourg a guide of the institutional landscape entitled 'Luxembourg, European capital' which includes a map of a guided walk, descriptions of the monuments and street names closely connected with the European Union. The Hague, described on the Internet site of the city, like a city of justice and peace in reference to the International Court, could be also quoted. Recently, Geneva also entered this market. The Swiss ministry of Foreign Affairs thus published in 2003 a small book entitled: 'Droits de l'homme, droit international humanitaire, droit des réfugiés: Genève entre les origines et le XXIe siècle', in which the name of Geneva is astutely associated with various legal and philosophical comments on Human rights. For example, in the book, it says that 'Geneva of the Human Rights offers an undeniable intellectual opportunity by allowing at the same time an insight the history of Human Rights and international Law relating to the human rights' (p. 19). There seems to be a double objective: on one hand, to attract tourists by proposing a juridico-humanitarian walk, and on the other hand to invite humanitarian international organizations to choose Geneva as the place to register their offices. Cities or States which can make use of such inheritance are certainly rare, but the economic advantage that they receive is far from negligible from an economic and political point of view.

Legal Systems Subject to Representations of Justice

Legal systems are subject to the influence of the representations of Justice.[1] However, such systems have largely contributed to produce some of these representations, which often return in a distorted form caused by a boomerang effect. For example, popular legal culture has an important influence on members of a jury in a court. In the same way, popular representations of law constitute a determining component of the legal market, in particular because they determine clients' expectations. Lastly, certain transversal legal concepts, like the general principles of law or the concept of natural justice are particularly favourable for cognitive projections.

Law Is the Place where Representations of Justice Conflict

During the Trial, the judge is confronted with the claims from the parties, and also with their representations of litigation.[2] Except in a situation of absolute bad faith, each one of them thinks that their vision is the one which must take precedence, because it would confirm the notion of fairness and Justice. Consequently, the judge's mission is indirectly to adjudicate among these visions and to give form to one of them. Let's take the example of the emergence of restorative Justice, which is probably related to an increasing need to reconcile Law and Justice.

Contrary to distributive Justice which is focused on transgression of norms and the consequent sanction, restorative justice seeks to release the emotional suffering caused by the offence. Herein restorative Justice characterizes a new way of thinking Law which tends to implement the best action possible in order to restore harmony within Society and to reduce individual or collective behavioural disorders created by an offence. However, the emotional suffering is mainly determined by the representation that the victim has of the offence. Everyone does not

---

[1]   See in this volume: Pascale Duparc Portier and Laurent Pech, 'The Portrayal of the Judicial Process in the French and Irish Media'; Barbara Villez 'Representation of the Legal Profession on Television.Professional Ethics and Client Expectations'; Judith Resnik and Dennis E. Curtis, 'From 'Rites' to 'Rights' of Audience. The Utilities and Contingencies of the Public's Role in Court-Based Processes'; Dr. Theo Gavrielides 'Deconstructing 'Justice' and Reconstructing 'Fairness' in a Convergent European Justice System. An Aristotelian Approach to the Question of Representation of Justice in Europe.'

[2]   See in this volume: Susan S. Silbey, 'Talk of Law: Contested and Conventional Legality'; Judith Resnik and Dennis E. Curtis, 'From 'Rites' to 'Rights' of Audience. The Utilities and Contingencies of the Public's Role in Court-Based Processes'; Claire Micheau and Alexander Conrad Culley, 'Representation of the European Court of Justice. Conscience of the People of Europe or Political Juggernaut?'; Bruno Deffains and Samuel Ferey 'Representation f Justice in Law and Economics.'

react in the same way to an infringement. To define the expectations of each person, corresponds thus to seek their representations of social relations and of Justice in order to translate them into law. In this respect, distributive justice proceeds no differently, with the only difference being that representations of Justice involved here have a societal scope. In fact, the Law itself is a cognitive system, wherein interests involved are treated on a hierarchical basis, according to standardized systems of representations.

Legal Systems Have Recourse to Representations of Justice

Justice needs representations.[3] During a recent dinner with one of the judges of the Court of First Instance of the European Union, the judge explained to me that the architecture of the new court should be able by its enormous proportions to impress Heads of Member state governments. Undoubtedly, the ambition is to put back in line the most eurosceptic of them. Examples of this type are numerous, because Justice always needed strong symbols to consolidate its place and to hide its own weaknesses.

Studying how Justice is represented in Society is thus interesting not only for citizens who want to understand the popular culture but also for lawyers. Furthermore, to try and give an overview of the question of the representations of Justice and its implication over various aspects, this book brings together some of the most reputed specialists from various disciplines. It is divided into three parts: the first one is dedicated to the representation of Law and Justice in popular culture, the second attempts to analyze the social and political implications of the representation of justice and finally, the last part explores the economic dimension of this topic.

We hope that this book will be a source of inspiration for the reader.

---

[3] See in this volume: Claire Micheau and Alexander Conrad Culley, 'Representation of the European Court of Justice. Conscience of the People of Europe or Political Juggernaut?'

PART I

LAW, POPULAR CULTURE AND REPRESENTATION OF JUSTICE

Allegory of Justice and Representation of Punishment in Crime Fiction

A Franco-Irish Comparison

Dominique JEANNEROD

Trinity College, Dublin

'To understand the power of Law, we must stop looking so much at the commands of legal institutions and start looking at the legal imagination'

P. W. Kahn, *The Cultural Study of Law, Reconstructing Legal Scholarship*[1]

I. Introduction

The scope of this paper is not to deal with mechanisms of Justice in France and Ireland but to see how legal issues are reflected in the cultural realm in these two countries. It argues that an understanding of the cultural context of Law is necessary in order to understand its Institutions, in the same way that the meaning of Legal Texts is dependent upon the understanding of Legal theory. It argues further that literature, viewed as a system of protocols of the depiction of human behaviour and inner representations can provide tools for a firm grasp of the manner in which law functions in society. With this in mind, the importance of detective fiction, which can be perceived entirely as a literature which reworks legal prescriptions, rewrites legal procedures, and gives life to legal abstractions, appears to have been surprisingly underestimated until recently. In the same way that scholarly criticism has, after decades of reluctance, turned towards crime fiction, aware of the narrative and thematic impact it had on general literature, it seems that Legal scientists and sociologists nowadays face the prospect of discovering how crime literature can contribute to the implementation of Law.

---

[1]   University of Chicago Press, 1999, p. 135.

The need for a few methodological clarifications will be addressed in a preliminary section (II). After introducing the allegorical representation of Justice in crime literature (III), a Franco-Irish comparison of such representations will then be dealt with in three steps. Firstly by presenting how Justice is embodied in the works of two authors of detective fiction in these two countries (IV); secondly by focusing on the portrayal of Justice made in their novels (V); and thirdly by discussing the alternative to a Legal understanding of Justice as suggested and the signal it sends to systems ruled by the Law (VI).

Lawyers do not usually take the theme of Law and Literature very seriously. The place allocated to it, albeit rare, within Legal conferences is transitional, somewhat recreational and generally dispensable: a sometimes refreshing, sometimes tiring excursion of the mind, before getting back to what really matters, to the core discussion on articles of positive Law.[2] It serves thus as a means of recalling that Lawyers are humanists after all. The main reason for such prejudice, albeit benevolent, and such superficiality, albeit unconscious, may lie not only in the narrowness of the approach, but also in the conventionality of such an expectation.[3] Such approaches, selecting works from the literary canon wherein the legal content is guaranteed, such as Kafka's *Trial*, Shakespeare's *Merchant of Venice*, Balzac's *Contrat de Mariage*, or Racine's *Plaideurs* and which are read for preconceived themes, are dually reductionist. Reducing literature to the classics, and the classics to some of their leading themes, they also often tend to look for a confirmation of the Lawyer's intellectual framework and representation of society.[4] They are therefore condemned to find in literature what the Lawyers already know. Moreover, their focus on a literature which is already

---

[2] Forgetting altogether, in so doing, J. Hermann von Kirchmann's much quoted statement from his 1848 conference paper, *Die Wertlosigkeit der Jurisprudenz als Wissenschaft, reprint*, Heidelberg, Manutius, 1988, p. 28, and according to which 'three correcting words of the legislator and whole (legal) libraries become rubbish'.

[3] For R. Posner, a leading figure in Law and Economics Studies but also as the author of several contributions on Law and Literature, 'The comparative study of Law and Literature will change neither the Study of Law, nor that of Literature'. (R. A. Posner, *Droit et littérature*, transl. by Chr. Hivet and Ph. Jouary, coll. Droit éthique et société, Paris, PUF, 1996, p. 413).

[4] However, remarkable examples of legal studies of literature include classical articles such as Georg Jellinek's pioneer publication in the *Grünhutszeitschrift*, 1882, T. IX, p. 438; J. M. Gest's in the *American Law Review*, 1912, Vol. 46, p. 481 or Hans Fehr's *Das Recht in der Dichtung*, Bern, A. Francke, 1931. For further classical references, see Posner, p. 29-31. More recently, several books by François Ost offer a great wealth of though-provoking confrontations with literary texts: *Sade et la loi*, Paris, O. Jacobs, 2005; *Raconter la loi. Aux sources de l'imaginaire juridique*, Paris, O. Jacobs, 2004.

deemed classical but which is cut off socio-historically from contemporary preoccupations, as well as the blind eye they turn to literature which engages with Legal issues in current societies, prevent them from finding workable examples of literary representations of Law in action.[5] Because literature is seen as a way of 'embellishing' the discourse on Law, thereby placing legal scientists in a culturally more favorable light, such endeavours fail to make a heuristically valuable use of it. Lacking a cultural-studies methodology for questioning literary texts and hampered by cultural reverence, such attempts which occasionally marvel at how good Kafka, Balzac or Shakespeare might have known the respective Law of their respective societies, do little more than merely reinforce the socio-historical findings about the literary works already made in diverse ways by Literary criticism.[6]

Literary criticism, in turn, had until recently, never showed much interest in studying Legal texts as a specific form of literature or as a coded systems of signs. It can not be said about Lawyers that they encouraged a methodological acculturation of modern literary criticism, of semiology or of deconstructionism in their own field either. If Binder and Weisberg have, in their important work, *Literary Criticism of Law*,[7] showed the potential contribution of the Humanities, and of hermeneutics, in particular, to Legal Studies, Richard Posner, in *Law and Literature*, warns Lawyers against borrowing techniques of literary interpretation. One of the acknowledged objectives of this monograph is to protect the Law and the Constitution against the assaults of literary criticism, and more so even against Lawyers using it unduly.[8]

II. Literature and Legal Consciousness

It appears that a methodological confrontation between the two disciplines is still required. It would have to begin with a reflection on the construction of the object of study and on the definition of the methods of such research situated at the edge of the two disciplines.[9] One aim of

---

[5] See for example the recurrence of similar patterns of analysis of Shakespeare's Play, starting with Ihering's seminal *Der Kampf ums Recht*, Wien, Manz, 1873; Andrew's, *Law versus Equity in the Merchant of Venice*, Boulder, University of Colorado Press, 1965; Posner, *op. cit.*, p. 106-134.

[6] For a theorisation of a socio-poetic approach of the writer's referential world and its textualization, see Viala, A. *Approches de la réception*, PUF, 1993. As representative of a socioanalytical turn in literary studies, see: *Le Dictionnaire du Littéraire*, A. Viala *et al.* (dir.), Paris, PUF, 2004.

[7] G. Binder, R. Weisberg, *Literary Criticism of Law*, Princeton University Press, 2000.

[8] R. A. Posner, *op. cit.*, p. 20.

[9] See for example: A. Teissier-Ensminger, *La Beauté du Droit*, Descartes & Cie, 1999.

this paper is to contribute to a broader definition of the body of the literary texts accessible for a legal reading, by extending somewhat the traditional canonical scope to crime fiction. It hopes to testify for the possibility of an interdisciplinary cultural theory of Law[10] as an efficient tool in the hands of the comparatist who attempts to grasp the structural differences between Legal systems. If comparative Law, is, as Otto Pfersmann puts it 'the part of legal theory that allows us to understand normative structures in different contexts',[11] then the study of the literary context, and generally popular literature, appears to give a good indication as to the level of expectancies and the representations of Justice shared by the reader. It can be seen as an auxiliary science to comparative Law, a discipline which is in itself a cultural reflexion about societies, as a comparatist like P. Legrand aptly demonstrates.[12] Legal perceptions and representations are a cultural phenomenon. The topic of the social perception of Justice lies hence at the crossroads of cultural studies. This legitimizes an attempt to use the reflection of contemporary culture upon the regulations of contemporary society in order to show how literary expression can theorize and rework the understanding of Justice in two societies and also indeed highlight the convergences between them. In this sense, taking literary representations of Law and Justice seriously, which means adopting a non-institutional approach of legal phenomena takes the focus away from the usual abstract formal level, in order to replace it with a focus within the symbolic order. It recalls the too often neglected fact that legal appropriations by the subjects of Law happen at this symbolic level. Moreover, due to the abstract general formulation of Law, it needs this symbolic operation in order to become concrete. The body of literary texts dealing overtly or covertly with the realm of the legal gives life and substance to norms that mostly consist of mere definitions. By doing so, literature acts as a text for which legal prescriptions are merely titles. This text, because it is read by the Justice seekers and informs their legal practices, at least as a subtext, cannot be ignored by either the institutions of Justice or by legal scientists attempting to analyze the processes of the implementation of Law. Literature's ability to show Institutions of Justice what they ignore, or what they choose not to reflect on about themselves, is thus the result of a creative consideration of opinions about the function of Law in society. In this respect, it associates itself

---

[10] P.W. Kahn, *op. cit.*

[11] O. Pfersmann, 'Comparative Law as Interpretation and as Theory of Law', *Revue Internationale de Droit Comparé*, 2001, p. 275-288.

[12] P. Legrand, *Le droit comparé*, coll. Que sais-je, Paris, PUF 1999. For a review see B. Rudden, *RIDC*, 1, 2000, p. 275; P. Legrand, 'Comparer', *RIDC*, 1996, p. 279-318; P. Legrand, 'Sur l'analyse différentielle des juriscultures', *RIDC*, 1999, p. 1053-1071.

with the contemporary branch of Legal Consciousness Studies.[13] The focus of this field of studies on patterns of everyday life induces an interdisciplinary approach.[14] The study of 'popular' literary genres from both a legal and a literary perspective can in this respect be seen as a way of approaching the general popular perception of the norm. This is reinforced by the fact that literature not only reflects, but in turn itself produces representations of values, and consequently modifies legal behavior.

III. Detective Fiction as an Interpretive Practice

There have been, so far, more investigations on literature and criminal Justice than, as attempted here, on criminal literature and Justice.[15] And, in a certain way, it seems to be a paradox to expect some clarification from detective fiction, when its narrative function blurs and conceals in such a way as to keep the reader interested. Insight is deferred, the resolution is delayed, the understanding is postponed until the very last second when the author ultimately reveals all. Nonetheless, crime fiction, as an account of the protagonists' perception of Law and as a narrative of subjective interpretations of Legal processes can easily be placed in the perspective of Ewick and Selbey's narratives of legal experiences.[16] The crime novel thus becomes a legal narrative.

Firstly, it is detective fiction, more than any other literature which uses Law as a trope. Albeit fictitiously, it portrays Law in action. Even though a counterfeited authenticity is at the core of popular culture, there is a documentary interest to its representation of Justice which is deprived of its rationality, its abstraction and its blindness. Far from taking the classical high/low culture divide too seriously, which considers detective fiction as non-artistic, we should benefit from its literary representation of Justice. Not simply because the sense of Justice is sentimentalized, but also because it gives an indication of aspirational representations of Justice. Crime fiction is therefore a literature which reflects at the same time the reality of the judicialisation of human relations and offers an idealized vision of social Justice. It is, on the one

---

[13] For an overview of this relatively new field of research, see J. Pélisse, 'A-t-on conscience du droit? Autour des *Legal Consciousness Studies*', *Genèses*, No. 59, 2005, p. 114-130.

[14] J. Jurt, G. Krumeich, Th. Würtenberger, *Wandel von Recht und Rechtbewußtsein in Frankreich und Deutschland*, Berlin Verlag, 1999.

[15] Cf. P. Verdaguer, 'Représentants de la Loi dans le roman policier français', in *Europe*, No. 876, 'Droit & littérature', April 2002, p. 164-179.

[16] P. Ewick, S. Silbey, *The Common Place of Law: Stories from Everyday Life*, Chicago University Press, 1998.

hand, the only literature which places its protagonists permanently under the eye of the Law, by which their acts and relations are defined. On the other hand, it gives a specifically dark vision of Justice, largely due to the requirements of the genre, but voicing in doing so a radical criticism which is seldom expressed in official reports. In other words, the crime genre operates a 'recodification' of the Law by confronting it with narrative codes and novelistic patterns. This makes it an interdisciplinary narrative which deals at the same time with Law, Culture and Literature.

Secondly, Justice is itself an allegory, represented through images. When dealing with diaegetic Justice, the detective novel is concerned with the context, the shared referent of an extra-diegetical Justice, common to the author and the readers. At this level, the detective novel also involves a non-literal form of expression. Since it comprises an active reading process prompted by the classical 'whodunnit', it also involves the reader more directly. There is a transmission from the context of the text to the context of the reader's surroundings. Contrary to representations of Justice as observed in official allegories (such as official iconography or architecture) representations through the medium of the novel are more critical. With regard to legal theory they present a way of bridging the gap between the popular idea of Justice and its institutional reality. Literature serves as a way of contributing to an understanding of its representation by non experts, who are indeed almost the totality of the people subjected to the Law. The realistic content of the detective novel, on the one hand, and its broad public appeal on the other, renders it an interesting place to observe Justice as felt by the writer as citizen, and moreso how it is presented to citizens as readers.

The broader readership of crime fiction compared to general fiction makes it more telling as an indicator of a general social consciousness. Since it is a type of writing which has an impact on the reader, there are repercussions to be found in the reader's conception of Justice. Crime literature is thus a popular form of legal rhetoric. In a similar way, and from the perspective of Roger Chartier's work, the influence of popular culture can be seen in the changes of paradigms which the Law must ultimatively consider.[17] Feelings of desacralization, for example, may induce a shift in the paradigm of representations of the public sphere. They can serve to highlight contestations of the norms or even publically anticipated Legal changes. In this respect, the *clichés* of the genre deserve investigating as much as or more than Legal culture itself because they influence the popular conception of Justice and therefore

---

[17] R. Chartier, *Les origines culturelles de la Révolution française*, Seuil, 2000.

the acceptance of its institutions. Legal Culture is thus not the result of exposure to legal texts, but to the mediatised reworking of them.

IV. Justice in French and Irish Crime Fiction

The detective fiction genre is rooted in a long french literary tradition and often indebted to Vidocq and Balzac. However, in the Anglo-American tradition, many founders of the genre such as Conan Doyle, Peter Cheyney and Raymond Chandler, all were of Irish origin. In order to investigate specificities, as well as convergences in the representation of contemporary Justice and its institutions in France and in Ireland as illustrated in crime fiction, two contemporary crime writers have been selected. Ken Bruen, and (amongst the numerous French authors dealing explicitly with French society such as Daeninckx, Vargas or Belaïd), Maurice G. Dantec have been chosen for the many similarities existing between them. Both belong to the generation of writers born in the 1950s, but who came relatively late to the public eye. They are both 21st-century writers and their works which are discussed here, Bruen's Taylor Tetralogy published with Brandon Press and Dantec's *Villa Vortex* were published in this millenium and may be arguably considered as their countries most interesting literary prospects in recent years within the crime genre. Both are stylists of crime fiction, but both are still extremely prolific. Both enjoy a broad popular acclaim and critical recognition.[18] Comparisons can further be made between their violent protagonists: they both choose as first person narrative voices addictive, destructive detectives; Bruen's Jack Taylor is an alcoholic and cocaine-adept Ex-Guard and Dantec's Inspecteur Kernal is a police officer who experiments with drugs and falls from grace with his superiors.

In both cases, there is an attempt at a representation of Justice, although it is significantly distorted. Bruen's opening opus, *The Guards*, is dedicated 'to the Minister for Justice'.[19] For Dantec, criticism of Justice is a way of politicizing the text. For both, crime fiction is also consciously used as a narrative in order to convey broader meanings,

---

[18] Bruen's book *The Guards* was a finalist in the 2004 Edgar Allan Poe award for crime fiction. He won the 2004 Shamus Prize. Dantec is published in the prestigious *Série Noire* Gallimard and benefits from a critical acclaim unusual for a writer of detective novels, in spite of his controversial opinions.

[19] K. Bruen, *The Guards*, Brandon, Dingle, 2001, p. 5. A policeman, in Ireland, is colloquially known as a 'guard' which expression derives from the Irish language: An Garda Síochána. This translates to Guardians of peace. Hence a policeman is a Garda or a Guard. See also the thematisation of the role and duties of the Guards and of the citizen's expectations towards them, K. Bruen, *The Killing of the Tinkers*, Brandon, Dingle, 2002, p. 201 and p. 176.

where the politics of Justice merges with a metaphysics of Justice.[20] This is obvious in the different ways both authors put an emphasis on knowledge. In order to replace the failing Justice system, both Kernal and Taylor need to find the solution within themselves, and moreover in literary, philosophical, or spiritual books. The process of gaining insight into right or wrong follows the methodology of human sciences rather than that of the Law, as indicated, for example, in the endowment of Dantec's detective with a PhD in Psychopathology.[21] In this respect, Dantec and Bruen converge. The works referred to provide us with distorted but significant representations, since they are purposefully distorted.[22] Most importantly, Dantec and Bruen find a cross-over in the breadth and scope that their works encompass, making them a place where society, as structured by their cultural heritage, is continuously quoted and rewritten. The personal and curricular similarities between these two writers thus serve to highlight the structural differences of the respective legal background of the countries they come from and which they both in turn came to see from the distance of a self-induced exile.[23]

V. Justice as a Paralyzed Bureaucracy

The two authors portray two bureaucracies which are disconnected from popular concerns. In Bruen's, as in Dantec's novels, the possibilities of official Justice are increasingly limited. Through this literary treatment, Justice is shown as a site of trauma. The trial is not as much reenacted as it is overrun by the action of the diaegetic subject performing Justice for himself.

Justice is a central bureaucracy in Dantec's 2003 voluminous *Villa Vortex*. The investigation is made impossible by those in charge of its supervision. Sectorial rigidities and solidarity block the inquiries. The Truth is *locked.*[24] The most visible function of hierarchy is to embroil the detectives and delay their progress. The vortex of the book is an abyss where evil is a Justice system which just follows procedures; it is an endless file-collecting machine, working in complete meaninglessness and wasting the life of its agents, its instruments. Although

---

[20] Bruen has a PhD in Metaphysics, Dantec has published *a Journal of Metaphysics and Polemics.*

[21] M.G. Dantec, *Villa Vortex*, Paris, Gallimard, 2003, p. 40 and p. 128.

[22] See for example the transposition and reworking of the controversies surrounding in the late 1990's the closing of the Magdalene penitential institutions in K. Buren, *The Magdalen Martyrs*, Brandon, Dingle, 2003.

[23] Dantec opted for living in Québec, whereas Bruen, who lives now in Galway, spent twenty five years abroad.

[24] *Villa Vortex*, p. 589.

much more ambitious in its experimentation with narrative devices, *Villa Vortex* can also be read as an attempt to portray French administration and definitions of Justice at the turn of the millennium. The book opens with the depiction of the powerless machine, in which the protagonist is only a peg.[25] Starting with the death of the investigator, and ending with the discovery that the culprit had been dead for many years, the investigation portrays a world beyond the grave. Fittingly, only the victims seem to be alive in this investigation, due to an electronic device attached to their corpses, and which was probably inspired by *Eve Future* by Villiers de l'Ile Adam. The Justice-serving Administration is a Necropolis. The policemen are the purveyors of this nauseous half-dead Moloch. The Law dehumanizes its servants. The main protagonist, Kernal is, literally, a custodian of order, who recognizes that his Justice ideals are just lost in bureaucracy.[26] Policemen are archivists of death. 'Gérer, c'est enterrer.'[27] Instead of being solved, cases will be buried.

We find a similar attitude in Ken Bruen: The *mot d'ordre* is to forget to prosecute officials. The first book of the series, *The Guards* begins with Jack's dismissal from the force. Even though, as he puts it, 'It's almost impossible to be thrown out of the Garda Síochana',[28] that's what happened to him. Not so much because of alcoholism, as for his transgressive refusal to leave the driving offence unprosecuted. The belief in equality before the Law will ruin his career. When the T.D.[29] asks Taylor: 'Have you any idea who you are talking to?' Bruen shows the separation of the idea of Justice from the Institutions which apply it. His *œuvre* reveals an overriding and irrevocable sense of corruption. This is made clear in *The Killing of the Tinkers*, when Bruen's Taylor spends time in detention and gets out on bail as part of an illegal deal on whether to prosecute or not. Unlike Kafka's *Trial*, his novels do not paint the image of Justice as an uncontrollable machine with an unstoppable course. Instead Justice is represented as both static and dysfunctional, in danger of being stopped at any stage on its lengthy journey to reestablish order by the corrupt forces of Justice and Economics. In this respect, the passage in *The Killing of the Tinkers*, in which Taylor, who has been placed in detention, is freed thanks to the intervention of relatives of the criminal, is particularly interesting.[30] Justice is thus

---

[25] *Ibid.*, p. 22.
[26] *Ibid.*, p. 41.
[27] *Ibid.*, p. 583.
[28] *The Guards*, p. 7.
[29] A *Teachta Dála* is a member of the Irish Parliament (*Dáil Éireann*)
[30] The different staging of the opposition between Taylor and his ex colleague Clancy, who chose to compromise with the system and got promoted after the injustice of

represented as a blind machine, a mechanism which can make the right decisions as long as it is sent on the wrong track. Similarly, in Dantec's *Villa Vortex*, rules are portrayed not as protecting the rights of people, but as being inefficient and obstructive. One of the recurring sub-stories within *Villa Vortex* portrays the French Al Qaida suspect, Zacharias Moussoui escaping the surveillance before 9/11.

Both authors reach similar conclusions: the investigation needs to be done outside a respect for the Law, in fact in complete contradiction with procedural Justice.[31] Justice can not be done without the guardians of Law committing infractions,[32] such as breaking and entering or violating rules of competence. The investigator is alone, his investigation is illegal. On the one hand, the investigator, in Dantec pretends to establish and maintain order, but on the other hand, he decides to adapt it: 'to sacrifice the Law for the sake of the truth.'[33] It is no different for Bruen whose character concedes: 'even as a guard, I was poor at regulations.'[34] As a result, the service of Justice appears in both cases as a function that has become impossible to perform.[35] It is, in Bruen, the ex-Guard himself who silences the official voices of the Institutions of Justice, filtering them almost to oblivion through his abuse of drugs and alcohol. In Dantec, victims speak beyond death and they testify to the horrific incompetence of the Justice system that failed to protect them: their voice is never to be silenced. This contrasts sharply with the voice of Justice, a voice turned to a mere ritual) and that becomes almost inaudible due to its sheer, meaningless repetition.[36] Justice, as depicted here, is in a terminal state and the failure of public institutions will never be redeemed.

Bruen's Taylor is also in a perpetual process of loss himself, which seems paradigmatic for the loss of the ideas his presence is meant to serve. This shows the loss of the legitimacy of the idea of Justice. In both Dantec's and Bruen's novels, judges are insulted. Bruen's judgment on Justice is without ambiguity: 'It's dispensed badly.'[37] The mechanisms of Justice posited by the Law have failed to deal with social injustice and indeed to protect social values against corruption, privi-

---

Taylor's devotion are also of interest: *Killing of the Tinkers, op. cit.*, p. 35-37 and p. 222-223.

[31] *Ibid.*, p. 435, 436.

[32] *Ibid.* See amongst other examples, p. 480-481.

[33] *Ibid.*, p. 542.

[34] K. Bruen, *The Dramatist*, Dingle, Brandon, 2004, p. 99.

[35] *Ibid.*, p. 55.

[36] *Villa Vortex*, p. 64.

[37] *The Dramatist*, p. 33.

leges and prejudices. For Bruen's detective, the Law can no longer sustain its claim to be 'the common sense of the community'. His literary portrayal of Justice, offers a testimonial of its dysfunctionality. Justice does not stop violence, it generates it: the narrator's voice, as subjective incarnation of the Law functions as a site of further violence. This is of course partly due to the very structure of the text in the crime genre. This type of literature can not afford, for reasons of narrative economy, to engage in the representation of the trial. The due process of Law needs to be kept to a minimum. The Justice process, while omnipresent, is but a background, of which the narrative is only a distorted echo. Thus, representations of the Institutions of Justice are rendered in an elliptical mode. The main distortion inherent to the genre, is to consider Justice from the point of view of the enforcement authorities. The police force is studied and depicted with great detail and accuracy in both novels. On the one hand, of course it lends the novel an element of picturesque, or as Roland Barthes put it, an *'effet de réel'*. But this endeavour occults the Institution of Justice itself, whose rationalities are ignored or dramatized. In the crime genre, there is a relentless focus on tragedy, one which is completely antagonistic with the pacifying function of the trial, whose liturgical dramatization aims at ending the community conflicts. There is an elimination of the rationality of the court order and instead an emphasis on the brutality of police Justice. The discourse of the police replaces the absence of a legal discourse. In addition, the formalities of the Trial may be seen as a form of oppression towards the culturally disadvantaged. Beyond Bruen's displayed desire to render Justice *readable* to the people in a language they understand and with punishments they can recognize, there operates the idea of decentralizing Justice.

What differentiates further the two universes is that the French police officer can easily state a non-procedural speech and act in an illegal way, even within the police force. For the Irishman, who was forced to leave the force, on the contrary, the respect for legal rigidities characterizes all the colleagues encountered in the dealing of criminal business. But in both cases, effective Justice happens outside, in the parapolice, even in private Justice.

VI. The Temptation of the Vigilantes

Since the healing function of the trial is denied in the novels of Bruen and Dantec, there can be no social recovery. After the apparent collapse of the Institution of Justice, effective Justice through due process of Law is no longer possible. 'People are tired of the legal way of dealing with things.'[38] The theme of vigilantes is present in all the novels of the series. In *The Dramatist* we learn 'there's talk about a vigilante group in town'.[39] They have their own agenda and target those they feel are allowed escape the judicial system. Punishment is at the core of the idea of Justice held by such vigilantes, who are in fact guards in disguise. They are, as Taylor calls them, an 'Urban legendith Guard shoes'.[40] The organization of Justice is dual: official Justice is leading nowhere, and civil vigilantes are needed to reinforce it. In *The Dramatist*, published in 2004, these vigilantes represent the return of Irish history. They call themselves Pikemen, in honor of the patriots who took Vinegar Hill in Wexford in the rebellion of 1798. Coming from the past where it was possible to read the idea of rights in a simplistic system of dualist values (Irish against foreigners, Yeomen versus Pikemen), they present themselves as servants of a new Justice. Fighting as they say, 'the evil that goes unpunished', they cry: 'We are the new guards.'[41] The problem of the vigilantes is ultimately solved in The Dramatist but in a way that we see Jack Taylor being trapped: as the narrative instrument and conveyor of Justice, he is guilty as well.[42] Not only does he share the same disbelief in Justice as the criminals he is investigating, but his methods of punishing them are the same as theirs.[43]

This is echoed by Dantec who draws the same conclusion about the inefficiency of the Justice system, and he will himself become its *ultra vires* instrument. But the very word for Justice has disappeared from his terminology.[44] The Law no longer applies. Law at this stage, has revealed itself as a text no less fictional than fiction. If the two authors find a link in the metaphorical interrogation their works embody, differences appear in relation to the metaphysical foundations that have to support an alternative Justice system. While France's constitutional order is based upon the principle of secularism, Dantec seems, in his global rejection of the administration of Justice to advocate a turn towards jusnaturalism, towards natural Law, when the main protagonist, Georges Kernal (fittingly sharing his forename with the Catholic writer Bernanos) claims not represent God's Justice: 'Nous sommes le bras de la Justice de Dieu.' Not surprisingly in this symmetry of inverted cultural positions, it is the Irish author Bruen, who, on the contrary, re-

---

[38]   *Ibid.*, p. 188.
[39]   *Ibid.*, p. 104.
[40]   *The Dramatist*, p. 177.
[41]   *Ibid.*, p. 171.
[42]   *Ibid.*, p. 203.
[43]   *Ibid.*, p. 236.
[44]   *Villa Vortex*, p. 585.

marks that 'True faith does not promote Justice'.[45] However, his dismissal of the rationality of Justice also ends in his resuming of an old practice. The last page of *The Dramatist*, shows him in a pub just about to resume drinking, solving the case in oblivion.

What we can see re-emerging in both cases, through this cultural enterprise are remnants of old beliefs and behavior patterns. More importantly, we can see how the two authors work together in popular culture, with media-induced fears and how they reject the existing Institutions of Justice. Neither of these writers are aiming at a reform of the Law, nor at an improvement of the Law, but just a simple rejection of it.

VII. Conclusion

The myth of the neutrality of a blind Justice system is reversed through the notion of the private eye, who reveals the application of Law, as well as through his presumed ability to discern and judge between what is right or wrong. The detective novel's appropriation and reworking of the Law starts not from the norm but from an anti-modern representation of right or wrong. The Police force is the last emblem of a degraded Justice system. Justice is degraded in that it makes the assumption possible, that to be effective it has to be freed not only of formal regulations but also of principles. The spectacular character of the diegetic Justice system leads to an overwhelming brutality that effectively silences the discursive quality of due process. The replacement of the police force is revealed as the symptom of a larger crisis. It is that of the Public bond within the state, where there is no longer such a thing as the shared ideals of Justice. However apocalyptic Dantec's nihilism about French institutions is, Bruen goes further still in his reporting of the decomposition of the commonly shared public idea of Justice. For the French novelist, the police force becomes the ultimate public utility of a State whose final frontier is located in the monopoly of repression but still serves an idea of Public Justice. For Bruen, on the contrary, the explosion of the public idea of Justice is complete: it results in a fragmentation of Justice into Justice-like behaviours, an atomization of the police force. The ultimate degradation of Justice is organized through its privatization, through the rough-justice of the vigilantes on the one hand, and through the intrusion of corporate entities in the solving of official Justice, on the other.

For those structural Franco-Irish differences, what strikes one as evident is the cultural proximity, indeed the community of representations between two supposedly divergent systems that are supposed to be the

---

[45] *The Dramatist*, p. 14.

very example of divergences, not only between the French Roman-German system of Law on the one hand, and Anglo-Saxon Law on the other, but also between a former colonial system and a post-colonial one. A process of homogenization of the particular cultures of Law is at work here. This process is highlighted in the identical evolution of the dispenser of Justice at the end of this Franco-Irish itinerary through the representations of Justice in the crime genre. In the *œuvre* of M.G. Dantec as well as in K. Bruen, we can see the transition from an alienated servant of Justice to a paranoid vigilante. The only difference is the emphasis placed by each author: Dantec focuses on in the alienated servants of the bureaucracy of the Justice system, while Bruen focuses on ethylic and narcoleptic vigilantes. This psychological convergence can be explained by the predominance of American culture exemplified by both writers. It is visible even in the diaegesis itself, where the narrator confesses this preconditioning cultural exposure. When Jack Taylor visits Mountjoy prison in Dublin, he confesses that he expected it to be to be like in the movies.[46] When fictional ex-guards identify no more with Institutions of Justice than with Television or Literature, their Legal consciousness certainly does not point to inherited national Legal traditions, as is sometimes assumed by historians,[47] but to their increasing meaninglessness. Indeed, the issue of Legal consciousness could here be reformulated. How much does identification with the Institution of Justice actually mean for the subjects of Law? Not so much, if we are to believe Bruen and Dantec. They both offer a disappearance of the Legal system as a social framework, in favour of a paranoid mediated representation of it.

References

M. E. Andrews, *Law versus Equity in the Merchant of Venice*, University of Colorado Press, 1965.

R. Binder, G. Weisberg, *Literary Criticism of Law*, Princeton University Press, 2000.

K. Bruen, *The Guards*, Brandon, 2001.

K. Bruen, *The Killing of the Tinkers*, Brandon, 2002.

K. Bruen, *The Magdalen Martyrs*, Brandon, 2003.

K. Bruen, *The Dramatist*, Brandon, 2004.

R. Chartier, *Les origines culturelles de la Révolution française*, Seuil, 2000.

M. Dantec, *Villa Vortex*, Gallimard, 2003.

---

[46] *Ibid.*, p. 39.

[47] Cf. G. Krumeich, 'Rechstbewusstsein und Mentalitätsgeschichte', in J. Jurt, G. Krumeich, Th. Würtenberger, *op. cit.*, p. 13-25.

P. Ewick, S. Silbey, *The Common Place of Law: Stories from Everyday Life*, Chicago University Press, 1998.

H. Fehr, *Das Recht in der Dichtung*, A. Francke, 1931.

R. von Ihering, *Der Kampf ums Recht*, Manz, 1873.

J. Jurt, G. Krumeich, Th. Würtenberger (eds.), *Wandel von Recht und Rechtbewußtsein in Frankreich und Deutschland*, Berlin Verlag, 1999.

P. Kahn, *The Cultural Study of Law, Reconstructing Legal Scholarship*, University of Chicago Press, 1999.

J. von Kirchmann, *Die Wertlosigkeit der Jurisprudenz als Wissenschaft*, 1848, *reprint*, Heidelberg, Manutius, 1988.

G. Krumeich, 'Rechstbewusstsein und Mentalitätsgeschichte', in J. Jurt, G. Krumeich, Th. Würtenberger (eds.), *op. cit.*, 1999, p. 13-25.

P. Legrand, *Le droit comparé*, Coll. Que sais-je, PUF 1999.

P. Legrand, 'Sur l'Analyse différentielle des juriscultures', *Revue Internationale de Droit Comparé*, 1999, p. 1053.

F. Ost, *Raconter la loi. Aux sources de l'imaginaire juridique*, O. Jacob, 2004.

F. Ost, *Sade et la loi*, O. Jacob, 2005.

J. Pélisse, 'A-t-on conscience du droit? Autour des *Legal Consciousness Studies*', *Genèses*, No. 59, 2005, p. 114.

O. Pfersmann, 'Comparative Law as Interpretation and as Theory of Law', *Revue Internationale de Droit Comparé*, 2001, p. 275.

R. Posner, *Droit et littérature*, transl. by Chr. Hivet and Ph. Jouary, PUF, 1996.

A. Teissier-Ensminger, *La Beauté du Droit*, Descartes & Cie, 1999.

P. Verdaguer, 'Représentants de la Loi dans le roman policier français', in *Europe*, No. 876, 'Droit & littérature', April 2002, p. 161.

A. Viala, *Approches de la réception*, PUF, 1993.

The Administration of Justice as Portrayed in *Le Charivari* and *Le Journal Amusant* at the End of the 19th Century

Scepticism and Derision

Solange VERNOIS

University of Poitiers

In the preface of the famous book, *Les Tribunaux Comiques* [Comical Courts] by Jules Moinaux, Armand Silvestre takes pleasure in reminding readers that the theatre did not disappear in that particular year, 1888, but rather that

> It has moved, that's all. It has taken up residence at the court where magistrates who are not as proud as comedians, but who are just simple lawyers and who, it is true, have not graduated from the 'Conservatoire', are in the presence of brave defendants, not excessively troubled by recidivism – always still agree to provide us with daily and obligatory preformances.

The author adds 'That comedy is never idle, each person taking turns – the rascals through a right to conquer and the decent people as witnesses to the rascals' conquests'.[1]

Through its theatrical style, the courts have always intrigued the caricaturists. It is however well known that it was Daumier who popularized satirical criticism against the wealthy, namely the Judiciary between 1845 and 1848, contributing at the same time to the success of the *Le Charivari*, a daily founded in 1832 by Charles Philipon, which had the originality of being the first and unique newspaper to publish 'a sketch a day' in black and coloured ink.[2] The collaboration between Daumier and

---

[1] A. Silvestre, preface of the Jules Moinaux book, *Les Tribunaux Comiques*, illustrated by Stop, 3rd series ed. 1888, Chevalier-Marescq & Co. editors.

[2] *Le Charivari*, Paris, publishing a new sketch every day. Daily satirical newspaper, 23x31 format, fonded on 1st December 1832 by Charles Philipon. Interrupts its publication in 1893. At the turn of the century, Henriot takes over management. The sub-

Philipon, both of whom were imprisoned for having infringed censorship, actually coincided with the glorious years of Le Charivari. Originally influenced by extreme-left beliefs, the newspaper defied the 1835 laws, became liberal in 1841 and interrupted publication in 1849. Suspended in 1870, it reappeared in 1895. The less glorious period of the Third Republic, after Daumier, is marked by the abandon of political caricature in favour of satires on everyday life. Hence, new artists, such as Henriot, Draner or Stop, were brought in to contribute to Le Charivari by regularly providing sketches under the 'News' heading (Actualités). Matters concerning the courts were alluded to discreetly, though constantly. This was a seemingly valued subject for Stop, a former lawyer, as well for Henriot, a Doctor of Laws, who was to take over management of Le Charivari in the early 20th century.[3]

Indeed, the law of 29th July 1881 was beneficial to the press. Neverthless, the Third Republic represents a less glorious era in the days of Le Charivari, which became a light weight paper. Other periodicals, such as L'Éclipse or Le Grelot, took over the political torch and were active at the time of the 'Affairs' (Panama and Dreyfus). Le Charivari, more discreet, maintained nevertheless its double political and social aim and interrupted publication in 1893.[4]

Criticism with regard to the parliamentary and judicial worlds is still apparent and plays a role of 'insinuation'. Caricatures of famous personalities like Emile Durier, President of the Bar of the Law Society, sketched by Bianco on 7th January 1889, are now seemingly rare.

---

title then becomes 'Journal satirique et politique'. See C. Saint-Martin, Dictionnaire Solo, plus de 5000 dessinateurs de presse et 600 supports en France, de Daumier à l'An 2000, Aedis, 2004, p. 159.

[3] The glorious years of Le Charivari were those of Daumier, which became famous. We shall thus study the end of the 20th century through two periodicals: Le Charivari and Le Journal Amusant both founded by Philipon. The main artists whom we shall talk about are:
- Cham Amédée de Noé (1819-1879) nicknamed the 'pencil journalist' for his love of illustrated stories.
- Stop Louis Morel-Retz (1825-1899).
- Draner Jules Renard (1833-1926), also signs 'Paf'.
- Henriot Henri Maigrot (1857-1933), also signs 'Pif', was scarcely interested in politics but was attaché to the French Ministry of the Interior.
- Baric Jules (1825-1905). Humorist interested in the fashions of the day and to rural lifestyles.

[4] Le Charivari indirectly evoked the 'affairs' in contrast to the other Republican periodicals, such as L'Eclipse (founded in 1868) or Le Grelot (founded in 1871), which were much more virulent. Jean-Louis Forain (1852-1931), despite his conservative ideas and being an anti-Dreyfus militant, he attacked the wealthy, including the justice

A certain number of artists were otherwise collaborating with *Le Journal Amusant*, a humorous weekly founded in 1856 by the same Philipon, though having a lighter tone.[5]

Sketches of a graphics quality, sometimes quite insignificant, often neglected to the benefit of captions and depicting stereotype scenes, tend to leave the art historian with a dissatisfied feeling. In this context, the era following Daumier is, without doubt, a period of decline, Forain [French Impressionist painter and caricaturist] on his part preferring to express his ideas in other spheres.[6] Having said that, although the caricatures of *Le Charivari* and *Le Journal Amusant* do not reflect a fighting strategy like that of *Père Peinard*, they are nevertheless proof of how contemporaries perceive the legal profession.

In these common places portraying the ridiculous, we can decipher all the scepticism and disillusion, when faced with the usefulness of proposed reforms, in these pictures of everyday life.

I. Common Places of Judicial Unrest

During the second half of the 19th century, the comedy of the courtrooms was far too well known for the artists of *Le Charivari* or *Le Journal Amusant* to attempt to seek originality in this area. On the contrary, we are indeed surprised by the number of recurring themes over the years and decades, a same sketch occasionally benefiting from different captions. The most traditional scene is, nevertheless, that of the accused being tried or of the witness in the box.[7]

Of course, Draner, Henriot or Baric, for example, are content most of the time to evoke, in an almost stereotype manner, the 'ordinary' faults linked to the legal microcosm: the judges are apathetic, somnolent or totally impassive, almost confined in indifference. A sketch in *Le Charivari*, dated 20th March 1893, incidentally shows a Magistrate discreetly benefiting from a heater hidden behind the podium.

---

[5] *Le Journal Amusant, journal illustré, journal d'images, journal comique*, founded in January 1856 by Ch. Philipon (Format 31x44). The sub-title varies. Was not published from October 1870 to March 1871 (Dico Solo, p. 456).

[6] The caricaturists present their sketches under the heading 'News'. The exact paging is, however, not always mentioned. The sections concerning Justice particularly appear in *Le Charivari* (e.g. 5th March 1872 – 'Réorganisation de la magistrature'; 17th March 1872 = 'Les réformes judiciaries'; 5th May 1872 – 'Juges d'instruction'; 21st May 1901 - 'Tribunaux Comiques'). The references are mainly taken from *Le Charivari*. Those concerning *Le Journal Amusant* will be directly mentioned within the text.

[7] Draner, 'Le juge d'instruction', *Le Charivari*, 16th September 1899; and A. René, *Le Charivari*, 17th September 1899. Draner takes up the same theme: e.g. *Le Journal Amusant*, No. 1968, 19th May 1894 and *Le Charivari*, 20th November 1902.

Besides, it is not without irony that the new inventions contribute opportunely to strengthening the impersonal character of Justice.

On 24th April 1891, we can wonder at a machine which automatically judges blatant offences before the magistrate.

On 28th December 1897, Draner pondered about the value of a magistrate's oath by telegraph and predicts, no doubt with a wry smile: 'Let us wait and see judges follow trials over the telephone.' Already on 24th March 1882, the so-called 'itinerant' judges, had to respond to urgent orders from the station master: 'Hurry up! You only have five minutes more.' In a still more offhand manner, Cham recommended, on 17th May 1872, that judges ought to stand on rollers to make them less irremovable. Expeditious to the point of adapting to the constraints of train timetables, the courts, as we already know, are blind. Such blindness is however not always synonymous with fairness. Such is the lesson that we can draw from a sketch dated 20th November 1902 where, much to our regret, a judge having poor eyesight is not completely blind: we could have entrusted him with a sensitive case.[8]

No less commonplace is the reputation of a lawyers artfulness in a purposeful comparison with a doctor, the two practitioners also being deficient when carrying out their duties.[9] Most often corrupt and unscrupulous, lawyers often fall into disgrace when defending disreputable persons, but are in the least concerned when innocent persons are convicted. Born manipulators, these masters of eloquence come to an agreement, often to the detriment of their own clients to whom they incidentally make no illusion.[10]

---

[8]   Draner, 'Au Palais', *Le Charivari*, 20th November 1902. See also Draner, 'Au Palais de Justice', *Le Journal Amusant*, No. 2022, 1st June 1895.

[9]   *Le Charivari*, 24th December 1896, 7th November 1897 (Paf); 20th November 1897, p. 241.

[10]   Draner, *Le Journal Amusant*, No. 1991, August 1894. See Baric, *Le Charivari*, 17th April 1885, p. 74; Stop, *Le Charivari*, 13th October 1883.

Ill. 1: Baric, 'Nos Paysans', *Le Journal Amusant*, 3 février 1894, No. 1953, p. 2, coll. S. Vernois.

Moreover, the business acumen and hunger for money govern relations between members of the Bar and those who are called upon to defend, whatever the circumstances. Being closely in contact with the bad characters, lawyers can become as crafty as their clients.[11] These born comedians seek, whatever the price, the right pardon from judges by developing a seduction strategy towards them. We find this, for example, sketched by Stop on 10th May 1894 at the law courts' bar:

'Would Your Honour care to accept a little 'mêlé-cassis' [black-currant & alcohol mix]?' asks the obsequious. Although a gifted speaker with appropriate gestures to soften the jury, the lawyer knows that he can be malicious and indeed takes advantage of such right. Henceforth, we realise the scepticism of an artist like Henriot with regard to the authenticity of the arguments elaborated by these professionals of Law.[12] Does this not recall the extraordinary metamorphosis of a bad boy into a man of Justice?[13]

The portraits of judges or lawyers, which are not unlike the physiologies sought after in the mid-century, can indeed be recorded in the context of social history. But apart from these traditional studies on custom and habit, we can guess from the caricaturists the criticism of the legal profession's collusion with the political authorities and the economic leaders which the profession strives to protect. Hence the notion of 'secret' manipulation or conspiracy.

It does in fact seem that the judges intentionally abuse the respect resulting from their status, in order to intimidate witnesses. 'Well, sirs, let us not forget that we are the High Court' reads the caption of a Dorville sketch published in *Le Journal Amusant* dated 25th November 1899.[14] Of course, secrecy arouses public suspicion, even when the topic is treated with flippancy, or with slight imagination. 'Why not have the High Court established at the top of the Eiffel Tower? Moreover, it would have been spared from indiscretions?' asked Draner on 3rd May 1889.[15] For the readers of *Le Charivari*, at least it would have been comical to see the dignified magistrates hanging from the famous tower, the then attraction of World Exhibition.

Generally speaking, as soon as well-known persons are implicated, arrests are no longer made. In a sketch dated 24th December 1898, the

---

[11]   Stop, *Le Charivari*, 28th January 1898, p. 20.
[12]   *Le Charivari*, 9th December 1899 (not signed). See also 29th July 1902.
[13]   Draner, 'Les coulisses du Palais', *Le Charivari*, 13th February 1890.
[14]   Dorville, 'Défilés des Témoins', *Le Journal Amusant*, 25th November 1899. Noël Dorville (1871-1938).
[15]   *Le Charivari*, 3rd May 1889, p. 83.

Presiding Judge of the High Court is seemingly content just to note the absence of the accused.[16] The theory of a complicity between the political and judicial authorities appears several times in the sketches. Such theory suggests, however, a prior arrangement by players in court. Moreover, as of 21st January 1887, Henriot foresees the threat hanging over the judges, who are hidden behind barricades to protect themselves from the civil commotion. Learning from recent debate, the Presiding Judges of the Assizes shall take precautions when judging political trials.[17] As for the High Court, it is compared to a mountain giving birth to a mouse (24th November 1899).

The instructing magistrates are especially suspected of being involved in delaying proceedings. On 18th May 1889, Stop depicts them in a significant manner-perched on giant tortoises![18] The deference of the investigating magistrate, with regard to the rich and the powerful, seems clear in a sketch by Albert René dated 9th November 1902: 'I am obliged to question the defendent. However, if the accused would care to accept to have lunch with me, we could talk about the matter whilst dining.' The intrigues and manoeuvres of the investigating magistrate are exposed during the Bompard trial in June and July 1890. The sketch by Paf dated 20th July 1890 is quite explicit in that sense:

- Eyraud, did you pass the cord with the right hand or with the left hand? (asks the investigating judge).

I don't remember.

Yet another enquiry ... You have fifteen days to recollect your thoughts.[19]

As for the lawyers, without any doubt, they favour the interests of the community or the party, rather than those of their clients, who they will possibly ask to make a sacrifice, just for the 'good cause'. Hence, the feeling that reforms, particularly those concerning criminal records, should first be applied to politicians. 'So, why not oblige each Deputy to have his criminal record with him at all times?' asks Henriot 'innocently' on 18th September 1899.[20]

---

[16] René, *Le Charivari*, 24th December 1898. Albert René also signs 'Albrene'. See also Baric, *Le Charivari*, 11th February 1893.

[17] Henriot, *Le Charivari*, 21st January 1887, p. 15. See also *Le Charivari*, 6th September 1886.

[18] See also *Le Charivari*, 17th September, 2-5th October 1896. Stop, *Le Charivari*, 18th May 1889, p. 92. One of the projects for *Le Charivari* was to replace the painting of the Justice by that of Pénélope (24th January 1888).

[19] Paf, *Le Charivari*, 20th July 1890. Stop, *Le Charivari*, 24th June 1890.

[20] Gabriel Lion, *Le Charivari*, 18th October 1899. Gabriel Lion (Paris, c. 1875) was an expert in caricatures. Draner, 3rd March 1890, *Le Charivari*, p. 43.

Hence, we can see, like sandwich men, two 'honourable' deputies exhibiting notices on which are written dates linked to compromising political events for the good memory of the public. Hence, the denouncement appearing under the 'News' heading of *Le Charivari* concerning a justice of distinction, afflicting victims all the more due to having to bear the cynicism by magistrates and lawyers. On 28th February 1896, Draner portrays a defendant complaining of the lack of compensation despite his innocence. His counsel nevertheless sarcastically proposes that he take away the notes and sketches from the anthropometric department. 'It will amuse your family', said he laughing. On 26th May 1891, the judge himself intervenes, accusing the innocent defendant of having been fed and watered with impunity in prison, and asks the guards to take away the criminal who will be prosecuted for contempt of Court.[21]

It goes without saying that the caricaturists, in favour of the destitute, are under no illusion as to the efficiency of reforms. Hence, Draner, in *Le Journal Amusant* dated 19th May 1894 considered it ridiculous to abolish lawyers who cost nothing to the State, rather than abolishing policemen who cost so much.[22]

The authority of the investigating judge, arbitrarily using his right of pre-trial detention, is often considered as abusive. The magistrate's supreme authority is incidentally denounced in detail in a sketch dated 15th November 1890 depicting the investigating judge like a monarch, crowned and carrying a sceptre: 'With all authority in their hands, why not give them the insignia of their duties?' questions the caption.[23]

Indeed, the investigating judges should refrain from any inconsiderate declaration dictated through intimidation and, due to the law of 8th December 1897, the defendants could benefit from counsel. However, public condemnation is emerging. A song by Xanrof, illustrated by Lourdey and published in *Le Journal Amusant* dated 6th November 1897, adopts a lamenting tone in this regard. As we listen to the verses, we learn that the investigating judge has 'everyone within a ten miles radius put inside', offers two 'louis' coins to witnesses to pay for their omnibus and has even the cheek to employ a character 'of which one should be careful', to make puns in order to 'bring light relief' and to be sure to make the clerk laugh'.[24]

---

[21] Maurice Marais, *Le Charivari*, 26th May 1891. Maurice Marais (1852-1898).

[22] Draner, 'La suppression des avocats', *Le Journal Amusant*, No. 1968, 19th May 1894. Henriot, 'La suppression des avocats', *Le Charivari*, 19th March 1886 and 5th March 1896, p. 45.

[23] Draner, *Le Charivari*, 26th September 1892, p. 190 and 15th November 1892, p. 292.

[24] 'Les juges d'instruction', Words and music by Xanrof. Sketch by Lourdey (Maurice Lourdey, 1860 1934), *Le Journal Amusant*, No. 2149, 6th November 1897, p. 5.

According to Baric, out in the country, the innocence and lack of culture of the farmers increase injustice.[25] One can only be struck by the apparent poverty of these miserable wretches with their patched up clothes, brought to trial before self-satisfied judges. The adult defendant, however, does not forget on the day to assert his civil rights, becoming recalcitrant, sometimes foolishly: 'Yes, I told the Prosecutor that he should not count on my vote when he is up for election', says he impertinently.[26]

On 15th May 1902, the magistrates are again strongly condemned for miscarriage of justice. Indeed, a commoner being accused of having stolen thirty-two shillings, responds to the investigating judge: 'It is perfectly true, but if I had stolen one hundred million, you would perhaps not attempt to be so clever.' *Le Charivari*, however, does not have the political claims of the *Père Peinard* [an anarchistic newspaper]. Dignified though resigned, the commoner lacks the energy of the 'good chap' and, on the contrary, often withdraws into total silence.[27] In conclusion, the caricatures relate to us in pictures the chronicle of an ordinary court life, especially the petty tricks of the District Court, the theme of a sketch by Paul Léonnec in *Le Journal Amusant* dated 8th April 1893.[28]

Nevertheless, the cynical side of justice is fortrayed by Draner in the portrayed case of a child accused of pickpocketing on 13th February 1890. However terse it may be, the caption stirs the conscience of the reader-spectator as though a scathing condemnation: 'The commitment of man depends upon the vivacity of is desires', Duclos. Léandre on his part is under no illusion as to the possibilities of the destitute climbing the social ladder: 'Yes, dear members of the jury', proclaims the lawyer, 'just as the humblest of citizens can have the noblest of ambitions to climb upwards, my client will buy a grocery business.'[29]

---

[25] See Baric, *Le Journal Amusant*, No. 1953, 3rd February 1894. Barthélemy Gautier (1846-1893) touched upon this theme. See Draner, *Le Charivari*, 6th February 1885, March, 3rd November 1889.

[26] Stop, *Le Charivari*, 17th October 1882, p. 209. See Stop, *Le Charivari*, 29th August 1882, p. 173.

[27] In May 1902, Humbert affair (15th May-31st May). Baric, *Le Charivari*, 16th June 1893.

[28] Léonnec, 'À la Justice de Paix', *Le Journal Amusant*, No. 1910, 8th April 1893, p. 60. Paul Léonnec (1842-1899). Draner, *Le Charivari*, 12th April 1894. Henriot, *Le Charivari*, 10th November 1900.

[29] Charles Léandre, *Le Journal Amusant*, No. 2190, 20th August 1898. Charles Léandre, (1862-1934). See also 'Le témoin', *Le Journal Amusant*, 3rd December 1898.

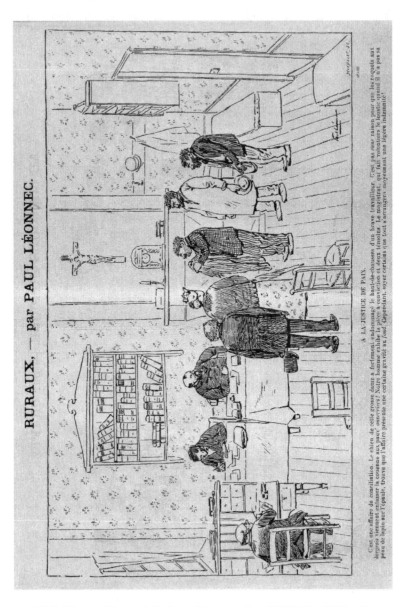

Ill. 2: Léonnec, 'Ruraux', *Le Journal Amusant*, 8 avril 1893, No. 1910, p. 6, coll. S. Vernois.

II. The Tricks of Appearance

Easily considered as a true vocation, a magistrate's duty in the 19th century comes with a great social prestige. It is probably not to be denied that the robe worn by these notables from the small provincial towns provides added dignity in the eyes of their fellow citizens.[30] However, for the caricaturists of the time, such regalia is very often only a decoy aimed at concealing the wrongs of justice. Despite its strictness, the robe is sometimes claimed as an item of style. Hence, in a sketch by Draner dated 9th March 1874, entitled 'Ball at the Commercial Court', a man of law is looking at himself in a mirror, not without self-satisfaction, like a young girl admiring the assured effect of her seductive power. In contrast, the learned magistrates lose some of their gravitas when more informally dressed. On 3rd March 1872, Cham recommends, for example, that the Court, during the warmer season, may sit wearing open-necked robes.

A few years later, on 29th July 1889, Henriot proposes to equip members of the High Court with a costume combining the respectability of a judge with the high temperatures of the summer season.[31] In this regard, it is easy to note the irony of the artist, not in the least ill-placed, in associating the insignia of duty – cap, ermine fur and a pair of scales, the court's emblem – with an ordinary pair of bathing trunks! Most of the time, however, indication of the costume enables the caricaturist to reveal the faculties of the Judiciary to adapt to the most varied situations. Hence, the magistrates by Draner are not afraid to dress up as Mandarins in order to be in harmony with the recent 'chinoiseries' ['Chineseries' = unnecessary complications] of proceedings (4th December 1899). As for the accessories, interchangeable headgear for example, they prove the connivance between the Justice and the armed forces, whichever the corps.[32] Hence, in order to shelter from possible attack, judges are advised to wear a fencing mask and when particularly in view, for example, members of the High Court, to wear a knight's amour.[33]

Generally speaking, by identifying the studied responses to the vagaries of women's fashion, the artists hardly appear to believe in the long-lasting reorganisation of the magistracy. On 3rd March 1872, Cham

---

[30]   M. Rousselet, *Histoire de la Justice en France*, PUF, 2e ed., 1948, p. 88.

[31]   Henriot, *Le Charivari*, 29th July 1889, p. 142.

[32]   Henriot, *Le Charivari*, 13th March 1882. See Draner 'Coiffure à la réforme judiciaire', *Le Charivari*, 7th April 1882.

[33]   Draner 'Modification à apporter au costume des juges pour les mettre à l'abri des projectiles des condamnés, Coiffure à la réforme judiciaire', *Le Charivari*, 7th April 1884, p. 69. Joseph Belon, 'Costume pour la Haute Cour', *Le Charivari*, 19th September 1899. Joseph Belon (1862-1927).

thus expresses the wish that the judges robes be brought into line with day-time dress. On 29th June 1883, Draner announces in turn 'The reorganisation of the magistracy' by asking: 'Why not brighten up old costumes by varying the robes and materials according to the rank?'[34] We can thus admire, on display in the window of a shop, a sumptuous cashmere robe designed for members of the Appeal Court and proposed at 150 francs, a very pretty taffeta robe reserved for judges of the Magistrates' Court, a charming chamber robe assigned to the Court of First Instance for the modest sum of 35 francs.

The specific clothing of the legal profession was going to provide an opportunity for their contemporaries to take up a fundamental question in a jocous manner – that of women acceding to the rank of lawyer.

Although the debate had been continuing since 1892, it became newspaper headlines in 1897, namely when Jeanne Chauvin requested on 24th November, before the First Chamber of the Paris Appeal Court, her admission into the lawyers association.[35] Yet, already on 26th August, *Le Charivari* had printed the title 'Long-live female lawyers'. On 10th October the same year, a sketch signed by Paf represents Mademoiselle Chauvin, 'the wonder one of the Bar', submerged under a pile of letters and beginning to regret the enthusiasm of her clients. Be it as it may the wearing of the lawyers robe enabled a group of detractors to take issue in the criticism in the judiciary in the case of Jeanne Chauvin, in relation to wanting at all costs, to keep the profession as a male preserve. On 13th August 1897, Draner, for his part, jokingly says with all pretence. 'In order that in law courts', he says, 'there is no confusion between female and male lawyers, *Le Charivari* requests that the latter wear low-necked robes.' On the 12th December 1900 the same artist continues the controversy and suggests, through the mouth of one of his heroines, a clothes' exchange between the men and women of the Bar. 'Seeing as you have monopolised the 'robe', sirs, it seems only logical for us to adopt breaches and a morning coat to distinguish ourselves from you.'[36] Are we to understand in all that, the abandoning of all male chauvinism by *Le Charivari* readers, masculine in their majority? In fact, caricaturists, as always, are fond of ambiguity. Hence, they never miss an opportunity to stress the pernicious effects of the feminine condition in a social context within the profession: child birth, problems of child-care. When these ladies go back to their knitting between consultations, it is heredity itself that becomes a threat. Implicitly, the female applicants are

---

[34] Draner 'La réorganisation de la Magistrature', *Le Charivari*, 29th June 1883, p. 132.

[35] J.-P. Royer, *Histoire de la Justice en France, de la Monarchie à la République*, Paris, PUF, 2001, p. 666. Paf, 'Croquis', *Le Charivari*, 10th October 1897.

[36] Draner, 'Les femmes avocates', 12th December 1900.

accused of jeopardizing their family, and beyond the family, the entire social order.[37] 'Woe betide the husband of the Lady President of the Bar, who shall make use of her symbols of office in the event of disagreement' launches a mocking Draner on 26th August 1897. Nevertheless, it is indeed masculine cynicism which, although does not necessarily win, at least enables to close all debate. We witness such words from a divorce candidate bragging to woo a female lawyer: 'I shall promise to wed her so that she will plead divorce with my wife with more conviction.'[38] At other times, the decency expected of the handsome sex is opportunely evoked in order to exclude women from sex cases.

The caricaturists even insist on the absurdity of certain situations, whereby female lawyers have to imagine themselves in the situation of their male clients:

And it is us, Sirs, who are being accused of committing this rape.

But look at me, Sirs, this accusation makes no sense.[39]

In the end, the natural role of the women is the seduction. Henriot's sketch dated 25th December 1888, entitled 'It just goes to show that the female lawyer can have some good', is perfectly clear on this point.[40] We can see an attractive young lady, admittedly wearing the lawyer's robe, though with the bosom completely naked and out in the background the judges scrutinising the pleadings through their binoculars. Failing an advantageous low neckline, the short robe is considered as a necessary modification in order to distinguish female lawyers from their colleagues. Moreover, these ladies have a gift for repartee to know how to defend themselves, even though attempts at familiarity from clients are still to be feared.[41] However, it seems that they hardly take any notice, if we are to believe a sketch by Henriot dated 23rd January 1899. 'Good gracious! This costume seems a little daring', points out an honourable cautious-looking man. The enticing-looking lady retorts quite plainly: 'Phryné was even more audacious, my dear sir.' However, the great danger no doubt comes from the fact that feminine seduction is likely to be used as a weapon, having the sole aim of destabilising the jury and magitrates.[42]

---

[37] Stop, 'Les femmes du Barreau', *Le Charivari*, 27th May 1892, p. 140. Draner, 'Vivent les avocates', *Le Charivari* 26th August 1897.

[38] Draner, *Le Charivari*, 12th December 1900. See also 26th August and 5th November 1897 (p. 225).

[39] Draner, *Le Charivari*, 28th August 1897.

[40] Henriot, *Le Charivari*, 25th December 1888, p. 248.

[41] Henriot, 'Nos avocates', *Le Charivari*, 2-3 January 1899.

[42] Draner, *Le Charivari*, 26th August 1897. See also Henriot, 20th October 1897.

Hence, Pif advises the State Prosecutor to make eyes at the Presiding Judge in order to restore the balance. Besides, it would certainly seem that the feminine solidarity reserves some surprises, despite the inevitable jealousy. 'Remember, my dear', advises a senior female lawyer, 'that one can steal a lover or a husband, but a client will never come back.' (Draner, 26th August 1897).

If fear of smutty drifting shows through in some captions, a little sauciness finally surpasses the equality of the sexes. The moral of this whole story appears in fact in a sketch dated 1st August 1897 signed by Paf. Two members of the Bar leaving court can be seen conversing

- 'The idea of seeing female lawyers at the courts does not revolt you?' asks one with a worried look.

'On the contrary … it will perhaps prevent the Court from falling asleep during hearings', answers the other laughing.[43]

Hence, to fight against boredom, there is only one remedy in the eyes of contemporaries: chivalry.

Any excuse, in fact, seems good for distracting the austere men of law, even the passing of a pretty silhouette amidst the sombre robes of the court rooms. Draner also mentions the 'little perks' of the judges, by noting that the graphic reconstitution of a rape is the only consolation for the judiciary.[44] As for Henriot, he feigns on 17th December 1897 to bemoan the gloomy night duties of magistrates deprived of their spouse. As for Jack Abeillé, he is content simply to stress the benefits of the 'refreshing massages of judges, exhausted after so many pointless sessions' in the presence of pretty female spectators.[45] Just like the public, the jury does not escape from the temptation of voyeurism. In a sketch dated 22nd January 1891, we can see a young man, extremely pleased to recount in the worldly salons every minor detail of a session in camera. A member of the audience nevertheless strongly criticises him for having acquitted the female defendant because she was pretty.

Hence, frivolity, which constitutes the very essence of humour in 1900, emerges victorious from the gloomy atmosphere, as though no doubt to remind that despite appearances, authenticity is often quite difficult to discern.

---

[43] See also Draner, *Le Charivari*, 26th August 1897.

[44] See Draner, 'Les coulisses du Palais', *Le Charivari*, 27th February 1890. See also 17th July 1895 & 26th January 1899 'Leurs petits bénéfices', Henriot, *Le Charivari*, 26th January 1866, p. 14.

[45] Jacques Abeillé, called 'Jack', born in 1873. 'La permanence de nuit des magistrats', *Le Charivari*, 17th December 1897, p. 257, *Le Charivari*, 5th January 1900. See also: Henriot, *Le Charivari*, 22nd January and 9th March 1891, Draner, 31st July 1901.

III. The Right to Decide to the Extent of Absurdity

People's good sense often offers the best response to the prevarications of Justice. In the case of the caricatures of *Le Charivari* and *Le Journal Amusant*, the subtleties of a purely graphic humour readily give way, it must be amitted, to silly puns and a simplister play on words.[46] Whether through strategy or ingenuity, the accused exercice their rights in a forceful and disconcerting manner, with their responses often being recorded profoundly in the wrong in relation to the judicial system. In other words, through humour whether or not at their expense, the accused portrayed by Cham, Stop, Draner ou Henriot do not belong within the social norms, nor within a typical logic. In a drawing by Draner dated 26th July 1887, we can see the accused, a commoner, haranguing the stunned judges. 'For the safety of the honourable court which gives me the honour of attending the proceedings', says he, 'I request, Your Honour, that we first set up an emergency service in order to maintain, in the event of an accident, a free conscience.' In the same line of thought, his fellow accused are called in to attend as witnesses in order to request damages to the Presiding Judge, should the latter resort to insulting remarks.[47]

The impertinence, however, is at its height when a bad character called to trial audaciously requests dismissal of the State Prosecutor as his defence. Of course, the civilities and the claim of a legal right are fallacious excuses, used as tactics in a defence. The artist, Mars, illustrates a curious dialogue: to the Presiding Judge asking the accused what he was doing prior to arrest, the latter retorts that he cannot reply because he does not want to give a preview of his memoirs.[48] A murderer arrogantly claims a premium for his confessions, having, in his opinion, amply assisted the police.[49]

As a general rule, the logic of the argumentation is in line with the interests of the accused. 'Each execution costs 23,000 French francs to the country. Plead for me in terms of cost', confides the prisoner to his lawyer.[50]

---

[46] Draner, *Le Charivari*, 7th November 1891, p. 216.

[47] Henriot, *Le Charivari*, 12th January 1891, p. 5.

[48] Draner, *Le Charivari*, 26th June 1902. Mars, *Le Charivari*, 23rd November 1889, p. 24. Mars (1849-1912).

[49] Draner, 'Les Echos du Palais', *Le Journal Amusant*, No. 2188, 6th August 1898, p. 6.

[50] Paf, *Le Charivari*, 15th January 1899.

GENS DE JUSTICE

— Cette affaire me trouble beaucoup... une gaffe peut me causer de réels préjudices... en résumé, pour un juge d'instruction, les criminels ne sont réellement dangereux que lorsqu'ils sont arrêtés !

Ill. 3: Henriot, 'Gens de Justice', *Les Maîtres Humoristes*, 2ᵉ série, No. 8, 1909, coll. S. Vernois.

It can happen, however, that injustice leaves a bitter taste for the defendant, for reasons that can affect common sensitivities: 'Six months in custody for a crime that I did not commit', screams a man in the middle of proceedings. He continues: 'I request at least to commit the rape of which I am wrongly accused.'[51] As for the murderer sketched by Baric on 12th May 1894, he is proud to prove his good will by asserting that during his second crime, he killed only one person instead of two.[52]

Certain words actually reveal in passing the political consciousness of the accused, such as the burglar refusing point-blank to be compared with crude forgers and blackmailers. Ferocious irony or an act of bravado, the future convict, leaving for New Caledonia shouts: 'Your Honour, I am in favour of colonial expansion.'[53] As a general rule however, the degree of absurdity in the answer is comparable with the dramatic nature of the situation and the extent of desperation. The evocation of death sentences particularly provides caricaturists with an opportunity to broaden their scope of dark humour. We can also see the convict becoming the center of attention by prison staff, who are afraid that he will catch a cold.[54] The latter attempts an ultimate subterfuge by refusing to climb onto the scaffold as long as the local council has not sorted out the question of gas. (4th February 1902).

The nobleness of attitude takes on, however, a suicidal air when the convict waiting to be beheaded is informed by his lawyer at the very last minute that there is no room left for execution; nevertheless the convict roars with determination, 'I demand application of the law. It's my right, yes or no?' (26th July 1902).

Hence, the humorist seems to say, when injustice prevails, anything is possible, and leniency is not necessarily a reassuring factor. If an innocent person is shown to fully rejoice at the idea of finally having a criminal record for contempt of court, this is only a mockery.[55] He indeed knows that such past criminal record is known to any new judge, thus enabling the accused, under the Bérenger Law, known as the reprieve law of 26th March 1891, to be released from sentence where he had not been previously convicted. Hence, the culprit of the sketch by Draner dated 6th September 1901 indulges in every challenge. Indeed, he does not deny having stolen from his mother-in-law, but he claims: 'Since this was the first time for me to do this, I request, just like the others, to be granted benefit from the Bérenger Law.' Reacting against

---

[51] Draner, *Le Charivari*, 19th January 1891.

[52] Baric, *Le Charivari* 12th May 1894, p. 93.

[53] *Le Charivari*, 2nd October 1894. See also Draner, *Le Journal Amusant*, 1er June 1895.

[54] *Le Charivari*, 25th July, 25th September 1890.

[55] Marais, *Le Charivari*, 16-17th August 1895.

such leniency, Henriot proposes a prudish law on 25th April 1895, a project devoted to the chaste Bérenger by *Le Charivari*.

In this fanciful world, sanctions are hencforth totally out of proportion with the crime. Hence, according to Article 12, the woman who, by winking or making other signs, shall have aroused guilty ideas in men, will be liable to the death penalty.

As for the juries, they are also suspected of indulgence, as not content just to acquit the authors of crimes of passion, we are told, they always end up by granting them medals of honour and crowns of laurel leaves.[56]

Although indulgence is not the ideal solution, revolt also takes on absurd airs. Did not that old woman hide a bomb in her corset when she was tried before the judge? (18th April 1891). Nevertheless, the respectability of the Court, forced to adjourn the hearing for one week, seems quite pathetic when the accused, carrying 6 kg of dynamite, screams: 'One more word and I will sit on it and blow up the Court.'[57]

Without doubt, we can guess similarities of opinion with the *Père Peinard* when the old man [newspaper] evokes the Mazas prison with nostalgia.[58] In any event, the political options are always tainted by the absurd. Hence in their fantasies, the most eccentric of artists imagines the broadest permissiveness inside the prisons, conferring henceforth an idyllic aspect therein. Since the court is a theatre, why not rejoice when seeing the comedian Coquelin Cadet arrive among the juries?[59] And in this world where everything, according to the caricaturists, is simply fiction, it is not surprising that the minor-ranking clerks study Law from serialised novels (Draner, 27th February 1890).

We again find the height of absurdity in a sketch showing a labourer with a tattoo on his arm reading, 'Long live anarchy'. He exclaims: 'I say that it's a scandal. Those people are no longer respected by judiciary.'[60]

Beyond the inherent exaggeration in caricature and the strings of an often easy humour used by artists regularly associated with periodicals, it is clear that the sketches by Cham, Stop, Draner, Henriot and several others, reflect to some extent the state of mind of their times. The witty eloquence that provided the reputation of *Le Charivari* during the

---

56 Henriot, *Le Charivari*, 27th December 1894, p. 256. See Rousselet, *op. cit.*, p. 115.

57 *Le Charivari*, 21st May 1901, p. 221.

58 See Henriot, *Le Charivari*, 15th November 1897, p. 221. René, 18th July 1898, p. 146.

59 René, *Le Journal Amusant*, 22nd July 1899, No. 9. Draner, 'La Réforme pénitentiaire', *Le Charivari*, 25th September 1890.

60 René 'Le respect de la magistrature', *Le Charivari*, 10th December 1899.

glorious years has disappeared. In many respects, however, we can consider that the political claims, particularly expressed during the major 'Affairs', have been taken up by other periodicals, the *Père Peinard* being the most virulent, prior to *L'Assiette au Beurre* which joined the scene at the beginning of the 20th century.[61] Nevertheless, *Le Charivari* and *Le Journal Amusant* maintained, to a lesser extent, the originality of combining moral perspective with a political conscience.

Besides, it is interesting to note that the caricaturists take up, in a minor way, certain themes developed by the *Père Peinard*, for example, the one where the commoner confronts his judges, or the one depicting a blatant miscarriage of Justice.[62]

However, it seems that the recurrent subjects, coming back repeatedly, are proof of the overall weariness.

The truth coming out the well in front of the French National Assembly building is itself surprised that one comes again to fetch it on 13th November 1895. Indeed, it is quite difficult to determine whether the lack of a significant artist on the staff of *Le Charivari* and *Le Journal Amusant* contributed to this general impression of scepticism, or if, on the contrary, despondency caused the decline of the satirical witty eloquence of *Le Charivari.*

The sketches concerning Justice and Politics reflect in any case a disenchantment which is not only linked to the loss of respectability of magistrates or members of the Bar, but which reflects the doubts of society in relation to itself. Over the years, the judicial world is scarcely any longer a cause for mirth. The argumentation between the lawyer and the investigating judge seems quite pathetic (6th January 1898), and in the tiny theatre of the court, the judges are intentionally portrayed as puppets on a string manipulated by politicians.[63] In the end, this terse phrase stated by a lawyer in a sketch dated 27th February 1890 is quite significant: 'In justice, the legal right is not always a reason to assert it.'[64] Already in 1888, in his preface of *Les Tribunaux Comiques* by Jules Moinaux, Armand Silvestre notes 'the modern indifference that makes this turn-of-the-century a completely dishonest era', and referring just as much to the well off rogues to the rogues in rags, the writer reveals that conscience with them is dead. The spirit of the time of the so-called 'Belle Époque' was thus a nihilistic one. In this context, the

---

61 *L'Assiette au Beurre*, weekly founded in 1901.

62 *Le Père Peinard*, weekly anarchist newspaper published from 1889 (ed. Emile Pouget).

63 *Le Charivari*, 18th September and 24th November 1895. Henriot, 'Magistrature idéale', *Le Charivari*, 15th November 1902.

64 *Le Charivari*, 18th February, 27th April, 1890.

caption of the sketch by Albert René dated 1st March 1900 has a particularly emblematic value:

> - Mister, I knew an officer who was a crook! Get rid of the army, it will not happen again...
>
> Mister, a magistrate has been arrested for false entries! Get rid of the magistracy...
>
> Sirs, everyday, civilians are arrested for theft and assassination! Get rid of the civilians...[65]

References

Le Charivari, 1832-1937.

Le Journal Amusant, journal illustré, journal d'images, journal comique 1855-1932.

J.-P. Royer, *Histoire de la Justice en France, de la Monarchie à la République*, Paris, PUF, 2001.

C. Saint-Martin, *plus de 5000 dessinateurs de presse et 600 supports en France, de Daumier à l'An 2000*, Dictionnaire Solo, Aedis, 2004.

A. Silvestre, preface of the Jules Moinaux book, *Les Tribunaux Comiques*, illustrated by Stop, 3rd series ed. 1888, Chevalier-Marescq & Co. editors.

---

[65] A. Silvestre, *Les Tribunaux Comiques* by Jules Moinaux, *op. cit.*, p. IX. René, *Le Charivari*, 1st March 1900. Henriot, *Les Maîtres Humoristes*, No. 08, Société d'Édition et de Publications, March 1909.

Decoding Justice

Intellectual Discourse
and the Trial of the Malagasy Deputies

Mairéad Ni BHRIAIN

IRCHSS scholar, National University of Ireland, Galway

> La justice et la vérité sont deux pointes sues subtiles,
> que nos instruments sont trop mousses pour y toucher
> exactement. S'ils y arrivent, ils en écachent la pointe, et
> appuient tout autour, plus sur le faux que sur le vrai.
>
> Blaise Pascal

I. 'La France et la justice': Attachment of the French to Ideal of Justice

In his introduction to *Histoire de la Révolution Française*, Jules Michelet writes: 'Je définis la Révolution, l'avènement de la Loi, la résurrection du Droit, la réaction de la Justice. [...] La Révolution n'est autre chose que la réaction tardive de la Justice contre le gouvernement de la faveur et la religion de la Grâce.'[1] The prominence accorded to the notion of justice by one of France's most renowned historians of the French revolution is indicative of the primacy of law within the Republic and the central role accorded to the ideal of justice within the revolutionary heritage.

With the advent of the French Republic and the *État de Droit* came a new *credo*, a new religion, and at the heart of this republican *credo* was a new, improved 'absolute' ruler: the law. No longer subjects of the King, all men were now subject solely to the law. In theory, no man was above the law and, as the law was to be recorded by the written word, each man was equal in the eyes of this immovable force in which his

---

[1] J. Michelet, *Histoire de la Révolution Française*, Tome 1, Bibliothèque de la Pléiade, Gallimard, Édition 1961, p. 21.

rights were enshrined. Thus, the very foundations of the French Republic relate to the ideal of justice which is to be attained and maintained
through the creation and implementation of *les lois écrites*.

A. Justice in the Colonies: 'La Dualité des Lois'

The *Déclaration des Droits de l'Hommes et du Citoyen*,[2] which
enumerates and safeguards the rights of the individual, records the
centrality of equality to the French conception of a democratic republic,
further reinforcing the assertion that representations of France and
French identity are contingent on the law and, more generally, the
notion of justice. This vision of an egalitarian society differentiates the
French republican ideal from that of the United States which places
Liberty at the centre of its republican ideology. Betrayal of this sacred
republican value has been and is often perceived as a threat to the very
essence and identity of the French nation. The Dreyfus affair is undoubtedly the most striking example of this identification between *une
certaine idée de la justice* and *une certaine idée de la France*, specifically between republican justice and the French nation.[3] Within this
context, representations of French republican justice exported to the
colonies were to come under scrutiny as they frequently seemed incon-
gruous to the republican ideal of justice, based on the equality of all in
the eyes of the law. Gilles Manceron has termed this phenomenon the
'republican paradox'.[4] Bancel *et al.*[5] argue that the republican paradox
manifests itself, not only in the negation of human rights in the colonies,
but in the very concept and existence within what claims to be a democratic, republican and, most importantly, egalitarian regime of a parallel
colonial regime based on inequality and oppression.

The native inhabitants of the colonies were placed outside the category of citizen and remained subjects of the French Republic. Therefore
they were not subject to the same laws as French citizens. This 'duality
of law'[6] – symbolised, for example, by the *Code de l'indigénat*[7] – within

---

2 Adopted by the French National Assembly on 26 August 1798.

3 For a more detailed account to the exemplarity and symbolic value of the Dreyfus
affair, see O. Baruch et S. Duclert, *Justice, politique et République, De l'affaire
Dreyfus à la guerre d'Algérie*, IHTP/CNRS, Éditions Complexe, 2002, p. 23.

4 G. Manceron, *Marianne et les colonies, une introduction à l'histoire coloniale de la
France*, La Découverte, 2003, p. 18.

5 See N. Bancel, P. Blanchard, et F. Vergès in *La République coloniale, essai sur une
utopie*, Éditions Albin Michel, 2003.

6 This expression is borrowed from the writings of Montesquieu in *De l'esprit des lois*,
Tome 1, Éditeur Jean de Bonnot, 1999.

7 In 1887, the French government imposed the *Code de l'indigénat* in all of its colonies. It was this code which provided for a separate status for the natives of the colo-

the 'One and indivisible French Republic', provided a legal structure which facilitated the ideological contradictions inherent in French colonial discourse and thus ensured the institutionalisation of 'inequality' and what has become known as the 'colonial exception'.

The ideal of republican justice thus became distorted through its function both as an instrument of oppression and an instrument of justification of that oppression with the colonies.[8] The discrepancy between an 'ideal (or sense) of justice' and the 'practise (or application) of the law' was therefore all the more evident within the colonial context. Consequently, references to justice in discourse relating to the colonies often prove ambiguous, whereby 'Justice' becomes an elusive ideal, a hollow conception which refers to everything and yet represents nothing specific or tangible.

This paper shall endeavour to demonstrate the manner in which the ambiguity often surrounding the concept of justice can lead to its usage as a codeword or a 'mantra'. The term mantra is, in this context, borrowed from the writings of Lévi Strauss who defines it as 'une valeur indéterminée de signification, en elle-même vide de sens, et donc susceptible de recevoir n'importe quel sens, dont l'unique fonction est de combler un écart entre le signifiant et le signifié'.[9] Roland Barthes draws from this definition in his essay on *La Grammaire Africaine* and identifies the term *honneur* as a french-mantra. Describing it as an empty space used for the collection of all the 'hidden', 'unspeakable' meaning, *honneur*, claims Barthes, is the noble equivalent of generic, ill-defined terms such as *truc* or *machin* meaning 'thing'. The analysis that follows suggests that the term justice also functions as french-mantra. We will argue in support of the claim that 'Justice' (in the Kantian sense) was used as a rhetorical device by certain French intellectuals – Albert Camus and Jean-Marie Domenach being important examples – as they commented upon the workings of 'Justice' (meaning the justice system)

---

nies, making them subjects of the French empire rather than citizens and therefore subject to different laws and sanctions. The *Code de l'indigénat* placed numerous restrictions and restraints on these 'subjects' (forced labour, curfews at night, heavy taxes and requisitions) and violation of these laws was punishable by imprisonment. This exceptional system of laws remained in force until 1946, some eight years after the Geneva Convention (23th April 1938) which precluded all forms of forced labour. Although the *Code de l'indigénat* was abolished on 7th April 1947, the tradition of legal exception to which it had contributed left an indelible mark on both the colonial and the French psyche.

[8] For a detailed account and analysis of the use of the justice system as an instrument of colonial oppression, see S. Thénault, *Une drôle de justice: Les magistrats dans la guerre d'Algérie*, La Découverte, 2001.

[9] Cited in R. Barthes, 'La Grammaire Africaine', *Mythologies*, Éditions du Seuil, 1957, p. 156.

in relation to the French colonies throughout the period of decolonisation.

B. Intellectuals[10] and Justice

The workings of the law and the ideal of justice have traditionally occupied a central place in French intellectual discourse. The legislature was seen by many of the *philosophes* as a sacred function. Montesquieu, Voltaire and Rousseau each endeavoured to articulate conceptions and representations of *l'Égalité*, *La Loi* and *La Justice* in society. In post-revolutionary France, however, it was primarily the safeguarding of these laws and of republican justice which became the 'sacred function' of the intelligentsia. Zola's intervention in the Dreyfus affair is perhaps the most historic and symbolic example of this function. His famed article, 'J'accuse', which condemned the violation of one man's right to justice and called upon the government to protect the Republic by safeguarding her ideals, provided a model for later generations of intellectuals who drew inspiration from this act of engagement. Zola was seen to have made his own the cause of 'justice' as a universal value. He thus served as the *clerc désintéressé*[11] par excellence in Julien Benda's essay on *La Trahison des clercs*, his ostensibly perfect intellectual profile being set in sharp contrast to that of intellectuals such as Barrès. Benda accused Barrès and other members of *Action française* of having betrayed the sacred function of the intellectual in choosing to defend political causes over universal values.

C. Wartime Experiences and the Burden of Responsibility

However, the vision of the *clerc désintéressé* and the very notion of justice became obscured and seemingly unattainable in the years imme-

---

[10] As with the notion of justice, the term intellectual is, in itself, extremely problematic and difficult to define. Various definitions for the term have been advanced by scholars. However, amid this plethora of categorisations, one common factor is clearly identifiable: the irrefutable link between the Dreyfus Affair and the advent of the intellectual as a public figure. Sirinelli, Ory, Winock and Drake each use this episode in French history as their starting point in recounting the history of the French intellectual. The present study defines as intellectuals those individuals who choose to intervene, become engaged or bear witness in the public domain with purpose, their intent being to challenge or change the status quo. Included in this would-be category of intellectuals are writers, artists, members of the 'academy' and various figures involved in (what may be termed) higher-journalism.

[11] Originally, Julien Benda defined the *clercs désintéressés* as: 'cette classe d'hommes dont l'activité ne poursuit pas des fins pratiques, mais qui demande sa joie à l'exercice de l'art ou de la science ou de la spéculation métaphysique, c'est-à-dire à la possession d'un bien intemporel.' Benda. Julien, *La Trahison des clercs*, Grasset, 1975, p. 10.

diately following the Liberation. The humiliating defeat in 1940, followed by four years of German occupation, had shaken the very foundations of the French nation. Liberation by the American (Allied) forces, followed by the emergence of a new bipolar world-order in which France was no longer one of the great and powerful nations, exacerbated this French *crise d'identité*. The safeguarding of a certain idea of France and of the French republican heritage of universal values was seen as a means by which French pride and reputation could be restored. Consequently, the French intelligentsia, which was to play a key role in this reconstruction of French national pride and identity, could ill afford the luxury of being *désintéressé*.

This is evidenced by the purging of the national community, wherein the thirst for vengeance among members of the intellectual community was particularly remarkable. Concepts of an 'ideal' justice gave way to retributive justice. Tony Judt has drawn attention to the persistent failure of intellectuals to produce any form of consensus or definition of the notion of justice during this post-war period.[12] Judt's analysis gives priority to the confusion and conflict among intellectuals surrounding representations of justice in relation to the Cold War paradigm, accusing many communist fellow travellers of intellectual irresponsibility due to their refusal to condemn soviet injustices.[13] Links between conflicting visions of justice and the question of intellectual responsibility or irresponsibility are further illustrated by disputes surrounding the trial and subsequent execution of Robert Brasillach (1945).[14]

Undeniably, the trial represents a forum through which the implementation of law and, by extension, the fulfilment of the ideal that is 'Republican Justice', takes place and is debated. Accordingly, intellectual discourse generated by colonial-related trials also reveals tensions and inconsistencies as to the definition and understanding of 'republican justice'. This paper centres on intellectual representations of justice within the colonial context and more specifically that of decolonisation. Consequently, the indictment and trial of the Malagasy nationalist deputies, which took place in the months following the 1947 Malagasy Revolt shall form the focal point for analysis of this intellectual discourse.

---

[12] 'The absence in post-war France, of any consensus about justice – its meaning, its forms, its application – contributed to the confused and inadequate response of French intellectuals to the evidence of injustice elsewhere', T. Judt, *Past Imperfect, French Intellectuals 1944-1956*, University of California Press, 1992, p. 75.

[13] *Ibid.*, p. 101.

[14] I refer here in particular to the public debate which took place through the medium of journalistic articles between Francois Mauriac and Albert Camus, the former arguing against the execution of Robert Brasillach.

II. The Malagasy Case[15]

On the night of 29 March 1947, Malagasy nationalist forces mounted an attack on numerous French military bases throughout the eastern part of the island, their aim being to overthrow the French administration and thus bring about independence for Madagascar. Malagasy nationalism had been accelerated by the Second World War, an experience which resulted in the politicisation of much of the population. Concessions made to the colonial peoples as a result of the Brazzaville (1944) conference, whereby Madagascar ceased to be a colony and became an overseas territory, allowed for Malagasy political representation in the French National Assembly for the first time since 1896. This gave rise to the creation of a new, vibrant national party in Madagascar, namely the MDRM.[16] The party experienced considerable success in 1946 with three members being elected as deputies to the French National Assembly.

The success of the MDRM, adding to the existing nationalist fervour in Madagascar, soon came to be seen as a threat to French sovereignty and the colonial status quo. Accordingly, the 1947 nationalist revolt was seized upon by the colonial administration as an opportunity to disband and outlaw the MDRM and to reassert French authority over the island. While a swift and brutal repression of the rebellion, resulting in the death of 80,000 Malagasies, saw to the latter of these objectives, the elimination of the MDRM proved to be a more lengthy process, involving the trial of three Malagasy deputies to the French National Assembly, namely, Jacques Rabemananjara, Joseph Ravoahangy and Joseph Raseta.

The three MDRM parliamentarians had their diplomatic immunity revoked, following debates and a vote on the question in the Assembly on 1st August 1947.[17] However, it should be noted that two of the deputies had been imprisoned since 12th April, despite their right, under constitutional law, to diplomatic immunity. Only Joseph Raseta remained free until June 1947 as he was in Paris when the events occurred. The police accused the deputies of having incited the revolt by

---

[15] Unless otherwise stated, all historical information pertaining to the Malagasy revolt was sourced from three principal works: Rabearimanana, L., *La Presse d'opinion à Madagascar de 1947 a 1956, contribution à l'histoire du nationalsime malgache du lendemain de l'insurrection à la veille de la Loi-Cadre*, Librarie Mixte, Madagascar, 1980, P. Stibbe, *Justice pour les Malgaches*, Seuil, 1954 and J. Tronchon, *L'Insurrection malgache de 1947*, Karthala, 1986.

[16] Mouvement Démocratique de Rénovation Malgache. (Democratic Movement for Malagasy Renovation).

[17] Raseta's immunity had been revoked on 6th June 1947.

means of a coded telegram.[18] They were indicted for conspiracy against the state and endangering national security.[19] Their trial took place from 22nd July 1948 to 4th October 1948. The principal witness (Samuel Rakotondrabe), said to have incriminated the deputies, was shot three days before the commencement of the trial. Moreover, much of the evidence against the deputies was said to have been obtained through the use of torture. Despite the fact that these 'judicial irregularities' were brought into question during the trial, Joseph Raseta and Joseph Ravoahangy were sentenced to death while Jacques Rabemananjara received a life sentence. Raseta and Ravoahangy were granted clemency and their sentences commuted to life imprisonment. All three deputies were granted amnesty in 1956.

Among the numerous texts written by intellectuals relating to this affair, it was the left-wing liberal Catholic monthly *Esprit* that published the highest percentage of articles dealing with Madagascar although other left-wing publications, such as *Humanité* and *Franc-tireur* and *Témoignage Chrétien*, also published numerous protests. The centre left non-communist publication *Combat* also registered opposition. Interestingly, *Les Temps Modernes*, which, according to David Drake, was later to become known as *the* anti-colonial newspaper due to its protests against the war in Indochina, remained relatively silent in relation to the 'events' in Madagascar and the subsequent trial of the Malagasy deputies.[20]

The most prominent personality to voice an opinion was Albert Camus in an article entitled 'La Contagion' which appeared in *Combat* on 10th May 1947. This will be the first of two articles under analysis in this paper. The second text was written by Jean-Marie Domenach[21] for

---

18   The message called upon people to 'maintain absolute calm and coolness in face of manoeuvres and provocations (of) all kinds destined to stir up troubles (among the) Malagasy population and to sabotage peaceful policy of the MDRM'. Cited in Sorum, Paul-Clay, *Intellectuals and Decolonisation in France*, University of North Carolina Press, 1977.

19   They were accused and arrested according to the concept of *flagrant délit continu*.

20   Although *Les Temps Modernes* did publish a dossier by Roger Stéphane on the affair, this gesture came late in the day (October 1948), when the verdict had already been read. Thus, it offered no real opposition to the manner in which the trial was carried out, but rather a retrospective commentary on what had taken place.

21   Born in Lyon in 1922, into a catholic family, Jean Marie Domenach belongs to the lift-wing liberal catholic category of French intellectuals, often categorised by their affiliation with the review *Esprit* (founded by Emmanuel Mounier in 1932). Having fought in the Resistance, Domenach was eager to become involved in intellectual debates concerning France's future. He joined *Esprit* in 1946. In 1957 he assumed direction of the review, a position which he held until 1976. A strong critic of colonial abuses he sought to promote, through his writings, a sense of moral responsibil-

Esprit's special edition on Madagascar in February 1948 and is entitled 'Union Francaise sans mensonge'.

A. Albert Camus Justice as Improved Colonialism

A native of French Algeria, Camus' engagement in colonial affairs has been widely associated with the Algerian conflict. Consequently, relatively little research has been carried out pertaining to his involvement or engagement in other colonial crises during the period of decolonisation. His interest in the Malagasy affair lies in the fact that certain journalistic reports of the investigation betray the presence, in France, of racial prejudice. The author's accusation is based on the fact that certain journalists have prematurely judged and labelled one of the Malagasy deputies as *L'assassin Raseta* despite the fact that the investigation into the affair is ongoing. Camus sees this as a sign that racism is taking hold of French society:

> Un journal du matin titre sur plusieurs colonnes, en première page: 'L'assassin Raseta.' C'est un signe. Car il est bien évident que l'affaire Raseta est aujourd'hui à l'instruction. [...] la question est de savoir si M. Raseta est un assassin ou non. Il est sûr qu'un honnête homme n'en décidera qu'une fois l'instruction terminée. En tout état de cause, aucun journaliste n'aurait osé un pareil titre si l'assassin supposé s'appelait Dupont ou Durand. Mais M. Raseta est malgache, et il doit être assassin de quelque façon.[22]

Camus also raises the question of torture, albeit briefly, as he affirms that *Combat* has discovered the existence of *la chambre d'aveux spontanés* in Fianarantsoa. However, he avoids engaging with this issue and its more far-reaching significance and implications of these injustices for the mission civilisatrice and the future of the French Union on any deep level, claiming, as he frequently does in other articles, that the problem is of another order. ('Je n'aborderai pas le fond du problème qui est d'un autre ordre'). This is a rhetorical device frequently used by Camus in his writings on the colonial question, through which he skirts the issues of colonialism, advocating only the need for reforms within the system while failing to question the legitimacy of the system itself.

In acknowledging this failing, it is also worth noting that as 'La Contagion' does raise the issues of racism and perceived French superiority, it goes further than any other of the Camusian repertoire pertaining to the colonies in actually broaching the origins of French colonialism and the ideology which underpins it, though the author remains consistent in

---

ity. For more information, see J Julliard, and M. Wincok, *Dictionnaire des intellectuels français, Les personnes, les lieux, les moments.* Éditions du Seuil, 2002, p. 434.

[22] A. Camus, 'La contagion', *Combat*, 27th Mai 1947.

his failure to acknowledge this 'racial superiority' as characteristic of colonial mentalities. Instead, Camus presents this concept of racism and injustice in the colonies as though it were a developing malady: 'il est impossible d'accepter sans révolte les signes qui apparaissent, ça et là, de cette maladie stupide et criminelle', thus ignoring the centrality of 'race' in the colonial rhetoric of the Third Republic. Equally, the image presented by Camus of 'les signes qui apparaissent, ça et là' implies that racially motivated injustice, or ideals of justice conditioned by race, represented the exception as opposed to the rule.

Camus does, nonetheless, situate the Malagasy affair within a broader historical context as he draws parallels between the French wartime experiences of torture and the conduct of the French police and military forces in the colonies: 'Pourtant le fait est là, clair et hideux comme la vérité: nous faisons, dans ces cas-là, ce que nous avons reproché aux Allemands de faire.' This reference to the wartime experience is indicative of the lens through which justice was conceived of and understood in post-war French society. Camus attempts to inspire in his readers a desire for justice on behalf of the Malagasies through his evocation of the French experiences of injustice at the hands of the German occupier as he criticizes French passivity and indifference to the treatment of both Malagasy and Algerian natives. 'Trois ans après avoir éprouvé les effets d'une politique de terreur, des Français enregistrent ces nouvelles avec l'indifférence des gens qui en ont trop vu.' Camus' development of this argument regarding French reaction to torture in the colonies, may be seen as a critique of French perceptions or understandings of justice which would seem to be conditioned by a sense of racial superiority:

> Si aujourd'hui, les Français apprennent sans révolte les méthodes que d'autres Français utilisent parfois envers des Algériens ou des Malgaches, c'est qu'ils vivent, de manière inconsciente, sur la certitude que nous sommes supérieurs.

Aimé Cesaire remarks upon this tendency in the western world to place more value on a European life, in his critique of European colonialism:

> Il vaudrait la peine d'étudier [...] les démarches d'Hitler [...] et de révéler au très distingué, très humaniste, très chrétien bourgeois du XXe siècle que [,,,] ce qu'il ne pardonne pas à Hitler, ce n'est pas le crime en soi, ce n'est pas l'humiliation de l'homme en soi, c'est le crime contre l'homme blanc [...] d'avoir appliqué à l'Europe des procédés colonialistes dont ne rele-

vaient jusqu'ici que les Arabes d'Algérie, les coolies de l'Inde et les nègres d'Afrique.[23]

Thus, the criticisms voiced by Camus serve to expose within French society a certain ethnocentric conception of justice whereby non-whites are not perceived as being subject to the same laws or form of justice as white Europeans. The assumption that natives of the colonies may be viewed as subject to different laws is a belief which stems from traditional colonial mindsets, for although the *Code de l'indigénat* had officially been abolished in April 1947 (a mere month before *La Contagion* was published), the sense of superiority it embodied remained entrenched in the French psyche.

Although Camus criticises the manifestation of such racial prejudice within France, he does not necessarily condemn the actual concept of French superiority. In fact, he declares France to be the 'least' racist country known to him – though he does not stipulate the other countries to which he is referring: 'Il n'est pas douteux que la France soit un pays beaucoup moins raciste que tous ceux qu'il m'a été donné de voir.' This statement is in itself a declaration of French superiority. What the author opposes is the manner in which this 'supposed' superiority is being illustrated in the colonies, that is, unjustly, through the use of torture: 'ils vivent, de manière inconsciente, sur la certitude que nous sommes supérieurs en quelque manière à ces peuples et que le choix des moyens propres à illustrer cette supériorité importe peu.' Camus goes on to assert that real French superiority lies in the ability of the French to recognise the signs of racism and preserve the country from it: 'Il s'agit de détecter les signes d'un racisme qui déshonore tant de pays déjà et dont il faut au moins préserver le nôtre. Là était et devrait être notre vraie supériorité et quelques-uns d'entre nous tremblent que nous la perdions.'

The article thus serves as a warning as to the threat apparently posed to French honour by the 'contagion' of racism, through the assertion that this malady is already dishonouring other countries. The emphasis placed on French exceptionality evokes France's humanist discourse and the self-image of a nation entrusted with a vocation to civilise. Within this context it becomes clear that the 'real superiority' to which Camus is referring is not necessarily biological in nature or racial as it would be understood today, but rather a moral or cultural superiority which, according to French humanist discourse, is implicit in more advanced civilisations. It is to this shared sense of moral and cultural superiority that Camus appeals as he intimates that behaviour such as

---

[23] A. Césaire, *Discours sur le colonialisme*, Éditions Présence Africaine, 2004, p. 14.

torture is beneath the French nation. Should France resort to the use of such barbarous methods it would mean the disintegration of the myth upon which French colonial expansion was justified, namely the difference between barbarism and civility. Equally, any behaviour comparable to that of the German occupier threatened the high moral ground upon which Resistance memory was built and further heightened the shame of French wartime collaboration.

Thus, Camus' primary concern appears to be for France as evidenced by the urgency of his appeal that 'at least' France be preserved from the racism which infects other countries. That the author fails to display the same urgency in claiming that 'at least' the colonies or the inhabitants of the colonies be preserved from such racism, of which they are the primary victims, is symbolic of the franco-centric nature of his discourse. Ultimately, France is presented as the victim of this racism and the Malagasy deputies remain a mere catalyst for French self-analysis.

Consequently, Camus' proposed solution to the biased treatment of the Malagasy deputies, to torture in the colonies and to the apparent rise of racism within French society, as exposed by the Malagasy affair, is 'Justice': 'Et c'est la justice qui devrait représenter la France' This may be seen as a bid for an improved French colonialism as the lesser of two evils, France being less racist than other unnamed countries, and justice representing French civility and moral superiority in the face of barbarity, 'Justice' in this context may be considered a codeword for 'improved colonialism'.

B. Jean-Marie Domenach Justice as Progressive Emancipation

Despite a more central position being accorded to the revolt in Madagascar and the investigation surrounding the pending trial of the deputies, Jean-Marie Domenach's article also reveals franco-centric tendencies, the notion of justice serving once more as a mantra of French greatness. Domenach's editorial introduces *Esprit*'s special edition on Madagascar and provides a more detailed account of the 1947 revolt than the previous text. This may be due to the fact that Camus' article appeared less than two months after the Malagasy revolt (May 1947) and during the very early stages of the judicial investigation, while *Esprit*'s team, publishing a dossier in February 1948, had the benefit of additional information regarding the indictment and subsequent treatment of the three Malagasy deputies, resulting in a more direct critique of the injustices suffered by the members of the MDRM and colonial abuses in general. Domenach directly criticises, for example, one of the principal characteristics of French colonialism, namely, economic exploitation of the colonies. In so doing he also reveals the possibility of communist ideological influence upon post-war intellectual discourse, as certain aspects of Marxist rhetoric are present in his argument regarding the oppressed and overexploited Malagasy worker under the French regime:

> Plus grave que la succession de gouverneurs souvent médiocres est l'état stationnaire d'une économie d'exploitation: quelques grands trusts florissants sur la misère populaire, une terre dont on a surtout consommé les richesses immédiates sans l'équiper pour la production de richesses durables, un capitalisme avide qui s'est dispensé d'investissement et d'équipement.[24]

This critique of capitalism also impacts upon the manner in which Domenach's use of the term justice might be interpreted, as economic justice or even social justice are more specific in meaning than the more fluid kantian evocation of the term. In identifying economic exploitation as the primary injustice, Domenach does not discount the possibility that republican justice can still prevail through the implementation of reform.

However, Domenach does not confine himself to condemning economic injustice as themes of torture and public ignorance regarding these methods are also raised, with Domenach echoing Camus' comparison between colonial and Nazi torture.

> Nous avons lu attentivement le rapport de la commission d'enquête parlementaire qui contient le texte des aveux signés par les inculpés du M.D.R.M. Cette lecture est ahurissante; quiconque a la moindre connaissance de la Gestapo sentira immédiatement et sans même examiner le fond, que les aveux recueillis par des policiers (c'est la coutume à Madagascar) sont des aveux extorqués.[25]

In both instances the comparative allusion to Nazi terror represented a serious accusation against the French forces in Madagascar, as images of the traumatic Second World War experience were still carved into French memory. Domenach, however, goes further than Camus in the seriousness of his accusations, using the term Gestapo as opposed to German and describing torture as 'un instrument ordinaire de la justice' in Madagascar. This evocation of torture as an ordinary instrument of justice as early as 1948 and in reference to Madagascar (as opposed to Algeria) is particularly significant and perhaps prophetic and serves to shed light upon more recent debates concerning the systematic use of

---

[24] J.-M. Domenach, 'Union Française sans mensonge', *Esprit*, May 1947.

[25] *Ibid.*

torture by the French Republic during the Algerian conflict.[26] This juxtaposition between torture and justice is particularly striking as it emphasises the idea that 'justice' was being brought about through the use of torture which is inherently unjust. It also calls into question the very legitimacy or authority of *la justice* in Madagascar. This issue relating to the transfer of legal authority and of republican justice from France to the colonies evokes the main argument proposed by Domenach, which centres on the location of the trial, a key element in debates concerning the trial of the Malagasy deputies. Domenach asserts, on more than one occasion throughout the article, the need for the trial to be held in France rather than Madagascar:

> Mais alors, où sont les responsables? [...] La justice en décidera peut-être, si le procès est jugé en France et il doit être jugé en France. [...] Tous les journalistes qui ont si bien célébré le cinquantenaire de l'affaire Dreyfus-François Mauriac, pourquoi pas? Qu'ils demandent comme nous que le procès des chefs du M.D.R.M. soit soustrait à une caricature de justice, pour être jugé dans la métropole.[27]

This second reference to the location of the trial, claiming that the only way justice can be served is through the transferral of the trial from Madagascar to France, exposes French failure to export republican values to the colonies and may be considered an indirect acknowledgement of the corruption within the colonial judiciary and accordingly a clear representation of the 'republican paradox', whereby the republican legal system has been transformed into an instrument of oppression. It is an indication that the author believes true justice can only be served on 'French soil'. Domenach thus reaffirms France as the ultimate site of legal authority, arguing that a trial in Madagascar would be nothing more than a mockery of justice ('une caricature de la justice'). The reference to the Dreyfus affair is also significant, as it invokes a more universal understanding of the ideal of justice and suggests that the self-image of the French intellectual at this time sought to associate itself with the dreyfusian tradition of intellectual engagement.

Despite the implications of corruption within the colonial administration, Domenach's representation of the ideal of 'justice' is essentially a positive one as his argument places considerable faith in metropolitan justice/justice system on condition that the trial takes place on French soil. Within this context, the concept of justice or more specifically French justice has been elevated by both authors and presented as a

---

26   For more detailed information concerning the use of torture and the oppressive nature of the justice system during the Algerian conflict, see Thénault, *op. cit.*, et R. Branche, *La torture et l'armée pendant la guerre d'Algérie*, Gallimard, 2001.

27   Domenach, *op. cit.*

solution to the Malagasy dilemma. Similarly, notwithstanding his earlier criticisms of colonial abuses, Domenach's final image of the French Union and French presence in Madagascar is in actual fact optimistic. He does not entertain the idea of independence and reasserts his/*Esprit's* belief in the 'possibilities' offered by the French union. As the final paragraph calls for the implementation of reforms in Madagascar which would improve the standard of living for the Malagasy people and prove to them that France can offer what they need to achieve what Domenach terms 'l'émancipation progressive'. Although this call for reforms in the colonies displays genuine concern for the fate of the natives, it must also be pointed out that domestic motivations are also prevalent in Domenach's text: 'Nous avons faibli et les peuples qui grandissent s'aperçoivent que nous les laissons démunis, quand d'autres nations pourraient les satisfaire.'

This statement, pertaining to the weakening of France's position as a result of the war, provides an insight into the manner in which intellectuals engaged with colonial crises such as the Malagasy revolt in French post-war terms, constantly using France's position and needs as a frame of reference as opposed to engaging more specifically with the colonial question. In an attempt to resurrect the greatness of the French nation within a new emerging bi-polar world order, and whilst grappling with the need to reconstruct French republican identity, French intellectuals frequently identified the empire as a means by which past grandeur might be restored.

Conclusion: Discourse of Victimisation: Justice as a Gift

Thus, each author looks towards France for a solution to the Malagasy problem. Independence is not an option and neither grants any form of political agency to the Malagasies themselves. They are not portrayed as playing any role whatsoever in the outcome. In fact, the Malagasies are presented by Domenach as a neutral, collective entity. Even the deputies, who are at the centre of the trial in question, remain virtually anonymous. They become the faceless other, the miserable worker, the victim. This discourse of victimization, particularly prevalent in Domenach's editorial, is symptomatic of the manner in which decolonisation was perceived in France, that is to say, in French terms, with the metropolis, domestic politics and ultimately French identity remaining at the centre of all viewpoints, arguments and interpretation.

Camus' criticism of French racist tendencies is mild and backed up with much praise for the French when compared to other unnamed countries. Equally, Domenach it at pains throughout the editorial to emphasise the fact that the review is not anti-French and attempts to pre-empt any criticisms or accusations of anti-French sentiment by declaring, echoing Peguy, that the aim is to protect France, i.e. it is for patriotic reasons that he and the members of the review wish to see justice done:

> On mesure maintenant le mal fait au people malgache et a la France par ceux qui nous accusent, parce que nous dévoilons les crimes dont ils sont les vrais coupables, d'être de mauvais français et les complices d'entreprises étrangères, qui s'autorisent aujourd'hui de leur impéritie.[28]

The dilemma of the French intellectual during this postwar period is therefore highlighted, as both texts raise the problematic question of the role of the intellectual, to stand up for universal morals and rights or to defend their country and the honour of the French nation. In response to this dilemma, both Camus and Domenach attempted to do both. They sought to defend 'Justice' as a universal value by condemning apparent injustice, while presenting French republican justice as the only possible solution to such injustice. Justice is thus presented as a gift from France, the site of all moral, cultural and legal authority, to the inhabitants of the colonies.

Projected as a mantra of French superiority, 'justice' is identified by both authors as a solution not only to the indictment and trial of the Malagasy deputies but also as a remedy for France's weakening position on the world stage. Consequently, their respective representations of justice remain true to French humanist images of 'la mission civilisatrice'. In reply to revolt they propose reform, for which they invoke a justice which is franco-centric in nature and in reality functions as a euphemism for terms such as improved colonialism or progressive emancipation. As a value and concept central to republican ideology and French metropolitan identity, 'justice', in the colonial context, thus becomes equally integral to notions of French superiority and functions as a mantra used simultaneously in attempts to reassert French greatness while camouflaging unspeakable realities brought about by French weakness.

References

Primary sources

A. Camus, 'La contagion', *Combat*, 27th Mai 1947.
J.-M. Domenach, 'Union Française sans mensonge', *Esprit*, February 1948.

---

[28] *Ibid.*

Secondary sources

N. Bancel, Nicolas, Blanchard, Pascal et Vergès, Françoise, *La République coloniale, essai sur une utopie*, Albin Michel, 2003.

R. Barthes, *Mythologies*, Seuil, 1957.

O. Baruch, et V. Duclert (dir.), *Justice, politique et République, de l'affaire Dreyfus à la guerre d'Algérie*, Complexe, 2002.

J. Benda, *La Trahison des clercs*, Les Cahiers Rouges, Grasset, 1975.

R. Branche, *La Torture et l'armée pendant la guerre d'Algérie*, Gallimard, 2001.

A. Césaire, *Discours sur le colonialisme*, Présence Africaine, 2004, p. 14.

D. Drake, *Intellectuals and Politics in Post-War France*, Palgrave, 2002.

T. Judt, *Past Imperfect, French Intellectuals 1944-1956*, University of California Press, 1997.

J. Julliard, et M. Winock, *Dictionnaire des intellectuels français, Les personnes, les lieux, les moments*, Seuil, 2002.

G. Manceron, *Marianne et les colonies, une introduction à l'histoire coloniale de la France*, La Découverte, 2003.

J. Michelet, *Histoire de la Révolution française*, Tome I, (Édition établie et commentée par Gérard Walter), Bibliothèque de la Pléiade, 1952.

Montesquieu, Baron de la Brède, *De l'esprit des lois*, Tome 1, Éditeur Jean de Bonnot, 1999.

L. Rabearimanana, *La Presse d'opinion à Madagascar de 1947 a 1956, contribution à l'histoire du nationalisme malgache du lendemain de l'insurrection à la veille de la Loi-Cadre*, Antananarivo, Librarie Mixte.

P.-C. Sorum, *Intellectuals and Decolonisation in France*, University of North Carolina Press, 1977.

P. Stibbe, *Justice pour les Malgaches*, Seuil, 1954.

S. Thénault, *Une drôle de justice: Les magistrats dans la guerre d'Algérie*, La Découverte, 2001.

J. Tronchon, *L'insurrection malgache de 1947*, Karthala, 1986.

J. Julliard, et M. Winock, *Dictionnaire des intellectuels français, Les personnes, les lieux, les moments*, Seuil, 2002.

Developments in Law and Popular Culture

The Case of the TV Lawyer

Peter ROBSON

University of Strathclyde

I. Introduction

The study of law has been slow to look beyond its narrow professional concerns at the social cultural context in which it operates. In the
past decade some work has been started in the cultural field, particularly
literature and film. Lawyers figure prominently in film and have been
the focus of a significant body of scholarship in the past decade. TV
lawyers have been largely overlooked. There is a paradox here. Television reaches the vast majority of the population. It provides news,
dramas, documentaries and comedies seven days a week, twenty four
hours a day. Cinema, the previous major player has declined from being
the major source of popular entertainment and is now a feature in the
lives of a small proportion of the population in Western societies. In the
studies that have been undertaken into the role and impact of popular
culture on people's legal consciousness, the overwhelming majority of
this work has taken place on film. This essay looks at how and why this
has come about and what the future is likely to hold as interest in law
and popular culture continues to expand.

II. Background

A. Popular Culture and Legal Education

The role of arts and culture as part of the education of lawyers has
long been recognised as important.[1] The same kind of thinking is encountered in relation to the potential of law and literature to expand the

---

[1]   P. Robson, *Law and Film Studies: Autonomy and Theory*, in Freeman, 2005, p. 21.

perspective of lawyers.[2] The early rationale for inclusion of subjects beyond the day-to-day courtroom forensic and document drafting skills of the practitioner was to ensure that lawyers were fully-rounded individuals capable of relating to ethical issues as human beings not just as lawyers.[3] In Britain legal education has been dominated by the vocational demands of the profession and the need for a work force well versed in the basics of the law. In exchange for recognising the University degree as the passport into the practice, the legal profession traditionally dictated an emphasis on vocational subjects and a blackletter approach. With the shift of training of lawyers from offices to fulltime study in the Universities in the 1960s this whole question of the relationship between education and training was a focus for discussion. The thinking behind extending the core curriculum beyond the 'practical' was to be found in the Ormrod Report of the early 1970s with its stress on making lawyers more effective practitioners.[4] This suggested that in the scheme of training for the practice of the law, the objectives of the academic stage should be to provide the student with:

- a basic knowledge of the law, which involves covering certain 'core' subjects …

- an understanding of the relationship of law to the social and economic environment in which it operates; and

- the intellectual training necessary to enable him to handle facts and apply abstract concepts.

Although this was principally taken as a fillip for teaching law contextually and for socio-legal studies, for some scholars this notion of the 'social and economic environment' has taken the form of an engagement with the cultural landscape within which law and justice operate. Courses covering law and literature, law and film and law and popular culture are now far from unusual.[5]

In the rather less constrained context of American legal education with each State controlling a separate post-Law School route into practice Ray Browne suggested a similar kind of strategic thinking at a Conference of scholars on popular culture in 1993. Noting that law is the matrix in which the forces of development and restraint collide and play out, he suggested that

---

[2] I. Ward, *Law and Literature*, Cambridge UP, 1995, p. xi.

[3] P. Robson, 'Housing and the Judiciary', Strathclyde University, Glasgow, Ph.D. Thesis, 1979, Chapter 2.

[4] G. Osborn, 'Border and Boundaries: Locating the Law in Film', in Machura and Robson, 2001, p. 167.

[5] Although some may still lurk within more traditional offerings like Jurisprudence.

Lawyers are the machine operators who keep the conflicting forces from overheating and destroying the central core. Thus, lawyers can and should be very much interested in the culture in which these forces operate.[6]

Other American writers have drawn attention to the empowering aspect of teaching using popular cultural texts. John Denvir indicated that when discussing issues like the 'rule of law' using movies as opposed to the traditional sources of constitution, codes and cases, a democratic ethos was encountered. Students benefited from a level intellectual playing field.[7] This may stem from the kind of approach which David Black has criticised in his comments on how law teachers engage with film theory[8] and a narrow professional approach to film texts.[9]

On a slightly different tack Anthony Chase urged scholars to engage with popular culture as a means of providing an alternative to what he perceived to be the arid deconstruction of critical legal studies.[10] Despite the emergence of a body of work in relation to popular culture in the 1990s, Austin Sarat still felt this to be minimal and worth drawing attention to in his Presidential Address to the Law and Society Association at the end of that decade.[11]

The various stimuli to work in this field, then have been very different. The starting point, though, has been a working hypothesis that law and popular culture have a significant relationship. The work of Richard Sherwin in the field is posited on the notion that popular culture feeds indirectly into decision-making in jury trials. Successful advocates tell their stories by adapting familiar narrative forms featuring recognizable character types. Trials are about stories being told effectively. This is best done when they resonate with popular culture.[12]

Michael Freeman, for his part, stresses the relationship between legal change and the zeitgeist. He has indicated the way in which legal issues are a central and ever-present aspect of culture from the Old Testament and Greek epics and plays through Shakespeare and Dickens to Hemingway and J.K. Rowling.[13] Introducing a collection of essays on law

---

[6]   R. Browne, 'Why Should Lawyers Study Popular Culture?', in Gunn D, 1993, p. 7.

[7]   J. Denvir, *Legal Reelism: Movies as Legal Texts*, University of Illinois Press, 1996, p. xii.

[8]   D. Black, *Law in Film*, University of Illinois Press, 1999, p. 116.

[9]   P. Robson, *Law and Film Studies. Autonomy and Theory*, in Freeman, 2005, p. 38.

[10] A. Chase, 'Towards a Legal Theory of Popular Culture', *Wisconsin Law Review*, 1986, p. 527.

[11] A. Sarat, 'Imagining the Law of the Father', *Law and Society Review*, Vol. 34, 2000, p. 7.

[12] R. Sherwin, 'Law and Popular Culture', in Sarat, 2004, p. 101.

[13] M. Freeman, *Law and Popular Culture*, OUP, 2005, Introduction *passim*.

and popular culture he noted the potential for these works to effect social transformation. They do this through having an impact on the debates with which they engage. The work of authors and film-makers, then alters the context for debate. Issues, for example, like abortion, sexuality or homelessness then are placed in the public domain. There, then, has been a range of different forces pushing the study of law into areas of popular culture.[14]

B. Range of Popular Culture Streams in Legal Studies

Academics both within Law Schools and in cognate areas of scholarship have engaged with various areas of popular culture. Courses have been developed which encompass law and literature as well as law and film.[15] There is also evidence of some interest in other areas such as music,[16] cartoons[17] and legal humour.[18] Insofar as there has been engagement and activity in relation to law and television it has occurred within the broader area of law and popular culture.

This, as indicated in the Law and Popular Culture edited collection[19] has involved writers engaged in debates about pressing moral and legal issues in their work and such themes continue to be found in modern literature. As Freeman notes, however, a considerable body of the scholars attracted to contribute to the 2003 Colloquium focused their study on the more modern genre of film.[20] Of the essays published from

---

[14] Work on the Continent has emerged from outwith Law Schools from Sociology of Law or has focused more on intellectual property rights than socio-legal aspects of popular culture – see below.

[15] Birkbeck College, London; Greenwich; Queen's University, Belfast; Strathclyde; Westminster – are amongst those which feature such courses.

[16] M. Ball, 'Doing Time and Doing It in Style', in Freeman, 2005, p. 303; and Tetzlaff, Thilo, 'Why Law Needs Pop: Global Law and Global Music', in Freeman, 2005, p. 316.

[17] M. Doherty, 'Heroes and Villains: moral panic and the anti-comic book campaign of the 1950s', M. Phil thesis, Q.U. Belfast, 2000.

[18] M. Galanter, *Lowering the Bar: Lawyer Jokes and Legal Culture*, University of Wisconsin Press, 2005.

[19] *Ibid.*

[20] M. Doherty, *op. cit.*

this meeting some seven were on literature,[21] fourteen on film and only three mentioned television.[22]

There has been little attention paid to the phenomenon of television in relation to lawyers in general. The portrayal of other aspects of the justice process on television have figured such as the police and the prison system.[23] Whilst the operation of the law includes the apprehension, deliberation and disposition phases of the legal process the separation of these phases within popular culture means that it is not unrealistic to consider each of these phases separately. In simple terms, the deliberation phase featuring lawyers does not feature in the vast majority of police or prison dramas. Inaccurate though this is, there is no sense from popular culture that the various phases inter-relate. Unrealistic and unhelpful though this is, it is worthy of a separate study which is being undertaken.[24] This seeks to explore the connections between the various phases of what comes under the umbrella of the 'justice system' and the portrayal of institutional isolation encountered in television programmes.[25] The separateness, then, of the trial process is a consistent feature of a considerable body of programmes in Britain as well as the United States[26] and the lawyer sub-genre ranks along with other dramas such as the cop show, the prison drama, hospital programme and the

---

[21] To indicate the lack of link with TV the titles are noted here – 'Where the Wild Things Really are: Children's Literature and the Law' Desmond Manderson; 'The Absence of Contradiction and the Contradiction of Absence: Law, Ethics and the Holocaust' David Seymour; 'Popular Fiction and Domestic Law: East Lynne, Justice and the Ordeal of the Unpredictable' Marlene Tromp; 'Law's Agent: Cultivated citizen or Popular Savage? The Crash of the Moral Mirror' Melanie Williams; 'Law's diabolical Romance: Reflections on a New Jurisprudence of the Sublime' Leslie Moran; 'Re-Imagining the Practice of Law; Popular Twentieth – Century Fiction by American Lawyers/Authors' David Ray Papke; 'The Materiality of Symbols: JG Ballard and Jurisprudence; Law Image, Reproduction' Adam Gearey; 'L'Oeil qui pense: The Emotive as Grounds for the Pensive in Phenomenological Reflection' Claire Vallier; 'Public and Private Eyes' Lawrence Friedman.

[22] J. Milbank, 'It's about this: Lesbians, Prison, Desire', in Freeman, 2005, p. 449; and P. Bergman, and M. Asimow, *Reel Justice*, McMeel & Co, 1996.

[23] Rafter, Nicole, *Shots in the Mirror*, OUP, 2000.

[24] TV Lawyers Today (forthcoming).

[25] The linked approach of GF Newman's *Law and Order* series is the exception and is only occasionally mirrored in miscarriages of justice themes which have featured in such series as *Rumpole* and *Kavanagh Q.C.* Most recently *Outlaws* featured some interplay between the lawyer protagonists, the Crown Prosecution Service and individual police officers in the context of plea-bargaining and securing clear-up rates. The underlying narrative drive of *Judge John Deed* is the active role of the 'Establishment' in seeking to determine judicial decision-making to favour their interests.

[26] Even the apparent exception to this convention of phase separation, *Law and Order*, comprises effectively freestanding components of apprehension and trial.

neighbourhood soap. It seems reasonable to explore the nature of the programmes and their development over the years and to note what scholarship this sub-genre has attracted.

III. TV Lawyers in Britain

There have been programmes centring on the legal process ever since television emerged in the United Kingdom as a mass medium. As we have noted in practice there has been a distinction between the three crucial stages in the operation of the legal process: apprehension, deliberation and disposition. Popular culture has always made a clear distinction between police programmes, lawyer shows and prison dramas. The apprehension and disposal phases of the legal process are not the subject of this current essay. They have operated in isolation from the other phases in dramatic, news and documentary terms and can be analysed separately in the first instance.

A. The Early Procedurals

Initially television groped for a way of presenting law in a socially responsible and public educational way. The first example we have in British TV of the coverage of the middle phase of the legal process is from the days of the single public service channel. The first steps in British TV coverage are through the means of a drama documentary centring on the Juvenile justice system. By means of 5 programmes of an hour's duration each the action followed a trainee probation officer as she observed different aspects of the legal system. This included the operation of the lower criminal courts.[27] This paved the way for a range of programmes depicting the procedures of the legal system in an almost documentary style. They operated within the limits of the technology of the time using a couple of cameras, were shot in the studio with very limited movement.

The first commercial Television channel in Britain commenced operation in 1955 and one of its first popular drama successes was a weekly half hour programme Boyd Q.C. It featured a courtroom lawyer who defended people and took on a role a private detective. He was assisted by his faithful amanuensis. This was written by a single writer and ran for some 9 years and over 70 episodes.[28] It was influential in that it demonstrated that there was an audience for stories about the prob-

---

[27] Magistrates Courts – as in the 21st century.

[28] A court official called Jack Roffey who was also the scriptwriter on such legal dramas as *Hostile Witness* (1966) and *Justice is a Woman* (1968). The former became a film with Ray Milland in 1968 and the latter provided the vehicle for the return of a Margaret Lockwood who later starred in *Justice* (below).

lems of the legal system. It showed that achieving justice might be thwarted but that there was someone who could rectify this – the lawyer. This theme was complemented by the arrival of American imports, *Perry Mason* and *The Defenders* although these did not appear until 1961 and appeared on British screens in 1962.

The final style in the early years of British television were 'jury' formats. The case would be presented with no background story to a jury of the general public who would reach a verdict on the basis of the presentations of actors on a contemporary theme. This format was borrowed from the United States and ran for a number of years in its initial title and variant.[29]

The early programmes, then were court centred with minimal background and focusing on the courtroom battles and forensic skills of disembodied professionals. It was in line with the vogue for cheap-to-produce courtroom dramas which produced by the Bristish cinema of the 1930s.

B. The Human Lawyer

What distinguishes the next phase of representation from the earlier works is the way in which there is a shift of focus away from the court-room as a separate locus for the revelation of truth to the representation of the judicial process as involving human beings with views and per-spectives. We see this first in comic and light dramatic vein with two adaptations of the work of the professional judge and part-time author, Henry Cecil. In the early 1960s two series featured first a young barris-ter starting out at the Bar and his personal and professional encounters[30] and then a short series focusing on the work of an experienced judge.[31]

In the 1970s a new trend built on this focus on the lawyer as a per-son. Dramas were produced which centred on a character and their life outwith the court as well as their performance therein. These all looked at the personal context in which the lawyers operated as well as the professional lives. There was background to both the solicitor David Main (*The Main Chance* 1969-75) and the barrister Harriet Peterson (*Justice* 1971-74). Their personal and professional lives and how these interacted were a world away from the lawyer as mere effective profes-sional. Similarly when we see the position of a public prosecutor, the Procurator Fiscal, John Sutherland (*Sutherland's Law* 1973-76) and the

---

[29] The idea reappeared in a long-running afternoon TV product when television expanded its output in the 1970s – see below.

[30] *Brothers in Law* (1962).

[31] *Mr Justice Duncannon* (1963).

pressures on him from both the public and the world of politics. From this era however, it is Horace Rumpole (*Rumpole of the Bailey* 1978-79; 1983; 1987-89; 1991) which had both the greatest longevity and impact. The writer John Mortimer developed a three level structure of court-room, office and home. We see the professional work of Rumpole defending in court as the centerpiece of each episode. This is comple-mented by the development of minor characters and their professional and personal lives in the legal Chambers where Rumpole works. The other individuals, like Rumpole are all self-employed barristers working in a range of matters in court. Sometimes they defend like Rumpole but they also are found prosecuting. Unlike Rumpole's work which we witness, we normally only hear of their work. There are, however in-stances where we get a flavour of their style when they are on the oppo-site side from Rumpole. In terms of impact Horace Rumpole is the first of the TV lawyers to be preserved for ever on video/DVD. His is one of the names students in the 21st century recall when asked to name any British TV lawyers.[32] In addition he has sparked a worldwide apprecia-tion of the 'rounded lawyer' dealing as he does with arrange of issues from freedom of speech to racism and sexism.[33]

C. The Law as Everyday Life

Throughout the 1970s and early 1980s, *Crown Court* provided a reli-able vehicle for afternoon television's expanding demand for the cheap and easily produced programming. This took the jury format from *You, the Jury* and applied it over some 700 episodes throughout the 1970s. TV prime time was dominated by American 'business' imports like *Dallas*, *Falcon Crest*, *Dynasty* and *Knott's Landing*. *Rumpole of the Bailey* and the imported *L.A. Law* in the 1980s provided the evening image of the TV lawyer in the 1980s. *L.A. Law* took the notion of the lives of a major protagonist to a new level with its adaptation of Steven Bochco's multi-layered story lines and distinct major characters used to such effect in *Hill Street Blues*. The almost soap approach saw *L.A. Law* carry some 8 lawyers as main characters) who both interacted with clients, their colleagues and the support staff. Subsequent British products sought to replicate either one of these successful multi-series models.

The mantle of Rumpole which had in its later four series and Spe-cials featured much higher production values and attained the status of 'heritage TV' was taken on by an established TV star in a retake on the

---

[32] Strathclyde 1st year students study conducted by the author on the opening day of 1st term, 2004; 2005; 2006. The same sort of pattern was also found when the same task was set to Westminster University students.

[33] J. Mortimer, *Rumpole*, Folio, 1994, Introduction, p. ix.

split between home/office/court in *Kavanagh Q.C.* This series from the 1990s had fewer light moments than its predecessor but did allow for the airing of controversial social issues like the 'double' trial of rape victims, vigilantism and military discipline.

D. New Twists on Old Themes

The reaction of programme makers and the speed from commissioning to the arrival of new product meant that it was not until a decade after *L.A. Law* came to a close that we find what we can take as attempts to replicate the formula of group interplay without a single focal point.[34] Between 1996 and 2002 there were 5 series with varied casts. One very cheaply made series looked at life in the lower courts and with those involved in prosecuting – *Crown Prosecutor*. We had two series about sets of barristers' Chambers outside London – *Wing and a Prayer* (1997-99) ran on the new commercial channel 5 and *North Square* set in Leeds. There were also 3 series providing a slightly less bourgeois image of the lawyer – *Close and True* featured a bizarre couple of lawyers in Newcastle flung together through necessity and *Fish* featured a lawyer with family problems as well as a commitment to the under-privileged. These series were not conspicuous critical or ratings successes and a return 'upmarket' was found in the most glitzy of the series to appear looking at the world of the corporate lawyer in *Trust* (2002). None of these series survived beyond a short run despite this being the aim of their producers.[35] The only one which has both run into multiple series and reached DVD status has the novel twist of centring the action on the life and loves of a serving 'maverick' judge. *Judge John Deed* takes on the shadowy 'Establishment' and poses a threat to the dark behind the scenes politica fixes of Government. Like the 21st century vogue for spy and 'alternative' police programmes this series thrives for its efficacy on the growth of the democratic deficit and the resultant re-emergence of conspiracy theories as a way of accounting for how power is exercised.

---

[34] For the sake of completeness there were two shortlived 1994 series – one was based in Edinburgh and looked at a group of advocates – Scottish version of barristers *The Advocates* (Scottish Television series); the other was a pilot which never came to anything with a solicitor with a life in mess but a nose for justice – Milner (BBC with Mel Smith).

[35] It is worth noting, however, that a number of the major protagonists have been established actors like Robson Green, Alan Davies and Martin Shaw. They may wish to avoid stereotyping by shifting fictional personae on a frequent basis rather than unknowns who might be content to be forever the new Rumpole/Kavanagh QC.

E. Towards Realism?

In addition to the styles of the drama series with their varying kinds of lawyers and clients moving towards the less wealthy and occasionally seedier end of the market there has been a very small amount of coverage of actual trials. Until the mid-1990s the one feature of British TV that has distinguished it from that of the United States has been the restriction on cameras being allowed routinely into courts. This was approved by the Supreme Court in 1981 and resulted in both ad hoc coverage and since 1991, the Court TV channel. In Britain there has been no equivalent of Court TV and only one example of the simulated Court TV of Judge Judy and her ilk.[36] The nearest we have come to this phenomenon are a handful of documentaries from Scotland which have shown the operation of the Scottish courts. These have, however taken place in strictly controlled conditions with the final emission vetted by the authorities and providing vetoes to the accused and juries against being shown. Hence the debates about the narrow focus on the sensational and law becoming mere entertainment have not taken place in Britain.

The future for both dramatic and documentary TV is far from clear, writing in 2006. The two most recent dramas adopt very different approaches. In *Outlaws* (2005) we have a light cynical world-weary perspective of the bottom end of the legal world, the magistrates' courts. This is the world of mere humans. There are no superheroes here. Rather we are observing the world peopled, in essence, by inadequates – both clients, police, lawyers and judges. Everyone is just getting by. This is the law as ordinary rather than inspirational. It is to *New Street Law* (2006) that we have to look to see the return of the obsessive fighter for justice – albeit in a 'posse' setting. It shares with *Outlaws*, however, the trope that the system does not offer much guarantee of justice. It returns to a more traditional heroic lawyer stance, though, in its demonstration that lawyers can make a positive difference to the process.

IV. Towards a Taxonomy of TV lawyers

Whilst it is true to say that there have been many different representations of law and lawyers it is worth developing some sort of classification scheme to enable any analysis of the changes in the representation of small-screen lawyers to have some kind of effective purchase. As indicated there is a world of difference between the law that we see practiced in reality TV and that which is encountered in TV dramas. Fiction and non-fiction can become blurred when we see real people

---

[36] *People's Court (UK)* ran for 12 weeks in 2005 and was not recommissioned.

appear before real judges in simulated judicial settings such as *Judge Judy* or *People's Court*. There is however, some purchase at least in making a distinction between these two worlds in our initial assessment of the possible impact of TV on public perceptions of how justice operates.

In any assessment of the changing was law and lawyers are portrayed we need to distinguish, though not simply between fiction and non fiction. The categories of comedy and drama also feature in this classification. Whilst some dramas are easily categorised as being serious, there are some like Rumpole which have comic elements but whose underlying purpose and impact is dramatic. The writer of Rumpole in fact has written of seeking to soften the politics of injustice through the medium of the character of Horace Rumpole. He never appears to be on a soapbox.[37] The comedies featuring lawyers though, for the most part centre on dysfunctional personalities or clashes of age/lifestyle in which the legal setting is peripheral to the comedic thrust of the series. Thus, in *Law and Disorder* the comic construction of a Thatcher-like arrogant self confidence of Penelope Keith is merely located into a different setting from her other sitcoms. The law itself is merely the vehicle for the comedy of a strident woman in a male bastion. Similarly the self-absorbed misfits of *Chambers* could be working in advertising or PR. The comedy is about them as personalities rather than any comment on law and its operation.[38]

By the same token it seems worth noting a clear distinction between legal dramas and those fictional programmes which have as their essence solely the courtroom interaction. Here in what I would dub 'courtroom procedurals' law and its mediation is not contextualized. Law is reduced to a complex technical process of persuasion. Guilt and innocence are here simply an issue of credibility, which may be enhanced by the level of performance of the hired mouthpiece. By contrast dramas have the potential to locate the legal within the social. Law and how individuals interact with both other individuals and the various arms of the State apparatus is a contingent matter. It depends on a host of class, gender and ethnic intersections. These determine how social power relations impact differentially on some groups of individuals more than others. It allows us to see how it is that the State legal apparatus provides different kinds of protections to some individuals whilst leaving others to the vagaries of their class/gender/ethnic fate. These narratives vary in the extent to which they imply that these forces are entirely within the control of individuals. In seeking a richer perspective on the changes in

---

[37] Mortimer, 1994, *op. cit.*

[38] The similarities between this series and the PR centred *Absolute Power* are striking.

the portrayal of law and justice over the years it is possible to discern some links between the rise of individualist politics and the decline of 'lawyer hero'. This is a theme I explore elsewhere in more depth.[39]

V. US and European TV Lawyers

As indicated the work on law and popular culture has ranged far and wide. There is a quite separate sub-field of work in law and literature with which this work is not concerned other than to point out that there is little common focus or shared methodology. Apart from some work on adaptation[40] the fields do not intersect and few people work in both areas.[41] The work is becoming more specialized and internally referential and the principal focus in terms of screenlawyers continues to be the world of film. There are some exceptions but there is as yet only a limited focus on the small screen. That said it is worth noting that some of the early work on images of lawyers quite happily jumped from film to TV in the discussion of images. Thus we find in early American work on the significance of popular culture Stephen Stark[42] looking at early TV lawyers and cop shows and Stewart Macaulay[43] mentioning both film and television. Despite this early interest we have only very occasional forays into the world of the TV lawyer in the form of essays on *LA Law* and *Ally McBeal*.[44] The vast bulk of the work in English in collections of essays, books and journals takes as their principal focus the lawyer and the justice experience encountered in the cinema.[45]

---

[39] *British TV Lawyers* (forthcoming)

[40] S. Machura, and P. Robson, *Law and Film*, Blackwell, 2001; Meyer, Phil (2001) 'Why a Jury Trial is More Like a Movie Than a Novel', in Machura and Robson, 2001, p. 133; Sarat, Austin, 'Imagining the Law of the Father', *Law and Society Review*, Vol. 34, 2000, p. 3.

[41] Moran is one of the few who has written in both areas.

[42] S. Stark, 'Perry Mason meets Sonny Crockett: The History of Lawyers and the Police as Television Heroes', *University of Miami Law Review*, Vol. 42, 1987, p. 229.

[43] S. Macaulay, 'Images of Law in Everyday Life', *Law and Society Rev*, Vol. 21, 1987, p. 185.

[44] Elayne Rapping's fascinating polemic on the rightward drift of reality TV in the past 20 years – *Law and Justice as Seen on TV*, NYU Press, 2003, and Barbara Villez comments on US TV lawyers in Villez, Barbara, *Séries télé: visions de la justice*, Paris, PUF, 2005.

[45] T. Harris, *Courtroom's Finest Hour In American Cinema*, Scarecrow Press, 1987; Denvir, John, *Legal Reelism: Movies as Legal Texts*, University of Illinois Press, 1996; Bergman, Paul and Asimow, Michael, *Reel Justice*, McMeel & Co, 1996; Black, David, *Law in Film*, University of Illinois Press, 1999; Rafter, Nicole, *Shots in the Mirror*, OUP, 2000; Machura, Stefan and Robson Peter *Law and Film*, Blackwell, 2001; Greenfield, Steve, Osborn, Guy and Robson, Peter *Film and the Law*, Cavendish, 2001; Chase, Anthony, *Movies on Trial: The Legal System on the Silver*

In Europe, in their discussion of the impact of popular culture, Machura and Ulbrich take as their departure point about the amount of lawyer images which are available to a viewer of TV in Germany at the start of the 21st century.[46] Similarly, more recently Machura has analysed the impact of TV law images on secondary school students.[47]

There are a number of studies emanating from Spain although the focus of this work is more Hollywood orientated. The series of monographs published by Tirant lo Blanch include volumes of essays on a range of themes in cinema.[48] In addition in this series there are two overviews of the field of cinema and law. In *Derecho y Cine en 100 peliculas* Rivaya and De Cima provide both a review of the whole development of the field of law and film as well as short commentaries on what they select as 100 films which they regard as basic to the new genre of 'law film'. This comments section has something of the style of Bergman and Asimow's pioneering *Reel Justice*. There is also another Spanish volume which looks at law as it appears in film from the viewpoint of a lawyer and a film theorist. Of the 24 films selected for examination, 23 of them are Hollywood films.[49] There is, however, at the time of writing, no work on TV lawyers published.

In France both taught courses[50] and written work takes as their principal concern the cinema. The 2002 collection in the journal *CinemAction*[51] ranges over a number of themes – the political process; cinematic lawyers' tricks; American Justice; Prison. Of the 32 essays in the volume over half are on American productions and Hollywood directors. There are, however, a dozen essays on French cinema. These include coverage of such central cultural issues as Jeanne d'Arc, French criminal scandals and courts martial. There is extensive coverage of the

Screen, The New Press, 2002; Moran, Leslie, Christie, Ian, Sandon, Emma and Loizidou, Elena, *Law's Moving Image*, Glasshouse, 2004; and Sarat, Austin *The Blackwell Companion to Law and Society*, Blackwell, 2004.

46 S. Machura, and P. Robson *Law and Film*, Blackwell, 2001.

47 Unpublished paper 2006.

48 Blade Runner: El derecho, guardian de la diferencia Javier de Lucas (2003); Vencedores o vencidos Francisco Munoz Conde and Marta Munoz Aunion (2003); Unnhombre para la eternidad Mercedes Albi Murda and Gabriel Martin Olivares (2003); Senederos de Gloria: Obedecer, a que derecho? Fernando Flores (2005); Anatomia de un Asesinato Virgilio Latorro Latorro (2005)

49 Francisco Soto Nieto y Francisco J *Fernandez Imagenes y Justicia: El Derecho a traves del Cine*, La Lay-Actualidad, 2004.

50 Master 2 course at Lyon 3 2006 Droit du Cinema, de l'Audiovisuel and du Multimedia and the Master Professionel Droit et Administration de l'Audiovisuel at Paris 1 2006.

51 F. Puaux, *La justice à l'écran*, Cinemaction, 2002.

image of French TV lawyers, on the other hand, in Barbara Villez's 2005 examination of both American and French TV lawyers.[52] Villez looks at the different kinds of law programmes on television ranging from telefilms, multi-part serials and series with freestanding episodes. She notes that in these series particularly there is a focus on the individual relationships of the lawyers rather than on legal controversies. This is a contrast to their American counterparts[53] which she also looks at and to the British material noted above.[54]

The work which focuses on British films and TV has thus far been limited. There have been collections and books produced by British authors[55] but these have not, hitherto, sought to make a distinction between those films and TV programmes emanating from the United Kingdom or from the United States. Interest in the 'local' film industry[56] and TV lawyers[57] is relatively recent. This essay is part of that process of seeking to develop a more grounded perspective. This examines the specific historical circumstances in which different kinds of TV law programmes have been seen and how these developments relate to broader themes of social, political and economic developments.

VI. The Future for Law and Popular Culture

There is a sense in which the focus on the product of cinema might not be as strange as at first blush. Whilst the plain statistics demonstrate that cinema as a locale for watching films lags behind the popularity of television this is only part of the story.[58] Television is the forum where not only are TV series, news and documentaries shown but films as well. Hence people who have not visited a cinema in years may well have access to reruns of major law films as well as the expanding DVD market. Half the income of film production by 2005 was estimated to come from DVD sales so that whilst cinema attendance figures continue

---

[52] B. Villez, *Séries télé: visions de la justice*, Paris, PUF, 2005.

[53] *Ibid.*, p. 105.

[54] The version in English under preparation in 2006 will expand the impact of the scholarship.

[55] S. Greenfield, '*Hero or Villain? Cinematic Lawyers and the Delivery of Justice*', in Machura and Robson, 2001, p. 25; S. Machura, and P. Robson, *Law and Film*, Blackwell, 2001; and L. Moran, I. Christie, E. Sandon, and E. Loizidou, *Law's Moving Image*, Glasshouse, 2004.

[56] 'The Strange Malaise of the British Law Film' Peter Robson *Entertainment Law in Context* 2007 (forthcoming).

[57] 'The British TV Lawyer' Peter Robson *International Journal of Law in Context* 2007 (forthcoming).

[58] BFI Handbook 2005.

to be modest compared to the 1930s and 1940s, the product is still reaching a wide audience.[59]

There are, nonetheless sound reasons why the two kinds of product need to be differentiated in analysis. The nature of the TV series is very different from the 90/120 minute film. Even allowing for the popularity of 'franchise' film with sequels[60] it remains the fact that we have no modern filmic equivalent of Rumpole and its 45 episodes, Kavanagh QC and its 29 separate 90 minute dramas or Perry Mason with its 245 episodes. The process of consumption is, of course, different too, with the cinema film being an event shared with many others in a theatrical setting. TV is watched increasingly alone with built-in interruptions. These can be commercial with advertisments as well as external visitors or simply the ability to press the record or pause button. Thus far little attention has been paid to how this impacts on our view of Atticus Finch as opposed to Judge John Deed.

What seems clear, is that there is growing awareness of the value of developing a more sophisticated approach to the cultural products of television as well as cinema. Not only do these need to be looked at separately but local work needs to be differentiated from the material of the dominant cultural producer, the United States. Developing in the first place a roster of what has been produced in individual countries and investigating how this has related to imported versions of the legal process is crucial for those with a particular interest in legal consciousness). In 2005 it was suggested that the issue of different methodologies be addressed in a search for some kind of broadly comparable criteria.[61] This notion has been developed so that a book discussing methodological issues in the field is in preparation in Paris at the time of writing. The contributing scholars are from France, Germany, Israel, Italy and the UK.

Focus on a principally aesthetic and film studies analysis of law and film can also be seen as limiting the value of law and popular culture in terms of the impact of the work. Although there has been empirical work on the impact of film on the consciousness of some actors this is limited in its scope. In addition to Machura's work in Germany one study from 2005 covered the sources of perceptions about justice of first year law students. It did not, however, go beyond seeking to assess the

---

[59] *Ibid.*

[60] *Rocky* I-V; *Police Academy* I-8; *Godfather* I-III, etc.

[61] P. Robson, *Law and Film Studies: Autonomy and Theory*, in Freeman, 2005, p. 21.

group's own influences which they felt had impacted on them.[62] The impact of television has also been examined in one study, again of first year law students expectations of their lives as lawyers.[63] This lack of empirical work, however, has meant that law and popular culture has tended to occupy a marginal position in meetings and writings on law and society.[64]

To this end the formation in 2006 of networks like the Images of Justice group and the formation of the RCSL Working Group on Law and Popular Culture indicate a serious desire to a more culturally specific approach to images of law and lawyers. The unstated assumption that there is a shared cultural and artistic heritage on which we can all draw and which informs our understanding of the nature of screen representations does not really bear thorough examination. The problem is that, hitherto, because we do share a common experience of films and TV shows we have been able to write effectively about this at perhaps a superficial level. Work has not differentiated between the different sectors of production and consumption leaving analysis in a broad zeitgeist mode.

This is, then, an interesting moment for law and popular culture. Increasingly the extent of the literature and the emergence of permanent transnational groupings mean that the individual efforts of a smallish group of individuals over the past decade are, in effect, creating a series of fixed reference points which will both encourage and enable new scholars and researchers to enter the field with a range of choices. These groups will permit newcomers to have the benefit of seeing the breadth and nature of many years' work. It will, hopefully put an end to the assumption that showing a few film clips is per se somehow novel, valuable and self-explanatory. It should help to provide a clearer perspective on the relationship between the machinery of justice and the social forces at work in society.

---

[62] M. Asimow, S. Greenfield, S. Machura, P. Robson, R. Robson, C. Sharp, G. Jorge, 'Perception of lawyer – A transnaitonal study of student views on the image of law and lawyers', *International Journal of the legal profession*, Vol. 12, 2005, p. 407.

[63] V. Salzmann, and Ph. Dunwoody 'Do portrayals of lawyers influence how people think about the legal profession?', *Southern Methodist Univ. L. Rev.*, Vol. 58, 2005, p. 411.

[64] The number of papers delivered on law and popular culture over the past decade at meetings of the Law and Society Association and RCSL have been very limited – Annual Meeting Programs/Programmes 1993 – to date.

References

M. Ball, 'Doing Time and Doing It in Style', in Freeman, 2005, p. 303.

P. Bergman, 'Emergency! Send a TV Show to Rescue Paramedic Services Paul Bergman', in Freeman, 2005, p. 130.

P. Bergman, and M. Asimow, *Reel Justice*, McMeel & Co, 1996.

BFI *Yearbook*, British Film Institute, 2005.

D. Black, *Law in Film*, University of Illinois Press, 1999.

T. Bradney, 'An educational ambition for 'law and literature', *International Journal of the Legal profession*, Vol. 7, No. 3, 2000, p. 343.

R. Browne, 'Why Should Lawyers Study Popular Culture?', in Gunn D, 1993.

A. Chase, 'Towards a Legal Theory of Popular Culture', *Wisconsin Law Review*, 1986, p. 527.

A. Chase, *Movies on Trial: The Legal System on the Silver Screen*, The New Press, New York, 2002.

L. Cooke, Les *British Television Drama: A History*, BFI, 2003.

Ch. Corcos, 'Colombo goes to School: or, some thoughts on the use of television in the teaching of law', *Loyola of Los Angeles Entertainment Law Journal*, Vol. 13, 1993, p. 499.

J. Denvir, *Legal Reelism: Movies as Legal Texts*, University of Illinois Press, 1996.

M. Doherty, *Heroes and Villains: moral panic and the anti-comic book campaign of the 1950s*, M. Phil thesis, Q.U. Belfast, 2000.

P. Ewick, and S. Silbey, *The Common Place of Law*, Chicago UP, 1998.

M. Freeman, *Law and Popular Culture*, OUP, 2005.

L. Friedman *Law, Lawyers and Popular Culture*, Vol. 98, Yale Law Journal, 1989, p. 1579.

M. Galanter, *Lowering the Bar: Lawyer Jokes and Legal Culture*, University of Wisconsin Press, 2005.

L Gies, 'Explaining the Absence of the Media in Stories of Law and Legal Consciousness', *Entertainment Law*, Vol. 2 (1), 2003, p. 19.

S. Gillers, 'Taking L.A. Law More Seriously', *Yale Law Journal*, Vol. 98, 1989, p. 1607.

S. Greenfield, 'Hero or Villain? Cinematic Lawyers and the Delivery of Justice', in Machura and Robson, 2001, p. 25.

S. Greenfield, G. Osborn and P. Robson, *Film and the Law*, Cavendish, 2001.

D. Gunn, *The Lawyer in Popular Culture: Proceedings of a Conference, Littleton*, ed. Fred B. Rothman & Co, 1993.

T. Harris, *Courtroom's Finest Hour In American Cinema*, Scarecrow Press, 1987.

O. Kamir, 'Feminist Law and Film: Imagining Judges and Juries', *Chicago-Kent L Rev*, Vol. 75, 2000, p. 899.

S. Macaulay, 'Images of Law in Everyday Life', *Law and Society Rev*, Vol. 21, 1987, p. 185.

S. Machura, 'Rechtsfilme und Rechtsalltag', *Richter ohne Robe*, Vol. 10. 1989, p. 39.

S. Machura, and P. Robson *Law and Film*, Blackwell, 2001.

S. Machura, and S. Ulbrich, *Recht im Film*, 1998.

S. Machura and S. Ulbrich in Machura and Robson, 2001.

Ph. Meyer, 'Why a Jury Trial is More Like a Movie Than a Novel', in Machura and Robson, *op. cit.*, 2001, p. 133.

J. Milbank, 'It's about this: Lesbians, Prison, Desire', in Freeman, *op. cit.*, 2005, p. 449.

L. Moran, I. Christie, E. Sandon and E. Loizidou, *Law's Moving Image*, Glasshouse, 2004.

J. Mortimer, *Rumpole*, Folio, 1994.

G. Osborn, 'Border and Boundaries: Locating the Law in Film', in Machura and Robson, *op. cit.*, 2001, p. 164.

F. Puaux, *La justice à l'écran*, Cinemaction, 2002.

N. Rafter, *Shots in the Mirror*, OUP, 2000.

E. Rapping, *Law and Justice as Seen on TV*, NYU Press, 2003.

P. Robson, 'Housing and the Judiciary', Strathclyde University, Glasgow, PhD Thesis, 1979.

P. Robson, *Law and Film Studies: Autonomy and Theory*, in Freeman, *op. cit.*, 2005, p. 21.

Ch. Rosenberg, 'An *L.A. Lawyer* Replies', *Yale Law Journal*, Vol. 98, 1989, p. 1625.

V. Salzmann and Ph. Dunwoody 'Do portrayals of lawyers influence how people think about the legal profession?', *Southern Methodist Univ. L. Rev.* Vol. 58, 2005, p. 411.

A. Sarat, 'Imagining the Law of the Father', *Law and Society Review*, Vol. 34, 2000, p. 3.

A. Sarat, *The Blackwell Companion to Law and Society*, Blackwell, 2004.

A. Sarat, L. Douglas and M. Umphrey, *Law on the Screen*, Stanford University Press, 2005.

R. Sherwin, *Law Goes Pop*, NYU, 2000.

R. Sherwin, 'Law and Popular Culture', in Sarat, *op. cit.*, 2004.

S. Stark, 'Perry Mason meets Sonny Crockett: The History of Lawyers and the Police as Television Heroes', *University of Miami Law Review*, Vol. 42, 1987, p. 229.

T. Tetzlaff, 'Why Law Needs Pop: Global Law and Global Music', in Freeman, 2005, p. 316.

B. Villez, *Séries télé: visions de la justice*, PUF, 2005.

I. Ward, *Law and Literature*, Cambridge UP, 1995.

Appendix: British TV Series (Chronological by category)

Year	Reality	Comedy	Procedural	Drama
1950				In Pursuit of Justice
1956-65				Boyd Q.C.
1959-63			The Verdict is yours	
			You, the Jury	
1962		Brothers in Law		
1963				Mr Justice Duncannon
1967-68; 1971		Misleading Cases		
1969-75				The main Chance
1970-73			Crimes of Passion	
1971-74				Justice
1972-84			Crown Court	
1973-76				Sutherland's Law
1978-79; 1983; 1987-88; 1991				Rumpole of the Bailey
1985				Black Silk
1989-94		May to December		
1994				The advocates
1994				The Justice Game
1996-2000				Kavanagh Q.C.
1992-94			Accused	
1994		Law and disorder		
1994				Milner
1994	Sheriff Court Case			
1994	The Trial			
1996				This Life
1996			The Verdict	
1996				Crown Prosecutor
1996		Is it Legal		
1997-99				Wing & a Prayer
1998				Mortimer's Law
2000				Close & True
2000				North Square
2000				In Defence
2000		Chambers		Fish
2001 -				Judge John Deed
2002				Trust
2004			The Courtroom	The Brief
2005				Ooutlaws
2005				The Brief II
2005	Teens on Trial			
2005	People's Court (UK)			
2006	Glasgow Sheriff Court			

The Portrayal of the Judicial Process in the French and Irish Media[*]

Pascale DUPARC PORTIER[*] and Laurent PECH[**]

[*] Lecturer in French Law, National University of Ireland, Galway
[**] Lecturer in EU Law, National University of Ireland, Galway

I. Introduction

It is often assumed that different legal traditions and, accordingly, different legal institutions and rules may explain a different portrayal or representation by the media of the judicial process and its practical manifestations. To a certain and limited extent, and as we shall first see, this diagnosis is accurate (Part II). However, the differences should not be overstated. In particular, Article 10 of the European Convention on Human Rights (ECHR), dealing with freedom of expression and freedom of the press, has led to a relative 'harmonization' of judicial practices throughout Europe (Part III). Moreover, from a more sociological point of view, in both Ireland and France, we note a similar media interest for the same type of litigation, i.e., criminal trials involving public figures and/or abhorrent crimes, media interest which has led in turn to shocking miscarriages of justice (Part IV).

II. Legal Framework

Differing legal tradition and laws could explain a different portrayal of the judicial process by the media in France and in Ireland. Varying sets of national rules, governing freedom of expression and therefore determining the freedom of the media, can indeed impact on the material reported to the public. Do French and Irish rules differ? Are the limita-

---

[*] This article is based on a paper presented in Dublin at a conference on Representations of Justice in France and Ireland organised by Antoine Masson at Trinity College, Dublin, Ireland.

tions on press freedom similar? Are the consequences for such rules different in each country?

Both France and Ireland provide for legal sets of rules governing and limiting freedom of expression and its competing rights. In France, there are numerous legal rules governing freedom of expression. The right to freely express oneself is not without limitations, however, and these limitations apply equally to the print media. The French Freedom of the Press Act issued on 29th July 1881 clearly states that the press is free to report (Article 1). This statute is the principal legal basis for press freedom. It is a liberal piece of legislation drafted by the law-makers of the 3rd Republic who were themselves inspired by the Declaration of Human and Citizen Rights, 26th August 1789 and its Article 11 which states: 'The free communication of thought and of opinion is one of the most invaluable rights of man: any citizen can thus speak, write, print freely, except where it is tantamount to the abuse of this liberty as determined by the law.'

This statute itself and French law in general also offers a comprehensive set of rules restraining media freedom in the name of several competing rights and interests.[1] The Statute of 29th July 1881 has been constantly amended and supplemented by a number of subsequent statutes to accommodate those competing rights and interests. As far as individual rights are concerned, the right to privacy is of particular importance, the infringement of which is sanctioned in the Civil Code.[2] The tort of privacy exists and is widely used both for individuals and for public persons. There is, under French standards, an important body of case law which interprets Article 9 of the Civil Code. Sanctions for privacy infringements are provided for in the Criminal Code, mainly in Article 226-1 and 226-2 Criminal Code.[3] Other competing rights are the right to dignity (Article 16 Civil Code[4]) and the right to be presumed

---

[1] See generally L. Pech, *La liberté d'expression et sa limitation*, PU Clermont-Ferrand/LGDJ, 2003.

[2] Article 9 of the French Civil Code provides that: 'Everyone has the right to respect for his private life. Without prejudice to compensation for injury suffered, the court may prescribe any measures, such as sequestration, seizure and others, appropriate to prevent or put an end to an invasion of personal privacy; in case of emergency those measures may be provided for by interim order.'

[3] Article 226-2 of the French Criminal Code is to be read in association with Article 42 Statute of the 29th July 1881 on freedom of the press and with Article 93-3 of the Statute, of the 29th July 1982 on broadcast communications. Both of the latter Articles provide for sanctions of fines and imprisonment.

[4] 'Legislation ensures the primacy of the person, prohibits any infringement of the latter's dignity and safeguards the respect of the human being from the outset of life.'

innocent (Article 9-1 Civil Code[5]). As far as public interests are concerned, we can add in particular the preservation of the authority and impartiality of the judiciary.[6] In practice, French courts have demonstrated their eagerness to sanction the media when the media compromise the right of the defendant/accused to be presumed innocent or his right to privacy (see e.g. *Jacques Brel* case[7]) or when the dignity of an individual is at stake (see e.g. *Préfet Erignac*[8] case).

The same rights and interests are obviously all protected in Ireland. However, it is important to note that some are constitutionally recognised rights. Some Irish freedoms are not only simple legislatively or statutorily recognised rights, but also enumerated or unenumerated constitutional rights.[9] Article 40.3.2 of the Irish Constitution is a significant article in this context as it provides for the protection of the 'personal rights' of the citizen. Subsection 2 of section 3 of Article 40 goes

---

[5] 'Everyone has the right to respect of the presumption of innocence. Where, before any sentence, a person is publicly shown as being guilty of facts under inquiries or preliminary investigation, the court, even by interim order and without prejudice to compensation for injury suffered, may prescribe any measures, such as the insertion of a rectification or the circulation of a communiqué, in order to put an end to the infringement of the presumption of innocence, at the expenses of the natural or juridical person liable for that infringement.'

[6] Article 434-25 of the French Criminal Code provides that: 'The attempt to publicly discredit a court's act or decision by actions, words, documents or pictures of any type, in circumstances liable to undermine the authority of justice or its independence, is punished by six months' imprisonment and a fine of 7,500 €.

The provisions of the previous paragraph are not applicable to technical commentaries or to acts, words, documents or pictures of any type oriented towards the amendment, cassation or revision of a decision. [...]'

[7] Court of Appeal Paris (Cour d'appel de Paris, 1re chambre), 9th July 1980, Le meilleur et autre c. Consorts Brel; French Supreme Court (Cour de cassation, 2e Ch. Civ.), 8th July 1981, Dlle Bamy c. Soc. Gogedipresse Paris-Patch, Consorts Brel et Mme Camerlan.

[8] Cour de cassation, 1re civ., 20th December 2000: Légipresse, No. 180-III, p. 57, note Derieux, Dalloz 1998, juris., p. 225, note Beignier. In this case, a picture taken by photographers of murdered Préfet Erignac's corpse covered with blood was deemed to have violated the right to human dignity.

[9] See Article 40.3.2° of the Constitution of Ireland. In Ryan v. The Attorney General [1965] I.R. 294 at 313 (S.C.), Kenny J. stated that: 'The next matter to be considered [...] is whether the general guarantee in Article 40, section 3, relates only to those personal rights which are specified in Article 40 or whether it extends to other unspecified personal rights of the citizen. [...] It follows, I think, that the general guarantee in sub-s. 1° must extend to rights not specified in Article 40. Secondly, there are many personal rights of the citizen which follow from the Christian and democratic nature of the State which are not mentioned in Article 40 at all – the right to free movement within the State and the right to marry are examples of this. This also leads to the conclusion that the general guarantee extends to rights not specified in Article 40.'

further in stating that the State 'in particular' should protect the life, person and good name and property rights of the Irish citizens. The inclusion of 'in particular' has enabled the courts to interpret this provision as providing also for the right to privacy.[10]

The limitations to press freedom are also to be found in the Constitution, namely in Article 40.6.1, which guarantees freedom to express opinions and convictions subject to considerations of public order and morality.[11] The test applied by the Supreme Court in *Cullen v. Toibin*[12] by O'Higgins, C.J., is that the freedom of the press 'can only be curtailed or restricted by the courts in the manner sought in these proceedings where such action is necessary for the administration of justice'. Theoretically, the freedom of the press and of communication cannot be lightly curtailed, but, interestingly, Irish courts seldom invoke Article 40.6.1 in support of media freedom.

The constitutional right to privacy has not been sufficiently tested so far. Judges have to use other legal paths to protect privacy issues: mainly defamation,[13] contempt of court[14] and, in England,[15] the equitable remedy of breach of confidence has been used to protect privacy interests. Defamation laws are very strongly in favour of political figures and other well known people in Ireland. Some journalists claim that decisions such as *Campbell-Sharp*, a case taken against the *Irish Independ-*

---

[10] Although privacy is not enumerated in the Constitution, the Irish Supreme Court has stated that the right to privacy is among the unenumerated rights protected by the Constitution. See, e.g., the judgment of O'Higgins C.J. in Norris v Attorney General [1984] I.R. 36 (S.C), where he explained that the right to privacy was not, however, unqualified, but may be subject, as were all other rights, to the constitutional rights of others and to the requirements of the common good. For a more recent judgment, see Foley v. Sunday Newspapers Ltd. [2005] 1 I.R. 88 (H.C.).

[11] Article 40.6.1° of the Constitution of Ireland provides that: 'The State guarantees liberty for the exercise of the following rights, subject to public order and morality: i. The right of the citizens to express freely their convictions and opinions. The education of public opinion being, however, a matter of such grave import to the common good, the State shall endeavour to ensure that organs of public opinion, such as the radio, the press, the cinema, while preserving their rightful liberty of expression, including criticism of Government policy, shall not be used to undermine public order or morality or the authority of the State. The publication or utterance of blasphemous, seditious, or indecent matter is an offence which shall be punishable in accordance with law.'

[12] [1984] I.L.R.M. 577.

[13] See, e.g., Foley.v. Sunday Newspapers Ltd. [2005] 1 I.R. 88 (H.C.).

[14] See, e.g., Irish Times Ltd. v. Ireland [1998] 1 I.R. 375.

[15] See, e.g., HRH Prince of Wales v Associated Newspapers Ltd [2006] E.W.H.C. 522 (Ch. D.); Harrods Ltd v. Times Newspapers Ltd and others [2006] E.W.H.C. 83 (Ch. D.).

ent, endanger freedom of expression.[16] Irish media representatives think that the defamation laws are outdated and neither focus on individuals' rights nor on the media's right to freedom of expression, which is significantly limited by those laws.[17]

By comparison with French judicial practice, Irish courts appear more willing to prevent or sanction any conduct likely to compromise the administration of justice and use the notion of contempt of court. Contempt of court can be explained historically[18] and has been applied in a number of cases taken against the press to sanction their reporting of certain trials.[19] It is defined as an offence created by the common law to protect the administration of justice. Contempt of court is usually invoked in support of the preservation of the authority of the judiciary and the right to a fair trial. An illustration of this legal and judicial trend is the Irish Supreme Court case of *Kelly v. O'Neill* which states that 'the power to punish for contempt was designed to protect the constitutional right of the accused to a trial in the due course of law'.[20] Contempt is frequently used against freedom of expression when the press is involved in the litigation. Criminal contempt is quite relevant to this discussion. Indeed, among others, a journalist cannot refuse to give his sources of information if asked during proceedings without facing charges of contempt *in facie curiae*. In France, the Code of Criminal Procedure[21] protects journalists and journalistic sources. However, this

---

[16] See Campbell-Sharpe v. Independent Newspapers High Court, unreported, 6th May 1997; Frazier, S., 'Liberty of Expression in Ireland and the Need for a Constitutional Law of Defamation', *Vanderbilt Journal of Transnational Law*, Vol. 32, 1999, p. 391.

[17] See 'Press Freedom & Standards' a speech delivered by Frank Cullen at the *PRII forum* on the 23rd March 2004 where he stated that 'the media operate within a defamation framework that is discriminatory, inequitable and out of date. The Irish defamation laws serve neither to protect the individual's reputation and good name nor to encourage a free and vibrant press, which is the cornerstone of democracy. [...] The State has an obligation to protect freedom of expression, which is at the core of a properly functioning democracy [...] If the State does not bring about change, it is likely to be forced to do so at a European level. This would regrettable.' The text is available at http://www.nni.ie/ppresrel21.htm.

[18] See M. McGonagle, and K Boyle, 'Contempt of Court: The Case for Law Reform', in McGonagle, M., *Law and the Media The Views of Journalists and Lawyers*, Round Hall Sweet & Maxwell, 1997, p. 128.

[19] See, e.g., The Director of Public Prosecutions v Independent Newspapers (Ireland) Ltd and another, High Court, unreported, Dunne J., 3rd May 2005.

[20] [2000] 1 I.R. 354.

[21] Article 109 of the French Code of Criminal Procedure provides that: 'Any person summoned to be heard in the capacity of a witness is obliged to appear, to swear an oath, and to make a statement, subject to the provisions of Articles 226-13 and 226-14 of the Criminal Code. Any journalist heard as a witness in respect of information collected in the course of his activities is free not to disclose its origin. If the witness

protection might well be compromised by the obligation to reveal their sources of information according to some interpretations of the Statute Perben II.[22]

More generally, the authors would argue that Irish courts, in practice, appear less often concerned with the protection of individual rights than with the preservation of the authority of the judiciary and the right to a fair trial.[23] The case of *Dermot Desmond v. Mr Justice Michael Moriarty* is an interesting case deciding that matters of urgent public importance should be dealt with in public which may outweigh privacy rights.[24] In comparison, the 'respect due to the judiciary' provided for in the French Criminal Code[25] has been very liberally interpreted. In France, in order to succeed in an action against the press, the prosecution must demonstrate that contentious 'abusive' comments are aimed at a particular

---

does not appear or refuses to appear, the investigating judge may, on the request of the district prosecutor, order him to be produced by the law-enforcement agencies.'

[22] *Le Monde*, 16ʰ September 2004.

[23] In Denham J. in D. v. Director of Public Prosecutions [1994] 2 I.R. 465 at 474, Denham J. stated 'The applicant's right to a fair trial is one of the most fundamental constitutional rights accorded to persons. On a hierarchy of constitutional rights it is a superior right. '

[24] Desmond v. Moriarty [2004] 1 I.R. 334 at 370 (S.C), Denham J. stated 'although the exceptional inquisitorial powers conferred upon the tribunal may interfere with a person's constitutional right to privacy, the exigencies of the common good require that such matters of urgent public importance be inquired into in public and this may outweigh a particular person's constitutional right to privacy': Redmond v. Flood [1999] 3 I.R. 79.

[25] Article 434-24 of the French Criminal Code, which deals with offences against the authority of justice, provides that: 'Abuse by words, gestures or threats, written documents or pictures of any type not publicly available, or the sending of any article to a judge or prosecutor, a juror or any other member of a court acting in the course of or on the occasion of the discharge of his office and liable to undermine his dignity or the respect owed to the office which he holds is punished by one year's imprisonment and a fine of 15,000 €. If the abuse occurs at a hearing by a court, tribunal or any judicial forum, the penalty is increased to two years' imprisonment and to a fine of 30,000 €.'

Article 434-25 of the French Criminal Code provides that: 'The attempt to publicly discredit a court's act or decision by actions, words, documents or pictures of any type, in circumstances liable to undermine the authority of justice or its independence, is punished by six months' imprisonment and a fine of 7,500 €.'

The provisions of the previous paragraph are not applicable to technical commentaries or to acts, words, documents or pictures of any type oriented towards the amendment, cassation or revision of a decision.

When the offence is committed through the press or by broadcasting, the specific legal provisions governing those matters are applicable to define the persons who are responsible. Criminal proceedings are time barred after three months from the day on which the offence defined by the present article was committed, if in the meantime no act of investigation or prosecution has taken place.

judge or prosecutor or at the judiciary in general. Since journalists usually pinpoint a specific judicial decision and not a judicial figure, the French Criminal Code provisions have not been applied to any significant extent.

Beyond those differences, it is noticeable that both Ireland and France provide for public hearings as a principle. Justice has to be done and to be seen to be done in any democratic country. Article 34.1 of the Irish Constitution provides for public hearings as a legal principle and in camera trials as an exception.[26] Article 34.1 states that '[J]ustice shall be administered in courts established by law [...] and, save in such special and limited cases as may be prescribed by law, shall be determined in public'. Those particular areas are sensitive areas like incest and rape. Irish law prohibits publications that would lead to the identification of the victims and of the alleged author.[27] The press is still allowed to come and attend trials of offences of a sexual nature if they safeguard the anonymity of the party.[28] Additionally, family law matters and issues pertaining to minors are areas where the media are usually excluded in Ireland.

A distinction may be drawn in the Irish case law between pre-trial publicity[29] and contemporaneous reporting[30] of trials. Pre-trial publicity can constitute a serious impediment to the fairness of a trial. Whether and to what extent publicity of a trial is permissible is decided on the basis of a case-by-case analysis undertaken by the trial judge considering the facts and the consequences of publicity on the impartiality of the jury and on himself. The main criteria is whether publicity will or will not impair (or has or not impaired) the fairness of the trial. Moreover, as

---

[26] See M. McGonagle, *Law and the Media: The Views of Journalists and Lawyers*, Round Hall Sweet & Maxwell, 1997, at Ch. 8 for further analysis.

[27] See, e.g., s. 20 (3) of the Criminal Justice Act, 1951; s. 6 of the Criminal Law (Rape) Act, 1981 as amended by s. 11 of the Criminal Law (Rape) (Amendment) Act, 1990; s. 2 of the Criminal Law (Incest Proceedings) Act, 1995 etc.

[28] See judgment of O' Flaherty J. in Irish Times Ltd. v. Ireland [1998] 1 I.R. 375 at 387-396 (S.C.).

[29] See, e.g., The Director of Public Prosecutions v. Independent Newspapers (Ireland) Ltd. and another, High Court, unreported, Dunne J., 3rd May 2005.

[30] See, e.g., Irish Times Ltd v. Ireland [1998] 1 I.R. 375 at 385-386 (S.C.), Hamilton C.J. quoting Morris J. in Irish Times Ltd v. Ireland [1988] 1 I.R. 359 at 374 (H.C.) where he stated that the learned High Court Judge (Morris J.) had properly concluded that 'before a judge presiding over a trial imposes a ban on reporting he must be satisfied of two things: (a) that there is a real risk of an unfair trial, if contemporaneous reporting is permitted, and (b) that the damage which such improper reporting would cause could not be remedied by the trial judge either by appropriate directions to the jury or otherwise'.

O'Flaherty, J. put it in the *Irish Times* case,[31] publication of evidence may be postponed by the decision of the judge:

> Aside from such statutory provisions, however, it has been recognised for a long time that it may be necessary to postpone publication of evidence on occasion. [I]ndeed the right of the public to know may also be restricted since the jury must be unprejudiced when reaching its decision, in such instances pre-trial publicity is a considerable obstacle to an objective hearing of the case.

The French New Code of Civil Procedure provides for the public hearing principle. As occurs in Ireland, some particular cases will be heard as *in camera* proceedings (in particular, family law matters). The French Code of Criminal Procedure also provides for the public hearing of trials[32] except in case of rape, torture, etc., where the victim can require *in camera* proceedings which are granted as of right by the court. French pre-trial publicity is prohibited for the sake of the presumption of innocence.

In France, the first step of the pre-trial criminal process, i.e., the exercise of public prosecution and judicial investigation is held in camera.[33]

---

[31] See judgment of O' Flaherty J. in Irish Times Ltd.v. Ireland [1998] 1 I.R. 375 at 393.

[32] Article 306 of the French Code of Criminal Procedure provides that: 'The hearing is public unless publicity would be dangerous for order or morality. In such a case, the court so declares by a ruling made in open court.

The president may nevertheless prohibit access to the courtroom for minors, or for certain minors. In the case of a prosecution for the offences of rape or torture and acts of barbarity accompanied by sexual aggression, a hearing in camera is granted as of right where the civil party victim or one of the civil party victims so requires; in the other cases a hearing in camera may only be ordered where the civil party victim or one of the civil party victims does not oppose it. Where a hearing in camera has been ordered, this applies to the reading of any judgments that may be made in respect of any procedural objections considered under Article 316.

The judgment on the merits must always be read in open court'

Article 400 of the French Code of Criminal Procedure provides that: 'Hearings are public. Nevertheless the court, after ascertaining in its judgment that a public hearing would be prejudicial to public order, the orderly conduct of the hearing, human dignity or the interests of a third party, may order by means of a judgment made at a public hearing, that the hearing will take place in camera…The judgment on the merits must always be read at a public hearing…'

Article 698-9 Article 306 of the French Code of Criminal Procedure provides for in-camera proceedings in case publicity constitutes a threat to national defence confidential information. The judgment on the merits takes place in public.

[33] Article 11 of the French Code of Criminal Procedure provides that: 'Except where the law provides otherwise and subject to the defendant's rights, the inquiry and investigation proceedings are secret. Any person contributing to such proceedings is subjected to professional secrecy under the conditions and subject to the penalties set out by Articles 226-13 and 226 14 of the Criminal Code. However, in order to pre-

On the reporting of criminal trials, the French Criminal Code, in Articles 434-16, provides that the publication, prior to the pronouncement of the final judicial decision, of commentary on anything that influences the statements of witnesses or the decision of the judicial investigating authority or trial court is punishable by six months' imprisonment and a fine of 7,500 €. When the offence is committed through the press or by broadcasting media, the specific legal provisions governing these matters apply in identifying the persons who are responsible. Moreover, Article 38 of the 1881 Freedom of the press Act, amended by the Statute of 22nd September 2000, prohibits the publication of the charging of any individual with a criminal offence or any other matter in relation to criminal charges before such matters are announced in a public hearing (the fine amounts to 3750 €).[34]

Ordonnance No. 45-174 of 2 February 1945, on juvenile offenders, as amended, provides limitations ot the principle of the public hearing and lists the people permitted to attend the proceedings (the victim, the witnesses, the next of skin, the representatives of the underage offender, the lawyers, etc.). It also prohibits reporting on the trial in books, in the press, via broadcasting means or cinema and the publication through these means of any text or illustration on the identity and personality of the juvenile offenders.[35] The decision on the merits is given in a public hearing for the young offender. It can be published, but the name (and even the initials) of the young offender cannot be given.[36] When a judge decides that a newspaper has committed an offence in publishing, a apology must be published to compensate partly the damage done notwithstanding other sanctions.[37] Moreover, Article 32 of the 1881 Act sanctions defamation of individuals.[38]

It can be concluded that the tools used, namely privacy and contempt of court, can indeed reflect in practice differing schools of legal thought both putting limits on the freedom of the media to report trials. However

---

vent the dissemination of incomplete or inaccurate information, or to quell a disturbance to the public peace, the district prosecutor may, on his own motion or at the request of the investigating court or parties, publicise objective matters related to the procedure that convey no judgement as to whether or the charges brought against the defendants are well founded.'

[34] See Cour de cassation, Ch. Crim., X...et autre, 22nd June 1999: publication of documents in criminal proceedings before the reading of the said documents in public hearing.

[35] A fine of 6,000 €, in the event of a second offence, a two-years long imprisonment sentence can be imposed.

[36] A fine of 3,750 € can be imposed.

[37] Article 13 of the Statute of the 29th July 1881.

[38] A fine of up to 12,000 € can be imposed.

many other principles are common in both jurisdictions: the principle of hearing proceedings in public is watered down when family or criminal matters are being decided in order to preserve some anonymity. Similar procedural legal rules as regards publicity of trials protect individuals against abusive intervention of the media via rules which may differ slightly, but which all aim at a fair balancing of interests.

We come to the conclusion that the variations in laws in the two countries may explain subtle differences in the reporting of the trial by the media but that those differences are of no consequence and therefore we cannot infer that media reporting is hugely different in France and in Ireland by reason only of national sets of legal rules.

This point is confirmed by the impact of the harmonisation of rules within the European Court of Human Rights system. Indeed the European Convention of Human Rights tackles freedom of expression and its limits, emphasising the efforts of the signatories, among which France and Ireland, to produce consistency and harmonisation in spite of differing legal national positions as regards the media reporting of trials.

III. Harmonisation of Media Freedom: The Impact of the ECHR

Regardless of the different legal traditions and rules, it is important to stress that media freedom all across Europe is now governed by Article 10 of the ECHR.[39] France ratified the Convention in 1974. In 1981, the right to individual appeal was agreed on. With effect from the 1st of January 2004, the European Convention on Human Rights Act requires the Irish courts to interpret every judge-made law and statute law in a manner compatible with the provisions of the Convention.[40] Under the Convention, the right to freedom of expression and of information provided by Article 10 is not absolute.[41] The State may validly

---

[39] Article 10 (1) of the European Convention on Human Rights provides that: 'Everyone has the right to freedom of expression. This right shall include freedom to hold opinions and to receive and impart information and ideas without interference by public authority and regardless of frontiers. This Article shall not prevent States from requiring the licensing of broadcasting, television or cinema enterprises.'

[40] See D. O'Connell, 'Ireland', in Blackburn & Polakiewicz (eds.), *Fundamental Rights in Europe: The European Convention on Human Rights and its Member States, 1950-2000*, Oxford University Press in association with the Council of Europe, 2001. p. 423.

[41] Article 10 (2) of the European Convention on Human Rights provides that: 'The exercise of these freedoms, since it carries with it duties and responsibilities, may be subject to such formalities, conditions, restrictions or penalties as are prescribed by law and are necessary in a democratic society, in the interests of national security, territorial integrity or public safety, for the prevention of disorder or crime, for the

interfere with the right to freedom of expression. To withstand European judicial scrutiny, limitations or restrictions on media freedom must be 'prescribed by law', must 'pursue a legitimate aim' and, finally, must be 'necessary in a democratic society'. The interference is lawful only if those three factors are present.[42]

An example illustrating this point is the 1979 European Court of Human Rights case, *Times Newspapers Ltd. v. United Kingdom*.[43] It was held that an interference with the applicants' freedom of expression was not justified under Article 10(2) and, accordingly, that there had been a violation of Article 10. It was stated:

> Having regard to all the circumstances of the case and on the basis of the approach described in paragraph 65 above, the Court concludes that the interference complained of did not correspond to a social need sufficiently pressing to outweigh the public interest in freedom of expression within the meaning of the Convention. The Court therefore finds the reasons for the restraint imposed on the applicants not to be sufficient under Article 10(2). That restraint proves not to be proportionate to the legitimate aim pursued; it was not necessary in a democratic society for maintaining the authority of the judiciary [...] There has accordingly been a violation of Article 10.

The Convention posits a balancing of rights: the right to freedom of expression and the right to a fair trial. The test referred to is the following: is the relevant restriction on freedom of expression necessary in a democratic society? The test of 'necessity in a democratic society' is largely illustrated by the ECHR case law.

A practical consequence is that both Irish courts and French courts are required by the Strasbourg Court to undertake a *genuine* proportionality analysis or to balance the competing rights and interests at stake on a case-by-case basis. National courts of both countries must demonstrate a fair balance between freedom of expression of the press and competing individual rights (or public interests). Interestingly, one should note that Irish judges already used balancing methods before Ireland signed the ECHR when applying Constitutional provisions. However, when the constitutionally guaranteed rights of freedom of opinion and expression, including that of the freedom of the press, competed with the right to a

---

protection of health or morals, for the protection of the reputation or rights of others, for preventing the disclosure of information received in confidence, or for maintaining the authority and impartiality of the judiciary.'

[42] See L. Pech, 'Freedom of the Press: A Comparative Perspective', in Eoin O'Dell, *Freedom of Expression*, Ashgate, 2006.

[43] (1979) 2 EHRR 245.

fair trial, the right to a fair trial was nearly always paramount.[44] In *Irish Times v. Ireland*,[45] significantly reinterpreting Article 34.1[46] of the Irish Constitution, the Supreme Court ruled that a court may interfere with the rights of the media to publish contemporaneous reports of criminal proceedings where this is necessary in order to protect the right of an accused person to a fair trial. Trial judges have, therefore, to balance the community's right of access to the court with information about the hearing and the administration of justice.

Another more recent case, *Cogley v. RTE*,[47] offered an additional good example of a decision where judges attempt to 'weigh and balance the competing rights and values at stake'. In this particular case, the plaintiff asked the court to grant an interlocutory injunction (in ECHR-speak, 'a prior restraint order') against RTE in order for a programme on nursing home care not to be broadcasted. The interlocutory injunction was refused. The key legal issue was how the right of privacy may be balanced against the freedom of the press. The TV programme was deemed to be of the highest public interest and if privacy proved to be violated then damages would be an adequate remedy. The Court explicitly referred to the ECHR case law to confirm that 'the weight to be attached to the undoubted right of parties to privacy can vary significantly from case to case'. The influence of the ECHR is to give more weight to press freedom.

When comparing Irish and French cases, it seems that no significantly different conclusions can be drawn from the case law of French courts. The *Cour de cassation* case, *X ...et autre*,[48] where the Court applied Article 10, paragraph 2 of the ECHR to sanction the breach of Article 38, paragraph 1 of the 1881 Freedom of the press Act illustrates this point. The publication had been made by a journalist in support of

---

[44] In Irish Times Ltd. v. Ireland [1998] 1 I.R. 375 at 380 (S.C.), Hamilton C.J., quoting Morris J. in Irish Times Ltd. v. Ireland [1998] 1 I.R. 359 at 370 (H.C.), 'The learned trial judge in balancing these two rights clearly found that the accused's right to a fair trial was paramount and ranked higher in the hierarchy of rights than the right of the media to contemporaneous reporting. In this conclusion, he was undoubtedly correct (see the judgment of Denham J. in D. v. Director of Public Prosecutions [1994] 2 I.R. 465).'

[45] Irish Times Ltd. v. Ireland [1998] 1 I.R. 375 (S.C.).

[46] Article 34.1 of the Constitution of Ireland provides that: 'Justice shall be administered in courts established by law by judges appointed in the manner provided by this Constitution and, save in such special and limited cases as may be prescribed by law, shall be administered in public.'

[47] Cogley v. Radio Telifis Eireann, Aherne and others v. Radio Telifís Eireann, High Court, unreported, Clarke J., 8th June 2005.

[48] Cour de cassation, Ch. Crim., 22nd June 1999.

one of the involved parties to the proceedings, while the investigation was still ongoing.

The French Supreme Court, the *Cour de cassation*, has an extremely concise, abstract and sibylline style where the reasoning of the court hardly ever appears. It is thus difficult to identify the balancing exercise, although it must also underpin the French decisions. It is only in the lower courts that the identification of the balancing exercise can be made, given the more detailed nature of those decisions. However, in some cases, the French courts' decisions have been quashed, namely in *Fressoz and Roire v. France*,[49] and in *Colombani et autres v. France*,[50] for a breach of Article 10 of the European Convention. The case *Ekin v. France* illustrates a further violation of article 10.[51]

Interestingly, the European Court of Human Rights tends to lay emphasis on press freedom in cases where journalists are a party to the legal proceedings when balancing the competing interests because, for the Court, the press plays an essential role in a democratic society. Not only does the press have a duty to impart information, but the public has a right to be informed. Moreover, it is noteworthy to recall that the European Court of Human Rights[52] declared that the protection of journalists' sources is 'one of the basic conditions for press freedom' and that an order requiring a journalist to disclose his sources of information is not necessary in a democratic society and that such a measure must be justified by an overriding requirement in the public interest. The case *Roemen and Schmit v. Luxembourg*[53] illustrates a violation of journalistic sources during searches carried out at the first applicant's home and workplace and concludes that 'impugned measures must be regarded as disproportionate and that they violated the first applicant's right to freedom of expression, as guaranteed by Article 10 of the Convention'. It seems that neither France[54] nor

---

[49] Fressoz and Roire v. France (1999) ECHR 1. 'In sum, there was not, in the Court's view, a reasonable relationship of proportionality between the legitimate aim pursued by the journalists' conviction and the means deployed to achieve that aim, given the interest a democratic society has in ensuring and preserving freedom of the press. There has therefore been a violation of Article 10 of the Convention.'

[50] Colombani and Others v. France (2002) ECHR 521.

[51] Ekin Association v. France (2001) ECHR 473.

[52] In Goodwin v U.K. (1996) 22 EHRR 123, para. 39, the European Court of Human Rights stated that the 'Protection of journalistic sources is one of the basic conditions for press freedom'.

[53] Roemen and Schmit v. Luxembourg (2003) ECHR 102.

[54] Article 109 of the French Code of Criminal Procedure provides that: 'Any journalist heard as a witness in respect of information collected in the course of his activities is free not to disclose its origin. If the witness does not appear or refuses to appear, the

Ireland[55] has concretely followed the Court in its conclusions in that particular field up to now.

The 'public watchdog' is strong in cases where public figures are involved in proceedings against the press since they are part of the political scene. Consequently, primacy is given to freedom of the press when a public official is the target because that freedom affords the public the best means of being informed of political matters. When a private person is involved, the 'public watchdog' is not as active and the journalist should act in a more restrained way. On the issue of contempt of court, the overriding concern of the ECHR in cases where judges have come under criticism is the protection of the individual judge as opposed to the judiciary as a whole. The Strasbourg court operates a balance between the press and individual rights, the protection of 'reputation and rights of others' is a legitimate aim under Article 10, paragraph 2. Therefore, cases which are national defamation cases fall under this Article.

Article 6 of the ECHR guarantees the right to a fair trial in criminal and in civil matters.[56] Hearings in camera are expressly authorised. The grounds on which such hearings can take place are listed in Article 6. The right of privacy is guaranteed by Article 8 of the ECHR and has been commented on by the European Court of Human Rights.[57] Everyone has the right to respect for his private and family life, his home and his correspondence. The presumption of innocence is also provided for

---

investigating judgevmay, on the request of the district prosecutor, order him to be produced by the law-enforcement agencies.'

[55] See The People (D.P.P.) v. Nevin [2003] 3 I.R. 321 at 331 (C.C.A.), per Geoghegan J. 'Counsel for the applicant had submitted to the trial judge that she should order the journalists to disclose their sources. As he pointed out there is no doubt that, on the law as it stands, there is no such thing as journalistic privilege and this was confirmed by a judgment of this court in In re O'Kelly (1974) 108 I.L.T.R. 97. Nevertheless, it has been understood to be the practice in this jurisdiction and in other common law jurisdictions that a trial judge will exercise a certain element of discretion in ruling as to whether a journalist does have to answer a question about sources. The judge is entitled to satisfy himself or herself that the answer to such a question is properly relevant to the matters to be tried and that the interests of justice require that an answer be given.'

[56] Article 6 (1) of the European Convention on Human Rights provides that: 'Judgement shall be pronounced publicly by the press and public may be excluded from all or part of the trial in the interest of morals, public order or national security in a democratic society, where the interests of juveniles or the protection of the private life of the parties so require, or the extent strictly necessary in the opinion of the court in special circumstances where publicity would prejudice the interests of justice...'

[57] Von Hannover v. Germany (2004) ECHR 294.

by the ECHR.[58] Article 6(2) on the presumption of innocence has been applied in particular in the case, *Allenet de Ribemont v. France*,[59] which dealt with a high profile murder of a well-known person. The media announced that Mr. Allenet de Ribemont was the murderer before the trial could take place. After the Strasbourg court's decision which found that there had been a breach of the presumption of innocence, he was subsequently released.

In sum, the ECHR is a key factor of harmonisation in rules related to freedom of the press, the ECHR' willingness to back up press freedom as an essential item of democracy, its rather liberal approach to freedom of expression, all lead to illustrate that this ECHR harmonising factor establishes a common standard for press freedom in France and in Ireland in the reporting of trials.

The national legal element and the European legal component have to be supplemented with an additional sociological aspect which may in turn play a part in the process. Indeed, some variations in presentation of trials by the media may be explained sociologically.

IV. Sociological Significance

Irrespective of the impact of Article 10 of the ECHR on judicial practices, it is tempting to argue that media reporting would have nonetheless presented similar characteristics in France and Ireland. In both countries, national newspapers tend to refer to major crimes, while regional papers focus on local minor criminal issues. However, some reports which are published in the main Irish national newspapers would not be found in their equivalent French counterparts, but in the regional press. This is probably due to the difference in population and in the corresponding volume of cases in the two countries.

One finds in Ireland and in France rather sober newspapers with a high standard of morals and less objective ones: broadsheets and tabloids respectively. In both countries, journalists have a linguistic and pedagogical role of explaining litigation while reporting the trial. Hence, they report in easy to understand language or seek to simplify legal terminology. In French newspapers, journalists specialise in the reporting of legal matters and in particular of trials. They are referred to as '*chroniqueurs juridiques*' or 'legal correspondents'. In Ireland, it is not

---

[58] Article 6(2) of the European Convention on Human Rights provides that: 'Everyone charged with a criminal offence shall be presumed innocent until proved guilty according to law.' Everyone charged with a criminal offence has the following minimum rights: (a) to be informed promptly, in a language which he understands and in detail, of the nature and cause of the accusation against him.'

[59] (1995) 20 EHRR 557.

as widespread. Common features also appear as regards the way the media report trials. For instance, it is typical for the media to report quotations from the oral arguments of the lawyers of the victims and the defence made by the accused. On the negative side, trials are also marked by the same excesses: press rumours, accusation anticipated by the media, photographs of the accused, leaks to journalists (despite the *secret de l'instruction*, i.e. respect of the professional secrecy of the process), etc. Indeed, excesses by the media can be illustrated both in France (*affaire d'Outreau*) and in Ireland (Nevin case).

In France, the general traditional tendency of journalists is to comment on facts rather than to report on them. This can lead to a higher level of unjustified and unfair comments. In Ireland, equivalent newspapers tend to stick much more to the facts of the case. Therefore, French papers are regularly sued on the grounds of privacy infringement. It seems that Irish papers are rarely sued for infringement of privacy, since they seem mostly objective in the way they report. When they are sued, it is mostly for inaccuracies (especially where names or charges are inaccurate because journalists have the right to take down notes, but do not have a right to access legal court documents).

Irish and French journalists cover predominantly and extensively the same types of trials. In France, it is particularly clear that civil law and administrative law do not attract the same media attention as criminal law. Only civil cases involving a 'public figure' (e.g. *Bernard Tapie*),[60] political parties (e.g. *Urba* case in the 1990s)[61] and/or a subject of public concern (victims of asbestos dust)[62] are reported. Administrative litigation, because of peculiar procedural rules (mainly the almost exclusive written character of the procedure), interests the media even less. However, one famous case heard in the Administrative Supreme Court, the Muslim scarf case,[63] generated some interest. Moreover, civil and ad-

---

[60] Bernard Tapie, a French businessman with political connections, has been involved in a significant number of cases over the last 20 years.

[61] A vast number of cases have involved political parties and some of their leaders or members and many were reported during the 1990s. However, the most striking example of all the cases in the 1990s remains the Elf Aquitaine case, which was opened in 1997 by Judge Eva Joly, who subsequently wrote a book on the saga and the threats she endured after the years she spent trying to comprehend the financial imbroglio involving Loïc Le Floch-Prigent (a close friend of late President Mitterrand) and Alfred Sirven, Roland Dumas and his mistress Christine Deviers-Joncour.

[62] In France, a long series of asbestos cases have been dealt with by the courts and by the Cour de cassation, the French Supreme Court, since the 1990s and, owing to the considerable media reporting of the trials, the prohibition of asbestos came about in 1997.

[63] See Conseil d'État, Assemblée générale (Section de l'intérieur), application No. 346.893, 27th November 1989. In France, the scandal came about in 1989 when

ministrative judges do not seek out the media to defend their decisions. This has not been necessarily the case in the past in some criminal matters.

Leaving aside civil and administrative law, it seems possible to argue that in both Ireland and France, the criminal process captures press attention more than any other type of litigation. To quote Jean Carbonnier, criminal law being 'the most theatrical of all branches of law', it is understandable that the media find criminal litigation more easily newsworthy. This is especially so when crimes involve public figures (either as perpetrators or victims), or when crimes are particularly 'serious' and/or directed towards a specific category of society (children, minorities, elderly people, etc). In both countries, crime on children raises a lot of concern. Recently, the killing of young Cork boy Robert Holohan[64] attracted a lot of attention in Ireland. In France, paedophilia cases are typically the most sensitive today.

But the most widely reported cases in France are criminal cases involving politicians. In the 1990s, a huge number of such trials took place. In France, a number of criminal trials involving politicians might never have come to a conclusion if the media had not been covering them (*affaire du sang contaminé*, *affaire Elf Aquitaine*, etc.). The media fully played their role of being a counterweight against the political sphere in those cases. If they did not enjoy the freedom they have, many important trials and prosecutions would be stifled.

Why do similar criminal trials attract media attention and scrutiny in both countries? The specific social role of criminal law explains the greater media interest. Criminal prosecution sends a message to society as a whole. A criminal trial triggers catharsis. The people identify with the victims and a collective, acute desire for justice is engendered. The public's right to know, however, may lead to undue pressure on the judiciary and damage the lives of the people involved. In all times and across the world, individuals have always demanded from the courts exemplary sentences. As was stated in *Kelly v O'Neill*:

> There are special considerations, however, arising where the sentencing of convicted persons are concerned, which must at least be borne in mind. In

---

three schoolgirls came to school with a scarf. It was the beginning of the scarf affair, which lasted for 15 years until a law in 2004 prohibited wearing a scarf or any religious sign.

[64] See, e.g., 'Unanswered questions: a full report on facts (the semen, the phone call, the State case, Robert's last hour, the bicycle, the refuse bags, the second journey, burning refuse bags, the mud stains, the injuries)', *Irish Times*, 28th January 2006. This very long and detailed report would never be published in a French national broadsheet, but in the regional press.

such cases, depending on the nature of the publication, the inference may be drawn that a court responded to a popular demand for an exemplary sentence and such an inference, however unjustifiable, might, on one view, be regarded as damaging to the administration of justice.[65]

Of course, there are also financial reasons behind the choice of media to report on particular issues. Historically, crime reporting has always sold well.

Media reporting only differs to the extent that the legal actors involved in the criminal process and its construction are not identical. In France, wider criminal coverage might be explained in particular because it is easy to identify the juge d'instruction (the investigating judge) in charge of a file and shift all the discontent of the population from the judicial institution to one person who is the symbol of the institution. The specific role played by the *juge d'instruction* is worthy of note. A powerful figure, he/she is sometimes the subject of intense media interest at the pre-trial stage (e.g., in *Affaire of Little Gregory*). His/her power to send a defendant into custody before trial made him/her a powerful figure in the 1990s, when numerous politicians were prosecuted on corruption charges. Several cases (e.g., *Outreau*) where mistakes, officially called 'dysfunctions of justice', were made have since considerably damaged the reputation of judges and of the whole judicial system. Following the reporting of the latter case, the era of 'star' judges in France seems over.

What are the consequences of media coverage of trials in both countries? First, the media definitely play a role in the increase in criminal legislation in both countries. Following the paedophilia *Outreau* case, the French legislation on child protection is now being reconsidered. Second, they also put the judicial system into question with at times positives consequences. For instance, following some high-profile condemnations of people who were subsequently proven innocent, it was decided in 2000 to allow for a right to appeal against decisions of the *Cour d'assises* in France. Finally, wide coverage of events triggers, *inter alia*, fear and panic in the population in both countries, and probably a certain level of discontent or doubt towards the efficiency of the judicial machinery.

To put it in a nutshell, the sociological aspect of the reporting of trials seems to underline the common cross-border trends rather than the slight differences in reporting traditions and habits. In both countries indeed there is a fine line between on the one hand democratic reporting which serves its neutral informative purpose and may lead to sensational cases

---

[65]   Kelly v O'Neill [2000] 1 I.R. 354 (S.C.)

– which implicate some VIP's who would rather not be mentioned or some other shocking miscarriages of justice which trigger judicial reform and on the other hand the dubious money-driven journalistic impulse to produce papers that sell like hot cakes.

V. Conclusion

Although Irish and French laws have differing legal traditions, and, therefore, different remedies and legal actions, they have similar goals, i.e., to safeguard the freedom of the press and its competing rights. In both countries, a public hearing is the rule and the hearing *in camera* the exception, which means that journalists, as a matter of principle, have the right to attend trials and are the usual channel of information for the public. As Hamilton, C.J. opines in the *Irish Times Limited and Others* case:

Justice is best served in an open court where the judicial process can be scrutinised. In a democratic society, justice must not only be done but be seen to be done. Only in this way, can respect for the rule of law and public confidence in the administration of justice, so essential to the workings of a democratic state, be maintained.[66]

The European Court of Human Rights case law plays an important role in the harmonisation of legislation and case law. Under the ECHR, the media plays a pre-eminent role in state governed by the rule of law. More precisely, the media have a role as a 'watchdog'. And in addition to the media's right to impart information and ideas, there is the public's right to receive them. The ECHR case law is in favour of the freedom of the press, especially when the publications which are challenged in court cover events of a political nature. This should further lead to more liberalism in Ireland and in France.

Sociologically, modern Western societies, including France and Ireland, have the same or similar cultural, political, economic, sociological backgrounds. The public waits for the same or similar newspapers reports and, because papers have to make money, they tend to serve the same courses in both countries. Market demand has remained the same for centuries. In turn, media reporting shapes societies and thus legislation and judicial systems. Interestingly, the gulf between the press and judicial perceptions of the trial can be bridged. This bridging is in process. In both countries, the judiciary is slowly moving from its

---

[66] Irish Times Ltd.v. Ireland [1998] 1 I.R. 375 at 382 (S.C), per Hamilton C.J. See also R v. Sussex Justices, Ex parte McCarthy [1924] 1 K.B. 256 at 259 per Lord Hewart C.J.: 'a long line of cases shows that it is not merely of some importance but is of fundamental importance that justice should not only be done, but should manifestly and undoubtedly be seen to be done.'

traditional secrecy to more openness to enable journalists to do their work properly and to have the opportunity to report on the basis of legal documents instead of making mistakes when taking down names and charges during trials. Wrong information can put the judicial machinery at risk. Justice has to be understood by the people.

The judiciary and the media, which once were opposed, might find a compromise. The quality of reporting can be enhanced if journalists, who, for the most part, have high morals and respect a strict code of conduct, are provided the means to do their jobs properly, i.e., to report to the people what happens in courts as is necessary in a purportedly transparent democracy, instead of being considered troublemakers. In short, courts might then find an ally in the press instead of an enemy.

In this vein, Keane, J. (later Chief Justice) once wrote the following of today's information-driven society. 'In modern conditions, the media are the eyes and ears of the public and the ordinary citizen is almost entirely dependent on them for his knowledge of what goes on in court.'[67]

References

Articles and Books

S. Frazier, 'Liberty of Expression in Ireland and the Need for a Constitutional Law of Defamation', *Vanderbilt Journal of Transnational Law*, Vol. 32, 1999, p. 391.

M. Mc Gonagle, and K. Boyle, 'Contempt of Court: The Case for Law Reform', in McGonagle, M., p. 128.

M. Mc Gonagle, *Law and the Media. The Views of Journalists and Lawyers*, Round Hall Sweet & Maxwell, 1997.

D. O'Connell, 'Ireland', in R. Blackburn & J. Polakiewicz (eds.), *Fundamental Rights in Europe: The European Convention on Human Rights and its Member States, 1950-2000*, Oxford University Press in association with the Council of Europe, 2001, p. 423.

L. Pech, 'Freedom of the Press: A Comparative Perspective', in Eoin O'Dell, *Freedom of Expression*, Ashgate, 2006.

L. Pech, *La liberté d'expression et sa limitation*, PU Clermont-Ferrand/LGDJ, 2003.

---

[67] Irish Times Ltd. v. Ireland [1998] 1 I.R. 375 at 409 (S.C.).

Portrayal of Justice
on German Television

Ruth HERZ

Senior Associate Member, St. Antony's College, Oxford

An 18-year-old high school pupil was indicted for of raping his classmate in the girl's toilette of their school in a small town in Germany. The trial took place before a youth court, which in cases of serious offences is presided by a panel of one professional judge and two lay judges. The defendant denied the accusations claiming that the girl had not shown any resistance. Fighting her tears, the victim in the witness stand, described the event as a violent act against her clearly expressed will and consent. Her closest friends from school, who had accompanied her to court, were sitting in the audience giving her support. Her best friend testified to have seen her running out of the girl's toilette with her blouse torn, distraught and sobbing. Their schoolteacher described the alleged victim as a most reliable young woman. The prosecutor had presented photos of the injuries the girl suffered on her thighs and breasts, taken in the police station when she had come to report the event on the same day. The defence lawyer had put the victim-witness to a tough cross-examination, to the point that the judge reminded him to speak more adequately and gently with the vulnerable young woman. The lawyer argued that the only eyewitness, the victim, was a girl who bore a grudge against his client because he had always ignored her advances in the past. He also claimed that the act was quite out of character for the defendant. After deliberating the court came to the conclusion that the girl's version of the event was the truth beyond a reasonable doubt. The corroborating testimony of the other two female witnesses strengthened her version whereas the defendant's version was not credible and lacked any empiric evidence. The court found the defendant guilty of rape and sentenced the young man to a custodial sentence of one year in a youth institution.

The court proceedings were shown on television. The following morning, there was an outcry in the local newspaper, reproaching the local authorities for having hushed up the matter. Horrified parents came to speak with the headmaster, seeking information about the incident, which had taken place in the school their children attended. He had a hard time convincing them no crime had been committed at this school and that it was a staged case on television.

The fictional case was shown on television in a daily court series entitled *'Das Jugendgericht'* ('The Youth Court'). It was one of many typical cases shown on this program and subsequently on several other similar shows, which were aired on the main German television channels, blurring the line between reality and fiction. Youth courts in Germany deal with youth between the ages of 14 to 21 years accused of all offences except murder and manslaughter. In practical terms it is therefore a criminal court for young people rather than a children's or a youth court. The cases shown in the series were based on real cases heard in youth courts in Germany, which had been adapted to the television program by highlighting specific problems of youth in society and further adorned by colour and suspense. The series was therefore neither a reality show, nor a documentary nor a purely fictional program. The format of the television case has become a genre of its own, fitting nicely in between purely fictional courtroom dramas and documentaries as well as trial coverage by court reporters. The outstanding feature of the series was that, rather than an actor, a professional judge played the role of the judge. The producer of the program had possibly taken the idea from great film directors like Otto Preminger and Constatinos Costa-Gavras who had casted real judges to play the role of the judge in their respective classic courtroom films *'Anatomy of a Murder'* and *'Music Box'*. The same applied to the roles of the defence lawyer and the prosecutor. Consequently, the legal procedure and tone portrayed in the series were true to real life. On the whole neither the position of the justice system as an institution, nor that of the judge or the lawyers involved in the hearings was undermined. The authentic feeling was further enhanced with the amateur actors playing the parts of the defendants, witnesses, as well as their friends and parents. The almost true to life photos of the injuries sustained, had been taken with the help of generous make-up preceding the recordings.

The television program was extremely successful with ratings of around 25%, which accounts for about two and a half million viewers. It was especially popular amongst young viewers. Given the numbers of viewers, it may well be argued that these programs have become the main source of information on the German justice system for the majority of the population. The question is therefore whether such programs can be considered as an effective and legitimate form of portraying justice on television as an alternative to documentaries and trial coverage on the one hand and the purely fictional series on the other hand.

The obvious explanation for the success of the phenomenon of court room dramas on German television can easily be chalked down to their entertainment value, perhaps the most obvious objective of the television medium. However, no doubt deeper reasons are to be sought. The great popularity of the program has also made the questions arising from the presentation of justice in the media in all genres acutely apparent.

As the courts of law are a site, where societal conflicts take place, legal dramas undoubtedly shape meaning. This observation raises a whole series of issues: should for instance the success of court room dramas be attributed to the current political climate of insecurity, anxiety and fear? Do the drama respond to the public needs to be reassured through the portrayal of the court as an institution, which retains its authority and is able to cope with and solve serious societal problems? Does the justice system fulfil this role in society or is it rather constructed on television to meet the needs of the program and thus of commercial constraints? Does the general political climate influence the justice system itself and its portrayal on television? Are images in our visual world likely to reshape justice? Have the social functions of punishment and the affirmation of shared morals been transferred from the justice institutions to mass media entertainment? What are the possible implications of the increasingly blurred borders between reality and fiction?

To confront these issues it is necessary to examine not only the representation but also the construction of law and justice on German television. To do so one needs first of all to look into the German media presentation of justice more closely. The author, herself a judge in Cologne, was offered the role of the judge in the series '*Das Jugendgerich*' at its outset in 2001. The decision whether to accept this unusual offer was not an easy task. Television is often perceived by academia and by judicial circles to be lowbrow popular culture. Nonetheless, the president of the regional Supreme Court was very positively inclined towards the prospect of having one of his judges appear in such a television program. He enthusiastically supported the application to the Minister of Justice of Northrhein-Westfalia for my leave of absence. The Minister of Justice agreed to the request and appeared in favour of the program precisely because it promised to lift the veil of secrecy involving the judicial system, ensuring transparency while providing information on the youth court system. He preferred to see a professional judge whom he could trust in the television role rather than an actor. It promised to ensure that the court and the justice would be portrayed in a realistically and dignified manner.

117

As in all Western Democracies, Justice in Germany is the third power in the state and the pillar if not guardian of its democratic ethos. The role of the independent judiciary is to safeguard democracy by making rational and impartial judgments. Law and Justice, especially criminal justice, are indisputably the carriers of values of democratic society. In order to achieve and retain legitimacy justice must be done but also seen to be done. Few people ever set foot in a courtroom and therefore seldom have firsthand experience. Justice must be understood by the citizens and thus must be accessible to them. A recent study by researchers of the university of Bochum[1] has indeed shown that, German television court series have enhanced the reputation of a fair and impartial justice thereby bolstering its legitimacy. The justice administration hoped the court drama might provide an opportunity of satisfying the public's great curiosity and interest in the process of doing justice. They expected the program to deflect the media from trying to enter the real courtroom with cameras.

The launching of the program coincided with a ruling of the German Federal Constitutional Court in 2001,[2] which confirmed its earlier decision banning cameras from the courtroom when the court is in session. A commercial news channel wished to cover the criminal trial against Erich Honecker, the former Leader of the German Democratic Republic, charged with high treason and crimes committed during the existence of the East German State. The channel claimed the public had a right to follow the court proceedings on television, especially in such an important trial. The court argued that the presence of journalists in the trial ensured a proper public exposure while cameras were bound to disrupt the court proceedings and deprive it of its dignity.

The position of judges in court, according to the German penal procedure, is central, active and consequentially powerful. The judge's role in the German, as in many other continental European legal systems, is to examine the defendant, the witnesses and the experts in the quest for the truth. It is he or she who, together with the lay judges, decides not only over the guilt of the defendant but also hands down the sentence and elaborates its reasoning. The judge's role is dovetailed to the male, fatherly but strictly authoritative, safeguarding the rules of the trial. The authority, the judges wish to retain, inside and outside the courtroom, is acquired amongst other factors by rituals, symbols, architecture, language and clothing. The judges' authority is reflected in their status in society, which maintains their credibility and legitimacy, concerning

---

[1]   S. Machura, Das Ansehen von Anwaelten bei Jurastudenten', *Zeitschrift für Rechtssoziologie*, 25, 2004, Jg. p. 3.

[2]   Bundesverfassungsgericht, 1BvR 2623/95.

both their official capacity as well as their personal lives. In contrast to some other European countries, like France for example, neither has so far been questioned. The reason may be found in the fact judges in Germany are anonymous and rarely known to the public. As individual personalities, they are invisible behind their robes and little known for their political or public views. German judges claim they fulfil their role by applying the law, following its letter in a rational and unbiased way. They are rarely conscious of the fact, and certainly do not admit it, that they not only apply the law according to judicial knowledge and tradition but also according to the way they perceive and understand the law within changing societal climate. The judiciary fear that the image of the immaculate irreproachable judge embracing sublime values could change if and when cameras would be permitted into the courtroom. It is assumed that the presence of cameras, cameramen, cables, bright lights, noise and unrest would necessarily confuse judges. This intrusion might well undermine the judge's position by disturbing the orderly hermetic world of the court.[3] The court series, watched daily by several million people have already caused a shift in this respect. Inevitably, those judges acting in the court series are well known by name and are familiar to viewers. They have in fact turned into celebrities. This has lead to the blurring of borders between the real, fictional and virtual. The author of this article, for example, was often approached in restaurants, museums, airports or doing daily errands by viewers who were puzzled to meet her at the time she was expected to be in court on television. The loss of anonymity is no small matter and is bound to have an impact on the judicial culture in Germany.

The prosecutor and the defence lawyer whose task is to address and convince the judge alone with their arguments, in the absence of the jury in a German court, are therefore less dynamic, or active in a common law court. This renders them less telegenic, which is one of the reasons why the series gradually resorted to a presentation of the trial in a fashion resembling American court series. This inevitably leads to Americanization, or perhaps globalization of the portrayal of German justice. Consequently, judges in Germany are often incorrectly addressed as 'your honour!' or are expected to hold a gavel, which are both foreign to the German legal custom.[4] It still remains to be seen to what extent this will have an impact on the legal system even without cameras in the real courtroom.

---

[3] C. Vismann, 'Tele-Tribunals: Anatomy of a Medium', *Grey Room*, Vol. 10, 2003, p. 5.

[4] B. Villez, *Séries télé: visions de la justice*, PUF, 2005.

The Federal Constitutional Court further argued that television cameras might interfere with the order in the courtroom. Television media would automatically cater to its own needs, which are governed by commercial constraints. These are completely at odds with the aims of the justice system.[5] Journalists would therefore probably exaggerate emotions and thus introduce false emphasis into the trial coverage in order to make the court proceedings more attractive to the TV audience. The cameras would focus on details, which the media might consider interesting or revealing from their point of view but not from the judicial point of view. Normality is seldom newsworthy. This would lead to the preference of the sensational and the extraordinary. In fact that is precisely what happened to the court series, which started out portraying the justice system realistically but ended up sliding into the scandalous as soon as competition appeared on other channels. Now bizarre figures populated the courtroom, the language became rough and the *décolletés* of the actors lower. The defendant, witnesses and audience started communicating uninhibited in the courtroom compromising the authority of the judge. The judge ended up losing his traditional position and competing with the cameras. Peter Goodrich has described how the logic of the learned legal order is at odds with the medias instantaneous logic.[6] Moreover, the Federal Constitutional Court reasoned, the choice of cases portrayed in the media itself might distort the image of what courts normally deal with. The court was also concerned with the protection of the persons involved in the court hearing and saw this as another major argument against opening the court to the cameras. The situation for the defendant and the witnesses as well as the court itself is difficult and cameras would possibly influence their behaviour unfairly.

The German television court series, where the line between reality and fiction is hardly discernible, sparked criticism from the judiciary. Bad behaviour and rough language in court as well as the fact that many cases revolved around sex were commented on. The president of the judges' association went as far as to complain that the books on the judge's bench on the set, were standing the wrong way round i.e. for the audience to read rather than the judge. The latter point being perhaps petty, the general atmosphere in court, as portrayed on television, deserves attention and needs to be examined from a different perspective. There is little doubt that the dramatization may disrupt the order and solemnity of the proceedings as well as possibly even frighten viewers

---

[5]   A. Garapon, 'Justice out of Court: The Dangers of Trial by Media', in D. Nelken (ed.), *Law as Communication*, 1992, p. 236.

[6]   P. Goodrich, 'Europe in America: Grammatology, Legal Studies, and the Politics of Transmission', *Columbia Law Review*, Vol 101, 2001, p. 2075.

as potential clients of the justice system. On the other hand court rituals, language, and clothing have been perceived for centuries as the means of exercising state power. The unintended effect of the people's behaviour and language used on television could facilitate the viewers introduction to the legal procedure and thus contribute to the democratization of the courts. After all this is what the anti-authoritarian and liberal movement in the late 1960s in Germany was all about. Thus the successful degradation ceremony, as Harold Garfinkel defined the court proceedings, may be seeing its last days.[7]

The reasoning of the Federal Constitutional Court were confined to the disturbances inside the courtroom overlooking the impact which the introduction of the cameras in the court might have on law's legitimacy and on the shaping of legal meanings.

In a dissenting vote three of the eight judges of the Federal Constitutional Court though in full agreement with the majority's arguments, decided that cameras should nonetheless be admitted in the courtroom in exceptional cases. They argued that after all television is an integral part of life in contemporary society, which trusts and relies on television as one of its main source of knowledge and information. Many years of experience have taught the public how to consume television in a responsible way. The minority opinion also stressed that the media, being in fact a means of control of the third power in the state, should not be hindered in its task.

However, in order to pre-empt misunderstandings between the judiciary and the media, judges in Switzerland for example, are instructed how to speak with and keep journalists informed. In Germany each court appoints a specific judge as the contact person for the media, whose responsibility it is to inform the media and explain court decisions. Despite the decision banning cameras from the courtroom the courts clearly seek to retain and even strengthen trust and confidence of society in their justice institution. Notwithstanding the dithering attitude of the justice system towards television, judges themselves seek the opportunity of interviews on television. In our contemporary culture television is too attractive a media to be ignored even by members of the justice system, who claim to disregard such lowbrow culture. Television is the media par excellence by which one can attain the '15 minutes of fame' and thus gain status and power. Television makes events really happen and transforms the local into the global.

---

[7] H. Garfinkel, 'Conditions of Successful Degradation Ceremonies', *American Journal of Sociology*, Vol. 61, 1956, p. 420.

Journalists, not unlike judges, claim it is their role to uncover the real facts and expose the truth to the public. Both professions, therefore, seem to be in the same business of searching for the truth. However they neither complement each other nor are they competitors. Working together with one another would even undermine their respective positions. In a democracy journalism must remain critical, noncompliant and even troublesome at times. Journalists conceive their role as that of watching the courts carefully in order to convey precisely to the public what is taking place in this important area of the state. They aim to mediate between the court and the public, to 'translate' what happens in court. It is their role to make democracy transparent. The judiciary is well aware of this, and agrees, as a German high court judge put it 'to have a mirror held to us'. The claim of journalists, to uphold freedom of expression in the public interest is necessary and noble. In order to be able to fulfil their task journalists must be credible and trustworthy. The German press has a tradition of famous court reporters with an excellent reputation. Paul Schlesinger, better known under his *nom de plume* Sling, created this genre of specialized reporting from the courtroom during the Weimar Republic, describing the everyday courtroom dramas with irony and wit while avoiding sensationalism. Gerhard Mauz continued in this vein reporting from the courtroom for *Der Spiegel* from the 1960s until his retirement in 1990 and many followed suit since. This tradition acts as an incentive and a yardstick for court coverage on television.

When journalists claim they aim to lay bare the real truth by telling the real facts they refer to a model of investigative journalism without the sensationalist or intrusive touch. There is seldom one single truth; especially not in court where the whole point is to decide over a conflict between different parties each claiming different truths. A journalist entering the courtroom without knowledge of the law, without understanding the reasons for the behaviour, actions, specific questions of the court, will not translate, but relay his own impressions of legal procedure of the fact-finding, which he may find alien. How much of what is going on in court, which is for judges an integral part of doing justice, such as the quiet, the order and the dignity of the courtroom, will be translated to the public and how? More likely journalists will focus on the court setting and on the behaviour, language, appearance and emotions displayed by the people involved. They may even find actors in the drama, who have so far only played side roles and move them into the centre stage. One interesting example of the different priorities between justice and media is the increasing attention given to victims of offences and their families by the media as opposed to the attention by the court whose primary interest lies in establishing the guilt or non-guilt of the accused.

Fairness and impartiality, the concepts on which justice is based, may not be the first priority of journalists and reporters when they enter a courtroom. Commercial constraints and competition pressures cannot be ignored. They exert pressure on journalists to emphasize standards, which are at odds with the values of the judiciary. The success of television journalists depends on ratings. They will therefore have to keep an eye on what the public wants, also when reporting from the courtroom. They assume that viewers have a short span of attention and have very often responded to this. The public are by now accustomed to short scenes and fast sequences in an environment of instantaneous reporting practically saturated by images. Television journalists are therefore prone to a reduction of complexities and to simplifying events, conflicts and facts. On the whole, the simplification of justice conveyed by the media flattens out legal meanings and leads to an infantilisation of the viewers.

The decision of the Federal Constitutional Court seriously hinders trial reporting on television. Cameras may only enter the courtroom before and after the court is in session, so they are unable to show the actual event in the court. Television reporters and commentators therefore resort to showing the court building from the outside, the accused being brought into the courtroom flanked on each side by guards and the judges entering the courtroom with grave expressions on their faces. The next shot usually shows the doors of the courtroom closing. This in itself is a specific message to the public, obviously conveying the power of the courts, even *en passant*, through the architecture and the glimpses of the black robes and other icons of justice as well as hinting that they act secretly. Subsequently the journalist himself comes on air explaining the matter to be decided and giving a summary of the proceedings so far in a few short sentences, in a supposedly unbiased fashion. Given even the best of intentions here lies the trap of simplification. The television viewers get only a few snatches and glimpses into the courtroom and sometimes interviews with lawyers in the courthouse corridors. It is thus hardly possible to convey properly the atmosphere and the personalities involved in the trial.

Unlike in the United Kingdom, court reporting is hardly a daily staple on German television. The types of cases covered can be divided in two categories. The first encompasses cases which deal with basic constitutional rights of citizens, such as the banning of religious symbols from state school classes and the decision legalizing abortion. The second category covers criminal trials usually when murder or rape are in question. Obviously courts throughout the country deal with a large variety of conflicts and offences, so the choice of the cases portrayed is not representative of their day-to-day workload. Due to commercial constraints scandalous cases, with no obvious relevance for the public interest, tend to be increasingly covered by the media. The case of a television presenter is a typical example of the biased and sensationalist reporting. The celebrity was accused of raping a young woman whom he had met in a discotheque shortly beforehand. The defendant was shown on television being escorted into the courtroom by two prison guards, where his defence lawyers were already seated, immaculately dressed in a suit, a white shirt and a trendy tie with his face set in a serious and quiet look. His hair cut followed the latest style. The alleged victim was shown in blurred pictures and referred to with her initials; although this was meant to protect her, it also robbed her of her personality. During the trial the press disclosed the identity of the woman, further undermining her with stories of her alleged unstable personality. The lack of hard evidence finally led to an acquittal. Rather than sustain the integrity of the court, the press, deliberately oblivious to the proper legal procedures, expressed indignation at the fact that the circumstances of the event remained inconclusive.

The reporters' inevitable simplification of the events unfolding in the courtroom, not only tends to bring out the reporter's view but also to make it seem convincing, even obvious. This has further implications: as it is impossible for the public to follow the trial on television like a soccer game, this style of journalism conveys the message that courts are either being slow and heavy handed about something the public could have done more simply and quickly and therefore more cheaply. At the same time it questions professionalism, conveying the message that anyone in society with, or even with no legal training, can be a judge. Most people consider themselves the better soccer referees and at the same breath might tend to consider themselves as the better judges. It does not come as a surprise therefore that the author has been asked on more than one occasion whether a children's court, in which youngsters would decide on offences committed by young people, would be appropriate. Democratic standards and values are at stake as the reliability and stability of law and justice are questioned.

Another, possibly unintended, consequence of the simplification in television journalism entering the courtroom may be the strengthening of prejudices. A foreigner for example, will be portrayed as such by exposing his or her distinct foreign accent, clothing or traditions.

Documentary films are another obvious way of portraying justice on television. 'Der Prozess', a documentary film in three parts on the so-called 'Majdanek trial' made for television in 1984 by the director Eberhard Fechner is an excellent example. Faced with the problem of not being able to present the trial in action, Fechner's film consists of interviews with the court actors. He repeatedly interviewed the presiding judge, the prosecutors, the victim's lawyer as well as the defence lawyers. The film director also succeeded in interviewing some of the twelve defendants, amongst them the only woman defendant, a 'guard' in the concentration camp, as well as a number of witnesses. In addition he introduced some of the footage, which was also used by the court in the trial as evidence, to illustrate the scenes of the crimes dealt with in the trial. Every in-depth presentation has to cope with the problem that it is documented by the author who cannot but have his own view of the events he is dealing with. The film will inevitably convey his point of view and make it seem real and convincing. Even though the film appeared to be impartial, it did become clear on whose side Fechner's sympathies lay and that is in fact his strength. Fechner's excellent film, which did not succumb to short cuts and simple explanations, stands out as a model of a German court trial documentary film.

Present day documentaries, however, are loaded with fictional devices. They increasingly show re-enactments of key events, which are interspersed with footage to suggest credibility and truth. The source of the footage used is seldom quoted, so that this does not really ensure transparency. The films are often accompanied by a voice over of the commentator and also often with a suggestive music soundtrack, magnifying certain moments. This results in a dramatization and exaggeration of the court trial in fact distorting the orderly and quiet atmosphere of a trial in a German court. This style of documentaries is luring and even suggestive. It has become something of an entertainment genre attracting the attention of viewers who are accustomed to seeing this style in fiction and entertainment programs. Paradoxically rather than moving away from reality this style makes the television documentaries seem more authentic and therefore convincing. Real life stories are told with the tools of fiction. In this way the line between reality and fiction tends to vanish, much like the atmosphere in the 'semi fictional' German court series.

One example for such a contemporary television documentary is the film *Die Geschichte eines Testfahrers – Der Tag als ich zum Todesraser wurde'* (The Story of Test Driver – The Day I Became the 'Speeding Killer') by Samuel Schirmbeck. It documents a spectacular court trial in which a man who worked for Mercedes as a test driver was accused of having caused the death of a young mother and her small child in a fatal accident by driving with excessive speed on the motorway. The author followed the perspective of the defendant, who consistently denied having been the driver of the car in the fatal accident. This approach in turn encouraged the viewers to put themselves in the position of the judge who must decide the case in court. The film received a respected prize for best court trial documentary in 2006. Ironically in the congratulating speech the filmmaker was praised especially because he had succeeded in putting together the material so as to make it seem like a fictional crime story.

Besides airing US American popular fictional court series such as *Ally McBeal, Law and Order* and others on German television, Germany produces its own fictional law series One example of a high quality witty series was *Liebling, Kreuzberg* (1986-1998) based on stories written by the well-known serious German novelist Jurek Becker. The hero is an unconventional but smart lawyer by the name of Liebling, which means darling. The series is set in the multicultural, working class neighbourhood of Kreuzberg in Berlin thus giving a sense of the years leading towards the country's unification. Another very popular series with plenty of verve is *Edel und Starck* (2002-2005). The protagonists are male and female lawyers, professional partners, who like the lawyer Liebling fight for the just cause of their clients whilst contending with their own professional troubles as well as their personal romantic relationship. The title of the series is a pun on their names as Edel means 'noble' while Stark means 'strong'. These fictional series, rather than focusing and emphasizing the judge and his role in the justice process, as would have been more suitable to the German legal system, have taken the perspective of the defence lawyers fighting for the just cause of their working class clients. Like a detective, the series dwells at length on their investigations, their visits to the scenes of the crime and the interviewing of potential witnesses. This is quite unrealistic as these kinds of activities are foreign for German lawyers. In real life you find lawyers sitting behind their desks in their offices or on their way to and from court. The series tends to be riddled with legal inaccuracies and misconceptions for the sake of entertainment. Above all the German fictional series are strongly influenced by, and even sometimes based on, American popular legal series. While the pervasiveness of American television series is yet again established, paradoxically both fictional series show lawyers' and court's everyday business of quite un-dramatic and un-sensational bread and butter cases. On this account, they therefore evince a far more realistic picture than the court series or even real trial coverage and documentary films which mostly portray spectacular court cases.

In fact, the criticism against court series, that the prevalence of cases with a sexual connotation is not representative of the cases dealt with in court, can be made against all television formats and genres. The fact that it is usually only expressed against the series probably has to do with the fact that the series portrays court so realistically in most other aspects. The choice of mainly serious crime such as murder and homicide as well as sexual abuse is obviously made in order to attract viewers. This is the stuff entertainment is made of. On the other hand it conveys a distorted impression of what courts deal with in their day-to-day work. Above all they convey a distorted picture of the problems German society is confronted with. Considering that law reform is largely haphazard, depending for instance on chance events such as scandal or disaster or perhaps on celebrity cases, television crime portrayal may well shape the agendas of politicians instead of dealing with visions for the future of the democratic society.

The television portrayal of justice, whether in extensive news coverage, in documentaries, in court series or in fictional television programs, or expressed in the attempts to bring cameras into the courtroom inevitably blurs the line between reality and fiction. This is taking place while simultaneously society is changing in a barely perceptible process. Although the political atmosphere or *Zeitgeist* in Germany, as in any given country, is shaped by its own history and culture, a general sense of fear has been especially acute since the terror attack in New York in 2001, which by the way, coincided with the launching of *Das Jugendgericht*. This global sensitivity to terror has shifted the political climate and societal values. In Germany the historical political awareness of the horrors of the Nazi past lasted well into the 1980s. It had triggered amongst other concerns, a discussion about the role of judges in a democracy especially concerning their political affiliation and activity. This debate has been gradually put aside in favour of rational, objective and impersonal judges who are bound only by the law and the letter of the law. They therefore consider themselves and are deemed by society to be, impervious to the political atmosphere surrounding them. The individual background and experiences of the individual judges, their personal opinions and emotion s, which could color their understanding of the law, are firmly denied. The special understanding for, and humanitarian attitude towards, defendants as a reaction to the past has rather given way to the stressing of interests of the victims. The general political attitude and thus also the attitude of the judges seems to focus more on security and less to personal dignity and freedom. The result of this change of climate seems to be harsher sentencing. Another implication is less sensitivity to minorities by identifying them as marginal.

Despite the legacy of Germany's history, the German media seems to go along with the watering down of the citizen's basic rights and the slow erosion of civil liberties focusing rather on security. In insecure times and in 'liquid societies' as Zygmunt Bauman puts it, television seems to make society more secure by portraying justice as strong and fair, solving problems and strengthening common values. This is not only achieved by a portrayal of the courts but also by concentrating on themes like immigration and terrorism. These are topics where the media seeks to convey to the public the sources of conflict. Redefining the roles of men and women in society by showing women as weak or as victims who asked for it in rape trials is another way of projecting order in society.

The political atmosphere colours the information and education of TV journalism. Obviously market forces also have a great influence on the television topics. Giving economic constraints alone the blame for simplified and sensationalist court reporting would be too short sighted. Portraying a legal trial on television means dealing with issues beyond the actual trial proceedings. Courts of justice are sites where not only personal problems are dealt with but also where societal conflicts are disputed. Court trials shape cultural meanings for the whole of society. Portraying conflicts in the media and how the courts resolve them, delivers no uncertain message to the public. This message shapes expectations and attitudes and perhaps the prejudices of the public. In the context of a rape case, for example, the behaviour, role and situation of men and women in society is also dealt with because a shift of attitude may be imminent. Market forces, images on television and societal conflicts converge and become a very powerful force.

The impact of legal representation on television cannot easily be measured, but whether cameras are inside or still remain outside the real courtroom, they are exercising their influence on the public's perception of justice. A study conducted among German law students at the University of Bochum, confirmed that even students found news coverage and popular legal portrayal on television programs quite helpful in forming opinions about lawyers. Judges in Germany in general are oblivious to this, although they certainly are television consumers. Paradoxically they continue to remain secluded, by referring to their own framework, which they term 'the judicial tradition', much like the ivory towers of academia. They are adamant that in order to preserve 'tradition', the atmosphere in the court should not be altered. They would be well advised to realize that they are part of society and that the prevailing political climate and the shifting values in society therefore affect them. This partially explains why the judges are wary of the invasion of the medias cameras. As for now, the Judiciary still maintains sufficient power to inhibit the entrance and presence of the media with their cameras in court. But at the same time they are aware that the court cannot remain an opaque institution and transparency has to be introduced. In politics the increasing collusion between media and politicians has already taken place. The judiciary is dependent on the trust and the confidence of the people, which in Germany is still very much intact. To maintain the credibility, the judicial system has to reach out to the public, which is only effectively accessible through the media. There may not be a perfect way of portraying justice. However in today's world practically speaking, an event did not take place if the mass media is not present to report on it. The coverage of disasters in distant parts of the world makes them part of our lives. We are sometimes less aware of a decision made by local court around the corner from where we live if we have learnt about it from television. Television has certainly come to stay. It has become the main cultural agent shaping peoples knowledge and attitudes to society and democracy. The judiciary can therefore not ignore television.

References

A. Garapon, 'Justice out of Court: The Dangers of Trial by Media', in D. Nelken (ed.), *Law as Communication*, 1992, p. 236.

H. Garfinkel, Conditions of Successful Degradation Ceremonies', *American Journal of Sociology*, Vol. 61, 1956, p. 420.

P. Goodrich, 'Europe in America: Grammatology, Legal Studies, and the Politics of Transmission', *Columbia Law Review*, Vol. 101, 2001, p. 2075.

S. Machura, 'Das Ansehen von Anwaelten bei Jurastudenten', *Zeitschrift für Rechtssoziologie*, 25, 2004, Jg. p. 3.

B. Villez, *Séries télé: visions de la justice*, PUF, 2005.

C. Vismann, 'Tele-Tribunals: Anatomy of a Medium', *Grey Room*, Vol. 10, 2003, p. 5.

A History of Representations of Justice

Coincident Preoccupations of Law and Film

Jessica SILBEY

Professor of Law, Suffolk University Law School,
Boston, Massachusetts, USA

The American trial and the art of cinema share certain epistemological tendencies. Both stake claims to an authoritative form of knowledge
based on the indubitable quality of observable phenomena. Both are
preoccupied (sometimes to the point of self-defeat) with sustaining the
authority that underlies the knowledge produced by visual perception.
The American trial and art of cinema also increasingly share cultural
space. Although the trial film (otherwise known as the courtroom
drama[1]) is as old as the medium of film,[2] the recent spate of popular trial
films, be they fictional such as *Runaway Jury*[3] or documentary such as
Capturing the Friedmans,[4] suggests more then a trend;[5] it suggests an

---

[1] J. Silbey, 'Patterns of Courtroom Justice', *Journal of Law and Society*, Vol. 28,
No. 1, Blackwell Publishers, 2001, p. 97.

[2] Carol Clover has suggested that the first trial film – what she calls the courtroom
drama – was released to audiences in 1906. See infra discussion of *Falsely Accused!*
Clover, C., 'God Bless Juries', in N. Browne, *Refiguring American Film Genres*,
University of California Press, 1998, p. 259.

[3] *Runaway Jury* (Dir. Gary Fleder, 2003).

[4] *Capturing the Friedmans* (Dir. Andrew Jarecki, 2003).

[5] Just by way of example, consider the following trial films of the past decade: *A Time
to Kill* (Dir. Joel Schumacher, 1996), *Sleepers* (Dir. Barry Levinson, 1996), *Midnight
in the Garden of Good and Evil* (Dir. Clint Eastwood, 1997), *A Civil Action* (Dir.
Steven Zaillin, 1998), *Erin Brockovich* (Dir. Steven Soderbergh, 2000), *Returned to
Innocence* (Dir. Rocky Costanzo, 2001), *Murder on a Sunday Morning* (Dir. Jean-
Xavier de Lestrade, 2001), *Legally Blonde* (Dir. Robert Luketic, 2001), *Snap Decision* (Dir. Alan Metzger, 2001), *Chicago* (Dir. Rob Marshall, 2002), *Intolerable Cru-
elty* (Dir. Joel Coen, 2003), *Aileen: Life and Death of a Serial Killer* (Dir. Nick
Broomfield, 2003), *The Life of David Gale* (Dir. Alan Parker, 2003), *The Staircase*
(Dir. Jean-Xavier de Lestrade, 2004), *North Country* (Dir. Niki Caro, 2005), *The Ex-
orcism of Emily Rose* (Dir. Scott Derrickson, 2005).

inherent affinity between law and film. This article investigates this affinity, the cultural space it inhabits, and its destiny in terms of the evolving filmic culture and technologies of the 21st century.

The novelty that cinema brought to its audiences was its moving image quality, the significance of which is rooted in the ideological and yet overdetermined relationship between the image seen on film and the event that was filmed. From its beginnings in 1894, cinema generally (and the trial film specifically) were preoccupied with what it means to know through sight, with the relation between witnessing an event and judging its truthfulness and authenticity. The by-now mythic story of film's birth begins on 28th December 1895, during a showing of Auguste and Louis Lumière's *L'Arrivée d'un Train en Gare* – a short film of a train arriving into a station.[6] The film camera was positioned on the quay such that on screen the train grew larger and larger as it entered the station. Apparently, when the film audience saw the train coming toward them, unaccustomed to the illusion of reality that film creates, the audience members feared for their lives and ran from the theater.[7] This, the story continues, inaugurated the notion that film creates a particularly persuasive reality, producing in the audience the experience of bearing witness to some real event on screen.

At the same time as cinema was persuading its audiences of the authenticity of the event on screen, cinematic masters were developing a film language, the basis of which undermined the very possibility of truthful representation. Film, these masters taught, constructs a world and experience by exposing its story-telling mechanisms that play on the hermeneutics of seeing and believing. The power and influence of film's language derives from its self-reflexive, often self-critical, qualities. The quintessential early example is Georges Méliès' 1903 film *The Magic Lantern*, a story on film about how film tells stories. *The Magic Lantern* purports to tell the history of Western dramatic art, showing first a landscape painting, then a play, and then an image of the newly developed moving pictures. Film à la Méliès is simply the next step in the evolution of cultural (and largely fictional) forms. But by exposing the audience to the film's own ways of worldmaking[8] and thereby involving the audience in the illusions created, Méliès also showed how film's self-reflexive qualities are central to its authoritative claim. Méliès' point was to show how film does not reveal the world, but constructs it. By exposing the ways in which cinema is just another form of storytel-

---

[6]   G. Mast and B. Kawin, *A Short History of the Movies*, Macmillian Publishing, 1996, p. 22.

[7]   *Ibid.*

[8]   N. Goodman., *Ways of Worldmaking*, Hackett Publications, 1978.

ling, the film's self-critique also empowers the audience to judge the story being told, to stand apart from the film and question the images it projects. Presented with the story as told on film that incorporates a critical perspective on the illusion that film creates, the audience is empowered to judge the film version as credible and inescapable nonetheless. The result in the case of *The Magic Lantern* is that the place of film in the history of dramatic art appears preordained.

Cinema's play on the hermeneutics of seeing and believing and its self-reflexive tendencies raise questions of the epistemic foundations of filmic representation. One might ask these same questions of law and its processes as regards the relationship between evidence and judgment. As with film, the trial process is based on the believability of observable phenomena, on seeing, bearing witness and judging. Much like stories told on film, the story that evolves in a courtroom and through the evidentiary process is emboldened with the privileged status of truth because of its basis in observation and the integrity of the testifying witness. And yet, like film language, legal processes are self-reflexive and recursive in nature; by reflecting on the possibility of multiple and conflicting stories (the essence of the trial) and asking jurors to judge those stories, or by exposing legal judgments to appeal and citing those judgments as precedents, law exposes its own story-telling mechanism and reflects on the impossibility of certain, stable knowledge and impartial judgements. Law nevertheless concludes with judgment that is both authoritative and (most often) backed by popular belief. In this way, as with film, the legal trial sustains the knowledge it produces (the 'knowledge' of guilt or innocence, for example) with the authority of self-critique such that the trial's outcome (as with the filmic version) is often perceived as the most persuasive account of 'what happened'. This paper situates this phenomenon – the shared preoccupations of legal and filmic authority – in light of a history of law and justice as represented in the American trial film genre.

The history that follows traces the development of the American trial film genre (the courtroom drama) from cinema's inception in 1894 to the present. It shows how this genre, distinctly stories of law, matured into a genre along side and in conjunction with the developing mechanisms of film and the phenomena of spectatorship. The history will also show how this early genre of film was preoccupied with what it means to know through sight (visual evidence) and with the relation between witnessing and judging (watching film and making a claim to know what you see). These early preoccupations and questions of epistemology (both legal and filmic) were embedded in and shaped theories of

film and filmmaking from its early stages.[9] This history will also describe in greater detail the irony of filmic and legal representations being
perceived as both definitive accounts of true stories and self-critiques of
the possibility of certain knowledge.

Discussions of law and popular culture can take as their object any
myriad of legal subjects and popular cultural objects.[10] The history that
follows is only about representations in film of the American trial –
courtroom battles being the ubiquitous symbol of law and justice in
popular culture and film being a pervasive cultural medium that, along-
side its institutional growth, has matured a sustained intellectual critique. Moreover, an analysis of film must be in terms of what makes
film different from other popular cultural forms: its distinct way of
making meaning as a primarily visual phenomenon whose significance
is garnered in substantial part by the ideological and yet overdetermined relationship between the editing of filmed images on film
with the event filmed. The filmic experience of seeing and being seen
(the primary filmic semiotic), and the world and community that visual
experience constructs (its epistemologies, politics, and a legal order)
remain the grounding for the following analysis of filmic 'representations of justice'.

I. In the Beginning Was Skepticism and Play...

Film is said to have been born in 1894 in France, with the Lumière
brothers' actuality film *L'Arrivée d'un Train en Gare*[11] and its fright-
ened audience. [Photo 1] Despite the aborted viewing of the film, with
this film the French film empire was off and running. So, too, was the
notion that film has a peculiarly 'real' feel, enabling the audience to feel
as though they are bearing witness to some event projected on screen.

---

[9] One conclusion to be drawn from the history of the trial film genre that follows is
that the legal trial is particularly well-suited to representation in and through film
because the trial film genre shares with the more general strategies of film and of law
an authority that is grounded in the individual viewer whose claim to know and judge
the world is based on self-consciousness or self-reflexivity. J. Silbey, 'Patterns of
Courtroom Justice', *Journal of Law and Society*, Vol. 28, No. 1, Blackwell Publishers, 2001, p. 98 (describing this viewer subject as the 'liberal legal subject of trial
films').

[10] J. Silbey, 'What We Do When We Do Law and Popular Culture', *Law and Social
Inquiry*, Vol. 27, No. 1, University of Chicago Press, p. 145.

[11] G. Mast and B. Kawin, *op. cit.*, p. 22.

Photo 1: 'L'Arrivée d'un Train en Gare', Auguste et Louis Lumière, 1895.

The actuality films of the Lumière brothers are as close to a representation of 'things as they are', or what I have elsewhere called '*évidence vérité*', as one might find in the history of film.[12] As film scholar
Bill Nichols has written, the Lumière brothers' films

> are but a single shot and last but a few minutes, [but] they seem to provide a
> window onto the historical world [...]. The departing workers in Workers
> Leaving the Lumière Factory, for example, walk out of the factory and past
> the camera for us to see as if we were there, watching this specific moment
> from the past take place all over again.[13]

And so, in the beginning, moving pictures ('the movies') were a
marvel because of their apparently unique relationship to reality. Film's
so-called mythic capacity for total worldmaking began with what has
become the basic premise of film's unique language: the ontological
bond between the filmic representation and the thing or event filmed.
This indexical linkage gave rise to theories suggesting that film appears
to 'bear [...] unimpeachable witness to 'things as they are''.[14] However,
as even the Lumière brothers understood, a 'sense of photographic
realism, of revealing what life has to offer when it is filmed simply and
truly, *is not, in fact a truth but a style*. It is an effect achieved by using

---

[12] As I have defined it, '*évidence vérité*' is a kind of film evidence, such as filmed
interrogations or surveillance footage, 'that purports to be unmediated and unselfcon-
scious film footage of actual events'. J. Silbey, 'Judges as Film Critics: New Approaches to Filmic Evidence', in *Columbia Journal of Law and the Arts*, Vol. 29,
No. 2, Columbia University School of Law, p. 507.

[13] *Ibid.*

[14] R. Stam *et al.*, *New Vocabularies in Film Semiotics: Structuralism, Post-
Structuralism and Beyond*, Routledge, 1992, p. 185.

specific but unassuming, definite but self-effacing means'.[15] And so the reality that early film presented to its audience was an imagined one, one intentionally conjured by the film (and filmmaker) to project onto and reproduce in its viewing audience a specific rendering of how 'reality' might look and feel.

Around 1902, the actuality film genre (of which the Lumière brothers were the innovators) found narrative. With narrative, whatever 'reality' was contained in the actuality film was replaced with overt fantasy. The quintessential example of the transitional film genre is Georges Méliès' early film *A Trip to the Moon.* [Photo 2] Méliès' films looked like staged plays, the camera passive while actors run on and off stage and puppeteers move props and scenes with invisible wires. The unsophisticated frame composition hid a more complex story, however, involving the audience in its telling, and by consequence, involving them in the new art of cinema.

Photo 2: 'Trip to the Moon', Georges Méliès, 1902.

---

[15] *Ibid.*, p. 92 (emphasis added)

For example, Méliès' 1903 film *The Magic Lantern* is the first film of a film, telling the history of Western dramatic art, showing first a landscape painting, then a play, and then an image of the newly developed moving pictures. Self-reflexivity in film – drawing the audience into the film's storyteling – was born here. By placing film in the trajectory of Western representational art, Méliès' film says that film art is no more or less faithful to its subject than painting. It also piques spectators' attention, drawing them out of the passive experience of the spectacle and into a more active role of contributing to the meaning of the film. To recognize that the film they are watching is just one representational scheme among others is to acknowledge their complicity in the perpetuation of the illusion of film's omniscience and their participation in the film's popular and personal meaning. With Méliès, it became a common practice in early films to tell stories about telling stories through pictures. Although now a ubiquitous and varied featured of cinema – think of more recent films like *Adaptation*,[16] or classic films like *Rear Window*[17] – film's early self-reflexive tendencies were considered another way of commenting on its illusionism, of providing another mode of resistance to what André Bazin later dubbed the 'myth of total cinema'.[18] Moreover, this self reflexivity – a recognition of the individual's presence beyond the representational schema but integral to the meaning of that representation – is one feature that makes law and film, and their ways of knowing and judging the world, so compatible. It is, for example, how audience members might experience films as jurors might experience trials, isolated and apart from the storytelling spectacle on screen or in court but also acutely aware of their integral role in the justification for both the film and the law's power in society.

---

[16] *Adaptation* (Dir. Spike Jonze, 2002).

[17] *Rear Window* (Dir. Alfred Hitchcock, 1954); R. Stam and R. Pearson, 'Hitchcock's Rear Window: Reflexivity and the Critique of Voyeurism', in M. Deutelbaum and L. Poague (eds.), *A Hitchcock Reader*, Ames, University of Iowa Press, 1986, p. 193-206; R. Stam, *Reflexivity in Film and Literature: From Don Quixote to Jean-Luc Godard*, Columbia University Press, 1985.

[18] A. Bazin, *What is Cinema*, University of California Press, 1967, p. 17.

Photo 3: 'The Great Train Robbery', Edwin S. Porter, 1903.

Photo 4: 'The Cabinet of Doctor Caligari', Robert Wiene, 1920.

Also in 1903 (but on the other side of the ocean), Edwin Porter made his famous film, *The Great Train Robbery*.[19] [Photo 3] *The Great Train Robbery* is credited as the first pseudo-documentary, its narrative subject: 'how to rob a train.'[20] With the popularity of this film came the fears and hopes – that have not abated today – that film is the most effective teaching tool, encouraging both the perpetuation of crimes and the beneficial participation in civic society. Its effectiveness comes from its unique persuasiveness. Film, especially documentary film, appears to show its audience how a moment in history actually unfolded. Like the courtroom trial that recreates competing stories for the best and most persuasive one to emerge as the 'truth', narrative film convinces its audience through their participation in and their acceptance of the story's climax, that the story being told makes true sense.

Ironically, *The Great Train Robbery*'s other contribution to film is its innovative editing structure that would become a film mainstay. In addition to its documentary-like feel, *The Great Train Robbery* also pioneered relational editing in film: juxtaposing shots of otherwise discontinuous images to create narrative logic where none existed before. With its reliance on the spectator's contribution to narrative continuity, relational editing would become one staple for film meaning made even more famous with Porter's contemporaries, D.W. Griffith and Sergei Eisenstein.

Griffith developed film rhetoric through consistent uses of, among others, the close-up, flashback, deep focus, long shot and pan shot. He discovered that

> [f]ilms could recreate the activities of the mind [...] [and] had come to realize ... the importance of the interplay between events presented on the screen and the spectator's mental synthesis of those events. Griffith's 'discovery' was far more than mere technique [...] it was the way to make film narrative, storytelling with moving images, consistently coherent.[21]

Eisentein pioneered the montage technique, which is 'the creation of sense or meaning not objectively contained in the images themselves but derived exclusively from their juxtaposition'. The famous 'Kuleshov experiments' out of the Moscow Film School in the 1920s conclusively established the principle by quantifying (through experiments on students) how the meaning of a single shot could change dramatically depending on the images that preceded it. Where an actor's expression is identical in three different shots, but is juxtaposed with diverse objects

---

[19] *The Great Train Robbery* (Dir. Edwin Porter, 1903).

[20] G. Mast and B. Kawin., *op. cit.*, p. 37.

[21] *Ibid.*, p. 58.

(a plate of hot soup, a dead person, a small child playing with a toy), the context of the juxtaposed material evoked diverging emotion s in the audience (hunger, sorrow and joy, respectively), which was then projected onto the actor. Audience participation and editing created the emotions.[22] Any perception of reality experienced through the film originates in the audience and not in the film's phantom capture of past lived experience.

D.W. Griffith's legacy for film and its grammar is profound. But before he made what are now classics in film history, such as *Birth of a Nation* and *Intoleranc e*, in 1907, he first appeared in film in the biograph picture *Falsely Accused!*[23] *Falsely Accused!* is possibly the first trial film.[24] And it contains many of the trial film's generic markers that remain visible today. *Falsely Accused!* opens with a murder of an inventor and the false accusation that his daughter committed the crime. The daughter's boyfriend, dwelling on the crime scene, finds a motion picture camera, which miraculously had been running during the commission of the murder. He develops the film – which reveals the true murderer – and rushes it to the courthouse, where he shows it to the judge and jury in order to free his girlfriend. It has been argued that *Falsely Accused!* participates in the trial film genre by featuring the film audience as the diegetic trial's jury.[25] By showing the newly-discovered film of the crime in the courtroom that exposes the true killer, the jury within the film and the film's audience eventually share the same information about the crime that legitimates the unanimous verdict of not guilty. This emphasis on the coincidence of film audience and filmic jury oversimplifies the interesting quality of this film and of trial films generally. Film audiences are not simply like a jury in that they are made to judge based on the facts presented by the film, but also that the legitimacy of their judgment depends on the perceived independence of the simultaneous investigations of the audience and in the film. Moreover, the coincidence of judgment of the film audience and the diegetic jury depends on a missing piece of evidence that is itself film (a still photograph or moving image), that once developed solves the crime in a triumphant climax. This self-referential gesture – making film the star of the film around which the meaning of the story about law's relationship

---

[22] *Ibid.*, p. 176.

[23] Biographs were an evolved form of Thomas Edison's kinetoscope.

[24] C. Clover, 'God Bless Juries', in N. Browne (ed.), *Refiguring American Film Genres*, University of California Press, 1998, p. 259.

[25] *Ibid.*, p. 259; J. Silbey, 'Patterns of Courtroom Justice', *Journal of Law and Society*, Vol. 28, No. 1, Blackwell Publishers, 2001, p. 111 and p. 116 (concluding that the trial film genre positions its audience within the courtroom drama to participate in the judgment and justice).

to truth is structured – is central to the common epistemology of law and of film as well as to their claims to telling truth with authority.

The self-reflexivity in *Falsely Accused!* bolsters the experience of film as a mechanism for revelation and truth-telling as well as it critiques claims of film's totalizing knowledge. As the film gestures at its own constructedness – by featuring the film camera as the source of the story's narrative thread – it nevertheless glorifies the capacity of film to reveal and clarify the world. *Falsely Accused!* perpetuates the notion that once any elusive perspective or fact is expressed or displayed (e.g., as captured by the undeveloped film), a coherent story will emerge. In this way, the self-reflexivity of the film enables both a critique of film's fictive nature and the confirmation of film as an objective form of knowledge. Spectators understand that what they are viewing is a point of view – a filmic point of view – and, because they are made aware, they feel capable of making judgments about what they see as true. And so, as early as 1907, film is both evidence and the story of evidence. It is about how one comes to know and it is about the contingencies of knowing. Only seven years into the new century and twelve years after the birth of cinema, the incorporation of self-reflexivity and extra-diegetic juries (qua audiences) into the film's world-making and judgment were part of the story films told about law. The many trial films that follow will contain similar marks of the genre.

II. Learning Faith in the Storyteller

After the First World War, two European film movements developed in parallel, one in Germany and one in Russia, both working from the point of view of a single narrator with whom the film audience identifies. This is the development of film narrative from omniscient 'tell-alls' to singular, first person narratives. The development of the first person narrative capitalized on the film's capacity for intimacy and revelation, blurring the 'boundary between subjective and objective perceptions'.[26] In one sense, the first person narrative helped perpetuate the sense of singularity and wholeness in the viewing audience, the sense that they are seeing with their own eyes the events on screen as if live before them. In another sense, however, knowing and seeing, from that singular perspective, was problematized as based on the trustworthiness of the individual telling the story. A mere twenty years after the birth of film, the development of the first person narrative art was already critiquing film's purported omniscient qualities and its false sense of transparency.

---

[26] G. Mast. and B. Kawin, *op. cit.*, p. 136.

The first person narrative film style drove the film industry. Indeed, it drove the cinematic art from Europe to the United States. Although in the way just mentioned, it could be seen as problematizing the first person's view point, this narrative form flourished, in part, because it was also experienced as glorifying and legitimizing the individual as the source of meaning. Based in large part on the illusion of ontological coherence of the thing on film and the thing filmed, the mainstream film experience perpetuated the fantasy of the authentic, centered subject from where the meaning of the film originates.[27] Film theorists in the 1950s and 1960s would write that film, like language, is an instrument of ideology constituting the subject through its formal mechanisms of seeing and the appearance of being seen, the illusory delimitation of a central location, a perspective focused on the subject as center of the story, what Bazin called a 'bourgeois idealism'.[28] Narrative theories of the Classical Hollywood style, 'which present psychologically defined individuals as its principal causal agents',[29] only further the notion of cinema as encouraging the viewer-subject of film to construct the event of and in film as coherent and consistent and as hinging on their personal role and influence. This is simply an iteration of the dynamic in *Falsely Accused!* except that it is about the impact and authority of the individual juror rather than the collective jury.

It is here where we find the seeds of the liberal legal subject, the person who simultaneously stands apart from the film's story and yet is integral to its storytelling, the idealized juror or legal hero whose independence from law is necessary for his righteous participation in it. But as with the legal system and cinema, a subject is never independent of his context; where we depend on the individual subject to be the source of knowledge (testifying to what he saw, learning what he knows through his senses), all we have is his story, about which we must also render judgment. We learn quickly with the development of German Expressionism that filmic persuasiveness (much like legal authority) depends on our assessment of the quality of the person telling the story, a matter that relies on quintessentially human (as opposed to technological or institutional) capacities.

German Expressionism, from roughly 1919 to 1933, draws on this question of subjective judgment and point of view. Where Griffith's

---

[27] R. Stam *et al.*, *New Vocabularies in Film Semiotics: Structuralism, Post-Structuralism and Beyond*, Routledge, 1992, p. 186; J.-L. Baudry, 'Ideological Effects of the Basic Cinematographic Apparatus', in G. Mast *et al.* (eds.), *Film Theory and Criticism*, Oxford University Press, 1992, p. 302.

[28] R. Stam *et al.*, *New Vocabularies in Film Semiotics*, *op. cit.* (quoting Baudry).

[29] *Ibid.*, p. 189.

close-up signified intimacy, the close up of German Expressionism signified intrusion, raising the emotion al level to psychological drama. German films of this time became what Gerald Mast describes as 'mirror[s] [reflecting] the subjective feelings of a single character'.[30] *The Cabinet of Doctor Caligari*[31] of 1920 [Photo 4] is the exemplar of such films, in which the film audience thinks it's being told a tragic but true story by the main character, who turns out, in the end, to be telling a deluded and paranoid fable from inside a mental institution. At the other extreme of the same movement in style and time, is Fritz Lang's *M*,[32] from 1931, [Photo 5] a notorious trial film, if not because it depicts any recognizable national legal system, but because it tells the story of mob justice. The legal system being usurped by mobs – outlaws taking the reigns of law, for good or for ill – becomes a familiar paradigm in the years that follow. In this vein, consider films such as *Fury, To Kill a Mockingbird*, and *Inherit the Wind*,[33] all films in which a mob features prominently and as powerful (if not more so) than the rule of law. Both aspects of German Expressionism, deluded individualistic accounts and a crowd's overwhelming influence that usurps the strength and will of any one person, call into question the role of the individual, his perception and his storytelling in discerning and propagating truths and lies.

During these technical and narratological revolutions in film form, sound emerged. This is the story of the *The Jazz Singer*[34] – the first feature length talkie – which opened on Broadway on October 6, 1927. Imagine: all of this signification and all of this cultural capital was spinning and developing from 1894 until 1927 *without the aid of words.* This evidences the power and the peculiar affectivity of the visual. And for those concerned with how legal and filmic ways of knowing and world-making overlap, imagine that all of this legal knowledge and culture was solely created through images. This was law and legal authority without spoken or written language. This vast visual legal landscape – images of justice and the rule of law – still exist today. But with the advent of dialogue and the hegemony of the word, it is far too easy to overlook the affect and sway of the visual in our experiences of representations of law.

---

[30] G. Mast and B. Kawin, *A Short History of the Movies*, Macmillian Press, 1996, p. 136.

[31] *The Cabinet of Dr. Caligari* (Dir. Robert Wiene, 1920).

[32] *M* (Dir. Fritz Lang, 1931).

[33] *Fury* (Dir. Fritz Lang, 1936), *To Kill a Mockingbird* (Dir. Robert Mulligan, 1962), *Inherit the Wind* (Dir. Stanley Kramer, 1960).

[34] *The Jazz Singer* (Dir. Alan Crosland, 1927).

Photo 5: 'M', Fritz Lang's, 1931.

III. The Rise of the Liberal Legal Hero in Classical Hollywood Cinema

As the United States grew its political and economic power from the late 1930s to the 1950s, Hollywood learned from these early masters of cinema and then took the reigns of world film. Fritz Lang came to the United States and made films like *Fury*[35] and *The Big Heat.*[36] These films – both law and chaos kind of film (although *Fury* the only trial film) – bookend the film noir period, which is characterized by Chiaroscuro-style of filmmaking and the criminal underside of the post-war glory of American life and its institutions.[37]

Fury stars Spencer Tracy as Joe Wilson, who is wrongfully accused of kidnapping. While detained, we think he is killed by a mob who set fire to his jail cell. We, the film audience, see Joe's face through the flames. His burning face is reproduced in the film's diegetic newspapers and newsreels. In fact, Joe survives the fire, but only the film audience knows of this miracle. Here, the film within the film (newsreel footage shown in court of the jail burning and Joe's apparent demise) fails to reveal the truth that Joe survived, but instead perpetuates the lie of Joe's death. The film in pointing to itself (its moment of self-reflexivity revealing a lie) is a key to how the law in this film will *fail* to serve justice.

---

[35] *Fury* (Dir. Fritz Lang, 1936).

[36] *The Big Heat* (Dir. Fritz Lang, 1953).

[37] N. Rosenberg, 'Hollywood on Trials: Courts and Films, 1930-1960', *Law and History Review*, Board of Trustees of University of Illinois, 1994, p. 341.

Joe seeks revenge for his near-death. Instead of entrust ing the legal system with his exoneration, he manipulates the district attorney and conspires with his brothers to assist in the conviction of the mob for his 'murder'. When the jury is about to convict those in the crowd who set the fire – an example of the law failing to evince the truth of the matter – Joe dramatically enters the courtroom and halts the trial. This film marks a beginning of two decades of legal films that criticize the law's capacity for justice.[38] It also evidences the liberal legal subject as legal hero: that person who at first stands in opposition to the law but whose tenacity and self-possession forge a place within the legal system in order to right the institution that has strayed from its honorable goal.[39] While criticizing the legal system for failing its subjects, the legal hero adds strength to that system by showing how truth and justice through law depends on the participation of individual men.

Well known films of this ilk from this era are plentiful. Consider *Young Mr. Lincoln*[40] and the *The Paradine Case*[41] made by the influential 'auteurs' John Ford and Alfred Hitchcock, respectively.[42] This is also the time that film theory, such as auteur theory and film noir became the subject of scholarly attention in France. But as Hollywood grew even more dominant, the Classical Hollywood style overshadowed film noir.[43]

Classical Hollywood Style was an antidote to film noir. Some of the most famous Classical Hollywood trial films were made during this time. They created some of the most memorable and heroic lawyer characters on screen and launched hopeful commentaries about the off-screen American legal system as it was dramatically evolving to more generously provide civil rights and civil liberties to all Americans. In contrast to the skepticism that pervaded the representations of law in the 1930s and 1940s, these later films portray a more hopeful vision of

[38] *Ibid.*, p. 352.
[39] J. Silbey, 'Patterns of Courtroom Justice', in *Journal of Law and Society*, Vol. 28, No. 1, Blackwell Publishers, 2001, p. 116.
[40] *Young Mr. Lincoln* (Dir. John Ford, 1939).
[41] *The Paradine Case* (Dir. Alfred Hitchcok, 1947).
[42] A. Sarris, 'Notes on Auteur Theory', in G. Mast *et al.* (eds.), *Film Theory and Criticism*, Oxford University Press, 1992, 'p. 585-588. Similar films include *Knock on Any Door* (Dir. Nicholas Ray, 1949), *Stranger on the Third Floor* (Dir. Boris Ingster, 1940), *They Won't Believe Me* (Dir. Irving Pichel, 1947).
[43] D. Bordwell *et al.*, *Classical Hollywood Cinema: Film Style and Mode of Production to 1960*, Columbia University Press, 1985, p. 370.

American law and justice.[44] Consider *Adam's Rib*[45] – a path breaking film for women in the law and on screen, and one of the few comedic trial films. Consider also *Twelve Angry Men*,[46] Sidney Lumet's masterpiece starring Henry Fonda and Lee J. Cobb that glorifies the jury process and the contribution of every man to the law's endeavor. Or think of *Compulsion*,[47] based on the case against Richard Loeb and Nathan Leopold from 1924 (the 'Loeb Leopold case'[48]) in which Orson Welles plays the boys' attorney (the famous Clarence Darrow) and delivers what some say is the longest monologue to a film audience at approximately fifteen minutes.[49] Other similar films of the emerging trial film genre include *Inherit the Wind*,[50] Stanley Kramer's rendition of the Scopes Monkey trial, and *To Kill a Mockingbird*,[51] in which Gregory Peck brings to life Harper Lee's Atticus Finch and dramatizes the complicity of the American legal system with the personal and social tragedies of the Jim Crow era. These films exemplify liberal legalism as they embolden the viewer's expectations in law by rooting the promise of justice in the determined and enlightened individual. We come to believe that although the legal system can be a tortured place, a determined and enlightened individual (a legal hero, for example,[52] whose enlightenment comes from the film's self-conscious display) can successfully navigate the legal system, participating in and thereby enacting the justice he has learned to demand from the idealized rule of law. The subject of these Classical Hollywood trial films (the subject constituted by them and their descriptive content) is the liberal legal subject of American and continental legal theory, the subject whose distrust and critique of law's totalizing presence and of its systematized non-personalized process is integral to and becomes integrated in the legal

---

[44] N. Rosenberg, 'Hollywood on Trials: Courts and Films, 1930-1960', in *Law and History Review*, Champagne-Urbana, Board of Trustees of University of Illinois, 1994, p. 341.

[45] *Adam's Rib* (Dir. George Cukor, 1949).

[46] *Twelve Angry Men* (Dir. Sidney Lumet, 1957).

[47] *Compulsion* (Dir. Richard Fleischer, 1959).

[48] G. Geis, and L. Bienan., *Crimes of the Century: From Leopold and Loeb to O.J. Simpson*, Boston, Northeastern University Press, 1998, p. 13.

[49] During this speech Welles breaks with film's diegesis and in lieu of addressing the judge in the film addresses the film's audience, expounding on the horrors of the death penalty.

[50] *Inherit the Wind* (Dir. Stanley Kramer, 1960).

[51] *To Kill a Mockingbird* (Dir. Robert Mulligan, 1962).

[52] O. Kamir., *Framed: Women in Law and Film*, Durham, Duke University Press, p. 115, and 178.

investigation that manifests law's promise of individual and equal justice.

While Hollywood was creating and distributing these memorable stories of American justice and its pursuit of truth around the world as based on the indomitable foresight of the legal hero, the French were classifying these films in terms of the medium's peculiar way of making meaning, the most famous theories of which were memorialized in *Cahiers du Cinéma* by the cineastes André Bazin, Francois Truffaut and Jean Luc Godard. Bazin began with the basic premise of the ontological bond between film's photographic representation and the object or event being filmed – an indexical linkage suggesting that film "bears unimpeachable witness to 'things as they are'".[53] But he went on to show how this mythology of total cinema was just that: a myth. Based in large part on the illusion of visual coherence of the thing on film and the thing filmed, French theorists played up the fantasy of the film's authentic, centered subject who can make claims to know the world and to identify truth, the subject whose development began with Griffith and Eisenstein, and who was made omniscient in the aforementioned Hollywood courtroom dramas of the 1950s and 1960s. Ironically, as the French theorists described the illusion of reality that film creates through its aural and visual sensory experience, Hollywood perpetuated through the trial film genre an ideology of legal authority premised on each individual's ability to enact justice by testifying to that which each can claim to know through observation.

The French film theorists wrote that film, like language, is an instrument of ideology. Whereas spoken or written language interpellates addressees and addressors and defines the identities of those conversing or reading,[54] film constitutes its subject through its formal mechanisms of seeing and the appearance of being seen. Each film through its play of shot and counter-shot delimits an illusory central location, a perspective from which the film makes the most sense. This locus is the dominant film viewer, the subject at the center of the story whose perspective is perceived as objective (neutral) but which perspective is necessarily subjective (one perspective and not another). While evolving film theory described this omniscient subject as one ideological effect of the filmic apparatus, a partner in 'bourgeois idealism' whose politics ignore the

---

[53] R. Stam *et al.*, *New Vocabularies in Film Semiotics: Structuralism, Post-Structuralism and Beyond*, Macmillian Publishing, 1992, p. 185.

[54] *Ibid.*, p. 21; T. de Lauretis, *Alice Doesn't: Feminism, Semiotics Cinema*, Bloomington, University of Indiana Press, 1984, p. 8 (describing interpellation as the 'mapping of social vision into subjectivity' whereby the 'movement of film actually inscribes and orients desire. In this manner cinema powerfully participates in the production of forms of subjectivity that are individually shapped yet unequivocally social').

influence of institutions and aggrandize the power of individuals,[55] Classical Hollywood (and particularly the courtroom drama) dominated the film industry with its 'present[ation of] psychologically defined individuals as its principal causal agents'[56] and perpetuated the notion of the world (in and beyond film) as coherent and predictable, its epistemology based on the individual's righteous participation and influence.

These representations of justice have persisted. Consider more recent films, such as *Erin Brockovitch* or *A Civil Action*,[57] both of which are squarely in the Classical Hollywood tradition, their stories based upon the central, independent subject whose skepticism of law is undone by the filmic experience of revelation. Consider also how many recent trial films are a combination of a docudrama ('based on a true story') and the Classical Hollywood style, two genres that best perpetuate a 'bourgeois idealism' insofar as they triumph the liberal legal spirit who is the lone legal conqueror, devoted and idealistic (think not only of John Travolta in *A Civil Action* and Julia Roberts in *Erin Brockovich*, but also Paul Newman in *The Verdict* and Jodie Foster in *The Accused*)[58] These legal heroes prevail in a tainted legal system by making a difference through their participation. That many of these films are based on true stories makes this ideology of the capacity of the common person to triump in a legal bureaucracy even more authoritative and persuasive. And although many of thse films are not obviously self-reflexive in their film form, each film climaxes around a visual revelation: a found document, a testifying witness, or a discovered identity. The film's indices of 'truth' – achieving a just verdict through visual revelation – furthers the film's epistemological authority as it tells a story of law through sight. The truth told is both that seeing is knowing, and, as each viewer bears witness to law's achievement of justice, that the righteous participation of individuals is all that is required.[59]

---

[55] R. Stam *et al.*, *New Vocabularies in Film Semiotics: Structuralism, Post-Structuralism and Beyond*, Routledge, 1992, p. 186-87 (quoting Baudry).

[56] *Ibid.*, p. 189.

[57] *A Civil Action* (Dir. Steven Zaillin, 1998), *Erin Brockovich* (Dir. Steven Soderbergh, 2000).

[58] *The Verdict* (Dir. Sidney Lumet, 1982), *The Accused* (Dir. Jonathan Kaplan, 1988).

[59] Of course this ideological effect of the trial film, like any ideology, is not monolithic but full of fissures. In fact, film's ubiquitous self-reflexive tendencies (telling stories through pictures about telling stories through pictures) can be a way both to comment on its illusion by pointing to its constructedness and providing a mode of resistance to the 'myth of total cinema'. For example, feminist and psychoanalytic film theory exploits these self-referential gestures using classical film's ideology of gender against itself. (Classical Hollywood film inscribes patriarchal relations through structured gazes.) By showing how the audience participates in, and to some extent embraces, hierarchical gender relations through the mutually constituted desire of seeing

IV.   Conclusion and the Next Frontier?

As it turns out, a substantial number of trial films are based on true stories. In addition to the ones mentioned above, consider also *Anatomy of a Murder, Inherit the Wind, Reversal of Fortune, In the Name of the Father, A Cry in the Dark, Helter Skelter, Compulsion, Young Mr. Lincoln, North Country*, to name only a few.[60] These films 'based on true stories' are not necessarily popular because they are based on fact, but instead because they exemplify throughout the one hundred years of cinema the central ties that bind filmic worldmaking to legal worldmaking. From the screening of the Lumière brothers' actuality films when the audience ran from the theater worried the train would run them down to the premier of docudramas such as *A Civil Action* when audiences are made to worry that the legal system is not sufficiently capacious to condemn murderous polluters, these trial films play on the question of how we decide that we know what we do.

Ultimately, these 'truth tales'[61] and are about the difficulty and duty of judging. As we see the roots of early film in even the most recent of these legal docudramas – the unity of sight and knowledge (an issue of evidence and ways of knowing) and of being seen and being counted (an issue of subjectivity and the ideological importance of each individual) – we also see the roots of law and justice in early film. The authority of the meaning made through law and through film remains based in large part on the strategies of reflexivity to recuperate criticism (of totality and of illusion). And the epistemological authority of both the film and law portrayed is grounded on the claimed centrality of each individual participant (audience member, juror or legal everyman), drawing on the ideology of the liberal subject whose claim to rightly know and to legitimately judge the event at issue is based on the centrality of their

---

and being seen (film's central semiotic relation), scholars like Laura Mulvey sought (and succeeded at) making possible a new form of cinema – a 'women's cinema' or utopian film – that attempts to subvert these hierarchical relations by challenging traditional expectations for the role and meaning inscribed by the cinematic gaze. Orit Kamir provides some excellent examples of this feminist reinscription of power in trial films in her book *Framed: Women in Law and Film* demonstrating how law's life in film can serve as fodder for a jurisprudential critique by imagining a more inclusive, compassionate legal order. Kamir, O., *Framed: Women in Law and Film*, Duke University Press, 2006.

60   *Anatomy of a Murder, Inherit the Wind* (Dir. Stanley Kramer, 1960) *Reversal of Fortune* (Dir. Barbet Schroeder, 1990), *In the Name of the Father* (Dir. Jim Sheridan, 1993), *A Cry in the Dark* (Dir. Fred Shepisi, 1988), *Helter Skelter* (Dir. Tom Gries, 1976), *Compulsion* (Dir. Richard Fleischer, 1959), *Young Mr. Lincoln* (Dir. John Ford, 1939), *North Country* (Dir. Niki Caro, 2005).

61   J. Silbey, 'Truth Tales and Trial Films', in *Loyola Law Review*, Vol. 40, No. 3, Loyola Marymount University, 2007, p. 557.

perspective to the (legal or filmic) meaning of justice that is being conveyed.

How will the trial film genre evolve? What are the contemporary representations of justice that are circulating in popular culture today? Law's most current manifestation in cinema appears to be the documentary trial film, such as *Paradise Lost, The Staircase, Murder on a Sunday Morning* or *Capturing the Friedmans*.[62] Whereas trial films based on true stories, such as *Compulsion* or *The Accused*, are fictionalized accounts of notorious trials, the recent spate of documentaries about contemporary trials are nonfiction accounts of relatively unknown legal cases. In many instances, these truth tales are personal accounts, versions of the filmic biography and autobiography, made possible by the explosion of camcorders, personal film cameras and digital photography. How these new film forms affect the meaning produced by the documentary trial film (the importance of truth, the correctness of verdicts and their relationship to justice) may be a subject to develop more fully at another time.

Suffice it to say, however, that these nonfiction films attempt to correct an injustice by revealing certain truths. Capitalizing on the relative anonymity of the case being portrayed, the filmmaker can be the single and persuasive source of the facts to be readjudicated by the larger film audience. In this way, these documentary trial films are a kind of legal appeal, attempting to affect a legal outcome, whether reverse or correct as the case may be.[63] Fictionalized trial films are not activist in this way. For the most part, they end with a satisfying experience of closure as regards the viewer's role in that system or with a sense of a more complete understanding of the place of the trial (and the verdict) in history.[64] Whatever critique of law may have motivated the fictional trial film in the beginning, it has been deflated at the film's conclusion upon the legal hero successfully challenging the law to right a wrong or the law having evolved to include the contemporary community in its endeavor.

---

[62] *Paradise Lost: The Child Murders at Robinhood Hills* (Dir. J. Berlinger and B. Sinofsky, 2000); *The Staircase* (Dir. J.-X. de Lestrade, 2004); *Murder on a Sunday Morning* (Dir. J.-X. de Lestrade, 2001); *Capturing the Friedmans* (Dir. A. Jarecski, 2003).

[63] J. Mnookin, 'Reproducing a Trial: Evidence and Its Assement in Paradise Lost', in A. Sarat *et al.* (eds.), *Law on the Screen*, Stanford Univesity Press, 1995, p. 188-190.

[64] Indeed, it is the nature of the classical Hollywood genre and of the trial film specifically to satisfactorily conclude its story and to make its viewers feel like critical subjects who become satisfied with the film's moral tale. This satisfaction leads to a kind of complacency with regard to the viewing endeavor necessary to perpetuate legal and filmic authority. We are critical of law, but we are constructed as sufficiently participatory within a legal system that is constituted in and by the film that we feel we have done our part to affect a justifiable end.

Whereas both the documentary trial film (such as *Capturing the Friedmans*) and the fictionalized truth tale (such as *Compulsion*) rely on the force of observable phenomena (the events on film) to tell a persuasive story of justice, at the same time the mechanism by which the film's story is told (the film medium and the legal process) is shown to be inherently unstable. This is where the roots of film and its illusion of reality come full circle. The trial, by its nature, reflects the possibility of multiple and conflicting stories. Cinema's play on the hermeneutics of seeing and believing and its self-reflexive tendencies raise questions of the epistemic foundations of filmic representation. By asking jurors (or film audiences) to judge these stories of law on film, and also by exposing those legal judgments to appeal (or further contemplation by rendering them in film form), law and film manifest the impossibility of knowing anything with certainty. And yet, the overwhelming influence of both cinema and law in our culture is that each claim to narrate *the definitive story*. The irony is palpable. While both film and law rely on the incontrovertibility of observations by testifying witnesses (qua viewers) to tell their stories, these stories – even those that purport to be documentary footage of real events – manage to convince their audiences that no story is undeniable.[65] The future of the representations of justice in film therefore may be found only by reclaiming cinema's past and by recalling film's capacity to change and shape our expectations of the world (hopefully for good) through imagination and fantasy.

References

A. Bazin, *What is Cinema*, University of California Press, 1967, p. 17.

D. Bordwell *et al.*, *Classical Hollywood Cinema: Film Style and Mode of Production to 1960*, Columbia University Press, 1985, p. 370.

C. Clover, 'God Bless Juries', in N. Browne, *Refiguring American Film Genres*, University of California Press, 1998, p. 259.

G. Geis and L. Bienan, *Crimes of the Century: From Leopold and Loeb to O.J. Simpson*, Northeastern University Press, 1998, p. 13.

O. Kamir, *Framed: Women in Law and Film*, Duke University Press, 2006.

N. Goodman, *Ways of Worldmaking*, Hackett Publications, 1978.

G. Mast and B. Kawin, *A Short History of the Movies*, Macmillian Publishing, 1996.

J. Mnookin, 'Reproducing a Trial: Evidence and Its Assement in Paradise Loat', in A. Sarat *et al.* (eds.), *Law on the Screen*, Stanford Univesity Press, 1995, p. 153.

---

[65] J. Silbey, 'Criminal Performances: Film, Autobiography and Confessions', *New Mexico Law Review*, Vol. 37, No. 1, Albuquerque, University of New Mexico, 2007, p. 189.

J. Silbey, 'Criminal Performances: Film, Autobiography and Confessions', *New Mexico Law Review*, Vol. 37, No. 1, University of New Mexico, 2007, p. 189.

J. Silbey, 'Judges as Film Critics: New Approaches to Filmic Evidence', *Columbia Journal of Law and the Arts*, Vol. 29, No. 2, Columbia University School of Law, p. 493.

J. Silbey, 'Patterns of Courtroom Justice', *Journal of Law and Society*, Vol. 28, No. 1, Blackwell Publishers, 2001, p. 97.

J. Silbey, 'What We Do When We Do Law and Popular Culture', *Law and Social Inquiry*, Vol. 27, No. 1, University of Chicago Press, 'p. 139.

J. Silbey, 'Truth Tales and Trial Films', *Loyola Law Review*, Vol. 40, No. 3, Loyola Marymount University, 2007, p. 551.

N. Rosenberg, 'Hollywood on Trials: Courts and Films, 1930-1960', *Law and History Review*, Board of Trustees of University of Illinois, 1994, p. 341.

R. Stam *et al.*, *New Vocabularies in Film Semiotics: Structuralism, Post-Structuralism and Beyond*, Routledge, 1992.

PART II

JUSTICE IN ACTION: REPRESENTATION AND REFLECTION

Representation of the Legal Profession on Television

Professional Ethics and Client Expectations

Barbara VILLEZ

Professor, University of Paris VIII

I. Introduction

Television has been a source of legal culture for the American public since the late 1940s. The first television programmes concerning the law and justice were either reconstitutions of real cases or forums where lawyers discussed the issues of the times. In the 1950s, the first fictional legal series[1] brought regular characters to the small screen dealing with the law and justice in the context of stories capable of grasping the attention of a wider public. Through regular watching since then, television viewers have been able to acquire criteria with regard to how a courtroom is set up, what can happen on the witness stand, when to speak or not and to whom. They have also become familiar with the specific roles of judges, prosecutors, lawyers and jurors. Over the years, the narratives have become increasingly complex carrying more complex legal issues and echoing the debates of specific times.

One such question is that of professional ethics Television fiction in general, and a series in particular, are especially capable of bringing this sort of question to the public eye because dilemmas, the basic feature of ethical concern, can be conveyed not only through narratives but through images as well. Featuring an internal conflict in the narrative of an episode is one thing, showing the torment on the face of the character as he paces the floor, spends a sleepless night, looks desolately through a window into the dark city below, is another. These are silent though

---

[1] This is the author's preferred term for television fiction series although some Americans call them 'lawyer shows' or 'courtroom dramas'.

very eloquent statements of the loneliness and difficulty of making *the right choice*. What is more, the series have the advantage of being able to develop the torment of a dilemma over time. Whereas series prior to the 1980s used a simple episodic structure, with recurring characters but closed narratives,[2] today's series carry story lines which continue from episode to episode, disappearing into the background of other stories perhaps for a few weeks, thus giving a character a bit of respite in his torment, like in life. However the dilemma will return to the foreground, still unresolved, and as problematic, if not worse, than before. Like in life too, clients come back to see their lawyers again with new problems or with a new unexpected turn of their previous cases. This is an aspect of reality often neglected in the discussions about the reality of these fictitious situations.[3] In the earlier series, as in the majority of French ones over the last fifty years, the only permanent or recurring characters are the partners of a firm, secretaries, family members or lovers, which one can easily expect to have left little room for any questions of legal substance.

Professional ethics are an aspect of realism often neglected in French legal series. The ethics of judges and lawyers is a current debate in the United States and other Common Law countries and these questions have always been more or less present in the television narratives of these countries, and even more so in the last twenty years. *Perry Mason*,[4] the best known among the earliest series represented the lawyer as above error or dishonesty, but very soon another series, *the Defenders*,[5] brought professional doubt and dilemmas to the public awareness. This was as early as 1961 and since then, ethical questions have often been in

---

[2]   When the main story line of an episode has exposition, climax and dénouement all in one and the same single episode, then the narrative is closed. Many series of the 'new generation' since the mid 1990s, have open narratives where the development of a story line runs over several episodes. See B. Villez, *Séries télé: visions de la justice*, Paris, PUF, 2005.

[3]   People often express their preference for David E. Kelley's series *The Practice* (ABC, 1997-2004) over his other series of the same period, *Ally McBeal* (Fox, 1997-2002) saying the former was more realistic because of the more traditional cases dealt with by the lawyers. The cases handled by the attorneys of the latter were indeed often strange, but did not affect the realistic way of representing the life of a firm. However, the recurrent relations with clients seen in both series is a major element of realism and the odd cases of *Ally McBeal* served as metaphor for legal questions which were made more easily perceivable to a general lay public through their zaniness.

[4]   CBS, 1957-1966, 1973-1974.

[5]   CBS, 1961-1965.

the foreground.[6] In France, an ethical code of rules exists for lawyers, but not for judges and the debate has begun with respect to this sector of the profession, but on a much more modest scale.[7] Nevertheless, from watching French legal series, of which there has been a relatively small number over the last fifty years,[8] a television viewer could legitimately wonder whether French lawyers were at all concerned with correct professional conduct. Liberties are taken in handling cases, and especially conversations between characters indicate that doing things in an irreproachable way is of little concern; in fact it is a sign of professional naivety.

The French television viewer today is caught between this traditional representation of the legal profession nourished through a national series, and the representation coming out of the onslaught of US television series, purchased and broadcast by French television stations. These series, now accessible to everyone on terrestrial channels, most often dubbed into French, especially when broadcast in the afternoon or early evening, are well constructed, entertaining, but offer a very different representation of the lawyer, and more recently of the judge as well, than what the French have been used to seeing. The French representation of the legal profession finds its source in the traditional national imagery in which the legal system, the institution, is not to be trusted and lawyers are cunning and greedy, judges pompous, only the modest examining magistrate is a lone, honest bureaucrat.[9] Confronting the representation of professional ethics in the legal series produced in the United States with that of French series should quickly reveal the complexity of the questions asked in the former and the near absence of any such concern in the latter. Nevertheless, the greater presence of the American representation on French television contributes in an important way to the creation of a public imagery which exerts an indubitable influence over client expectations in France, or other countries where these programmes are seen.

---

[6]   For example, 1970s *The Young Lawyers*, 1980s *The Paper Chase*, 1990s *Law and Order*, 2000 nearly all series, particularly *Ally McBeal* and *The Practice*.

[7]   A lawyers' code of ethics under a 1970 law was revised into the Réglement intérieur unifié of 2005. As a code exists, there is little if any debate. For the question of judicial ethics, see for examble the work of the Cabannes Commission 2003-4, and D. Salas and H. Epineuse, *L'éthique du juge: une approche européenne et internationale*, Dalloz, 2003.

[8]   Over 100 legal series in the US between 1948 and 2006, hardly half as many in France during the same period.

[9]   The recent scandal of the Outreau pedophilia cases, as well as the media coverage of the much criticised handling by the 'juge d'instruction' or examining magistrate, have greatly jolted this traditional collective image.

II. Ethical Conduct

The variety of legal specialisations represented in American serial fiction covers criminal and civil cases[10] of course, but also divorce law and guardianship[11] juvenile court[12] and military justice.[13] In addition, there is variety in the points of view at the center of the various series (lawyers can be featured as well as prosecutors,[14] judges,[15] even paralegals[16]). The types of ethical dilemmas therefore are also more varied according to the professional position occupied. Behavioral choices are always law related and often echoed in the personal dilemmas of the characters in a single episode. Sometimes these choices are tied to the relations between the interlocutors in a particular situation. Is it possible to defend an accused if the opposing prosecutor is your roommate? Is it preferable to avoid mentioning something about a judge to your immediate superior interrogating you on this subject, if you know it could be interpreted erroneously and to his detriment? Is it possible to give a client's spouse advice in a divorce case? Can a trial lawyer be seen talking to a juror outside of the courthouse? Is it correct to plead before a judge with whom you are having an affair? Is it ethically wrong to sleep with a client?

It is not surprising that questions such as the last two are absent from French television series as they are absent from any ethical debates in France. What is one's personal business is gladly kept separate from the professional sphere. However, the anxiety over *doing the right thing*, adopting the correct behaviour in all situations is examined in greater detail, sometimes even to great exaggeration, on the American small screen. Exaggeration can serve as a tool however and what is bigger than life, on the small screen, is less likely overlooked by the television viewers, many of whom have become skilled in reading television discourse.

Hence the concern with conduct in the images and narratives of these programmes brings to the fore individual professional choices and, at the same time, attitudes and conceptions of responsibility and of the

---

[10] *Perry Mason*, CBS, 1957-1966; *Ally McBeal*, Fox, 1997-2002, *100 Centre Street*, A&E, 2001-2002.)

[11] *Civil Wars*, ABC, 1991-1993.

[12] *Judging Amy*, CBS, 1999-2005.

[13] *JAG*, NBC 1995-6, CBS, 1996-2005.

[14] *Law and Order*, ABC, 1990-present.

[15] *100 Centre Street* and many episodes of *The Practice*.

[16] *Kate Brasher*, CBS, 2001.

professional role. Judge Rifkind's[17] use of humour and kindness in dealing with the seedier elements of society in night court reflect his notion that his decisions affect the lives of people who appear before him nervously and who have never had much of a chance. This, he feels, makes it necessary for him to be the one to offer them that chance. His choice is often challenged by more conservative colleagues and the members of the judicial disciplinary board for a time during the first season. Although Rifkind appears to be sure of his vision of his role as a judge, a fatal error, brings the wrath of his superior and the criticism of the press upon him and causes such self doubt that he even considers leaving the Bench. The dilemma judges must face in dealing with young delinquents is thus brought to public awareness and no easy answer is offered by the series. Such is the lot of those who must, like Rifkind make decisions which determine people's futures. The public is thus made aware of the rather uncomfortable situation judges find themselves in day in and day out in trying to reconcile application of the law with serving justice.

As if the narratives were not enough, the images of Rifkind show his torment. Viewers see him, his hand on the top of his head which is facing down as he reads newspaper headlines accusing him of being too soft.[18] Later scenes have him lying on a couch talking to a fellow judge in her chambers about the unappreciated role of night court judges and the risk of erroneous judgments. One also sees him sitting in his kitchen with his wife who makes him a 'comforting cup of tea' while trying to ward off phone calls from intrusive reporters.

Professional error, such as Rifkind's, is of course not the only cause for worry. Attitudes are often called into question in these legal series. Is it just for a black female judge from the South, to have a strict conservative stance with regard to inner city youths?[19] Should a prosecutor try to force a witness to testify even when he knows the opposing party will use in retaliation information which will expose the witness to the risk of arrest and prosecution?[20] Should a lawyer take lightly his client's feelings? And in this case, is it ethical to put doubt in the client's mind about his fiancée's loyalty, in order to get him to sign a pro-nuptial

---

[17] *100 Centre Street*, A & E Entertainment, 2001-2002.

[18] Very early in the first season, he liberates a boy who, on leaving court, robs a grocery store and kills a rookie cop on her first day of service. *100 Centre Street*, A&E Entertainment, 'Queenie and Joe', season 1, episode 2, first aired 15th January 2001.

[19] Judge Atellah Sims, *100 Centre Street*.

[20] D.A. McCoy, *Law and Order*, episode 154 'We Like Mike', first aired on 30th April, 1997.

agreement?[21] In this particular episode of *Ally McBeal*, if it were not for McBeal's visual surprise at her colleague's behaviour, the public may not have grasped the problem. Ally quickly calls in a friend from another firm, to represent the future wife as 'outside counsel'. The public is thus made aware that it is unadvisable, if not unethical, for two lawyers from the same firm to represent two parties to an agreement.

Thus not only do the series bring the workings of the legal profession to the public's awareness, they actually put into circulation notions and issues which television viewers, laymen in terms of the law, may not have imagined to be problems in the first place. Most people have very little to do with lawyers in their lives, apart from perhaps an inheritance, and even then, if probate is uncontested, a person will not need seek an attorney's services. Therefore, if not for television, the public would remain mostly unaware of expected standard professional behaviour, and even less so of the discussions on questions of ethics which lawyers or judges have among themselves.

The few French series that have been on the air[22] have painted a very negative picture of lawyers and hardly any picture of judges at all. The lawyers in *Avocats et Associés*[23] are cynical, arrogant and even disdainful of their pitiful or equally dishonest clients. The brilliant young female lawyer in *Engrenages*[24] is overly ambitious, and goes to the extremes of lying and hiding evidence to maintain her dominance in a situation. Her only interest is her own cause which is consistent with French cultural representations of lawyers. The current French television programmes generally portray prosecutors or magistrates as well to be distant, uncaring or obstructed by the inertia of the system. If one of them does something potentially unethical, no dilemma is considered. If it is shown or suggested, a look, an angry voice is all one gets. Actions and decisions, whether good or bad, seem, on the whole, easy to undertake and pose no moral or professional problems. What is bad is seen rather as losing a client, causing financial repercussions or having to betray a longtime friend or family member caught up in a legal mess.

---

[21] *Ally McBeal*, 'The Pursuit of Unhappiness', episode 84, season 4, first aired on 26th March 2001.

[22] Most French programmes about justice have been documentaries or made-for-tv movies, with recurrent characters, but do not fall into the 'series' category. See B. Villez, *Séries télé: visions de la justice, op. cit.*, chapter 3.

[23] France 2, 1998-present.

[24] Canal +, 2006.

III. Dilemma

Using one's position to help or protect a family member, in breach of the law or of one's professional responsibility, is a recurrent theme in both French and American series. However, it appears to cause no dilemma in the former while it is a source of torment and often heavy consequences in the latter. Bobby Esposito, of *100 Centre Street*, begins the first season of the series as a brilliant young prosecutor in an overloaded night court. He soon has not only a promising career and the respect of his colleagues, but a budding romance with a beautiful newcomer who is there because she has chosen to do public service rather than build a rapidly lucrative career for herself as a corporate lawyer. These two committed young people exude honesty and dignity. Bobby comes from a modest but very warm and loving immigrant family. He has made it up the social ladder and had come to be seen favorably by his superiors. This makes it all the more poignant when his father suddenly calls on him one evening outside the courthouse to urge him to help his drug addicted brother avoid imminent arrest by erasing his previous record. This emotion al personal and yet professional dilemma will run through nearly all the episodes of the first season. At first Bobby's allegiance is to the law, to his professional responsibility and reputation. His conduct conforms to professional norms and is exemplary. However, as time passes, his commitment crosses over the border from professional to personal and he sacrifices himself to resolve this family problem. In the process, he throws his career out the window and is soon obliged to pay a big price for his act. Not only does the public witness his torment as he wavers, during several episodes, between the two unsatisfactory choices open to him, but they also see confirmation that this was professionally an unwise decision with serious consequences. Bobby's act is discovered, he is disbarred, and he must leave the District Attorney's office. He achieves some form of redemption later on when, with his sweetheart, he opens an inner city legal aid office in which he will serve as legal advisor while *she* does the pleading in court.

Judge Rifkind's decision, mentioned above, was, at first, only a minor dilemma: to give an inner city youth an expected sanction or a sign of generosity. Television viewers saw him in court, rubbing his head, a gesture soon to become a recurrent code for his dealing with dilemma, while he races to make the right decision in the limited time allotted to each case in overloaded night court. This lesser dilemma quickly grows into a series of major ethical questions for the judge, showing him to be above all a man doing his job. His moral and professional problems are brought to the audience both in narrative and visible form, as is the case in most of the series since the late 1990s. Must judges be held account-able for their decisions? If so, then to whom? Must a judge admit an error? Should a judge be disciplined for an error? Is misjudging a person's character a judicial error?

Lawyers like John Cage, a senior partner of the firm at the center of *Ally McBeal*, paces back and forth, often barefoot so as to think more efficiently, considering the ethical limits of his behaviour. His attraction to a female client causes him to doubt his ability to continue represent-ing her. The risks involved in such deviation from professional norma-tive conduct are made apparent to the audience in the discussions he has with fellow lawyers and this occurs in more than one episode. Discussions after office hours, and in such places of intimacy as the office lavatory, bring the ruminations of one's conscience within earshot of the television audience. Even if the public's legal culture does not attribute much importance to such problems, they are made aware of ethical codes of behaviour which are very present on the American professional scene.[25]

The look on a lawyer's face, in *Murder One*,[26] as he walks into a col-league's office to find him prepping a witness before courtroom testi-mony is sufficient to alert the audience to the concept of ethical conduct examined here. There are never very easy answers to such questions offered in the discussions following the initial image. When specific answers do exist, this information is inserted into the narrative. Conse-quently here the public learns that prepping a witness is a lawyer's obligation, but that formal guidelines exist as to what is permissible and what is not.

Hence the legal series serve the public as a source of ethical consid-erations. Where does an attorney's first obligation lie: to his client? to the firm? to the law? Which is the more ethical choice: freeing an obviously guilty defendant on a procedural error or keeping a potential recidivist off the streets? The line between moral choices and profes-sional ethics is not as clear as the lay viewers might think at first.

Judge Hiller in the *Practice*,[27] must choose between allowing ille-gally obtained evidence to be used in a murder case, or refusing it thus following a precedent set by the Supreme Court concerning warrant requirements. Deciding against the use of evidence obtained in a war-rantless search would not only challenge case law, but would immedi-

---

[25] The National Judicial College ABA Model Rules for Judicial Disciplinary Enforce-ment, videotape produced by the State Justice Institute.

[26] ABC, 1995-1997.

[27] *The Practice*, 'Closet Justice', episode 53, season 3, first aired 28th March 1999.

ately put an end to the trial at hand, freeing the defendant. Her decision therefore concerns the threat of danger the defendant presents to society were he to be set free. She must decide between her judicial obligation to assure the application of the law, or her judicial obligation to challenge past decisions which may have become bad law. If she does the latter, she will likely cause the case to go to the court of Appeal and eventually even the Supreme Court, thus giving them the possibility of revising their stance on the warrant requirement. But which choice would better correspond to 'performing the duties of judicial office [...] diligently?'[28] Her dilemma clearly goes beyond the legal question of imposing limits on the warrant requirement. Judicial behaviour is also in question here. What is the primary responsibility of the judge, to the situation at hand, or to the preservation of a uniform coherent body of law? To make this dilemma more visible to the public, the episode contains the arguments of the two sides in court and a scene in private discussion between Judge Hiller and a fellow judge over the logic and 'embarrassment' of the warrant requirement. When she finally pronounces her decision, which goes in favour of legal coherence, applying the Supreme Court decision in the case, the tension in her voice, as well as the sounds of the immediate reactions of the public in her courtroom and the faces of counsel, make it clear to television viewers that this was indeed a very difficult and controversial decision to make. Respect for the law in this case causes tears of despair.

Judges and lawyers are confronted with ethical dilemmas in their professional lives, but the first place where such questions are asked is law school). *The Paper Chase* was a series which centered all its episodes in the context of legal education. Class discussions between professor and students, inside the ivied walls of a typical looking New England university, often hinged on ethical questions as well as the more technical, legal ones. Like in reality, these television law students had to find internships and begin working in the real world of the law. In one episode,[29] a student having obtained the position of intern in the public defender's office, is required by his superiors to defend a person wrongfully arrested, but who, television viewers know although he does not as yet, is the person who, in an unrelated act, aggressed and injured the student's professor. Once this comes out, all his fellow students repudiate him, which leads to heated discussions about professional and moral responsibility with the few friends still talking to him. 'What good is legal knowledge (asks one student pointing to the many volumes

---

[28] ABA Model Code of Judicial Conduct, Center for Professional Responsibility, 2000, p. 8.

[29] *The Paper Chase*, CBS, 'Burden of Proof', season 2, 1979.

of lawbooks on the shelves of the law library) if it is used to free a crook?'

The discussion following the question of prepping witnesses in *Murder One*[30] echoes aspects of legal ethics courses in law schools. Should a lawyer prepare witnesses? What are the limits to such preparation? Law students learn that there are precise rules covering this aspect of a lawyer's activity. It is possible to inform a witness of what may happen in court, that it is even an obligation to give him or her advice on strategies to adopt in answering questions: like not volunteering information, waiting to be asked a direct question, or when memory fails, not making up an answer.[31] Television viewers learn this too and also that telling a witness what to say goes far beyond acceptable advice on strategies, and crosses the borders of ethical conduct. In *Murder One* other questions of professional norms with regard to laymen in court are examined. The interaction between two jurors becomes a problem to one of the parties and the judge must decide whether or not to deal with it or call a mistrial. Judicial intervention in a case is less cut and dry than the public may have expected from watching *Perry Mason*. It is true that judges in the Common Law system are umpires and take a back seat to the confrontation in court. Nevertheless, as Judge Attelah Sims, of *100 Centre Street*, often reminds the television audience, in her court, she sets the rules as to how it should be run.

The frequent ethical issues dealt with in the television series produced in the United States thus echo the preoccupations of the legal profession and is part of legal education. These questions are shown to be a moment of impasse, of crisis, of both personal and professional conflict. The law is often perceived by the public as technical, efficient and cold, but these questions divulge a more tentative side of the legal profession. The question of what is right in today's ever more rapidly changing world subjects everyone, without exception, to evaluative judgment. Painting a more vulnerable, human portrait of lawyers and judges brings them closer to the erring mortals they must represent or judge themselves. If Perry Mason was a lawyer of unwavering integrity, with no personal flaws, nor any personal life, the modern television lawyer or judge is an erring, self-questioning, but caring servant of justice. This less slanted vision of the profession brought to the public eye in the modern series necessarily influences client expectations. Frequent viewing of legal activity and ethical considerations has brought

---

[30] ABC, 1995-1997.

[31] 'Cross Examining the Well Prepared Witness', mpg, DVD, The National Institute for Trial Advocacy, North Star Lit Technologies, 12th April 2006

audiences to develop an image of the lawyer in addition to the already acquired representations of place, activity, and attitudes.

IV. Client expectations

A. *Imagery*

It has been proved that television contributes to the formulation of audience expectations. Television viewers of medical series like *ER*[32] or *Grey's Anatomy,*[33] have acquired an image of what they may expect to experience in a hospital emergency room. They know that if not covered in blood themselves, they will have to wait a while before a doctor comes to see what has brought them there.[34] The public likewise has a mental image of how a courtroom is set up from watching legal series like *Perry Mason* or even *Ally McBeal,* which offer a sort of schematic regularity. Audiences have always seen a single judge as the only person wearing a robe in court. They have a picture in mind of him, or her, sitting, facing the court, saying little unless a question of order or a need for clarity arises. Television viewers know that judges call to order by banging a gavel on the bench table in front of him. They can conjure up an image of the jury sitting in a confined area to the right or left of the judge's bench. A foreman or forewoman, who is always the first person in the bottom row of jurors, the person nearest the judge, will be asked whether the jury has reached a verdict. The parties sit with their lawyers at tables facing the judge, their backs to the public in court. A uniformed attendant asks everyone to rise when the judge enters the courtroom, he goes to the door to call witnesses to enter and take the stand to give testimony. He holds the bible upon which witnesses take an oath to tell the truth.

Not only do American audiences have this mental picture, but it is shared by most French television viewers as well as those in other European countries whose local terrestrial and cable channels purchase and air these lawyer series produced in the United States. However viewing imported series is not the only basis for the French viewpoint on American courtroom organization. A surprising number of French courtroom dramas insert American features into their home produced series. Hence, contrary to French legal conventions, judges on television are addressed as 'Your Honour' rather than as Mister or Madam Presi-

---

[32] NBC, 1994-present.

[33] ABC, 2005-present.

[34] S. Chalvon-Demersay, 'La Confusion des conditions. Une enquête sur la série télévisée Urgences [ER]', *Réseaux*, No. 95, CENT/Hermès Science Publications, 1999.

dent which would be a preferable translation of 'Monsieur (ou Madame) le président'.[35] In French made-for-television movies, with recurring main characters, frequently a jury finds itself sitting separately from the judge in a confined area on his left or right. This would never happen in a French court where jurors sit on either side of the judges *with* whom they reach the verdict, and not on their own like in Common Law countries. Lawyers are not allowed to make objections interrupting counsel who address the court or conduct questioning, yet this is often what the French television viewer sees in home produced series. The obvious question is why does this happens. The less obvious answer is that it is not due to naivety or lack of information on the part of scriptwriters, nor does it result from the absence of legal advisors on the set. The explanation for such erroneous images is that French channels dictate these inclusions, sometimes over the protestations of writers and producers, because they feel audiences would be more at home with aspects of the law they recognize, even if these aspects belong to a system which is foreign to them, but which they ultimately know better than their own.[36]

The French have produced a greater number of documentaries than dramas about the law. The former most often focus on particular cases and lawyers' roles are minimized. This results from a director's choice in most cases, but it is also largely due to the fact that in the French inquisitorial procedure, lawyers are less active than their Common Law counterparts who basically run the show in court. Consequently the representation the work of lawyers, coming out of Common Law countries, offer more material for the collective French imagery because lawyers are the principal courtroom actors. Another reason that documentaries are lesser sources of mental pictures of trials is that they are largely composed of interviews. As yet the French government has not authorized the filming of trials, except on very rare occasions,[37] and even less so the airing of such films on television.[38] Interviews do not feed the imagination of television audiences today, whose culture is a visual one above all else. Even French television dramas involving lawyers offer very little representation of courtrooms. These pro-

---

[35] The French principle of collegiality puts a panel of three judges on the Bench in the Assises Court, in several other courts as well. The president of the court is the judge presiding over the panel.

[36] This information comes from interviews with scriptwriters Philippe Donzelot (several episodes of Femmes de loi, TF1, 2000-present) and Guy-Patrick Sainderichin (Engrengages, Canal +, 2006).

[37] Trials for crimes against humanity like that of Klaus Barbie 1987 in Lyon France, or that of Maurice Papon in 1997-8.

[38] 'Court Bans Film of Wartime Collaborator's Trial', Europe Press Release, 21st December 2002, http://www.rsf.org.

grammes, unlike a police series, focus the stories principally on the personal and social lives of the characters, over and above their professional activities. Consequently the setting for most of the lawyers' activities is limited mainly to offices, bedrooms and restaurants.

Thus, French audiences acquire much of their knowledge about the law and justice from American television programmes, largely dramas which attract them often for reasons other than their interest in the law. Images abound of lawyers and students in impressive law libraries, sometimes doing late night research on case law to find solutions to difficult cases. Viewers are used to seeing lawyers in conference rooms giving colleagues an update on cases. Many an episode of *Ally McBeal* or the earlier *LA Law*[39] opened with start-of-the-day conference room briefings. So many scenes of lawyers demonstrating their skills as fast thinkers and persuasive talkers have led television audiences well beyond a simplistic image of administrators with memorized knowledge of codes or precedents. Audiences know that the law is complicated and necessitates interpretation. They know too how much a person's case depends on skillful pleading before judges-of-fact. Television no longer makes lawyering or judging look easy like in the days of *Perry Mason*, and the public is aware of the late hours, the last minute discovery of a persuasive precedent, the dilemma of dealing with the technicalities of the law and nevertheless following the ideals of justice.

The law is represented in all its complexity in the series of the last fifteen years. Solutions to problems do not come simply and require teams of lawyers to sit behind piles of casebooks until one of them finds a precedent or an obscure law on which to base an argument. Audiences who are used to decoding televisual messages, recognize the signs of efforts spent and sleepless nights, in the red eyes, loosened ties and rumpled once crisp white shirts, the half filled coffee mugs sitting among scattered books and files on a big conference table, as the morning light appears from the window outside. It is not unusual then for the public to imagine that the lawyers, they might come to engage one day, would make the same efforts to defend them.

B. Trust

Television progamme makers give the public virtual insight into the modus operandi and quality of service, they could expect from attorneys. Contrary to the detached relationship for clients seen in many French dramas, American television lawyers are not only polite but surprisingly concerned about their clients' problems from the outset.

---

[39] ABC, 1986-1994.

This attitude does not go unnoticed by French audiences.[40] Advice also becomes an ethical dilemma for television attorneys, again echoing current debates in the profession. To the client's question of 'what should I do', television lawyers are frequently heard replying 'well, the choice is yours, but here are your options'. Lawyers, and especially lady lawyers whom writers have placed, intentionally or not, in traditional nurturing roles, must deal with the ethical choice of how far to go in advising clients. Laymen feel that lawyers have competence and experience and clients naturally want to rely on this to feel taken care of and secure. Explanations in simple language, set into the dialogues of episodes, not only inform television clients of their options under the law, they also educate television viewers who become more acute observers of the service carried out by attorneys. Advising clients, however, must not come to mean ignoring their autonomy or allowing the loss of their dignity. Lawyers must suggest possible end results but leave the ultimate choice to the client.[41] Here the legal series serve to correct rather than create client expectations since audiences learn that it is unprofessional for a lawyer to go beyond advice and defence and take decisions in place of his client.[42] Such discussions occurred frequently in scenes of series like *Ally McBeal* or *The Practice*, both written by the same lawyer turned scriptwriter. The team of caring lawyers in the zany law firm of Cage and Fish[43] were good listeners and careful advisors. Scenes that went as far as having a lawyer (a woman) cut a client's hair could be taken as metaphor for taking care of the whole person, protecting his integrity and inviolability.[44] At the time of writing, two new, yet ill fated, series in the United States presented a somewhat different picture of lawyers, that of ultra competent professionals who enter their clients' lives like bulldozers and take over everything.[45] The cancellation of these programmes may have something to do with the aggressive image that audiences were perhaps not ready to accept, or with the image of the

---

[40] B. Villez, '*Ally McBeal* and the French television viewer: a study of the reception of French legal and lay audiences with respect to the series', presentation given at the Conference on 'American Quality TV, Trinity College, Dublin 1st-3rd avril 2004. In the study conducted for this presentation, the French television viewers questioned, unanimously expressed surprise at the relatively intimate relationships between attorneys and clients in the episodes they watched.

[41] With regard to the debate on advising clients, see for example: W. H. Simon, 'Lawyer Advice and Client Autonomy: Mrs Jones's Case', in D. Rhode (ed.), *Ethics in Practice*, Oxford University Press, 2000, p. 165.

[42] *Ibid.*

[43] *Ally McBeal.*

[44] J.L. Baudoin, Preface in P. Pedrot (dir.), 'Éthique, Droit et Dignité de la Personne: Mélanges Christian Bolze', *Economica*, 1999.

[45] *Shark*, CBS, 2006 and *Justice*, Fox, 2006.

helpless client that today's audiences may be too sophisticated to tolerate.

Besides being caring and concerned defenders, the great majority of television lawyers are portrayed as being basically honest. Many of the conflicts they face arise from reconciling respect for the law and protecting a client against arrest. They know and acknowledge that it is unethical to conceal evidence of a crime from the police, but they also remind the audience that is a lawyer's responsibility to protect his client. How does one reconcile the confidentiality of information brought by a client, with one's obligation to respect the law? Honesty is also tested when, like in life, a television attorney must defend a client he believes to be guilty and does not like. Ellenor Frutt calms a client who refuses to plea-bargain by explaining that this offer is his best option and concludes: 'Look, you think that we don't like you, which is true. But you also think that because we don't like you, we won't do everything that we can for you, which is not true.'[46] The scene ends there with the subdued client nodding his head, and the message comes through to the audience as well.

Before an extensive study is actually carried out, it is only possible to speculate as to whether, like for American medical dramas, European audiences of lawyer shows have developed more trust in lawyers than they had before these programmes became so present on their airwaves. French dramas featuring lawyers certainly do not inspire such trust. The extensive media coverage of recent legal bungling in France has done little to convey to the public a sense of reliability and trustworthiness in the legal profession. Television legal dramas from the United States have most likely contributed more than anything else to the public's expectations of respectful, concerned lawyers who will work hard to protect a client's interests, without treating him like a child. Ethical questions examined before the public audience has had an important role in creating audience insight with respect to the complexity of certain legal dilemmas and in influencing client expectations. Programmes like *Ally McBeal* and *The Practice* especially, which, it is important to remember, are written by lawyers, deal very frequently with ethical problems. These recurring questions do not go unnoticed by regular watchers and the difference between such issues being placed at the center of stories in American dramas, in contrast to the absence of such interrogations in French dramas, strikes the occasional viewer as well.

Ethical choices take place in a personal space, inside one's conscience. Images make this invisible activity visible. They permit television viewers to confront what they see with what they hear, and to

---

[46] *The Practice*, 'Part One', episode 2, season 1, first aired 11st March 1997.

observe developments of a theme over several episodes, permitting the problem, and the reflection upon it, to grow as well, until the problem is resolved or turns into a new problem, showing the limits and the humanity of all men of law. The tension in choosing between what is *right* and what is *efficient*, is a question of limits. What is brought to the attention of the public is often clearer in borderline cases. Sometimes it is necessary to cross the borders of professional mores to do what is *just*, sometimes it is necessary to deny one's own sense of justice to act in respect of the law.

For audiences in the United States, as well as in many parts of the world, American cinematic and television representation of lawyers has created the *myth of the lawyer-saviour.*[47] This myth contradicts the American tendency to distrust 'ambulance chasers' and mock judges whose embarrassing media coverage has deprived them of the ability to serve as great models of wisdom. Yet the American public knows that there are honest self-questioning judges and lawyers who do have their clients' first interests at heart. French television viewers watching American legal series have become aware of this more ethical figure in recent years and many have, like the viewers of *ER* perhaps, come to expect to find French lawyers fitting this model.

Public awareness of ethical questions and acceptable conduct contributes to the formation of criteria with which potential clients can judge their legal system and evaluate the service of legal professionals. The profession's awareness of the public's awareness of normative conduct, may influence the ways in which they practice law. Thus, the public's expectations may also serve as a guardian of professional ethics. Men and women of the law will know that they may have to answer for their behaviour and acknowledge possible mistakes. Consideration of the public's expectations is a constant reminder to them to explain options and give full clear information to clients. The existence of a critical watchdog, outside the profession, can help keep legal professionals on their toes, forcing them to take their clients seriously, taking care to maintain the quality of the service that they provide, which is also an essential safeguard of democracy.

References

ABA, *Model Code of Judicial Conduct*, Center for Professional Responsibility, 1999, (2000 edition).

L. Cadiet (dir.), *Dictionnaire de la justice*, PUF, 2004, p. 469.

Charte européenne sur le statut des juges, Council of Europe, July 1998.

---

[47] See B. Villez, *Séries télé: visions de la justice, op. cit.*

G. Durand, *Six études d'éthique et de philosophie du droit*, Liber, 2006.

H. Epineuse, 'L'éthique et la déontologie des juges en Europe', in S. Gaboriau, and H. Pauliat (dir.), *Justice et démocratie*, Pulim, 2002, p. 145.

A. Etchgoyen, *La Valse des éthiques*, François Bourin, 1991.

A. Garapon, 'L'éthique du juge', *Le Juge et son éthique, Cahiers de l'IHEJ*, Décembre 1993.

Ph. Pedrot (dir.) *Ethique, Droit et Dignité de la Personne: Mélanges Christian Bolze*, Economica, 1999.

D. Rhode (dir.), *Ethics in Practice*, Oxford University Press, 2000.

D. Salas and H. Epineuse, *L'éthique du juge: une approche européenne et internationale*, Dalloz, 2003.

F. Stumpf, *ABA Model Rules of Judicial Disciplinary Enforcement*, The National Judicial College, State Justice Institute, 1996.

P. Truche, *Juger, être jugé*, Fayard, 2001.

P. Truche, 'L'éthique du juge: les dépendances du juge', in S. Gaboriau and H. Pauliat (dir.), *Justice et démoncratie*, Pulim, 2002, p. 141.

B. Villez, *Séries télé: visions de la justice*, PUF, 2005.

Talk of Law

Contested and Conventional Legality

Susan S. SILBEY*

*Professor of Sociology and Anthropology,
Massachusetts Institute of Technology*

I. Introduction

From February 8th to February 11th of 2006, the *Boston Globe* carried numerous articles, editorials, and letters about a six-year-old boy in the Brockton, Massachusetts public schools who had been suspended from kindergarten for three days for sexually harassing another child in his classroom. After the principal reported the incident-which consisted of the young boy putting his hand in the elastic of his classmate's pants, touching the skin on the back-the school superintendent forwarded the case to the Plymouth County district attorney's office. The prosecutors refused to bring charges, however, because the Commonwealth's juvenile criminal laws do not apply to children under seven.[1]

Very quickly, the story was picked up by the Associated Press and reported in news outlets across the continent including the *Wall Street Journal*, the *New York Daily News*, the *Ottawa Citizen*, and the *Calgary Herald*. The story erupted in the news media nine days after the suspension had taken place because the mother, Berthena Dorinvil, refused to

---

* I am particularly grateful for the extensive research support from Ayn Cavicchi as well as critical suggestions by the participants in the 2006 Clifford Symposium and the editors of the DePaul Law Review. The conception of a multi-plaited legality derives from a ten-year collaboration with Patricia Ewick appearing in The Common Place of Law: Stories from Everyday Life (University of Chicago Press 1998) and more recently Silbey, 'After Legal Consciousness' *Annual Review of Law and Social Science*, Vol. 1, December 2005, p. 323.

1   MGLA ch. 19, section 52, defines "Delinquent child', as 'a child between seven and seventeen who violates any city ordinance or town by-law or who commits any offence against a law of the commonwealth.' www.mass.gov/legis/laws/mgl/.

allow her son to return to school. Mrs. Dorinvil requested that her son be moved to another elementary school in the district because she feared that 'he would be treated differently' at his old school and would be 'stigmatized by the incident'.[2]

Within two days of the news blitz, and twelve days after the suspension, the Brockton School Department apologized for suspending the boy. The next day, his 'parents hired a lawyer to investigate the school system's handling of the matter'.[3] More than two weeks after the suspension, the story continued to generate activity in local and national media across the political spectrum-from *TalkLeft: The Politics of Crime* to *World Christian News* to the *Massachusetts GOP News*.[4] On March 8, 'one month after the story first made the news, a Brockton Superior Court judge ordered the city to provide the parents of the boy 'immediate access' to the boy's school records'.[5] During the six weeks following the boy's suspension, the school system had reportedly provided the parents with 'only the boy's health record and report card'.[6] After the court ordered the release of school documents, Mrs. Dorinvil reportedly stated that at the time of the suspension, her six-year-old had been 'told to sign a paper on which the principal had written an account of the incident'.[7]

As of the writing of this Article, the school system had transferred the boy to another school where he was reportedly happy.[8] It also began revising its system of reporting student conduct to better address inappropriate touching among young children; it would presumably no longer be labeled as sexual harassment.[9] In addition, legislators at the state capitol had discussed the case during debate on a bill that would

---

[2] R. Ranalli and R. Mishra, 'Boy's Suspension in Harassment Case Outrages Mother', *Boston Globe*, February 8, 2006, p. A1.

[3] T. Jan, 'In Brockton, Boy's Parents Hire Lawyer: School System Apologizes, to Alter Harassment Policy', *Boston Globe*, February 11, 2006, p. B1.

[4] See, e.g., Don't Shake Hands with Brockton School Principal Diane Gosselin, Massachusetts GOP News & Views Blog, http://gopnews.blog.com/548249 (8th February 2006 00:44 EST).

[5] M. Papadopoulos, 'Parents of Brockton First-Grader Wrongly Accused of Sexual Harassment Win Court Approval to See the Records in the Case', *Enterprise*, 9th March 2006.

[6] *Ibid.*

[7] *Ibid.*

[8] Jan, *op. cit.*

[9] M. Papadopoulos & Terence J. Downing, 'Touchy Subject', *Enterprise* 11th February 2006, available at http://enterprise.southofboston.com/articles/2006/02/11/news/news/news01.txt.

require sex education for children as young as pre-kindergarten.[10] 'This incident is a teachable moment for everyone concerned with young children', said Representative Geraldine Creedon, a member of the Massachusetts' Education Committee.[11] The outcome of the legislative discussion is not yet clear, nor is it clear whether the family will file suit against the school system.

This story illustrates the deeply layered and textured meaning of the rule of law in popular culture and understanding. Rather than a simple or singular phenomenon-a thing that can be placed on a shelf to be consulted when needed-the rule of law lives in the myriad practices and contradictory aspirations of a people. Neither entirely a set of disinterested rules and rational procedures for confining arbitrary power,[12] nor merely a terrain of unregulated, agonistic engagement,[13] the rule of law is an ambivalent, paradoxical phenomena that is a commonplace feature of everyday life in the United States. Its ambiguous, knotty constitution sustains, rather than undermines, its durability and its power to shape social relations.

In a recent essay rethinking Professor Robert Cover's *Nomos and Narrative*,[14] Professor Judith Resnik echoes this understanding of the rule of law when she claims that the nation's citizens '*live* law's meaning'.[15] Although 'in general, judges pronounce the meaning of law', she writes, they 'do not have to enact those meanings by themselves engaging in the activity that they require-by living the law that they make'.[16]

Resnik, like Cover, focuses primarily on the jurisgenerative work of the few centuries-old communities who have 'sustained remarkably distinct legal regimes across time, place, and enormous' socio-political and economic changes.[17] Resnik and Cover argue that these 'communities [are] instructive because they show [...] that the creation of *endur-*

---

10   M. Papadopoulos, 'Schools to revise harassment policy', *Brockton Enterprise*, 11th February 2006,

11   M. Papadopoulos, 'Schools to Revise Harassment Policy', *the Enterprise*, 10th February 2006, *available at* http://enterprise.southofboston.com/articles/2006/02/10/news/news/news01.txt.

12   See generally Ph. Selznick, *Law, Society, and Industrial Justice*, Russell Sage Fondation, 1969; Ph. Selznick, 'Sociology and Natural Law', Nat. L.F. Vol. 6, 1961, p. 84.

13   A. Leff, 'Law and', *Yale L.J.*, Vol. 87, 1978, p. 989.

14   R. Cover, 'The Supreme Court, 1982 Term – Foreword: Nomos and Narrative', *Harv. L. Rev.*, Vol. 97, 1983, p. 4.

15   J. Resnik, 'Living Their Legal Commitments: Paideic Communities, Courts, and Robert Cover', *Yale J.L. & Human.*, Vol. 17, 2005, p. 17.

16   *Ibid.*, p. 28.

17   *Ibid.*, p. 29.

ing legal meaning require[s] action, not just words'.[18] Members of these communities do not merely pronounce law, as judges do, they exemplify the process of 'living their law'.[19] Judges and most citizens are 'able to state their understanding of law without facing tests of their commitments to the principles they elaborated',[20] Resnik claimed. But, Mennonites, devout Muslims and Jews, or the orthodox Baptists Professor Carol Greenhouse wrote about in *Praying for Justice*,[21] are not always able to do so. When conflicts arise between the law of the state and the core beliefs of these communities, members are forced 'either to reaffirm or to abandon a set of core beliefs and, if reaffirming, either to suffer persecution or to migrate'.[22]

Cover feared-and history may yet prove him right-that '[t]he universalist virtues that we have come to identify with modern liberalism, the broad principles of our law', procedural justice, and due process considerations, would turn out to be 'system-maintaining 'weak' forces'.[23] Liberal relativism and procedural justice would eventually, he predicted, erode commitments to the rule of law.[24] The strong forces supporting a durable rule of law derive not from easily assented-to rules of procedure, but from more deeply sedimented habits, conventions, and ways of being in the world.

How *do* Americans live their law? When Americans talk about law, what are they referring to? What does the rule of law mean to ordinary Americans? In their classic account of how to study the 'law-stuff of a culture', Professor E. Adamson Hoebel and Professor Karl Llewellyn[25] laid out three investigatory paths to mapping 'legal culture' or 'legal consciousness)'.[26] The first path was ideological and traced the extant rules of social control for channeling and controlling behavior.[27] In this path, the scholar tries to map the official, formal norms of a society,

---

[18] *Ibid.*

[19] *Ibid.* (quoting Cover, *op. cit.*, p. 49).

[20] *Ibid.*

[21] C. Greenhouse, *Praying for Justice: Faith, Order, and Community in an American Town*, Cornell University Press, 1986.

[22] Resnik, *op. cit.*, p. 29.

[23] *Ibid.*, p. 30 (alteration in original) (quoting Cover, *op. cit.*, p. 12).

[24] Ph. Selznick, *The Moral Commonwealth: Social Theory and the Promise of Community*, A Centennial Book, 1992.

[25] K. Llewellyn & E. A. Hoebel, *The Cheyenne Way: Conflict in Case Law in Primitive Jurisprudence*, University of Oklahoma Press, 1941.

[26] See generally S. Silbey, 'Legal Culture and Consciousness', in N. Smelser & P. Baltes, *International Encyclopedia of the Social and Behavioral Sciences*, Vol. 13, p. 8623.

[27] Llewellyn and Hoebel, *op. cit.*, p. 20.

those rules of right behavior for which individuals-as distinct from the official organs of the community-no longer retain agency or authority to define. This is the traditional task of the legal academic. The second path of legal inquiry explored the patterns according to which behavior actually occurs.[28] This became the standard model of law and society research for several generations.[29] Finally, Hoebel and Llewellyn urged a third path that looks at 'instances of hitch, dispute, grievance [and] trouble', and inquires what the trouble was and what was done about it.[30] This Article follows the third path, although it is obvious that in any complete investigation of legal culture the three paths are intertwined:

> It is rare in a [...] group or society that the 'norms' which are felt or known as the proper ones to control behavior are not made in the image of at least some of the actually prevalent behavior; and it is rare, on the other hand, that [the norms] do not to some extent become active in their turn and aid in patterning behavior further.[31]

Norms build up over time with amazing emotion al and material power, often attaching moral meanings to what may have originally been accident or convenience. Hoebel and Llewellyn explain that '[i]nstances of hitch and trouble, as both moments of deviation and as grounds for repair, lay bare a community's norms'.[32] What was latent is made manifest, and what appeared consensual is the subject of open, explicit contest. By following what, in a different register, Cover and Resnik call jurispotent conflicts,[33] we may be able to trace the threads of legality that compose the rule of law.

Following the models of trouble cases and jurispotent conflicts, this Article revisits the case of the six-year-old suspended for sexual harassment. Part II traces the lines of analysis and interpretation that quickly emerged in the public media to identify the diverse conceptions of law circulating in American society. Part III analyzes how, as an ensemble rather than discrete distinguishable threads, this collection of legal narratives works to constitute a hegemonic legal consciousness, or

---

[28]   *Ibid.*, p. 21.

[29]   See, e.g., R. Abel, *The Law and Society Reader*, NYU Press, 1995; S. Macaulay, *Law and Society: Readings on the Social Study of Law*, Norton Publishing, 1995; J. Sutton, *Law/Society: Origins, Interactions, and Change*, Pine Forge Press, 2001.

[30]   Llewellyn & Hoebel, *op. cit.*, p. 21.

[31]   *Ibid.*

[32]   *Ibid.*

[33]   J. Resnik, *op. cit.*, note 15, 25, n. 37. Resnik mentions that Cover is more often cited for jurisgenerative and jurispathic than jurispotent. Resnik more often uses the term jurisgenerative in her interpretation of Cover's work *op. cit.*, note 15 and, 26, 28, 34, 40, 42, 47, 48, 53. R. Cover, 'The Supreme Court, 1982 Term – Foreword: Nomos and Narrative', *Harv. L. Review.*, Vol. 4, 1983, p. 15.

what we might call the 'rule of law'. Part IV concludes with a different 'trouble' case that has also occupied the press in Massachusetts and elsewhere: the local convention of reserving-with milk crates, chairs, or other physical objects-shoveled-out parking spots on public streets. In this movement from the six-year-old sexual harasser to the claims of property on public ways, I hope to show the variety of ways in which legality and the rule of law are performed in American culture, the difference between contested, ideological law and conventional, hegemonic law.

II. Contested Legality

The following reactions, pulled from the news accounts of the Brockton incident, display Americans' complex appreciation and enactment of the rule of law.

A. 'Educators Overreact, but Charge Deserved Attention'[34]

Start with the school administrators. Why would any reasonable adult report a six-year-old who puts his hands in another child's waistband-touching only skin on the back-for suspension, let alone criminal prosecution? According to the school officials, the law demanded their action; they were following legal mandates. 'This was done right by the book', said Cynthia McNally, a district spokesperson with whom I spoke and whose comments were reported in the media, it 'was throughly investigated'.[35] 'It's a situation within the parameters [of sexual harassment], and we're dealing with it within the parameters', McNally said.[36] The Brockton School System has a six-step process for reporting and investigating sexual harassment allegations.[37] The policy requires a written account of the alleged harassment submitted by the accuser and a meeting between the alleged harasser and a principal or other school administrator. The Brockton School system was acting in accord with the mandate of the Massachusetts Department of Education, which requires every school to develop a nondiscrimination policy that covers harassment and bullying.[38] In *Davis v. Monroe County Board of Education*, a 1999 case, the Supreme Court assigned responsibility and financial liability to school systems that failed to take action against

---

[34] M. Hancock, 'Educators Overreact, but Charge Deserved Attention', *Enterprise*, 12th February 2006.

[35] Ranalli and Mishra, *op. cit.* (internal quotation marks omitted).

[36] *Ibid.* (alterations in original) (internal quotation marks omitted).

[37] Editorial, 'Lessons Needed in Common Sense', *Boston Herald*, 9th February 2006, p. 34.

[38] *Ibid.*

harassment.[39] Although many school systems adopted policies on harassment prior to 1999, just about every system in the nation adopted similar policies after *Davis*.[40] The *Boston Globe* reported that '[c]ities and towns are liable if their school departments fail to take action against incidents of sexual harassment'.[41]

These interpretations of what federal and state law demanded of school administrations were not limited to the Brockton officials. Antonio Barbosa, principal of the F. Lyman Winship elementary school in Boston, said that children at his school are taught to 'keep one another at arms' length and to use words, rather than to touch'.[42] Barbosa claimed that he followed the Boston School 'system's six-page sexual harassment policy and that [the school] would treat all incidents seriously', although he could not 'recall an instance of a young child sexually harassing a peer'.[43] The Boston school policy calls for student suspension or expulsion for harassment, defined as 'inappropriate touching, massages, catcalls, whistles, patting, squeezing, or spanking'.[44] 'We take these things extremely serious [*sic*] these days', Barbosa said, 'whereas years ago, people might not have thought of touching as having a sexual connotation. We want to make sure children respect one another and that they don't get in each other's personal space.'[45]

Many school officials believe they have no room for discretionary judgment. '[Harassment] is something you have to address legally', a principal in Taunton, Massachusetts stated.[46] 'If you don't do something, then a child's civil rights have been violated and there are legal repercussions', said Joseph O'Sullivan, the president of the Brockton teach-

---

[39] 526 U.S. 629 (1999).

[40] Jodi L. Short, 'Creating Peer Sexual Harassment: Mobilizing Schools to Throw the Book at Themselves', *Law & Pol'y*, Vol. 28, 2006 p. 31.

[41] Editorial, 'Brockton Overreaction', *Boston Globe*, 11th February 2006, p. A10; see also D. E. Abrams & S. H. Ramsey, *Children and the Law: Doctrine, Policy and Practice* 291 (2nd ed. 2003) ('Over time other professionals, such as teachers and social workers, also became 'mandated reporters.''); A. Pearson, 'Eulogies, Effigies, and Erroneous Interpretations: Comparing Missouri's Child Protection System to Federal Law', *Mo. L. Rev.*, Vol. 69, 2004, p. 589, 591-92 ('Although the federal legislation provides some standards for defining and reporting abuse, state law varies. States differ as to who is required to report [...] suspicions of child abuse or neglect.').

[42] T. Jan and K. Burge, 'Case vs. Brockton Boy Stuns Officials', *Boston Globe*, 9th February 2006, p. B1.

[43] *Ibid.*

[44] *Ibid.*

[45] *Ibid.*

[46] M. Papadopoulos, 'Brockton Boy's Ability to Sexually Harass Girl Questioned', *Enterprise*, 8th February 2006.

ers' union.[47] 'Civil rights has no age limit on it, whether it's a 5-year-old or a 15-year-old or a 20-year-old', agreed a principal in Easton, Massachusetts; all such complaints must be taken seriously.[48] 'Teachers are mandated reporters. That's the standard that you have', according to O'Sullivan, 'You have a policy, you have to follow the policy, and we do.'[49] As Basan 'Buzz' Nembirkow, the Brockton Superintendent explained, 'Our procedures created the situation where [sexual harassment] was the only box you could check.'[50]

Two themes emerge from these comments. First, law is a necessary and appropriate response to serious social problems. It is not for petty, personal matters. Second, law not only specifies impermissible behaviors, but also identifies a range of legitimate and even required responses to the legal proscription. Both the officials involved and some critics invoked this sense of law as a set of shared aspirations and as recipes for action.

Child-to-child harassment is part of a serious 'pandemic of sexual violence' in elementary and secondary schools, according to Nan Stein, senior research scientist at the Center for Research on Women, one of the leaders of the movement to create the offense of peer sexual harassment, who was one of the experts liberally quoted in the media coverage of the case.[51] Since the 1970s, she has 'constructed and disseminated the narratives about peer harassment that were taken up by the media, schools, and eventually courts'.[52] From this perspective of peer sexual harassment as a social problem, the law has responded appropriately by mandating locally enacted antiharassment policies to control the injuries regularly inflicted on school children.[53] Officials must now take it

[47] Papadopoulos and Downing, *op. cit.*

[48] Papadopoulos, *op. cit.*

[49] Papadopoulos and Downing, *op. cit.*

[50] Jan, *op. cit.* (alteration in original).

[51] N. Stein, 'A Rising Pandemic of Sexual Violence in Elementary and Secondary Schools: Locating a Secret Problem', *Duke J. Gender L. & Pol'y*, Vol. 12, 2005, p. 33

[52] Short, *op. cit.*, p. 42.

[53] The actual history of the law on harassment is not as strong as the voices in Brockton seem to suggest. Legal construction of this heretofore normal, if undesired, behavior was transformed through a series of cases. Following Franklin v. Gwinnett County Public Schools, in which the Supreme Court held that schools could be sued for monetary damages if they ignored sexual harassment, many states began requiring schools to create sexual harassment policies. 503 US 60 (1992). However, Franklin was a case of adult school employees harassing a minor student; the analogy to peer harassment was not entirely clear. Short, *op. cit.*, p. 38. Although Davis, ruled that 'private damages may lie against the school board in cases of student-on-student harassment', the Court, over the vociferous dissent of four justices, set a high bar so that

seriously: 'School systems, businesses, churches and other institutions-if they know what's good for them-don't brush off allegations of harassment.'[54] Stein added in an interview, however, that zero tolerance is not the right approach.[55] Officials must follow rules once enacted, but within reason. In this case, Brockton failed to follow its own definitions and procedures, which called for suspension when there is '*repeated*, unwanted, or unwelcome verbalism or behaviors of a sexist [*sic*] nature'.[56] This was not even a case of sexual harassment, Stein asserted, so the invocation of the law 'was outrageous'.[57] Moreover, no one has suggested sexuality was involved in the six-year-old's hand touching his classmate's back.[58] In addition, she added, 'nobody knows whether this was the first or one hundredth incident with this child, irrespective of whether it was sexual in nature'.[59] Stein's interpretation was echoed by others who were less active and less professionally allied with the issue of sexual violence among children.[60] These nonprofessional actors also argued, however, that invoking sexual harassment for disciplinary issues that are normal aspects of child development only 'trivializes actual sexual harassment'.[61] Harassment is real, they agreed, and 'it should not

---

this action would apply 'only where the funding recipient acts with deliberate indifference to known acts of harassment in its programs or activities [...] that is so severe, pervasive, and objectively offensive that it effectively bars the victim's access to an educational opportunity or benefit'. 526 US 629, 633 (1999). Despite the Court's rather strong language, many states, Massachusetts included, required all school systems to prohibit sexual harassment. The school systems would, however, design their own complaint and sanctioning policies to comply with this high standard. Justice Kennedy's dissent predicted, however, that '[a]fter today, Johnny will find that the routine problems of adolescence are to be resolved by invoking a federal right to demand assignment to a desk two rows away'. *Ibid.*, p. 686 (Kennedy, J. dissenting).

54 Hancock, *op. cit.* ('[A]t least those in charge took the incident seriously [...]. [A]t least folks were paying attention. And that's a good thing.').

55 Telephone Interview with N. Stein, Senior Research Scientist, Ctr. for Research on Women, in Wellesley, Mass. (Mar. 15, 2006); see also N. Stein, 'Bullying or Sexual Harassment? The Missing Discourse of Rights in an Era of Zero Tolerance', *Ariz. L. Rev.*, Vol. 45, 2003, p. 783.

56 Editorial, '6-year-old Predator? Brockton Harassment Charge Defies Common Sense', *Worcester Telegram & Gazette*, 10th February 2006, p. A10 (emphasis added) (noting the difference between sexist versus sexual in policy).

57 Telephone Interview with N. Stein, *op. cit.*.

58 D. Rose, 'No Kiddin'! Boy, 6, in Sex Flap', *N.Y. Daily News*, 10th February 2006, p. 15 (quoting Christopher Murray about a six-year-old not having the capacity to be sexually gratified).

59 Telephone Interview with Nan Stein, *op. cit.*

60 Editorial, '6-year-old Predator?', *op. cit.*

61 *Ibid.*

be brushed off',[62] but this was not a case the law was meant to address. Thus, both the officials who believe they are following legal rules governing sexual harassment and people who find sexual harassment law necessary but inapplicable here agree that the law is a set of governing substantive and procedural standards.

B. 'Punishable by Emasculation'[63]

Some observers thought the Brockton school department's actions were necessary, others saw them as an unfortunate overreaction and a misinterpretation of a nonetheless serious social problem and reasonable public law. Some members of the public, however, saw this as just another instance of the overwhelming power of 'loony liberal[s]'[64] who pray at 'the altars of political correctness'.[65] 'Not even childhood is safe from excessive incriminations of the politically correct kind' whose 'invasion into our lives is appalling', according to the student newspaper at the University of Texas at Arlington.[66] Feminists, the argument goes, undermine classrooms and families and emasculate boys with their zero tolerance politics. This voice was not prominent on news pages in the *Boston Globe*, but did appear in letters to the editors in Boston newspapers and elsewhere, as well as on a half dozen or more webblogs. In addition, the *Boston Globe* reported that the Brockton superintendent of schools had been receiving 'hate mail from all over the country',[67] perhaps from those who saw him as part of this conspiracy of feminist political correctness.

Again, two themes emerge in the interpretations that saw the incident as part of national political struggles. First, the law has become a tool of feminists and others preoccupied with gender and sexuality. Second, sexual harassment laws have become an uncontrollable weapon that can be used to harass good people, as well as undermine important policies and rights. Officious bureaucrats and litigious citizens are different sides of the same unfortunate power struggle. According to these interpretations, the Brockton story is more about power than law. Gender and sexuality played several roles in the stories. Some perceived the incident as the logical outcome of the single-minded, unreasoned power of feminists to colonize and reinterpret ordinary social relations through their incessant harping about gender inequality. See what they have

---

[62] Papadopolous, *op. cit.*, note 46.

[63] Editorial, 'It's Tough Being a Boy', *Las Vegas Rev.-J.*, 11th February 2006, p. 10b.

[64] 'Don't Shake Hands with Brockton School Principal Diane Gosselin', *op. cit.*

[65] Editorial, 'It's Tough Being a Boy', *op. cit.*

[66] C. Dowden, 'Kindergartners Gone Wild', *Shorthorn U. Wire*, 14th February 2006.

[67] Jan, *op. cit.*

wrought! These responses were not entirely wrong. Many of these harassment policies were adopted with the advice and support of professional education managers and organizations spurred by an organized campaign that had been ongoing since the 1970s.[68]

Despite the vehemence of the claims, they were considerably muted in comparison to what had erupted in 1996, when a ten-year-old in Lexington, North Carolina was suspended for kissing a young girl in school.[69] At that time, the major media were mobilized, with TV news and public affairs programming carrying interviews with proponents of various positions in organized debates. The theme of this political interpretation was the same in 1996 as it was in 2006: '[L]ook at what you feminists have done' to little children.[70] Unfortunately, according to a child psychiatrist in Philadelphia, '[it's] an approach to answer 20,000 years of degradation of women by finding some 42-pound little fellow to take the fall for it'.[71] According to an editorial in the Quincy, Massachusetts *Patriot Ledger*, little girls are being mobilized by their politically correct parents; no little girl would know to claim sexual harassment.[72] Sexual harassment may be serious but it protects girls, not boys, some writers claimed; if a little boy were touched by a little girl, 'it would be passed over'.[73]

Prominent in the Associated Press report that was carried across the nation was the description of Mrs. Dorinvil, referring to her as a 'stay-at-home mom'.[74] In addition, the newspapers reported that this 'stay-at-

<hr>

[68] Short, *op. cit.*, p. 41-51.

[69] According to several of the stories, this type of incident had been reported in the news before. Editorial, 'Sex at 6?: First-Grader Punished for Sexual Harassment', *Tulsa World*, 13th February 2006, p. A15 ('It has happened before. A New York second-grader was suspended in 1996 for kissing a girl and ripping a button off her shirt. The boy said he got the idea from his favorite book, 'Corduroy', about a bear with a missing button.'); see also N. Onishi, 'Harassment in 2nd Grade? Queens Kisser Is Pardoned', *N.Y. Times*, 3rd October 1996, p. A1 (reporting that later in the year, 'a 6-year-old' was suspended for kissing a classmate on the cheek'); N. Weil, 'Read Their Lips: No Kissing', *St. Petersburg Times*, 26th September 1996, p. 1; 'Boy Banned for Kissing Gets Star Treatment', *Daily Telegraph* (Sidney, Austl.), 26th September 1996, p. P4.

[70] Telephone Interview with Nan Stein, *op. cit.*; see also Dvorak Uncensored, http://www.dvorak.org/blog/?p=4183 (9th February 2006, 02:02 EST) (depicting a cartoon of Jack and Jill).

[71] Rose, *op. cit.*, p. 15.

[72] Editorial, 'Brockton School's Reaction Was Overkill', *Patriot Ledger* (Quincy), 14th February 2006

[73] *Ibid.*, p. 18 ('If a male child told a teacher that a female student touched him, it would be passed off; but because it was a female student, it gets investigated.').

[74] See, e.g., Rose, *op. cit.*

home mother' was 'rais[ing] her only child in the conservative moral tradition of Haitian evangelicalism'.[75] She and her husband, 'a school bus driver in Boston, do not let [their son] watch secular television and have signed up for cable so he can watch religious cartoons'.[76] One message conveyed by this framing of Mrs. Dorinvil emphasized the disabling effect of the power of the dominant political culture. A religious stay-at-home mother-and a statistical minority-who has more time to devote to her child than working mothers, cannot protect her child from the over-whelming power of the feminized state.

The fact that the boy did not watch mainstream conventional television provided additional silage for those who saw the incident as a sign of the corruption of the public culture; the law was not a product of a feminist conspiracy, but of a sexualized media. Many of those who tried to explain what had happened-rather than evaluate it-linked the social problem of sexual harassment to sexual saturation of popular culture by the media.[77] In the first construction, the incident was a result of the power of feminist groups to colonize the law. In this second rendering, however, the incident was a consequence of the power of the media to suffuse our lives with sexuality. In both cases, it was about power. Indeed, Mrs. Dorinvil seemed to experience it as a matter of unjust power. No one contacted her about the incident or their concerns, she reported, until 'she was instructed to pick her son up from school'.[78] 'When I got there, they had all this paperwork in front of them', she said, 'They said they had already called the district attorney and school police.'[79] From Mrs. Dorinvil's perspective, the heavy arm of the law had fallen on her unannounced: 'I was shocked. I was crying. I was out of control because I see that this is not fair.'[80] She was unable to explain

---

[75] Ranalli and Mishra, *op. cit.*

[76] *Ibid.*

[77] E.g. Editorial, 'Allow Room for Innocence', *Calgary Herald*, 11th February 2006, p. A28; 'Unfortunately, lots of kids have much more 'sexual' knowledge then we think – even if they don't have the rest of the backgroun or context knowledge that relates it to sex – either from being abused, getting it from parents, or TV', http://www.bloggingbaby.com/2006/02/09/sixc-year-old-boy-suspended (posted at 6:30 am on 10th February 2006 by That Girl (downloaded 3/1/2006); 'Our culture protects and celebrate lewd and egregious forms of sexual chaos of all sorts in public, in print, in movies, on TV, in debate, in Super Bowl commercials, on cable, in inter-net, and on and on. We put real perverts on parade and are outraged if they are called perverts' http://www.worldmagblog.com/blog/archives/022494.html. posted by Joel Mark at 9th February 2006 8:33 am (downloaded 3rd January 2006).

[78] L. Crimaldi and C. Ross, 'Boy, 6, Hit with Sex Harass Rap', *Boston Herald*, 8th February 2006, p. 6.

[79] *Ibid.*

[80] *Ibid.*

to her son what was happening: 'He doesn't even know what the word 'sexual' is. I don't see how I'm going to explain it to him [...]. I can't. He's just too young for that.'[81]

This religious, attentive, stay-at-home mother was incapacitated by the combined power of the school officials, the threat of the police, the referral to the district attorney, and in the critics' accounts, the power of feminists and the media. Managing to keep the media at bay, she was unable to keep the law from her doorstep. In this situation, she did what a lot of people do under the circumstances: she found a way of resisting the bureaucratic procedures by following them literally.[82] Following the demand to remove her son from school, she did not return him to school. The school expected that the child would, of course, return to school following the three-day suspension. By insisting that the boy be moved to another school to avoid stigmatization, she required the school to fully embrace their own interpretation of the case as serious enough to warrant suspension and referral to the district attorney. Further, by insisting on the seriousness the school invoked in their literal use of policy, she directly challenged the school administration's prerogative to determine a child's placement.

Mrs. Dorinvil's resistance exposed to public view the power institutionalized in the school bureaucracy-a routinized, complacent authority that conventional procedures did not seem to restrain or moderate. Whether it was an example, as some commentators claimed, of 'cover your ass bureaucrats'[83] trying to hide behind badly drawn policies, or genuine concern about harm to the little girl, they sacrificed another child. His stay-at-home mother had the time, it seems, to resist. Her resistance was unexpected and almost inconceivable, thus prompting the scandal. Had this happened in Newton, Wellesley, Weston or Lexington-communities with considerably more affluent and professional populations than the blue collar, primarily black population of Brockton-then the young boy's family would have arrived at the school with lawyer in tow. The case would have been resolved on the spot without public notice, and it is unlikely that the child would have been suspended or assigned to another classroom.

---

[81]   Ranalli and Mishra, *op. cit.* (internal quotations omitted).

[82]   See P. Ewick and S. S. Silbey, 'Narrating Social Structure: Stories of Resistance to Legal Authority', *Am. J. Soc.*, Vol. 108, 2003, p. 1328.

[83]   See Editorial, 'Lessons Needed in Common Sense', *op. cit.*

C. 'Boy's Parents Hire Lawyer'[84]

A third line of interpretation involves this more familiar scenario in which a litigant retains counsel to regain rights threatened by another, which is of course the bread and butter of legal practice. In this account, we focus on the fact that once the story broke in the news, the Dorinvils did hire an attorney; 'I want to stand to defend my rights', Mrs. Dorinvil said.[85] Because she hired an attorney, she was able to secure her child's transfer to another school, receive an apology from the school system, and instigate a review of the school's policy that led to a formal change. A month after the original incident, again with the help of her attorney, Mrs. Dorinvil obtained court-ordered access to her son's full school record and all investigations of the incident so that she could find out what actually happened.[86] This legal engagement proved once again that we no longer live in 'the nonlitigious days of Dick and Jane'.[87] If the law is not seen as an absolute command as in the first telling, nor as a matter of brute political power as in the second set of interpretations, then in this third line of analysis, litigation is at least an option. There is room for maneuver, engagement, and discretion all along the way. Viewed as a tactical resource, the law need not be invoked categorically.

Many of the teachers, principals, and school officials contacted by the media described alternatives that the Brockton schools could have pursued short of suspending the boy and referring the case to the prosecutor. Joan Vodoklys, principal of the McCarthy Elementary school in Framingham, Massachusetts suggested that '[i]nstead of suspension [...] she would have first contacted the parents, and then would have asked a social worker or counselor to speak with the boy about his intentions'.[88] 'Giving the boy (and maybe the girl if she started it) some 'time-out' in the classroom might have been enough', as some reports have suggested.[89] A New York City school official said that the department does deal with sexual harassment by youngsters, but a typical punishment would not involve suspension. 'It does happen, kids get curious', but '[u]sually, the kids get put into counseling.'[90] The *Boston Herald* sug-

---

[84] Jan, *op. cit.*

[85] *Ibid.*

[86] Papadopolous, *op. cit.*

[87] Editorial, 'Sex at 6?', *op. cit.*

[88] Jan, *op. cit.*

[89] Hancock, *op. cit.*; accord Editorial, '6-year-old Predator?', *op. cit.* ('School officials said a girl in the boy's class told the teacher he had put two fingers inside the waistband of her pants. His mother said he told her he touched the girl's blouse after she touched him').

[90] Rose, *op. cit.*

gested that 'a stern lecture and a meeting between the teacher, the principal and the boy's parents' were all that was necessary, 'not a three-day suspension, a referral of 'evidence' to the DA and a permanent mark on th[at] little boy's reputation'.[91] The *Tulsa World* suggested that 'a quiet talk with the boy and maybe a report to the parents would have been sufficient'.[92] 'Rather than be suspended or branded a potential criminal', one letter written to the *Boston Globe* recommended, 'the child should have been corrected and counseled as to what constitutes inappropriate touching.'[93] A letter to the editor noted that 'a competent elementary school teacher could have, and should have, handled the little incident in the classroom'. They are just kids. Bravo to the mother for bringing it all public'.[94] The principal in another Brockton school said, 'Nine times out of 10 it's about sitting down with them, talking with them, telling them about respecting each other's personal body. And nine times out of 10, you will never see that child again.'[95] The general consensus was clear that 'talking to this child was all that was needed'[96] – by the teacher, the parents, or perhaps a professional counselor.[97]

Believing themselves constrained by the federal and state laws, and finding that 'sexual harassment' was the only applicable category listed on official forms, the Brockton Schools suspended the six-year-old. Without legal representation, Mrs. Dorinvil was unable to influence or persuade the school to act otherwise; she was unable to mobilize a review process. With legal representation, however, and certainly with media coverage, the legal mandate became considerably less rigid; alternatives were considered and negotiations ensued. With legal and media forces engaged, the school system became less confident of its own action, reconsidered its legal obligations, reinterpreted the legal mandate, and finally apologized to the Dorinvil family. Just as importantly, the system formally changed its policy, as well as the forms for referring incidents of abuse between children to higher authorities. With

---

[91] Editorial, 'Lessons Needed in Common Sense', *op. cit.*

[92] Editorial, 'Sex at 6?', *op. cit.*

[93] Editorial, 'Counseling Is What 6-Year-Old Needed', *Boston Globe*, 10th February 2006, p. A1.

[94] Editorial, 'School Wrong on Boy, 6', *Patriot Ledger* (Quincy), 18th February 2006, p. 14.

[95] Papadopoulos and Downing, *op. cit.* (quoting Frances Hoeg, the principal at Duval Elementary School).

[96] Editorial, 'Brockton 6-Year-Old', *Patriot Ledger*, February 17, 2006, p. 6.

[97] J. Porrazzo, 'Most Important Lessons Begin at Home', *Brockton Enterprise*, 12th February 2006, available at http://enterprise.southofboston.com/articles/2006/02/12/news/ news/news05.txt; see also Editorial, *6-year-old Predator?*, *op. cit.*

this apology and the policy revision, the school officials demonstrated their discretionary, rather than mandatory, authority. Rather than a fixed, inviolate set of commands, the school system's response to Mrs. Dorinvil's attorney enacted an understanding of public policy as malleable, adaptable, and the product of engagement.

III. Locating the Rule of Law
in Conventional (Hegemonic) Legality

Thus far I have displayed at least three interpretations of law that circulated in public discourse in response to the Brockton case. None of these accounts-whether the conception of law as (1) a set of procedures and rules of play that offer accessible and participatory decisionmaking, (2) a transcendent good that defers as it both confines and embodies coercive force, (3) a tool of power that subordinates as it promises justice-is able to sustain, by itself, the pervasive deference to law that saturates American society. Let me be clear that I am not disagreeing with colleagues who locate deference to law in procedures or in conceptions of rights and legitimacy. By themselves, they are simply not sufficient. A valid description of how law lives and survives as a taken-for-granted set of practices is needed to encompass this deeper understanding.

As an ensemble, rather than discrete distinguishable threads, the collection of legal narratives works to constitute popular legal consciousness), or what we might call the 'rule of law'. Any particular experience can fit within the diversity of the whole. Here, legality is understood to be both a set of ahistorical, universal principles and a set of pragmatic opportunities and strategies. It sustains itself, as hegemonic, because any singular account conceals the social organization of law by effacing the connections between the concrete particular and the transcendent general.[98] It is both beyond the mess of mundane reality and securely located within day to day affairs. To state the matter differently, legality is much weaker and more vulnerable where it is more singularly conceived. If legality were ideologically consistent, as our Platonic heritage has for so long urged, it would be quite fragile. For instance, if the only

---

[98] P. Ewick and S. Silbey, 'Common Knowledge and Ideological Critique: The Significance of Knowing that the 'Haves' Come out Ahead', in H. Kritzer & S. Silbey, *In Litigation: Do the 'Haves' Still Come out Ahead?*, Stanford University Press, 2003; see also Ewick and Silbey, *op. cit.*; P. Ewick and Silbey, 'Subversive Stories and Hegemonic Tales: Toward a Sociology of Narrative', *Law & Soc'y Rev.*, Vol. 29, 1995, p. 197. This argument derives from and is more fully elaborated in P. Ewick and S. Silbey, *The Common Place of Law: Stories from Everyday Life*, University Of Chicago Press, 1998.

thing people knew about the law was its profane face of crafty lawyers and media reported tort cases, it would be difficult to sustain the support necessary for legal authority. The aspiration for disinterested, procedurally regular decisionmaking serves to balance that cynical account, feeding the image of lady justice, the sacred, awesome, transcendent legality. However, a transcendent, reified law unleavened by familiarity (and even the cynicism familiarity breeds), would in time become irrelevant. Law that becomes entirely procedural without substance becomes legalistic.[99] Either way-as solely god or entirely an empty game-it would eventually self-destruct. Instead, legality is strengthened by the oppositions that exist within and among the narratives.

The Brockton case is both usual and unusual, banal and extraordinary. It is a very common example of what constitutes routine compliance-efforts to organize social relations in accord with legal requirements. As a relatively minor, street-level form of law enforcement, it is merely one of thousands-indeed, millions-of such acts that take place everyday that constitute daily life in America. On the other hand, it is unusual in that it is an incident that moved several steps along the litigation process, from a perceived injurious event (the boy's hands on his classmate's back), through the stages of 'naming, blaming and claiming'.[100] Although almost any social transaction could, in theory, become a matter of dispute and could lead to legal claims, few in fact do.[101] Even when people hire an attorney and then file suit, as Mrs. Dorinvil did, few cases actually go to trial, as the Dorinvil case did.[102] Thus, this incident is quite unusual, comprising one of the approximately three percent of court filings that actually go to trial, and the even smaller percentage that get media coverage.

When we speak of a 'rule of law', it is because most of legality lies submerged within the taken-for-granted expectations of mundane life. We might imagine this legality, this rule of law, as an iceberg whose mass lies beneath the articulated events of ordinary social life. Rather than contested and choreographed in the rare trial, legality 'rules' everyday life because its constructions are mostly uncontested and habitual. Law's constructions and mediations have been gradually sedimented

---

[99] L. Friedman, 'On Legalistic Reasoning—A Footnote to Weber', *Wis. L. Rev*, 1966, p. 148.

[100] W. Felstiner, Richard L. Abel and Austin Sarat, 'The Emergence and Transformation of Disputes: Naming, Blaming, Claiming', *Law & Soc'y Rev.*, Vol. 15, 1980-1981, p. 631.

[101] Galanter 1983, 1986, 1996; Hensler 1994; Kritzer 1980-1981, 1989; Kritzer, Bogart and Vidmar 1991; Miller and Sarat 1980-1981; Silbey 1980-1981; Trubek *et al.* 1983

[102] 'School system did not defend itself in the hearing', *Brockton Enterprise*, 9th March 2006.

and built up throughout the routines of daily living, just as each day of precipitation adds to the mass of the iceberg, some floating visibly above the waterline, the larger mass invisible below. Actions that become practices, habits and then conventions help us to go through life in more or less unproblematic ways, without having to think about each step we take as we drive cars, cross streets, pay for groceries, or take our children to school. The conventions that become law are not different, helping to organize social relations, often without having to invoke, display, or wield the law's elaborate and intricate processes-especially its ultimate, physical force.

Of course, this normative and legal sedimentation is never complete; we do not always stay within the boundaries of legally sanctioned expectations, and the reach of law is always disputed. Thus, much of the visible iceberg of legality is about what to do in the event of breach; some of those messes or matters of concern lead to litigation, and some even to trials. Importantly, however, these visible legal battles are the exceptions to the law's more routine dominance.

The law is a durable and powerful human institution because it invisibly suffuses our everyday life. As we go about our daily lives, we rarely sense the presence of the law. Although law operates as a means for making things public and mediating matters of concern, most of the time it does so without fanfare, without contest, and without notice. We pay our bills because they are due; we respect our neighbors' property because it is theirs. We drive on a particular side of the road because it is prudent. We register our motor vehicles and stop at red lights. We rarely consider the collective judgments and procedures through which we have defined 'coming due', 'their property', 'prudent driving', or why automobiles must be registered and why traffic stops at red lights. If we trace the source of these expectations and meanings to some legal institution or practice, the origin is so far away in time and place that the matters of concern and circumstances of invention have been long forgotten. As a result of this distance, sales contracts, property, and traffic rules seem to be natural and inevitable facts of life.

Legal objects, signs, forms, rules and decisions are understood, however, to be a special kind of fact-a legal fact. Perhaps we should collapse the distance between the words 'legal' and 'fact' to write *legalfact* to emphasize the procedures of law that are the grounds for constructing facts. That is *legalfacts*. In other words, jurisprudence recognizes at its core that its truths are created only through its particular processes and that the relationship between *legalfacts* and empirical facts is at best only approximate.[103] The habits sustained by law and the interpretations of social relations underwritten by legal concepts or authorities may also function as *legalfacts*.

As naturalized features of modern life, the signs and objects of law are omnipresent. Through historic as well as contemporary legal decisions that are no longer debated, countless matters of concern have been resolved, concretized, and objectified, literally written onto the surfaces and figuratively built into the very structures of ordinary social relations. Every package of food, piece of clothing, and electrical appliance contains a label that warns us about its dangers, instructs us about its uses, and tells us whether (and where) we can complain if something goes wrong. Every time we park a car, have clothes dry cleaned, or leave an umbrella in a cloak room, we are informed about limited liabilities for loss. Newspapers, television, novels, plays, magazines, and movies are saturated with legal images, while these very same objects display their claims to copyright.

Although much of the time, legal forms go unnoticed, they are imperfectly naturalized. At any moment, the stabilized, historical *legalfact* can reappear, perhaps becoming a matter of concern, debate, challenge, or resistance. Children attend school from ages five through sixteen in Massachusetts as the General Laws and convention have required for the last 150 years. The fact teachers monitor student interactions for sexual harassment and report such incidents to authorities has not yet become habituated or uncontested, despite the legal mandate. Here, the visible iceberg of legality cracks and hits a passing ship. Most of the time, however, legal regulation goes without consideration or challenge.

IV. One Final Illustration

My favorite illustration of this deeply sedimented, hegemonic law concerns the familiar practice in Chicago, Boston, New York and some other northern cities, of placing an old chair, traffic cone, milk crate, or other noticeable object in a recently shoveled parking spot on a snow-filled public street. 'Before snowfalls, a parking space belongs to the one who occupies it: you leave it, you lose it. In wintertime Chicago, however', writes Fred McChesney in an economic analysis of this practice and of the city's response to it, 'excavating one's car changes the system of property rights'.[104] Just so, says Richard Epstein, referring

---

[103] See B. Latour, *Reassembling the Social: An Introduction to Actor-Network-Theory*, Oxford University Press, 2005 (providing an extended discussion of the making of social facts, including scientific facts).

[104] F. McChesney, 'Snow Jobs', *Libr. Econ. & Liberty*, 15th October 2001, available at http://www.econlib.org/library/columns/mcchesneysnow.html.

to this practice as 'dibs'.[105] Although 'dibs reduces available parking spaces [...] it also rewards those who have put the effort into the job. Would the shovelers spend all that time if they only got to use the space just once?'[106] In this way, Esptein argues, dibs provides 'a trade-off not dissimilar to that found in the patent and copyright law. The initial digger of the spot is given a limited monopoly for its use'.[107] Although questions of duration of the monopoly preoccupy the economic analysis, my interest lies in the legality of the practice, in the sense I have been using the term, as a discourse of law. Like those who hire lawyers to protect their rights or negotiate a child's return to school, McChesney and Epstein express a pragmatic sense of law as negotiated contest rather than a transcendent good.

Dibs on parking spots enacts a form of justice, sustained by supply and demand, utility and exchange. At the same time, however, the practice of placing an old chair on a public street to hold a parking spot evokes a foundational conception of ownership and labor, which cannot be practiced or interpreted without legal concepts and cognitions, as our economic and legal commentators evidence. The chair placed in a parking spot on a public street, with or without a person in the chair, is understood to endow the chair's owner with use rights in the space. This understanding is not limited to our esteemed colleagues. My point is that this practice cannot be interpreted by those who engage in or observe it without invoking legal concepts and meanings. It is, without notions of property and trespass, unintelligible. However, unlike contracts, copyrights, traffic signs, or bills of sale, which are standard markers of legality, this chair in the snow is not the direct and intentional product of professional legal work. Instead, we might view these chairs as residue of that formal legal practice. Rather than a piece of professionalized law, this is a visual image of the law from the bottom up and from outside of legal institutions. The chair in the shoveled-out parking spot signals to the neighborhood, or any would-be parker, a type of ownership. In claiming ownership, that chair often elicits the same sorts of deference and respect accorded more conventional types of property. Other drivers park elsewhere. Similarly, the violation or transgression of this property claim by removing the chair and parking in the spot may lead to conflicts and disputes more commonly associated with property as formally defined by the legal system-informal claims of trespass.

---

[105] R. Epstein, 'The Allocation of the Commons: Parking on Public Roads', *J. Legal Stud.*, Vol. 31, 2002, p. 515.

[106] R. Epstein, 'Parking and Property', *U. Chi. Mag.*, No. 42, April 2003, p. 42.

[107] *Ibid.*

Without naming the doctrinal concepts of constructive or adverse possession, the person placing the chair in a clearing among mounds of snow implicitly invokes conventional and historic justifications for property on the basis of investment and labor, the same arguments that underwrote the emergence of liberal law in the 17th century. The heavy labor of shoveling out the mounds of snow is understood to endow the chairs' owners with use rights in those spaces. By placing a chair in a public parking place, the formal legal idea of private property is appropriated along with many of the rights associated with it, such as exclusive use. Yet, property here is construed very differently than its doctrinal sense demands or would allow. Even without registered deeds and titles, stamps and seals, the law is absent in its formal professional sense, but. it is continually and morally present in organizing social relations on a city street around this particular construction of the automobile, the parking space, and private property.

The public street becomes a forum with a particular 'set of procedures, its definition of freedom and domination, its ways to bring together those who are concerned [...] and what concerns them'.[108] The *legalfacts* of public space, the truth of who owns and who can use this space, for what and for how long, no longer command unremarked deference. Whether others defer to or contest the claims to the parking spots, the *legalfacts* of property rights, the city's services, and law enforcement now demand collective reconfirmation of their matter of factness.

The Brockton elementary schools, just as the public street with a milk crate holding dibs, become spaces of civic engagement for those concerned with children, schools, freedom, sexuality, and the law. The *legalfacts* of children's rights, of teachers' obligations, and of parental authority no longer command uncontested compliance. Whether others defer to or challenge a teacher's report of sexual harassment, a school system's authority to determine a child's placement, or a parent's desire to shield a child from hostile forces, legality now demands collective reconfirmation of the *legalfactness*. This is the rule of law enacted everyday by Americans.

References

R. Abel, *The Law and Society Reader*, NYU Press, 1995, S. Macaulay, Law and Society: *Readings on the Social Study of Law*, Norton Publishing, 1995.

K. Burge and T. Jan, 'Case vs. Brockton Boy Stuns Officials', *Boston Globe*, 9th February 2006, p. B1.

---

[108] B. Latour, *Making Things Public: Atmospheres of Democracy*, MIT press, 2005.

R. Cover, 'The Supreme Court, 1982 Term—Foreword: Nomos and Narrative', *Harv. L. Rev.*, Vol. 97, 1983, p. 4.

R. Epstein, 'The Allocation of the Commons: Parking on Public Roads', *J. Legal Stud.*, Vol. 31, 2002, p. 515.

R. Epstein, 'Parking and Property', *U. Chi. Mag.*, No. 42, April 2003, p. 42.

P. Ewick and S. Silbey, 'Narrating Social Structure: Stories of Resistance to Legal Authority', *Am. J. Soc.*, Vol. 108, 2003, p. 1328.

P. Ewick and S. Silbey, 'Common Knowledge and Ideological Critique: The Significance of Knowing that the 'Haves' Come out Ahead', in H. Kritzer and S. Silbey, *In Litigation: Do the 'Haves' Still Come out Ahead?*, Stanford University Press, 2003.

P. Ewick and S. Silbey, *The Common Place of Law: Stories from Everyday Life*, University Of Chicago Press, 1998.

P. Ewick and S. Silbey, 'Subversive Stories and Hegemonic Tales: Toward a Sociology of Narrative', *Law & Soc'y Rev.*, Vol. 29, 1995, p. 197.

W. Felstiner, R. L. Abel & A. Sarat, 'The Emergence and Transformation of Disputes: Naming, Blaming, Claiming', *Law & Soc'y Rev.*, Vol. 15, 1980-1981, p. 631.

C. Greenhouse, *Praying for Justice: Faith, Order, and Community in an American Town*, Cornell University Press, 1986.

B. Latour, *Reassembling the Social: An Introduction to Actor-Network-Theory*, Oxford University Press, 2005.

B. Latour, *Making Things Public: Atmospheres of Democracy*, MIT press, 2005.

A. Leff, 'Law and', *Yale L.J.*, Vol. 87, 1978, p. 989.

K. Llewellyn and E. A. Hoebel, *The Cheyenne Way: Conflict in Case Law in Primitive Jurisprudence*, University of Oklahoma Press, 1941.

Resnik, 'Living Their Legal Commitments: Paideic Communities, Courts, and Robert Cover', *Yale J.L. & Human*, Vol. 17, 2005, p. 17.

Ph. Selznick, *Law, Society, and Industrial Justice*, Russell Sage Fondation, 1969.

Ph. Selznick, *The Moral Commonwealth: Social Theory and the Promise of Community*, A Centennial Book, 1992.

S. Silbey, 'Legal Culture and Consciousness', in N. Smelser and P. Baltes *International Encyclopedia of the Social and Behavioral Sciences*, Vol. 13, p. 8623.

Ph. Selznick, 'Sociology and Natural Law', *Nat. L.F.*, Vol. 6, 1961, p. 84.

J. Short, 'Creating Peer Sexual Harassment: Mobilizing Schools to Throw the Book at Themselves', *Law & Pol'y*, Vol. 28, 2006 p. 31.

N. Stein, 'A Rising Pandemic of Sexual Violence in Elementary and Secondary Schools: Locating a Secret Problem', *Duke J. Gender L. & Pol'y*, Vol. 12, 2005, p. 33.

J. Sutton, Law/Society: Origins, Interactions, and Change, Pine Forge Press, 2001.

From 'Rites' to 'Rights' of Audience

The Utilities and Contingencies of the Public's Role in Court-Based Processes[1]

Judith RESNIK* and Dennis E. CURTIS**

*Arthur Liman Professor of Law, Yale Law School,
**Clinical Professor of Law, Yale Law School

I. The Public's Place

In this chapter, we examine the history of public displays of the power of rulers, who relied on the open rituals of judgment and punishment to make and to maintain law and order. We map how the ritualistic performance *for* the public became a right *of* the public to participate in and to observe adjudication.

Using the United States as an example, we show why courts can serve as rich sources of information about legal, political, and social conflict. Yet, despite new technologies facilitating access, information about conflicts and their resolution is being limited through laws, doctrines, and practices that devolve court authority to low-visibility tribunals inside administrative agencies, outsource decision making to private providers, and reformulate court-based processes to promote private management and settlement in lieu of public adjudication.

---

[1] This chapter is related to our lecture, 'Representing Justice: From Renaissance Iconography to Twenty-First Century Courthouses', given at the American Philosophical Society (12th November 2005) (See Proceedings of the American Philosophical Society, Vol. 151, June 2007, p. 139), to our book on that topic to be published by Yale Press, to the essay, J. Resnik & D. E. Curtis, 'Images of Justice', *Yale L.J.*, Vol. 96, 1987, p. 1727 [hereinafter Resnik & Curtis, 'Images of Justice'], and to Judith Resnik's 'Uncovering, Discovering, and Disclosing How the Public Dimensions of Court-Based Processes Are at Risk', *Chi.-Kent L. Rev.*, Vol. 81, 2006, p. 521. The authors retain copyright authority to publish the materials here, with acknowledgement of this publication.

These new processes reveal the contingency of the public's role and require analyses of the premises for public rights of audience. The argument we make for public processes relies not only on courts' capacity to provide insights into the uses of both public and private power but also on how court-based public practices generate and reflect democratic norms.

Open courts welcome popular input into the production of norms. Further, they provide an opportunity to observe the ordinary, bureaucratic imposition of authority. Whether expressing and creating commitments to human dignity, fair treatment of equals, and government accountability or demonstrating aggressive retribution that can foster sectarian strife, the display of conflicts (with its attendant cross-claims, fights over facts, decisions, and sanctions) enables contestation, change, or reaffirmation of the practices and rules shown. Open courts enact commitments to living in a social order in which disputes are neither the private and exclusive domain of those in disagreement nor owned by governmental authorities holding the power to impose law.

II. The Public Display of State Power

To maintain order and to enforce obligations, legal regimes do violence,[2] in that both civil and criminal judgments involve the relocation of rights to property or to personal liberty. Displays of the imposition of such violence – from the pageantry that once surrounded the infliction of punishments and executions (as Michel Foucault famously analyzed[3]) to contemporary courtroom dramas – demonstrate state force in an effort to reaffirm rulers' capacity to insist on obedience and to legitimate their exercise of power.

With a few dramatic exceptions (including the hanging of Saddam Hussein in 2006), punishments in many societies have moved largely offstage – from the scaffold and stocks of town squares into the prisons. Yet the public processes of trials, harkening back to Greek traditions and before,[4] have continued to be emblematic of criminal and civil

---

[2] R. Cover, 'Violence and the Word', *Yale L.J.*, Vol. 95, 1986, p. 1601.

[3] M. Foucault, *Discipline and Punish: The Birth of the Prison*, A. Sheridan, trans., Vintage Books, 1975 (2nd ed. 1995). See also S. Edgerton., *Pictures and Punishment: Art and Criminal Prosecution during the Florentine Renaissance*, Cornell U. Press, 1985; B. Berkowitz, 'Negotiating Violence and the Word in Rabbinic Law', *Yale J.L. & Humanities*, Vol. 17, 2005, p. 125.

[4] See A. Lanni, 'Spectator Sport or Serious Politics? oi periesthkotes and the Athenian Lawcourts', *J. Hellenic Stud.*, Vol. 117, 1997, p. 183-189; K. Slanski, 'Mesopotamia: Middle Babylonian Period', in R. Westbrook (ed.), *A History of Ancient Near Eastern Law*, Brill, 2003, p. 485.

adjudication.[5] Moreover, the activities of judges – under monarchies and in pre-democratic republics as well as in democracies – have influenced contemporary ideas about how governments ought to behave, both in dispute resolution and more generally.

Courts are understood as a place for spectatorship, which is the point made by the phrase 'theater of justice.'[6] But court activities (as distinct from rules of law and constitutional principles) are not much in focus in the literature on the 'public sphere', conceived to enable, through participatory parity, reasoned discourses about the development of norms.[7] Rather, when considering the public purposes of courts, contemporary legal writing focuses on the function of judgments in the production of legal rules and in the dissemination of information.

Our thesis is that the contributions made by adjudication's open practices are more far-ranging. Courts – and the discussions that their processes produce – are one avenue through which private persons come together to form a 'public.'[8] Court processes can facilitate participatory opportunities and can shift currents of authority among participants, including the government. If done before an audience, encounters in court can help to inscribe as well as to teach political commitments and to anchor certain behaviors as practices requisite to functioning democracies. Courts thus provide a communal space in which to enact, watch, debate, develop, contest, and materialize the exercise of both public and private power.

To see these utilities and contributions of courts, of course, is not to valorize them as the best or dominant resource for such activities.

---

[5] See J. Bentham, *The Works of Jeremy Bentham*, Edinburgh, W. Tait, 1843, Vol. VI, 355-70 (reprinting Bentham, Jeremy *Rationale of Judicial Evidence*, Vol. I, 1827); see also F. Cutler, 'Jeremy Bentham and the Public Opinion Tribunal', *Pub. Opinion Q.*, Vol. 63, 1999, p. 321.

[6] See Bentham, *op. cit.*, p. 356 (describing the roles of the audience in the 'theatre of justice' as well as of 'readers of the dramatical performances exhibited at that theatre'); Lanni, *op. cit.*, p. 183 (providing a description of the 'social drama' enacted in ancient Greek law courts, in which spectators 'played a crucial role'). See also K. Fischer Taylor, *In the Theater of Criminal Justice: The Palais de Justice in Second Empire Paris*, Princeton University Press, 1993; M. Ball, 'The Play's the Thing: An Unscientific Reflection on Courts Under the Rubric of Theater', *Stan. L. Rev.*, Vol. 28, 1975, p. 81.

[7] See J. Habermas, *The Structural Transformations of the Public Sphere: An Inquiry into a Category of Bourgeois Society*, T. Burger, trans., MIT Press, 1989; L. Goode, *Jürgen Habermas: Democracy and the Public Sphere*, Pluto Press, 2005; D. Zaret, *Origins of Democratic Culture: Printing, Petitions, and the Public Sphere in Early-Modern England*, Princeton University Press, 2000.

[8] See generally C. Calhoun, 'Introduction: Habermas and the Public Sphere', in C. Calhoun, *Habermas and the Public Sphere*, MIT Press, 1992, p. 1.

Moreover, through public disclosure, courts also impose costs on those whose 'private' pains become widely known. But understanding the history and customs that have produced 'rights of audience' in democracies is a predicate to assessing the import of the current trend toward the privatisation of court-based activities.

A. Ritual and Spectacle

That courts have long served as places for public performance can be seen from still-standing Town Halls dating from Europe's Renaissance. These multi-purpose buildings typically included rooms for holding court and pronouncing judgments. For example, contemporary visitors to Amsterdam's 17th Century Town Hall (now called the Royal Palace, due to its use in the 1800s by Louis Napoleon) may enter the Tribunal where judgments and sentences (including death) were imposed.

That marble chamber, shown in Figure 1, is on the ground floor, with windows open to the street enabling outsiders to watch the proceedings.[9] The ruling burgomasters of the town could also, from windows above in their second floor chambers, look down to oversee the procedure. Such displays gave rulers a means by which to show their power, insist on their capacity to command obedience, and give content to the practices with which they sought compliance.[10]

The public enactments also imposed a discipline on judges, whose authority derived from rulers (themselves often claiming their prerogatives by divine right). To remind judges of their obligations, many Town Halls showed allegorical scenes in which historical figures demonstrated their loyalty to the laws of the state by suffering personal pain.

For example, the Amsterdam Town Hall features a stone carving in which the Roman envoy, Brutus, is depicted ordering the death of his sons for joining a conspiracy against Rome. See Figure 2. Another scene along the same wall details the Greek story of Zaleucus, said to have found his son guilty of violating his edicts and imposing the mandated punishment – gouging out the eyes – but mitigating it by taking out one of his own as well as one eye of his son. See Figure 3.

These allegories (repeatedly used in various Town Halls) made the point that obedience to the law of the state came at a price for those who were its judges as well as for those who were judged. Moreover, the familial scenes served to analogize rulers to parental figures, who could

---

[9] See Figure 1 and K. Fremantle, *The Baroque Town Hall of Amsterdam*, Haentjens Dekker & Gumbert, 1959, p. 80.

[10] See generally M. Loughlin, *Sword and Scales: An Examination of the Relationship Between Law and Politics*, Hart, 2000, p. 65.

be understood as taking no joy from imposing punishment on subjects but who were obliged, nonetheless, to do so when violations of the law occurred.

Figure 1: A photograph of the Vierschaar in the Town Hall of Amsterdam, reproduced with permission of the Amsterdam City Archives.

The walls of Renaissance Town Halls reflected other injunctions to judges. For example, while parties once routinely gave 'gifts' to judges, rulers came to prohibit that practice by recasting such gifts as illicit 'bribes.'[11] Instructions against receipt of money from litigants can be found in many rooms in which judgments were made. A 1604 fresco from the Town Hall of Geneva, called *Les Juges Aux Mains Coupées*, shows a line of judges, all with their hands cut off. At one side is a phrase from the Old Testament warning that the taking of gifts 'blindeth the wise, and perverteth the words of the righteous.'[12]

Another painful example of the consequences of judicial misbehavior can be seen in a vivid diptych by Gerard David that once hung in the Town Hall of Bruges. On one of the panels, in a scene at the back, the corrupt judge Siasamnes is shown accepting a bag of money. In the foreground, that judge is removed from the bench at the behest of the ruling monarch, Cambyses. The second panel features the judge being flayed alive. In the rear of that panel, the judge's son Otanes has been anointed the new judge and forced by Cambyses to assume the seat of power on a bench made from the skin of his father.[13]

Today, we may read these scenes as directed against corruption. But the line between a permissible 'gift' and a 'bribe' was (and remains) unclear. Scholars of the Renaissance report that judges often supported themselves through the receipt of goods from litigants. By establishing a ban on gift-giving by parties, local rulers and kings were able to increase judicial dependence on the state (which funded their positions) and thereby to enhance their control over judges.[14]

---

[11] See N. Davis, *The Gift in Sixteenth-Century France*, University of Wisconsin Press, 2000, p. 86.

[12] *Ibid.*, p. 85 (providing a translation of the words, taken from *Exodus* 23:8). The image is reproduced in Resnik and Curtis, 'Images of Justice', *op. cit.*, figure 4, p. 1736. The fresco, from 1604 and by Cesar Giglio, was commissioned for the chambers; subsequent refurbishing covered the wall, and the image was not found again until 1901. See B. Roth-Lochner and L. Fornara, *The Town Hall of Geneva*, J. Gunn, trans., Switzerland, Chancellerie d'Etat, 1986, p. 10.

[13] This image is reproduced in Resnik and Curtis, 'Images of Justice', *op. cit.*, Figures 5a and 5b, p. 1737 and discussed p. 1749. See also H. van Miegroet, *Gerard David*, Mercatorfonds, 1989, p. 143; W. Weale, *Gerard David Painter and Illuminator*, Seeley and Co., 1895.

[14] See Davis, *op. cit.*, p. 86 (also noting that judges defended the practice on the basis that both sides gave gifts).

Figure 2: 'The Judgment of Brutus',
reproduced with permission of the Amsterdam City Archives.

Figure 3: 'The Blinding of Zaleucus',
reproduced with permission of the Amsterdam City Archives.

But, over time, such prohibitions have come to mean that, for decisions to be perceived to be fair, judges must not be beholden to the parties, including the state. Further, and through the development of democratic theories that the state's powers were themselves subject to constraint, the position of the judge was reconceived to be that of a specially-situated employee of the state, paid by the state yet insulated from its ordinary exercise of authority. Such independent jurists were empowered to sit in judgment of the state and, on occasion, to find rulers liable for breaches of their own laws.

Scenes and practices of pronouncing judgment produced other messages. The allegorical narratives placed inside Town Halls told stories of judgments predicated on reasons, tied to evidence, and based on even-handed decision making. For example, in rooms dedicated to resolving cases, one sometimes finds the Latin phrase, *Audi & Alteram partem* – 'Hear the other side as well.'[15] That premise helped to anchor the idea that the power of judgment could not be exercised in an utterly arbitrary fashion but instead required some justification, with outcomes reflective of the relevant facts and the governing customs and rules. In later eras, rules of evidence and procedure served not only to organize the imposition of state power but also to alter the distribution of power between litigants,[16] thereby beginning to shape the possibility of participatory parity.[17]

Courts came also to be associated with the safeguarding of information. For hundreds of years, in Europe and then the Americas, churches and courts provided locations for people to gather, to obtain information orally, and to create written documentation. By some time during the 12th century, common law courts were a place in which to verify facts. As Pollock and Maitland explain, courts were able to create 'indisputable evidence of. […] transaction[s]' in eras when forgeries 'were common.'[18] To make good on that function, communities used stone for

---

[15] The Town Hall of Amsterdam provides one such example. See Fremantle, *op. cit.*, p. 76 (describing the phrase in gold lettering above the entrance to the Magistrates' Chamber, a room in the Town Hall).

[16] See generally J. Langbein, 'Historical Foundations of the Law of Evidence: A View from the Ryder Sources', *Colum. L. Rev.*, Vol. 96, 1996, p. 1168.

[17] In later centuries, political theorists came to see this stance as a predicate to deliberative discourse. See N. Fraser, 'Rethinking the Public Sphere: A Contribution to the Critique of Actually Existing Democracy', in *Habermas and the Public Sphere*, *op. cit.*, p. 109.

[18] F. Pollock and F. Maitland, *The History of the English Law*, Vol. II, Washington D.C., Lawyers' Literary Club, 2nd ed. 1959 (reprinting a 1898 volume), p. 94. See also S. Milsom, *Historical Foundations of the Common Law*, Butterworths, 1969 (2nd ed. 1981).

courthouse buildings so as to preserve documents by reducing the risk of fire. Long before public archives and private title companies existed, courts (actually often rooms within multi-purpose Town Hall buildings) were government-based document repositories that, through recordation, permitted people beyond those immediately involved to know something about what had transpired.

B. From Rites to Rights

From allegorical images displayed in Town Halls around Europe and through the public rituals of judgment, information about the processes used to respond to conflicts became available to a diverse audience and shaped attitudes about what constituted legitimate decision making. Initially the public displays were 'rites' for the public, conceived as an observer without any ability to make demands on rulers for transparency or accountability.

But given that the processes were public, rulers could not always contain the effects of their own processes. The consequences ranged from uncontrollable crowds (as Foucault recounted[19]) to the generation of new information that brought private events into the public domain, which in turn affected the norms that governed those conflicts.

Moreover, trials were not only sources of information but also techniques to produce new information, both factual and normative, as members of the audience gained a role in the unfolding narratives. Jeremy Bentham identified some of these facets of adjudication's potential when arguing the utilities of open court proceedings. He insisted that the 'publicity' of tria ls served as a check on 'mendacity and incorrectness' – in that the wider the circle of dissemination of a witness's testimony, the greater the likelihood of truth and accuracy.[20] 'Many a known face, and every unknown countenance, presents to him a possible source of detection.'[21] Here, the imagined moment entails a spectator moving from passivity to action, to denounce a false statement.

Bentham also advocated a role for ordinary spectators to serve as reporters. He suggested that any member of the audience be permitted to make notes that could be distributed widely, and moreover that those 'minutes' would serve as insurance for the good judge and as a corrective against 'misrepresentations' made by 'an unrighteous judge.'[22]

---

[19] Foucault, *op. cit.*, p. 59.

[20] Bentham, *op. cit.*, Chapter X 'Of Publicity and Privacy, as Applied to Judicature in General, and to the Collection of the Evidence in Particular', p. 351.

[21] Bentham, *op. cit.*, p. 355 (quoting himself in an earlier volume).

[22] *Ibid.*

Further, while Bentham did not propose that judges be legally obliged to 'deliver' opinions in all cases, he argued that 'the performance' of decision making in public would make 'natural ... the habit of giving reasons from the bench', as judges would want an audience to understand the reasons for their actions.[23] They would, through an interaction with the audience, be motivated to communicate and be concerned about public opinion. Bentham's sense of the centrality of publicity in courts can also be seen from his use of the terminology of the trial as he argued for the 'Public Opinion Tribunal', an institutional fiction he deployed to capture his commitment to a communicative public, able to constrain the sovereignty of the state by judging its work and thereby influencing its activities.[24]

In short, in pre-democratic eras, rituals of judgment occurred in public spaces as a form of instruction and as a demonstration of ruling powers' capacity to enforce their edicts and secure some form of public acceptance. The audience had, however, no authority to command disclosure, to insist on access to state decision making, or to participate in the elaboration of its norms. As countries became more committed to democratic practices, the openness of courts and their information-forcing capacities enabled the public to play more active roles that, when coupled with the development of media and other forms of information exchanges, enabled interactions to thicken around both 'facts and norms.'[25]

Open courts continue to serve as visible demonstrations of rulers' power but, when functioning inside democratic states, help to form a more general presumption that government decision making ought to be transparent. Further, democracies have profoundly altered the scope of adjudication. Through normative commitments to individual rights under government, women and men of all colors gained access to law, and the public gained the 'right' to be in the audience. During this last century, the public dimensions of court processes became embedded in a language of entitlements under which the audience (media included) have the power to demand that proceedings and records be open and to insist (with caveats) on their ability to watch what transpires.

---

[23] *Ibid.*, p. 351.

[24] See O. Ben-Dor, *Constitutional Limits and the Public Sphere: A Critical Study of Bentham's Constitutionalism*, Hart, 2000, p. 193.

[25] Here, of course, we borrow from Habermas's *Between Facts and Norms: Contributions to a Discourse Theory of Law and Democracy*, W. Rehg trans., Polity Press, 1996. See also S. Benhabib, *The Rights of Others*, Cambridge University Press, 2004, p. 171.

Pronouncements of these rights can be found in transnational agreements as well as in national constitutions. The International Covenant on Civil and Political Rights proclaims: 'Everyone shall be entitled to a fair and public hearing by a competent, independent and impartial tribunal established by law.'[26] The European Convention for the Protection of Human Rights and Fundamental Freedoms offers a parallel guarantee, as well as explains its limits: 'Judgment shall be pronounced publicly but the press and public may be excluded from all or part of the trial in the interests of morals, public order or national security in a democratic society, where the interests of juveniles or the protection of the private life of the parties so require, or to the extent strictly necessary in the opinion of the court in special circumstances where publicity would prejudice the interests of justice.'[27]

Principles of openness are also part of the constitutions of many nation-states and can be found in doctrine[28] and text in the United States.[29] The obligations of the state to perform adjudication in public have also (in some jurisdictions) generated rights of access for non-parties not only to watch but also to read the documents filed in court.[30]

---

[26] See, e.g., Article 14 of the International Covenant on Civil and Political Rights, G.A. Res. 2200A (XXI), at 54, U.N. GAOR, 21st Sess., Supp. No. 16, U.N. Doc. A/6316 (December 16, 1966). The press and the public may be excluded under certain conditions.

[27] Convention for the Protection of Human Rights and Fundamental Freedoms art. 6 (1), *opened for signature*, November 4, 1950, Europ. T.S. No. 005.

[28] See, e.g., U.S. Const. amend. VI ('In all criminal prosecutions, the accused shall enjoy the right to a speedy and public trial'). That provision was understood as ensconcing rights of audience. See 'Public Trial: Exclusion of Spectators', *Yale L.J.*, Vol. 16, 1907, p. 341 (describing Roman practices of private taking of evidence that came to be associated with subsequent Ecclesiastical courts in England, the discretion accorded judges to close courts under an English statute of 1848, and the American commitment to public criminal trials in both federal and state constitutions). The author concluded that judges had discretion to exclude disruptive persons but not those of 'mature years and whose moral standard' were not 'notably deficient'. Judges, however, did not have the power to order 'a wholesale exclusion of persons not directly interested'. *Ibid.*, p. 344.

[29] See, e.g., Connecticut Const. art. 1, § 10 ('All courts shall be open'); South Carolina Const. art. I, § 9 ('All courts shall be public').

[30] In the United States, for example, debate has been had about whether public rights of audience extend beyond trials to pre-trial hearings and filed documents. In general, courts have concluded that these auxiliary processes are presumptively open. See, e.g., Press-Enterprise Co. v. Superior Court, 478 U.S. 1 (1986); Richmond Newspapers, Inc. v. Virginia, 448 U.S. 555 (1980). Court files are also presumptively open. See Hartford Courant Co. v. Pellegrino, 380 F.3rd 83, 96 (2d Cir. 2004). Not all common law jurisdictions share this view. Until recently, English law limited 'non-party' access, absent permission, to certain documents but recent rulemaking has provided more access. See Adrian A.S. Zuckerman, Civil Procedure 88-89 (2003); De-

These contemporary legal obligations are bolstered by the traditions of displaying judgments that were forged in the earlier centuries and by revulsion at totalitarian regimes characterized by secretive state processes. In democracies, courts' openness is taken for granted more often than not, but when justifications are required, jurists and theorists generally make utilitarian claims that openness is educational and supervisory, cathartic and communicative. As Bentham put it, courts are 'school[s] of the highest order.'[31]

III. New Technologies for Public Display

Identifying the continuity of certain aspects of adjudication over time and their social import should not, however, deflect the focus from how radically different are the ways in which judges work today. What constitutes 'openness' and the modes by which court-based information is gathered and exchanged have varied across time and place.

Before the 20th century, the public gained knowledge via the open doors and windows of courtrooms in which trials and hearings took place, through the episodic publication and dissemination of opinions, and by personal inspection of papers filed with courts. As courts developed practices of explanations, reduced to writing and published in opinions, they disseminated their findings – initially through a designated reporter and, more recently, by means of a marketplace of providers.[32] With the rise of the newspaper business, the press provided another route, as have commercial publishers of compilations, organized by subject matter or geographical location, to be sold to specialized practitioners.

Today's technologies have amplified the possibilities as well as the legal questions – such as whether a 'right to televised broadcasts' of court proceedings exists.[33] In addition to the publication of decisions

---

partment for Constitutional Affairs, Civil Procedure Rules, October 2006, 42nd Update, http://www.dca.gov.uk/civil/procrules_fin/contents/frontmatter/notes42.htm (last visited December 1, 2006).

[31] Bentham, *op. cit.*, p. 355. See generally J. Resnik, 'Due Process: A Public Dimension', *U. Fla. L. Rev.*, Vol. 39, 1987, p. 405 [hereinafter Resnik, 'A Public Dimension'],

[32] See T. Woxland, and P. Ogden, *Landmarks in American Legal Publishing: An Exhibit Catalogue*, West Publishing Co., 1990; J. Krause, *Towering Titans*, A.B.A. J., May 2004, p. 51 (discussing the legal publisher, West Publishing Company, and its competitors).

[33] See generally W. MacKay, 'Framing the Issues for Cameras in the Courtrooms: Redefining Judicial Dignity and Decorum', *Dalhousie L.J.*, Vol. 19, 1996, p. 139 (exploring whether, under Section 2(b) of the Canadian Charter of Rights, which

through the web and access to files through electronic databases, some jurisdictions broadcast court proceedings. For example, oral arguments before the Supreme Court of Canada are televised.[34] The proceedings of the International Criminal Tribunal for the Former Yugoslavia (ICTY)[35] are transmitted (in more than one language)[36] via a web link.[37] (When security problems exist, witnesses' images and voices can be scrambled.[38]) Although courtroom hearings are not generally televised is the United States' federal system,[39] both New York[40] and California[41] have experimented with doing so.

---

provides for freedom of the press and of expression, electronic media ought to have access to court proceedings).

[34] Most 'courtroom proceedings are televised by the Canadian Parliamentary Affairs Channel (CPAC)'. See Supreme Court of Canada, Frequently Asked Questions, http://www.scc-csc.gc.ca/faq/faq/index_e.asp (last visited 27th February 2006).

[35] All proceedings other than deliberations 'shall be held in public, unless otherwise provided'. International Criminal Tribunal for the Former Yugoslavia [ICTY], *Rules of Procedure and Evidence*, at Rule 78 (Open Sessions), ICTY Doc. IT/32/Rev.37 (29th March 2006), http://www.un.org/icty/legaldoc-e/basic/rpe/IT032Rev37e.pdf. When needed for protection of victims or witnesses or for reasons of security or justice, the trial chambers may make provisions for private or in camera processes. *Id.* at Rule 75 (Measures for the Protection of Victims and Witnesses), Rule 79 (Closed Sessions). Full transcripts and, when appropriate, video recordings are made. See *id.* at Rule 81 (Records of Proceedings and Evidence).

[36] The tribunal's working languages are English and French; in addition, the accused has a right to use his or her own language. *Id.* at Rule 3 (Languages).

[37] See ICTY, Courtroom Schedule: Online Broadcasting, http://www.un.org/icty/latest-e/schedule/proceedings-e.htm (last visited 27th February 2006).

[38] See ICTY, *Rules of Procedure and Evidence*, at Rule 75(B)(i)(c) (Measures for the Protection of Victims and Witnesses).

[39] See 'Bills Would Bring Rent Relief to Judiciary, Allow Cameras in Courts, Shape Judicial Security and Review, and Create Inspector General', *Third Branch*, Vol. 28, May, 2006, p. 3, available at http://www.uscourts.gov/ttb/05-06/rentbill/index.html (discussing the federal judiciary's policy to permit appellate courts, at their option, to televise oral arguments but to oppose 'cameras in federal trial courtrooms'). Proposed legislation, called 'The Sunshine in the Courtroom Act of 2005', would authorize district judges to permit, at their discretion, the televising of proceedings. See S. 829, 109th Cong. (30th March 2006), available at http://thomas.loc.gov.

[40] In 1987, the New York State Legislature authorized courts in their discretion to permit televising certain hearings. See generally N.Y. State Comm. to Review Audio-Visual Coverage of Court Proceedings, An Open Courtroom: Cameras in New York Courts (1997). Section 218 also included sunset provisions, which took effect in 1997. In 2005, the State's highest court concluded that no constitutional right existed to televise a trial and hence that the decision about whether to permit televised proceedings rested with the legislature. See Courtroom Television Network LLC v. New York, 833 N.E.2d 1197 (N.Y. 2005).

[41] See Cal. R. Ct. 980, providing that photography, recording, and broadcasting courtroom proceedings may occur if 'executed in a manner that ensures that the fair-

The world has recently witnessed that the new technologies are, like Foucault's 'unruly mob', beyond the state's control. On December 30 2006, Saddam Hussein was hanged – five days after he had lost an appeal of his sentence.[42] At first, the media reported that '14 Iraqi officials attended the hanging' at an unspecified location and that 'witnesses said Mr. Hussein was carrying a Koran and was compliant as the noose was draped around his neck.'[43] A few more details came from the small number of people sent to serve officially as witnesses to the execution.[44]

But within a day, a 'video recording appeared on the Internet [...] apparently made by a witness with a camera cellphone.' The tape showed the 'mocking atmosphere in the execution chamber' and recorded the taunts hurled at Hussein at his death.[45] While the organized media in different countries debated whether to air that video,[46] the media did not control the channels of distribution. The video was rebroadcast around the world and supplanted the description that guards had made 'a few insults' with a torrent of reaction to and comment about the timing, fact, and process of the execution. According to some press reports, the imagery of the hanging turned Hussein into a 'martyr', galvanizing appreciation for his 'dignity' and moving formerly hostile viewers toward sympathy for Hussein and anger towards those who had tried and executed him.[47]

The uncontrollability of the video of the hanging has its counterpart in thousands of ordinary actions that take place in low level tribunals.

---

ness and dignity of the proceedings are not adversely affected', and that judges are to decide whether to permit media coverage by considering more than a dozen factors including the '[p]rivacy rights of all participants, [...] including witnesses, jurors, and victims', available at http://wwwcourtinfo.ca.gov/rules/titlethree/titlethree.pdf.

[42] During the course of the trial, three defense lawyers were killed and two judges were dismissed. Moreover, the prosecution for the first trial had not included charges of genocide involving 180,000 Kurds. See J. Burns, J. Glanz, S. Travernise, and M. Santora, 'In Days Before Hanging, A Push for Revenge and a Push Back from the U.S.', *N.Y. Times*, 7th January 2007, p. A12.

[43] M. Santora, J. Glanz, and S. Travernise, 'Saddam Hussein Hanged in Baghdad; Swift End to Drama; Troops on Alert', *N.Y. Times*, 30th December 2006, p. A1.

[44] M. Santora, 'On the Gallows, Curses for U.S. and 'Traitors', *N.Y. Times*, 31th December 2006, p. A1.

[45] J. Burns and S. Marc, 'U.S. Questioned Iraq on the Rush to Hang Hussein', *N.Y. Times*, 1st January 2007, p. A1.

[46] B. Carter, 'Graphic Video of Execution Presents Hard Choices for U.S. Media', *N.Y. Times*, 1st January 2007, p. A7 (noting that Fox News and CNN both ran the video, and that Fox had followed Al Jazeera in doing so).

[47] H. Fattah, 'Hanging Images Make Hussein a Martyr to Many in the Arab World', *N.Y. Times*, 6th January 2007, p. A1; C. Krauthammer, 'The Hanging: Beyond Travesty', Op-Ed, *Washington Post*, 5th January 2007, p. A17.

Once events are accessible to an audience of third parties who are not themselves disputants, 'spectators and auditors' (to borrow Bentham's categories[48]) can put their descriptions and commentary into the public realm. These exchanges are rich, albeit sometimes pain-filled, sources of communicative possibilities. They empower diverse speakers, some of whom may respond by seeking vengeance and others by offering reasoned discourses but all of whom understand themselves as having authority to speak as a consequence of what they have witnessed or read.

Above, we outlined how these public rights of audience emerged from traditions of public ritual that have been reinterpreted through the lens of democratic commitments to transparent and accountable governance. Below, we examine the role that adjudication has come to play as a constitutive institution *of* democracy and, further, how democratic demands for adjudication are now (ironically) used as a justification for its devolution and privatisation. To do so, we shift from extraordinary moments such as the hanging of Hussein to the ordinary exchanges of civil litigants. We use experiences over a century in the United States to show both the growth in reliance on rights to public adjudication and the contraction of those opportunities, which in turn have limited the occasions on which the public can be present.

IV. Contingent Processes: The American Example

A. Expansive Vistas for Courts and Their Audiences

The bulk of America's lawsuits – many millions of cases – occur in state, not federal, courts.[49] Yet, through the confluence of several factors during the 20th century, the federal courts became a center of publicly-based dispute resolution. In the wake of the Depression in the 1920s, many saw national governance as a necessary and desirable response. Court-based rules reiterated themes of other projects of that era, eager to facilitate national economic capacities, welcoming of regulation, and embodying beliefs that fact-based inquiries would either prompt parties to settle or judges to make just decisions.[50] Federal procedure innova-

---

[48] Bentham, *op. cit.*, p. 356.

[49] Excluding traffic cases, one tally counts about forty-five million filings annually in the state systems. See Conference of State Court Adm'rs, Bureau of Justice Statistics, & Nat'l Ctr. for State Courts' Court Statistics Project, Examining the Work of State Courts, 2004, p. 13-14 (2005), available at http://www.ncsconline.org/DResearch/csp/2004_Files/EWOverview_Final_2.pdf.

[50] See generally J, Resnik, 'Procedure's Projects', *Civ. Just. Q.*, Vol. 23, p. 273 (A. Zuckerman ed., Symposium Vol., Sweet and Maxwell, 2004).

tions were part of a larger national constitutional project, relying in part on authorizing individuals and groups to come to court as rights-seekers and in turn on judges to respond, in public.

Specifically, in addition to increasing the number of federal judges, new rules of national procedure (the Federal Rules of Civil Procedure), which became effective in 1938, invented an obligation, 'discovery', requiring disputants to exchange information orally and to produce relevant documents in advance of trials.[51] These procedures not only enhanced the information available from adversaries but, by virtue of rights of public access to court filings, enabled others to learn about claims and evidence, whether or not a trial took place. Further, the new rule system simplified the process for filing in courts and thereby facilitated access to courts.

Reformers' aspirations succeeded on several metrics. Between the 1960s and the 1990s, caseloads within the federal system tripled, as hundreds of new statutory causes of action were enacted.[52] In response, Congress gave substantial resources to the federal courts, whose budget (in constant dollars) grew from about $250 million in the early 1960s to about $4.2 billion in 2006.[53] Those funds provide for some 30,000 federal judicial staff supporting 1,700 federal district, magistrate, bankruptcy, and appellate judges who are dispersed in about 800 locations nationwide.[54] These employees in turn respond to a docket that includes annual filings averaging about 350,000 civil and criminal trial cases, more than a million bankruptcy petitions, and about 65,000 appeals.[55]

---

[51] See Act of 14th September 1922, Pub. L. No. 67-298, 42 Stat. 837. In 1934, Congress authorized the United States Supreme Court to promulgate federal procedural rules that had the power to displace local practices with national norms. Rules Enabling Act, Pub. L. No. 73-415, 48 Stat. 1064 (1934) (codified as amended at 28 U.S.C. § 2072 (2000)).

[52] See J. Resnik, 'Trial as Error, Jurisdiction as Injury: Transforming the Meaning of Article III', *Harv. L. Rev.*, Vol. 113, 2000, p. 924, 957, 958, n. 119.

[53] See M. Galanter, 'The Vanishing Trial: An Examination of Trials and Related Matters in Federal and State Courts', *J. Empirical Legal Stud.*, Vol. 1, 2004, p. 459, and 501 [hereinafter Galanter, 'The Vanishing Trial'].

[54] Understanding the Federal Courts, Administrative Office of the United States Courts, p. 1, available at http://www.uscourts.gov/understanding_courts/80016.htm (last visited 3rd March 2006).

[55] See Admin. Office of the U.S. Courts, Judicial Business of the United States Courts 2005, at 11 (2006) [hereinafter 2005 Judicial Business], available at http://www. uscourts.gov/judbus2005/front/judicialbusiness.pdf. While well-provided for when compared with state courts and administrative agencies, members of the federal judiciary are concerned that their resources are insufficient, their courts seriously under-funded, and their capacity to sustain current services at risk. See 'Judiciary Seeks to Avert

The normative premises for this adjudicatory project were to welcome disputants who (in theory) participate as equals. Their conflicts were to be resolved through a 'due process model' of procedure[56] in which disputants exchanged information through public channels and made public presentations of claims and facts to state-empowered judges. Those officials in turn were obliged to respond by making public findings of fact and conclusions of law.[57] All of these events were 'on the record' – docketed, filed and, if entailing oral exchanges, generally transcribed. Given the building of courthouses around the United States to anchor a 'federal presence'[58] as well as rules making files open in civil cases, the federal courts became an excellent resource for gathering information. Revelations of toxic products (asbestos, leaded paint, cigarettes, and harmful drugs) followed revelations of discriminatory treatment of racialized minorities in schools and employment and of barbarous conditions in prisons and mental hospitals.

Moreover, the federal courts were not only the receivers and purveyors of information but also the producers and systematizers of knowledge.[59] In 1939, Congress gave the federal judiciary the administrative capacity to do its own record keeping and, in the 1960s, augmented the resources for research and education.[60] As of 2003, the federal judiciary's budget allocated about eighty-two million dollars for such activities.[61] Those funds permit the federal judiciary to produce its own periodical, a monthly newsletter called *The Third Branch*, disseminated in print and through the web,[62] as well as yearly publications providing

---

Cuts', *Third Branch*, Vol. 37, November 2005, p. 1, available at http://www.uscourts.gov/ttb/nov05ttb/avertcuts/index.html.

[56] See J. Resnik, 'Procedure as Contract', *Notre Dame L. Rev.*, Vol. 80, 2005, p. 593 [hereinafter, Resnik, 'Procedure as Contract']; K. Sanford, 'Methodology and Criteria in Due Process Adjudication – A Survey and Criticism', *Yale L.J.*, Vol. 66, 1957, p. 319.

[57] See, e.g., Fed. R. Civ. P. 12(b); Fed. R. Civ. P. 56(d). See generally, A. Miller, 'The Pretrial Rush to Judgment: Are the 'Litigation Explosion', 'Liability Crisis', and Efficiency Cliches Eroding Our Day in Court and Jury Trial Commitments?', *N.Y.U. L. Rev.*, Vol. 78, 2003, p. 982.

[58] L. Craig, *The Federal Presence: Architecture, Politics, and Symbols in the United States Government Building*, MIT Press, 1978.

[59] See R. Wheeler, *A New Judge's Introduction to Federal Judicial Administration*, Washington, D.C., Federal Judicial Center, 2003.

[60] See 28 U.S.C. §§ 601-613 (2000) (creating the Administrative Office of the U.S. Courts); 28 U.S.C. §§ 620-629 (2000) (creating the Federal Judicial Center).

[61] 'The FY 2003 Budget and the Federal Judiciary', *Third Branch*, Vol. 35, March, 2003, p. 2, available at http://www.uscourts.gov/ttb/mar03ttb/budget.html.

[62] See *The Third Branch: The Newsletter of the Federal Courts*, available at http://www.uscourts.gov/ttb/index.html (for *The Third Branch* online).

data on *The Judicial Business of the United States Courts*, filled with charts that track filings and dispositions by the kind of case and the level of court.[63]

But the insights that such data can provide are blurring as courts and legislatures revamp the procedures for dealing with cases. As is detailed in the next section, despite the growing number of filings, the number of cases tried is declining. Moreover, the opportunities for observing hearings of any kind are diminishing, as courts have outsourced those activities to other, far less accessible, venues.

B. Vanishing Trials and Diminishing Rights of Audience

In 2002, in the US federal courts, a trial started in fewer than two of one hundred civil cases filed. Both the percentage of civil cases tried and the absolute number of civil trials have declined over the course of forty years – producing a trend that lawyers and judges label 'the vanishing trial.'[64]

But trials are not the only events that take place in courtrooms. Judges hear arguments on motions, take guilty pleas and pronounce sentences, and sometimes convene conferences in courtrooms. One cannot therefore equate public processes with trials alone. Other data about opportunities for members of the public to witness the exercise of judicial power are available (with another study now underway) in response to inquiries from legislators asked to fund new building projects. Because the price of a courtroom and its adjacent office space is estimated at about $1.5 million and, therefore, new courthouse buildings cost tens of millions of dollars,[65] some legislators challenged the custom that each judge should have a courtroom of his or her own[66] and, more generally, wanted to know about how much time was spent in courtrooms.[67]

---

[63] See, e.g., U.S. District Court-Judicial Caseload Profile, http://www.uscourts.gov/ cgi-bin/cmsd2004.pl (select 'All District Courts') (2004).

[64] In 1962, 5,802 civil trials took place; forty years later in 2002, with many more cases filed, 4,569 civil trials were held around the United States. In percentage terms, the decline was from 11.5 percent to two percent in civil trials commenced during that time period. Galanter, 'Vanishing Trial', *op. cit.*, p. 461 (also noting that the drop has not been constant but rather was 'recent and steep').

[65] See Congressional Budget Office, 'The One Courtroom, One-Judge Policy: A Preliminary Review 2-3' (2000) [hereinafter CBO, One Courtroom].

[66] See, e.g., H.R. Rep. No. 106-1005 (Conf. Rep. Accompanying H.R. 4942, Making Appropriations for the Government of the District of Columbia and Other Activities), U.S. House of Rep. 106th Cong., 2d Sess. at 287-88 (25th October 2000).

[67] See U.S. Gen. Accounting Office, GAO-01-70, Courthouse Construction: Sufficient Data and Analysis Would Help Resolve the Courtroom-Sharing Issue, 57 app. IV

As a consequence, the US General Accounting Office (GAO) undertook a study of courtroom usage, defined as 'any activity' (including but not limited to trials)[68] – including those days when a courtroom had its 'lights on' for two hours.[69] With that metric, the GAO found a fifty-four percent usage rate of available days in the sixty-five courtrooms at seven locations on which it gathered data.[70] Also noted was that in all but two locations, 'courtrooms were used more often for nontrial purposes than they were for trials.'[71] In short, many courtrooms are regularly dark.

Declining opportunities for the public to exercise their rights of audience at the trial level are mirrored at the appellate level. No longer are appellate arguments routinely held in all cases and, if permitted, each side may be accorded only eight minutes for their presentations. In terms of the availability of judicial opinions, an increasing number appear in tabular form, with the words 'affirmed' or 'denied' listed by the name of a case. As of 2001, only about one fifth of the decisions rendered in the federal appellate system were denominated 'for publication' – meaning that litigants could subsequently cite to them as informative precedent.[72]

(2000) [hereinafter GAO Courthouse Construction 2000]. The economic retrenchment in the wake of 9/11, coupled with heightened security risks, reshaped the plans for courthouse construction. See *The Judiciary's Ability to Pay for Current and Future Space Needs: Hearings Before the Subcomm. on Economic Development, Public Buildings and Emergency Management of the H. Comm. on Transportation and Infrastructure*, 109th Cong. 92-98 (2005) (prepared statement of Hon. Jane R. Roth, U.S. Court of Appeals for the Third Circuit; Chair, Judicial Conference Committee on Security and Facilities), available at http://www.uscourts.gov/Press_Release/Roth062105.pdf (describing a two-year moratorium on more than thirty-five courthouse construction projects, a review of the judiciary's design standards, and a re-evaluation of space needs including renewed consideration of the question of individual courtrooms for each jurist).

[68] See U.S. Gen. Accounting Office, GAO/GGD-97-39, Courtroom Construction: Better Courtrooms Use Data Could Enhance Facility Planning and Decisionmaking 8-10 (1997) [hereinafter GAO Courtroom Construction 1997].

[69] GAO Courthouse Construction 2000, *op. cit.*, p. 8.

[70] GAO Courtroom Construction 1997, *op. cit.*, p. 10.

[71] *Ibid.*, p. 11.

[72] See generally P. Pether, 'Inequitable Injunctions: The Scandal of Private Judging in the U.S. Courts', *Stan. L. Rev.*, Vol. 56, 2004, p. 1435 and 1465; L. Robel, 'The Practice of Precedent: *Anastasoff*, Noncitation Rules, and the Meaning of Precedent in an Interpretive Community', *Ind. L. Rev.*, Vol. 35, 2002, p. 399. A 2006 rule revision now requires that litigants be able to cite to decisions, whether deemed 'published' or not. See Fed. R. App. P. 32.1 (stating that courts may not 'prohibit or restrict the citation of federal judicial opinions, orders, judgments, or other written dispositions that have been designated as 'unpublished', 'not for publication', 'non-precedential', 'not precedent', or the like').

One might conclude from these data that, as a relative matter, not much conflict exists, and hence, that there is not much in courtrooms to see. But by enlarging the context to consider alternative venues, one learns that a good deal of adjudicatory activity is underway outside of the courts. The Social Security Administration (SSA), for example, may well be 'the largest system of trial -type adjudication in the world',[73] serving 'over ten million beneficiaries' and resolving conflicts that involved expenditures of '$100 billion in FY 2002.'[74] Yet despite the SSA's import, this agency's website reveals relatively little about the bases for resolution of its cases or about the kinds and quantities of dispositions. Nor can one turn to some general database, akin to that provided for the 94 federal district trial courts, to learn about agency adjudication more generally.

Thus, while Congress significantly increased the number of life-tenured federal judges, Congress did not provide – and the federal judiciary did not press for – the hundreds of additional life-tenured judges necessary to respond to the demands for adjudicatory services that were generated through the interaction of democratic equality norms, new statutory rights, and judicial interpretations. Rather, public and private actors developed three strategies – delegation and devolution, outsourcing, and revamping internal procedures – to channel disputes elsewhere and to alter the ways in which they were processed. These innovations have, in turn, narrowed the occasions on which the public can play any role.

1. Delegation to Agencies

In the 1940s, Congress enacted comprehensive administrative law legislation that provided for Administrative Law Judges (ALJs) within agencies and for agencies to designate other line employees to serve as 'hearing officers.'[75] In the following decades, the United States Supreme Court conceptualized statutorily-conferred property rights as 'entitlements' that could not be terminated without 'due process', defined as requiring some form of impartial judgment, limited by a record.[76] Through this mixture of legislative and judicial oversight, administrative agencies became 'court' systems, hosting a volume of adversarial proceedings that far outstrips what takes place in the federal trial courts around the United States.

---

[73] P. Verkuil, and J. Lubbers, 'Alternative Approaches to Judicial Review of Social Security Disability Cases', *Admin. L. Rev.*, Vol. 55, 2003, p. 731 and 759.

[74] *Ibid.*, p. 738.

[75] See Administrative Procedure Act, Pub. L. No. 79-404, 60 Stat. 237 (1946) (codified as amended at 5 U.S.C. §§ 551-559, 701-706 (2000)).

[76] Goldberg v. Kelly, 397 U.S. 254 (1970).

Two charts illustrate this point. Figure 4 provides a comparison between the numbers of judges inside federal courts and those working in administrative agencies. About four times as many judicial officers serve outside courts than within.[77] Figure 5 provides a comparison of the occasions on which these two sets of judges hear evidence. By using a generous measure of counting any 'contested hearings [civil and criminal] at which evidence is presented'[78] before any judge (district, magistrate, or bankruptcy) sitting in a federal courthouse, one can identify under 100,000 such proceedings in 2001.[79] Such events take place 'in open court' and permit public attendance.

In contrast, by taking data from the high-volume SSA[80] and adding information from three other major federal agencies deciding disputes about immigration, veterans' benefits, and equal employment within the federal government,[81] we can estimate that more than five times as many evidentiary proceedings take place annually in these four federal agencies than in all of the 94 federal trial courts. See Figure 5. But these

---

[77] Figure 4 and Figure 5, below, are both copyright, Judith Resnik and are reproduced non-exclusively, as authorized.

[78] See Admin. Office of the U.S. Courts, Judicial Business of the United States Courts: 2001 Annual Report of the Director 24-25 (2002), available at http://www.uscourts. gov/judbus2001/front/2001artext.pdf [hereinafter 2001 Judicial Business].

[79] Specifically, life-tenured federal trial judges (both senior and active status) presided at 13,558 trials; magistrate judges at 10,663 proceedings, including 1,079 civil cases tried with the consent of the parties, 589 misdemeanors, 4,768 petty offense trials, 3,690 evidentiary hearings, and 537 mental competency proceedings. Bankruptcy judges presided at 67,140 adversary proceedings. 2001 Judicial Business, *op. cit.*, p. 25 and 30.

[80] See Soc. Sec. Admin., Performance & Accountability Report 46-47 (2004), *available at* http://www.ssa.gov/finance/2004/Full_FY04_Par.pdf. This number represents the hearings 'processed by OHA', which is the Office of Hearings and Appeals in which a hearing officer or a judge listens to sworn or un-sworn oral presentations so as to apply legal rules to factual claims.

[81] The definition of 'court proceedings' under the relevant regulations are those in which 'aliens appear before an Immigration Judge, and either contest or concede the charges against them'. Executive Office of Immigration Review, U.S. Dep't of Justice, FY 2004 *Statistical Yearbook*, at B1, available at http//www.usdoj.gov/eoir/statspub/fy04syb.pdf. Complainants can present direct evidence, and the immigration judge renders a decision based on the evidentiary record. 8 C.F.R. §§ 1003.12-1003.37 (2005). Our count of EEOC hearings involving federal employment includes proceedings in which a complainant presents evidence and the Administrative Law Judge 'issue[s] a decision on the merits of the complaint'. 29 C.F.R. §§ 1603.214, 1603.217 (2005). For determining hearings in the Board of Veteran Appeals, we considered those in which the Board 'receive[s] argument and testimony relevant and material to the [...] issue' in order to make a decision on the complaint. 38 C.F.R. § 20.700 (2005). For further discussion, see J. Resnik, 'Migrating, Morphing, and Vanishing: The Empirical and Normative Puzzles of Declining Trial Rates in Courts', *J. Empirical Legal Stud.*, Vol. 1, 2004, p. 783 and p 798.

many evidentiary hearings within agencies are invisible to most members of the public, who would be hard-pressed to find the rooms inside the government buildings where the proceedings occur. And, even if able to locate *where* to go, spectators are not, by regulation, permitted to attend all such proceedings.[82]

Efforts to read – rather than to see – the output are similarly unavailing. The decisions of Administrative Law Judges and hearing officers are routinely made part of files but not published more generally.[83] No 'reporter service' (either in print or online) regularly compiles and reproduces decisions of all of the various administrative judges and hearing officers. Rather, with rare exceptions, one would have to search case files or agency-by-agency databases to gather systematic information.[84]

---

[82] The EEOC limits access to those with information relevant to the complaint. 29 CFR § 1614.109(e). As for the Board of Veterans Appeals (BVA), the description of the hearings (informal, ex parte, etc.) does not detail a role for the public. 38 C.F.R. § 20.701 (2000) (stating that 'only the appellant and/or his or her authorized representative may appear and present argument in support of an appeal'). The agency considers the hearings closed and relies in part on the Privacy Act of 1974, Pub. L. No. 93-579, 88 Stat. 1896, which protects disclosures related to medical and education records. The Board of Veterans Appeals permits open s only if agreed to by the claimant. Access to immigration hearings vary with the issues (deportation, asylum, removal, and exclusion); exclusion hearings and certain kinds of other proceedings are closed while other immigration hearings are presumptively open. 8 C.F.R. § 1003.27 (2005) (providing that an Immigration Judge 'may place reasonable limitations upon the number in attendance at any one time with priority being given to the press over the general public' and that hearings involving an abused 'alien spouse' may be closed). After 9/11, federal courts disagreed about the constitutionality of a blanket closure by the Justice Department of deportation hearings. See N. Jersey Media Group, Inc. v. Ashcroft, 308 F.3d 198 (3rd Cir. 2002), *cert. denied*, 538 U.S. 1056 (2003); Detroit Free Press v. Ashcroft, 303 F.3d 681 (6th Cir. 2002). SSA hearings are open to the public unless the Administrative Law Judge, based on 'good cause', closes a hearing. 20 C.F.R. § 498.215(d) (2005).

[83] See 5 U.S.C. § 557(c) (requiring that '[a]ll decisions, including initial, recommended, and tentative decisions, are a part of the record' on appeal).

[84] See, e.g., Ninth Circuit Gender Bias Task Force, 'The Effects of Gender in the Federal Courts, The Final Report', reprinted in *S. Cal. L. Rev.*, Vol. 67, 1994 p. 745, (describing the method for researching social security dispositions) [hereinafter 'The Effects of Gender']. In contrast, the relatively small number of decisions rendered by the National Labor Relations Board administrative law judges are placed online. See http://ww.nlrb.gov/research/decisions/alj_decisions.aspx (last visited 1st December 2006).

Figure 4: A Comparison of Court-Based and Administrative Judiciaries in the US Federal System (as of 2002)

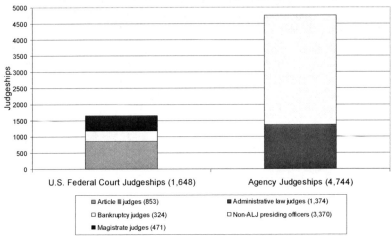

© 2007 by Judith Resnik

Figure 5: A Comparison of the Numbers of Evidentiary Proceedings in US Federal Courts and in Four Federal Agencies (2001)

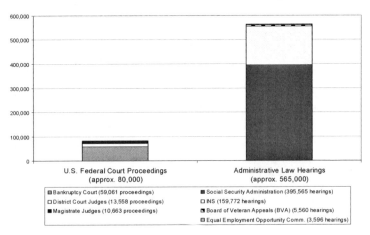

© 2007 by Judith Resnik

The lack of data stems in part from a lack of public and private financing for research on agency judgments. Congress has not funded bodies akin to those provided for the federal courts to collect inter-agency data. Further, because many agency-claimants do not often have the resources for lawyers (and in some, lawyers have been prohibited from participating), publishers have not focused on marketing opinion-databasing services to the bar. One is left instead to depend on special efforts.[85] Occasionally, and sometimes by virtue of in-depth press reports, distress at agency processes and outcomes produces an outcry, a congressional hearing, or a body of federal appellate law.[86] But these episodic exposures provide a very small (and often skewed) sample of the quality, quantity, and kind of decisions rendered.

In short, and borrowing from the language of political economy, during the course of the 20th century, through successful efforts of both public and private institutions and actors, the federal courts became the most prominent and the best-endowed court system in the nation. When trials occur in any of their hundreds of facilities, the public can attend. Decisions from its jurists can be read (even if not always 'published for citation') through online and print services.

In contrast, a large quantum of adjudicatory-like decision making goes un-compiled, under-recorded, and minimally represented in the public sphere. A good many trial-like procedures (more than half a million evidentiary proceedings annually in federal agencies) cannot be seen by any but the immediate participants. Delegation of adjudication to agencies may well provide many benefits (usually catalogued as informality, lower costs, expertise, and more judging for more claimants) but it also imposes significant costs in terms of reducing the openness of

---

[85] See Ctr. for Gender and Refugee Studies, U. of Cal. Hastings College of the Law, Case Law, http://cgrs.uchastings.edu/law (last visited 1st May 2006) (collecting decisions about women immigrants seeking to gain asylum); Transactional Records Access Clearinghouse: TRAC, About Us, available at http://trac.syr.edu/aboutTRACgeneral.html (last visited 1st December 2006) (gaining much of its knowledge by pursuing Freedom of Information Act requests).

[86] See, e.g., Benslimane v. Gonzales, 430 F.3d 828, 829-30 (7th Cir. 2005) (describing a 'staggering 40 percent' reversal rate of the 136 petitions reviewing the Board of Immigration Appeals that were resolved on the merits and concluding that 'the adjudication of [immigration] cases at the administrative level has fallen below the minimum standards of legal justice'); N'Diom v. Gonzales, 442 F.3d 494, 500 (6th Cir. 2006) (Martin, J., concurring) ('There are no doubt many conscientious, dedicated, and thorough immigration courts across the country. Unfortunately, their hard work is overshadowed by the significantly increasing rate at which adjudication lacking in reason, logic, and effort from other immigration courts is reaching the federal circuits.'). See also N. Bernstein, 'New York's Immigration Courts Lurch under a Growing Burden', *N.Y. Times*, 8th October 2006, Section 1, at 1.

dispute resolution processes and access to information about both processes and outcomes predicated on claims of public rights.

2. Outsourced by Contract

In addition to delegation from one public institution to another, outsourcing to private venues is another means of putting dispute resolution beyond public purview. Private resolution has a long history,[87] but during decades past, the law of the United States was ambivalent about enforcing obligations that required disputants to pledge, before a conflict emerged, to forgo access to public processes. Judges guarded their own monopoly power and regularly refused to enforce compulsory arbitration contracts.

Over the course of the 20th century, however, the attitudes of legislators and judges changed. In 1925, Congress enacted the Federal Arbitration Act, recognizing arbitration contracts as enforceable obligations.[88] Yet the statute was seen at the time as having a narrow range of applications. Through the 1970s, judges declined to enforce agreements that contained ex ante waivers of federal litigation rights. In such opinions, judges explained that arbitration was too lawless and too informal when contrasted with adjudication, which was esteemed for its regulatory role in monitoring adherence to national norms.[89]

However, in the 1980s, the United States Supreme Court revised its earlier rulings and upheld broad grants of authority to arbitrators as long as the alternative venue permitted vindication of federal statutory rights.[90] Instead of objecting to the informality of arbitration, judges

---

[87] See, e.g., L. Bernstein, 'Opting Out of the Legal System: Extralegal Contractual Relations in the Diamond Industry', *J. Legal Stud.*, Vol. 21, 1992, p. 115; R. Ellickson, *Order Without Law: How Neighbors Settle Disputes*, Harvard University Press, 1991.

[88] See United States Arbitration Act, Pub. L. No. 68-401, 43 Stat. 883 (1925) (codified as amended at 9 U.S.C. §§ 1-14 (2000 & Supp. III 2005)) and now commonly referred to as the Federal Arbitration Act.

[89] See, e.g., Wilko v. Swan, 346 U.S. 427 (1953). See generally J. Resnik, 'Many Doors? Closing Doors? Alternative Dispute Resolution and Adjudication', *Ohio St. J. on Disp. Resol.*, Vol. 10, 1995, p. 211 [hereinafter Resnik, 'Many Doors? Closing Doors?'].

[90] See Mitsubishi Motors Corp. v. Soler Chrysler-Plymouth, Inc., 473 U.S. 614 (1985); Dean Witter Reynolds, Inc. v. Byrd, 470 U.S. 213 (1985) (both upholding ex ante arbitration agreements as sufficient despite claims of violation of federal securities and antitrust rights). Thereafter, the Court enforced arbitration clauses despite allegations of discrimination under federal or state law. See Circuit City Stores, Inc. v. Adams, 532 U.S. 105 (2001); Gilmer v. Interstate/Johnson Lane Corp., 500 U.S. 20 (1991).

praised its flexibility. Judges did not only alter their attitudes toward arbitration; they also changed their views of adjudication, which came to be described as only one of several techniques appropriate for the resolution of disputes.[91] Today, law often sends contracting parties (including employees and consumers entering standard form contracts) to mandatory arbitration programs created by employers, manufacturers, and the providers of goods and services.[92] If questions of contract interpretation are raised, they must generally be presented first to arbitrators.[93]

Gaining knowledge about such private dispute resolution processes is difficult. Some private providers are free-standing institutions, such as the American Arbitration Association and the Better Business Bureau. Others are linked to a particular industry or are run, in-house, by the entity requiring the alternative procedure. No national obligations of producing data on decisions nor of providing access to procedures currently apply. Watching these providers at work is not an option offered to the public at large.

3. Conciliation within Courts

A third method of privatisation of public processes comes through the changes in the ways in which courts themselves respond to cases filed. Pressed by soaring caseloads, interested in more efficacious ways to deal with conflicts, and responding to criticisms about adversarialism, cost, and delay, judges and lawyers sought to retool court procedures. A movement emerged championing Alternative Dispute Resolution (ADR) and focused on augmenting or replacing adjudication with mediation,

---

Some constraints exist. Federal law requires that the 'alternative' provide an adequate means to vindicate federal rights. Thus, when litigants challenge contractual obligations, courts inquire into the adequacy of arbitral tribunals. On rare occasions, courts have found that a process was insufficient or that a form of contracting was unconscionable. See generally J. Stempel, 'Arbitration, Unconscionability, and Equilibrium: The Return of Unconscionability Analysis as a Counterweight to Arbitration Formalism', *Ohio St. J. on Disp. Resol.*, Vol. 19, 2004, p. 757.

[91] J. Resnik, 'Many Doors? Closing Doors?', *op. cit.*, p. 253.

[92] See, e.g., *Circuit City*, 532 U.S. 105; Green Tree Fin. Corp.-Ala. v. Randolph, 531 U.S. 79 (2000). See generally L. Demaine & D. Hensler, 'Volunteering' to Arbitrate Through Predispute Arbitration Clauses; The Average Consumer's Experience', *Law & Contemp. Probs.*, Winter/Spring 2004, p. 55. In a sample of contracts from moving companies, department stores, car dealers, hospitals, airlines, and credit card dealers, about one third included arbitration clauses in their contracts. Almost seventy percent of financial services (credit cards, accounting, banking) required arbitration. In some of the contracts, parties were prohibited from participating in class actions. Of thirty clauses that dealt with costs, about half provided that the consumer and service company would split the costs, unless the arbitrator decided otherwise. *Ibid.*, p. 58.

[93] See Green Tree Fin. Corp. v. Bazzle, 539 U.S. 444 (2003); Buckeye Check Cashing, Inc. v. Cardegna, 546 U.S. 440 (2006).

settlement conferences, arbitrations, and early evaluation of cases by 'neutrals.' Proponents succeeded in winning congressional attention and in altering court processes and doctrine.

The 1938 Federal Rules of Civil Procedure had not provided procedures for settlement of cases nor had those rules charged judges with the task of overseeing settlements. By 2004, however, the rules had been rewritten to call on judges to promote settlement. The changes, began in 1983 and codified in 1993, detail the powers of the managerial judge, now authorized to direct 'a party or its representative' to 'be present or reasonably available by telephone in order to consider possible settlement of the dispute.'[94]

Court-based ADR comes in various forms, some of which, such as arbitration, could be public. But that kind of court-based program is infrequently used. As of 2002, seven districts had operating programs that involved about eight percent of those districts' civil dockets.[95] But in only one district were court-annexed arbitrations listed as a part of the court calendar and conducted in courthouse rooms open to the public.[96] More common – and more private – are mediations and judge-run settlement conferences. These negotiations usually take place in lawyers' offices or in judges' chambers. A few federal courthouse projects now include plans to build ADR suites, but at least one such room (dedicated to mediation in a federal district court in Portland, Oregon) is tucked inside an area not regularly accessible to the public.

While bargaining *in* the shadow of the law is a phrase often used,[97] bargaining is increasingly a requirement *of* the law of procedure. Also increasing are ex parte contacts between judges and lawyers, licensed to facilitate settlement. Such discussions not only take place away from public scrutiny but also may be closed to some of the parties in the very case at issue.

What can be found in court files has also changed. The Federal Rules once required that all discovery materials be filed unless a court ordered otherwise. As the notes from a 1980 rule advisory committee explained,

---

[94] Fed. R. Civ. P. 16(c) (16) (1993). See J. Resnik, 'Managerial Judges', *Harv. L. Rev.*, Vol. 96, 1982, p. 374.

[95] See Administrative Office of the United States Courts, 2002 Annual Report of the Director: Judicial Business of the United States Courts 20, 56, tbl. S-12 (2003) [hereinafter Judicial Business 2002], available at http://www.uscourts.gov/judbus2002/front/jdbusiness.pdf.

[96] See E.D. Pa. R. 53.2 (5) ('Arbitration Trial […] The trial shall take place in the United States Courthouse in a room assigned by the arbitration clerk').

[97] See R. Mnookin, & L. Kornhauser, 'Bargaining in the Shadow of the Law: The Case of Divorce', *Yale L.J.*, Vol. 88, 1979, p. 950.

'while cumbersome in size for courts to store, such materials are some-times of interest to those who may have no access to them except by a requirement of filing, such as members of a class, litigants similarly situated, or the public generally.'[98] Amendments of 2000 now mandate the opposite: that 'discovery requests and responses must not be filed until they are used in the proceeding or the court orders filing.'[99] Only if materials obtained through discovery are reflected in or appended to motions or affidavits does that information make its way into the public realm.

Moving from the structure of rules to lawyering practices, 'privacy' or 'secrecy' (with the term chosen depending on one's vantage point) can also stem from party-negotiated and court-enforced agreements. Lawyers often bargain for settlements contingent on nondisclosure of information. In the federal system, parties may withdraw cases by filing notices of dismissal. Separate settlement contracts need not be made a part of the record. 'Confidentiality clauses' in settlement contracts appear to be commonplace.[100] One has no way to determine empirically the rate at which information is kept from the public through such contracts. In contrast, when settlements are filed with courts, sealing is generally not permitted.[101]

That settlement may hinge on agreements to make data inaccessible can be gleaned from the few cases that do make it into public purview. One vivid example is a sex-discrimination case against a major Wall Street firm[102] that had been accompanied by a good deal of advance media coverage. Shortly before the case was to be tried, a newspaper ran a headline: 'Women of Wall Street Get Their Day in Court.'[103] But

---

[98] See Fed. R. Civ. P. 5(d), which had originally provided that discovery materials were to be filed 'within a reasonable time'. This rule can be found at 308 U.S. at 669 (1938). The 1980s notes explain that 'this amendment and a change in Rule 30(f)(1) continue the requirement of filing but make it subject to an order of the court that discovery materials not be filed unless filing is requested by the court or is effected by parties who wish to use the materials in the proceeding'.

[99] See Fed. R. Civ. P. 5(d) (as amended in 2000).

[100] See generally A. Miller, 'Confidentiality, Protective Orders and Public Access to the Courts', *Harv. L. Rev.*, Vol. 105, 1991, p. 427.

[101] See R. Reagan, S. Wheatman, M. Leary, N. Blain, S. Gensler, G. Cort, D. Milotich, *Sealed Settlement Agreements in the Federal District Courts*, Washington, D.C., Federal Judicial Center, 2004.

[102] Some of the preliminary rulings were published. See EEOC & Allison Schieffelin v. Morgan Stanley & Co., No. 01 Civ. 8421, 2004 U.S. Dist. LEXIS 12724 (S.D.N.Y. July 8, 2004), aff'g in part 324 F. Supp. 451 (S.D.N.Y. July 2, 2004).

[103] See P. McGeehan, 'The Women of Wall Street Get Their Day in Court', *N.Y. Times*, July 11, 2004, § 3, p. 5. See also Susan E. Reed, 'When a Workplace Dispute Goes Very Public', *N.Y. Times*, 25th November 2001, § 3, p. 4 (discussing the sex discrimination litiga-

within days, the case was settled with promises of nondisclosure not only by the individual plaintiff but also by the Equal Employment Opportunity Commission (EEOC), the federal agency that had filed the lawsuit. The *Wall Street Journal*'s reporters explained that the EEOC 'had planned to introduce statistics about women's pay and promotion at trial' but the 'details on the alleged disparities between the firm's male and female employees were never made public.'[104]

In addition to such party-based negotiations and court rules stemming from ADR, other methods are available to keep information about conflicts from the public. Many states, as well as federal law, have created a privilege for information obtained in mediations.[105] Moreover, private providers of ADR can also make rules that mandate confidentiality.

Yet another facet requires note. Aggregate processing of cases and claims – through mechanisms such as the 'class action' or rules mandating that separately filed lawsuits be consolidated and dealt with as a unit – are now on the rise. These amalgams are the products of the volume of cases, the infliction of wide-spread harms across a sprawling group of individuals, entrepreneurial lawyers, and judges looking for economies of scale. While some decision making in such litigations entails public adjudication, such large-scale litigations also create incentives for settlement. The remedies, however, often require disaggregation to enable the individuals affected to recoup specific sums. Those allocations and distributions are often run by specially-created 'claims facilities' that combine features of courts, private dispute resolution centers, and insurance companies. Like other ADR providers, these facilities often work outside the public purview.[106]

---

tion against Merrill Lynch, its settlement with hearings, and efforts by unhappy litigants to bring the issues back to public attention, including through hiring an airplane to tow a banner, 'Merrill Lynch Discriminates Against Women').

[104] See K. Kelly, & C. DeBaise, 'Morgan Stanley Settles Bias Suit for $54 Million', *Wall St. J.*, 13th July 2004, p. A1; see also Susan Antilla, Op-Ed, 'Money Talks, Women Don't', *N.Y. Times*, 21st July 2004, at A19 (arguing that 'Morgan Stanley, and all of Wall Street, scored' by keeping the statistics private).

[105] See, e.g., 28 U.S.C. § 652(d) (2000) (requiring district courts to provide local rules for confidentiality in ADR). See generally L. Kartky Doré, 'Public Courts Versus Private Justice: It's Time to Let Some Sun Shine in on Alternative Dispute Resolution', *Chi.-Kent L. Rev.*, Vol. 81, 2006, p. 376; E. Deason, 'Procedural Rules for Complementary Systems of Litigation and Mediation – Worldwide', *Notre Dame L. Rev.*, Vol. 80, 2005, p. 553.

[106] See generally J. Resnik, D. Curtis and D. Hensler, 'Individuals within the Aggregate: Relationships, Representation, and Fees', *N.Y.U. L. Rev.*, Vol. 71, 1996, p. 296.

Above, we described the Federal Rules of 1938 as expressing a commitment to what we termed a *Due Process Model* of procedure. One way to capture the shift over the last several decades is to use the phrase *Contract Procedure* to denote the degree to which rules, statutes, and practices have been reframed to support conciliation and contractual agreements in lieu of adjudication. Such bargaining, conducted at the prompting of courts, results in the privatisation of process.[107]

V. The Happenstance of Observing the Ordinary

The production of new modes of dispute resolution raises serious questions about the durability of public rights of audience and about adjudication more generally. The new forms are themselves artifacts of public rights of audience, which enabled sets of participants to articulate criticisms that have proved influential.

The complaints came from different vantage points. Some objected to adjudication's failure to make good on its own promises, in that too many potential litigants have too few resources or subsidies to participate as adversarial equals. Other critics argued that litigants had to wait too long, pay too much, and gain too little through processes that were unduly combative and remedially limited. In contrast, some commentators pressed for revisions because they perceived access to adjudication to be too liberal – burdening economic innovation by imposing too many risks of liability and impoverishing interactions by promoting a culture of complaint.

The results (the devolution, outsourcing, and conciliation sketched above) are products of the success of some objectors, who had the political and economic capacity to bring about particular kinds of reforms. The impact of their work requires two levels of inquiry. One is to ponder whether certain functions performed by open courts can be provided by other institutions. Another is to question the normative premise that openness itself is a worthy aspiration.

A. Multiple Fora for Public Revelation

During eras when few institutions kept secure records of land transfers or of changes in personal status (such as citizenship, marriage, and adoption), courts provided social services not otherwise available. Today, archival and evidentiary systems in places such as libraries, municipal centers, and banks permit verification and provide repositories that make certain court-based record keeping unnecessary or duplicative.

---

[107] See J. Resnik, 'Procedure as Contract', *op. cit.*

Further, while courts continue through public trials to produce par-
ticularistic narratives (documented through transcripts, proceedings, and
exhibits[108]) about specific events,[109] courts are only one of many government-based investigatory mechanisms available to generate such
records. Other institutions – from South Africa's Truth and Reconcilia-
tion Commission to blue-ribbon investigatory panels focused on particular tragedies – augment the regularly-constituted oversight hearings
convened by legislatures. Generally open to the public, these institutions
serve functions comparable to courts.[110] Private sectors are also rich
resources; fictions (and reality shows), written or filmed, pour stories
into the marketplace. The web, bloggers, and the press also stream
information. Given that multiple – and new – fora exist for revelation,
courts do not need to fulfill all the functions served in prior eras.

Courts, however, distinguish themselves in one respect – their attention to the ordinary. As pre-existing institutions that do not rely on ad
hoc enabling acts or national traumas to prompt their creation, on selling
copies of their decisions, nor on responding only when something
'interesting' is at issue, courts are a window into mundane conflicts.
Courts respond to a myriad of daily disagreements as well as to rare
extraordinary moments. If members of the public have the inclination
and the stamina to watch, courts can enable insight into the kinds of
disputes that repeatedly display the harms that befall individuals and the
remedies (if any) provided.

By observing the redundancy of various claims of right and the processes, allegations, and behaviors that become the predicates to judgments, debate can occur about not only the particulars of a given procedure and its outcome but about what the underlying norms ought to be.
Public concerns and private interests interact repeatedly, and the multi-

---

[108] The Nuremburg Trials, whose sixtieth anniversary was marked in November of 2005,
are exemplary. See BBC News, Germany Marks Nuremburg Tribunals, *available at*
http://news.bbc.co.uk/2/hi/europe/4453790.stm (20th November 2005).

[109] See J. Resnik, 'A Public Dimension', *op. cit.*; E. Bazelon, 'Public Access to Juvenile
and Family Court: Should the Courtroom Doors Be Open or Closed?', *Yale L. &
Pol'y Rev.*, Vol. 18, 1999, p. 155.

[110] See, e.g., M. Minow, *Between Vengeance and Forgiveness: Facing History After
Genocide and Mass Violence*, Beacon Press, 1998; J. Simon, 'Parrhesiastic Accountability: Investigatory Commissions and Executive Power in an Age of Terror', *Yale
L.J.*, Vol. 114, 2005, p. 1419. As Zaret, *op. cit.*, p. 7 noted, in fifteenth century England, 'disclosure of parliamentary debate was a crime. Popular participation in political discourse was limited to the receiving end of symbolic displays of authority.' As
he mapped the rise in print culture, he also noted its dependence on 'commerce and
controversy, forged by the interest of authors and stationers in producing texts for
which popular demand exists'. *Ibid.*, p. 13.

226

ple iterations illuminate aspects of the social ordering that are otherwise not readily perceived.

The shaping of prohibitions against sexual harassment and against domestic violence provide two contemporary examples of how such reiterations, through and in public courts, helped to develop public agendas that altered extant norms. Both kinds of actions had been situated in the realm of the 'private' and were tolerated (if sadly so). Courtroom narrations – intersecting with legislative action and a world-wide movement framing women as equal actors entitled to control their own bodies whether at home, at work, or on the streets – catalogued the range of injuries incurred and what rights could (and could not) be enforced.[111]

And of course, a repeating pattern of alleged injuries made patent through courts can not only generate but can also limit rights. The political success of arguments that many tort injuries are overstated products of 'junk science', manipulated evidence, and deceived juries is one illustration of this point.[112] That contested view, supported by assertions that insurance premiums escalated as a consequence, has succeeded, in that new laws in the United States alter liability rules, police plaintiffs' attorneys, and impose caps on damages.[113]

Moreover, because even a few cases can make a certain problem vivid, social policies may be forged that respond in extravagant ways to harms that are less pervasive than perceived. Criminal sanctions are exemplary here, as public disclosures of particular crimes produce anger and vengeful consequences. Publicity itself has come back into vogue as a form of punishment. In the United States, for example, press coverage of individuals found to have sexually assaulted children prompted new laws that require individuals who are convicted of a wide array of offenses to register with government officials and to have their photos placed on the web so that, upon completion of prison sentences, poten-tial neighbors could be forewarned about their presence.[114]

---

[111] See J. Resnik, 'The Rights of Remedies: Collective Accountings for and Insuring Against the Harms of Sexual Harassment', in *Directions in Sexual Harassment Law*, C. A. MacKinnon & R. B. Siegel, (eds.), Yale University Press, 2004, p. 247.

[112] See, e.g., P. Huber, *Galileo's Revenge: Junk Science in the Courtroom*, Basic Books, 1991, See also Marc Galanter, 'An Oil Strike In Hell: Contemporary Legends About the Civil Justice System', *Ariz. L. Rev.*, Vol. 40, 1998, p. 717, 731 (describing media distortion of cases, including the litigation around the scaldingly-high temperatures of coffee served at the restaurant chain, McDonald's).

[113] See N. Marder, 'The Medical Malpractice Debate: The Jury as Scapegoat', *Loy. L.A. L. Rev.*, Vol. 38, 2005, p. 1267.

[114] See Connecticut Department of Public Safety v. Doe, 538 U.S. 1 (2003) (upholding the constitutionality of state laws requiring such registration and publication).

Further, the protected status of spectatorship has generated new legal questions about the demeanor of the audience and the freedom that viewers ought to have to express their opinions. Incidents of racialized injustice in American law made plain the power of the 'mob' to undermine the ability of courts to render judgment.[115] Media involvement with cases can similarly create a turbulent atmosphere.[116] But more complex questions are raised when spectators at trials make statements through their dress or by placards and buttons, for example, with pictures of a victim or ribbons denoting a particular cause.[117] Law can and should limit spectators' participatory rights by imposing temporal bans on certain forms of demonstrative behavior.

The prospect that a spectator could affect a proceeding is evidence of the potential generativity of rights of audience. The presence of witnesses *to* adjudication can alter the interactions of those *in* adjudication. Competing claims about what transpired and about the underlying events can make their way into the public discourse. Courts' communicative possibilities and public norm production operate to open up or to close off avenues of redress, or to reconfirm support for the status quo.

Public display does not necessarily trigger reasoned discourses or engender participatory parity. Nor is public spectatorship intrinsically supportive of progressive interventions. Further, one cannot make neat causal chains between events and outcomes. But what the publicity does enable is for Foucault's 'unruly crowd'[118] to respond in ways uncontrollable by those protective of their own powers and prerogatives. Discipline and control of those powers may (not will, but may) follow.

B. Democratic Practices of Power

That courts can – as an empirical matter – affect and sometimes generate public agendas addressing the intersections of private interests and public rights offers one justification for rights of audience. That courts do so by attending to a volume of mundane matters is relevant to another kind of justification for rights of audience in a democracy. Courts are a site of democratic valorisation of individual dignity, thereby

---

[115] See, e.g., Moore v. Dempsey, 261 U.S. 86 (1923); Frank v. Mangum, 237 U.S. 309 (1915).

[116] See, e.g., Sheppard v. Maxell, 384 U.S. 333 (1966).

[117] See, e.g., Carey v. Musladin, 127 S.Ct. 649 (2006); Holbrook v. Flynn, 475 U.S. 560 (1986).

[118] As Foucault detailed, government literally lost control in that, at times, the public processes of executions were sites in which crowds turned into mobs that were animated by protests of either the verdicts or the punishments. Foucault, *op. cit.*, p. 59.

rendering instruction on the values of a polity or insight into its inability to materialize those commitments.

Courts institutionalize democracy's claim that it imposes constraints on state power. In open courts, government judges have to account for their own authority by letting others know how and why power is used. Bentham's widely-quoted phrase captures this activity: 'Publicity is the very soul of justice [...]. It keeps the judge himself, while trying, under trial.'[119] Such accountability may be both desirable and anxiety producing, as one aspires to enable judgments in adjudication that are sensitive to context but do not aim to please. Yet such accountability has an egalitarian aspect when government officials as disputants are, like private litigants, subjected to scrutiny.

Governments do not only run courts. They are themselves either plaintiffs or defendants, obliged to comply with court rules and therefore subjected to the discipline of such constraints. Within the United States, for example, government litigants must bear the exposure that obligations of discovery impose, thereby exposing their past deeds, their files, and their e-mails. The importance of such obligations can be seen in the efforts to avoid them. After 9/11, the Executive branch in the United States repeatedly sought to enact legislation 'stripping' courts of jurisdiction over claims that the government had wrongly detained and tortured individuals.[120] The effort to create a separate 'tribunal system' is aimed at controlling access and information as well as limiting the rights of defendants and augmenting the powers of the state.

Openness limits government power in another respect, by undermining the ability of the government or the disputants to control the social meaning of conflicts and their resolutions. The lesson of the video of the hanging of Saddam Hussein is that its disclosure reduced our dependency on official reports. Without direct access, non-parties must rely on insiders to reveal events, inevitably translated through their perspectives. In contrast, public procedures themselves teach that conflicts do not belong exclusively to the disputants or to the government and give the public a place through which to interpret, own, or disown what has occurred. Courts are one of many public spheres that make possible reasoned, passionate, or irrational discourses about social norms.

Courts are also a place in which to insist on equal treatment or to argue about the failure to accord it. For example, during the 1970s and

---

[119] Bentham, *op. cit.*, p. 355, and Vol. IV, p. 316. See also N. Andrews, *English Civil Procedure: Fundamentals of the New Civil Justice System*, Oxford University Press, 2003, p. 79.

[120] *See* the Military Commission Act of 2006, Pub. L. No. 109-366, 120 Stat.2600 (to be codified at 10 U.S.C sections 948 et seq.; 28 U.S. C. Section 2241).

1980s, as women and men of color brought claims of discrimination to courts in the United States, they found that some judges responded that differential treatment was natural. Moreover, these litigants sometimes found themselves subjected in court, by opposing lawyers and judges, to some of the very behaviors to which they were objecting.

In response to such concerns, the chief justices of many state courts convened special projects, denominated 'fairness' or 'gender bias' and 'racial bias' task forces. From reports based on information obtained through 'court-watchers', transcripts, decisions, interviews, and surveys of participants, more than forty jurisdictions examined whether, when, and how opponents or judges demeaned certain claimants or lawyers. These projects identified areas of law (such as violence against women or sentencing decisions) in which doctrines and practices did not accord equal treatment.[121] Statutes, rulemaking, and case law resulted because materials, accessible to public scrutiny, showed behaviors at odds with the provision of 'equal justice under law.'[122]

Courts permit the possibility of another kind of equality, between litigants. Their rules can alter the relative status of private litigants. The right to sue is itself a property right, given to any person who has the resources to pursue a cognisable claim. When use of that right is subsidized (either through government support for lawyers, by waivers of fees for filings or transcripts, or by inter-litigant payments from either losers to winners or across a class), individuals gain voice and gain the power to require disclosures and accounting from adversaries. Participatory parity[123] is an express goal of courts, even if they do not always achieve it.

In addition to undermining the state's monopoly on power, forging community ownership of norms, demonstrating inter-litigant obligations, and equalizing the field of exchange, open courts can express another of democracy's promises – that rules can change because of popular input. By examining a particular conflict in depth in light of legal rules, courts teach that the appropriate solutions and remedies (as well as the underlying rights) are not necessarily fixed and, moreover, that decisions on liability and remedy do not belong exclusively to the disputants. The public and the immediate participants see that law varies by contexts, decision makers, litigants, and facts, and they gain a chance

---

[121] See, e.g., The Effects of Gender, *op. cit.*; J. Resnik, 'Asking Questions about Gender in Courts', *SIGNS: Journal of Women in Culture and Society*, Vol. 21, 1996, p. 952.

[122] These are the words inscribed on the front of the façade of the Supreme Court of the United States.

[123] See Fraser, *op. cit.*, (arguing that such parity is requisite to the functioning of Habermasian public spheres).

to argue that the governing rules or their applications are wrong. Through democratic iterations, norms are reconfigured.

To appreciate the political and social utilities of the public dimensions of adjudication is not, however, to ignore the costs and burdens imposed.[124] The immediate participants in a dispute may find the exposure to the public disquieting. Even the disclosure of accurate information can be uncomfortable. Further, the public dimensions of adjudication may inhibit parties' abilities to find common ground, thereby deepening discord. And, despite Bentham's confidence that public disclosure reveals falsehoods, many a court record is subsequently impeached as predicated on witnesses who lied. Returning to the hanging of Saddam Hussein, one can also see that the imagery fueled outrage and prompted some spectators to see valour in a person previously despised.

Moreover, one should not romanticize spectatorship. While watching state-authorized processes may prompt celebration, action, or dialectic exchanges that develop new norms, boredom can also result. Were every door to every one of the tens of thousands of administrative hearings to be open, one would not expect many (any?) to volunteer to see many of the proceedings. But it is the happenstance of observation that is at the front of what makes open courts an important facet of a functioning democracy. Extraordinary conflicts have many routes into the public sphere. The dense and tedious repetition of ordinary exchanges is where one finds the enormity of the power of both bureaucratic states and private sector actors. That is the authority that is at risk of operating unseen.

C. Neither Rites nor Rights

Our mapping of the declining public dimensions of conflict resolution is aimed at undermining the assumption that public access *to* courts is an enduring feature *of* courts. Procedures, laws, and norms have great plasticity. Practices that seemed unimaginable only decades ago (from the mundane examples of the relatively new reliance on court-based settlement programs to the stunning assertions by the US government of the legitimacy of according little or no procedural rights to individuals at

---

[124] While providing many explanations of the utility of public processes, Bentham also argued the costs of public disclosure as he analyzed justifications for privacy (such as protecting participants from 'annoyance', avoiding unnecessary harm to individuals through 'disclosure of facts prejudicial to their honour' or about their 'pecuniary circumstances', and preserving 'public decency' and state secrets). His view was that a presumption in favor of public trials should, upon occasion, give way. Bentham, *op. cit.*, p. 360.

Guantanamo Bay and elsewhere) are now parts of our collective land-scape. Given the volume of filings and the political reticence to commit the resources requisite to supporting robust public institutions of dispute resolution that welcome all of those now entitled to make claims, the reformatting of adjudication is underway.

What we have shown is that one cannot assume the inevitability of an equation of courts with publicity. Rather, and here again invoking Bentham, for courts to be vehicles of publicity requires active decision making. But neither ought one assume that secrecy is an essential characteristic of the alternatives (agencies, ADR, private providers) to courts. As the variety of rules and customs surrounding court-annexed arbitration suggest, even as judges and other dispute resolution providers move away from trials and focus on pretrial management and dispute resolution in chambers and conference rooms, it is possible to build in a place *for* the public or to wall off proceedings *from* the public.

Whatever places are constituted as authoritative provide opportunities to engender or to preclude communal exchanges.[125] As Bentham noted centuries ago: 'Considered in itself, a room allotted to the reception of the evidence in question [...] is an instrument rather of privacy than of publicity; since, if performed in the open air [...], the number of persons capable of taking cognisance of it would bear no fixed limits.'[126] Locating judgment in courthouses with windows to the streets and open doors makes publicity possible, but even then a question remains about how to secure an audience.[127]

Normative commitments, predicated on a political theory about the role that the audience plays in juridical proceedings, are the prerequisite to configuring spaces to enable justice to be seen as well as to be represented. This excursion into a mélange of cultural history, custom, practice, data, budgets, and rules is aimed at providing some of the contours of such an approach, supportive of rights of audience.

Familiarity with courts' public dimensions, as well as with the impressive new buildings in countries around the world, and the thousands

---

[125] J. Bentham understood this choice as he delineated between two means by which publicity occurred. First were 'natural' instruments of publicity – those 'without any act done by any person (at least by any person in authority) with the intention and for the purpose of producing or contributing to the production of this effect.' Second were 'factitious' opportunities, which were those 'brought into existence or put in action by the hand of power.' Bentham, *op. cit.*, p. 354.

[126] *Ibid.*

[127] Bentham considered whether to have public authorities require attendance as matter of duty or to provide compensation for attendance or to devise some other 'factitious means.' He also advocated that permission liberally be granted for the publication of information obtained and for its republication.

of stones and panes of glass that comprise them may lead some to assume the stability of the public institution of courts. We do not. The display of justice is on the wane in some of the venues in which it was once vibrant, and its relocation to other locations has not been accompanied by either rites or rights of audience. If limited to rare instances, the processes of judgment return to the realm of the spectacle, the audience becomes voyeuristic, and power flows back to the producers.

References

The History of the English Law, Vol. II, Lawyers' Literary Club, 2nd ed. 1959 (reprinting a 1898 volume).

N. Andrews, *English Civil Procedure: Fundamentals of the New Civil Justice System*, Oxford University Press, 2003.

M. Ball, 'The Play's the Thing: An Unscientific Reflection on Courts Under the Rubric of Theater', *Stan. L. Rev.*, Vol. 28, 1975, p. 81.

E. Bazelon, 'Public Access to Juvenile and Family Court: Should the Courtroom Doors Be Open or Closed?', *Yale L. & Pol'y Rev.*, Vol. 18, 1999, p. 155.

O. Ben-Dor, *Constitutional Limits and the Public Sphere: A Critical Study of Bentham's Constitutionalism*, Hart, 2000.

S. Benhabib, *The Rights of Others*, Cambridge Press, 2004.

J. Bentham, *The Works of Jeremy Bentham, Edinburgh, William Tait, 1843*, Vol. VI, 355-70, (reprinting Bentham, *Jeremy Rationale of Judicial Evidence*, Vol. I, 1827).

B. Berkowitz, 'Negotiating Violence and the Word in Rabbinic Law', *Yale J.L. & Human*, Vol. 17, 2005, p. 125.

L. Bernstein, 'Opting Out of the Legal System: Extralegal Contractual Relations in the Diamond Industry', *J. Legal Stud.*, Vol. 21, 1992, p. 115.

C. Calhoun, 'Introduction: Habermas and the Public Sphere', in C. Calhoun, *Habermas and the Public Sphere*, MIT Press, 1992.

R. Cover, 'Violence and the Word', *Yale L.J.*, Vol. 95, 1986, p. 1601.

D. Curtis, & D. Hensler, J. Resnik, 'Individuals within the Aggregate: Relationships, Representation, and Fees', *N.Y.U. L. Rev.*, Vol. 71, 1996, p. 296.

F. Cutler, 'Jeremy Bentham and the Public Opinion Tribunal', *Pub. Opinion Q.*, Vol. 63, 1999, p. 321.

N. Davis, *The Gift in Sixteenth-Century France*, University of Wisconsin Press, 2000.

E. Deason, 'Procedural Rules for Complementary Systems of Litigation and Mediation - Worldwide', *Notre Dame L. Rev.*, Vol. 80, 2005, p. 553.

L. Demaine & D. Hensler, ''Volunteering' to Arbitrate Through Predispute Arbitration Clauses; The Average Consumer's Experience', *Law & Contemp. Probs.*, Winter/Spring 2004, p. 55.

S. Edgerton, Jr., *Pictures and Punishment: Art and Criminal Prosecution during the Florentine Renaissance*, Cornell University Press, 1985.

R. Ellickson, *Order Without Law: How Neighbors Settle Disputes*, Harvard University Press, 1991.

K. Fischer Taylor, *In the Theater of Criminal Justice: The Palais de Justice in Second Empire Paris*, Princeton University Press, 1993.

M. Foucault, *Discipline and Punish: The Birth of the Prison*, A. Sheridan, trans., Vintage Books, 1975 (2nd ed. 1995).

N. Fraser, 'Rethinking the Public Sphere: A Contribution to the Critique of Actually Existing Democracy', in C. Calhoun, *Habermas and the Public Sphere, op. cit.*

K. Fremantle, *The Baroque Town Hall of Amsterdam*, Haentjens Dekker & Gumbert, 1959.

M. Galanter, 'The Vanishing Trial: An Examination of Trials and Related Matters in Federal and State Courts, *J. Empircal Legal Stud.*, Vol. 1, 2004, p. 459.

M. Galanter, 'An Oil Strike in Hell: Contemporary Legends About the Civil Justice System', *Ariz. L. Rev.*, Vol. 40, 1998, p. 717.

L. Goode, *Jürgen Habermas: Democracy and the Public Sphere*, Pluto Press, 2005.

L. Craig, *The Federal Presence: Architecture, Politics, and Symbols in the United States Government Building*, MIT Press, 1978.

J. Habermas, *The Structural Transformations of the Public Sphere: An Inquiry into a Category of Bourgeois Society*, T. Burger trans., MIT Press, 1989.

J. Habermas, *Between Facts and Norms: Contributions to a Discourse Theory of Law and Democracy*, W. Rehg trans., Polity, 1996.

P. Huber, *Galileo's Revenge: Junk Science in the Courtroom*, Basic Books, 1991.

S. Kadish, 'Methodology and Criteria in Due Process Adjudication – A Survey and Criticism', *Yale L.J.*, Vol. 66, 1957, p. 319.

L. Kartky Doré, 'Public Courts Versus Private Justice: It's Time to Let Some Sun Shine in on Alternative Dispute Resolution', *Chi.-Kent L. Rev.*, Vol. 81, 2006, p. 376.

J. Krause, 'Towering Titans', *A.B.A. J.*, May 2004.

J. Langbein, 'Historical Foundations of the Law of Evidence: A View from the Ryder Sources', *Colum. L. Rev.*, Vol. 96, 1996, p. 1168.

A. Lanni, Note, 'Spectator Sport or Serious Politics? oi periesthkotes and the Athenian Lawcourts', *J. Hellenic Stud.*, Vol. 117, 1997, p. 183.

M. Loughlin, *Sword and Scales: An Examination of the Relationship Between Law and Politics*, Hart, 2000.

J. Lubbers & P. Verkuil, 'Alternative Approaches to Judicial Review of Social Security Disability Cases', *Admin. L. Rev.*, Vol. 55, 2003, p. 731.

W. MacKay, 'Framing the Issues for Cameras in the Courtrooms: Redefining Judicial Dignity and Decorum', *Dalhousie L.J.*, Vol. 19, 1996, p. 139.

N. Marder, 'The Medical Malpractice Debate: The Jury as Scapegoat', *Loy. L.A. L. Rev.*, Vol. 38, 2005, p. 1267.

H. van Miegroet, *Gerard David*, Mercatorfonds, 1989.

A. Miller, 'Confidentiality, Protective Orders and Public Access to the Courts', *Harv. L. Rev.*, Vol. 105, 1991, p. 427.

A. Miller, 'The Pretrial Rush to Judgment: Are the 'Litigation Explosion', 'Liability Crisis', and Efficiency Cliches Eroding Our Day in Court and Jury Trial Commitments?', *N.Y.U. L. Rev.*, Vol. 78, 2003, p. 982.

S. Milsom, *Historical Foundations of the Common Law*, Butterworths, 1969 (2nd ed. 1981).

M. Minow, *Between Vengeance and Forgiveness: Facing History After Genocide and Mass Violence*, Beacon Press, 1998.

R. Mnookin & L. Kornhauser, 'Bargaining in the Shadow of the Law: The Case of Divorce', *Yale L.J.*, Vol. 88, 1979, p. 950.

P. Ogden & Woxland, Thomas A., *Landmarks in American Legal Publishing: An Exhibit Catalogue*, West Publishing Co., 1990.

P. Pether, 'Inequitable Injunctions: The Scandal of Private Judging in the U.S. Courts', *Stan. L. Rev.*, Vol. 56, 2004, p. 1435.

J. Resnik, 'Asking Questions about Gender in Courts', SIGNS: *Journal of Women in Culture and Society*, Vol. 21, 1996, p. 952.

J. Resnik, 'Due Process: A Public Dimension', *U. Fla. L. Rev.*, Vol. 39, 1987, p. 405.

J. Resnik & E. Curtis, 'Images of Justice', *Yale L.J.*, Vol. 96, 1987, p. 1727.

J. Resnik, 'Managerial Judges', *Harvard L. Rev.*, Vol. 96, 1982, p. 374.

J. Resnik, 'Many Doors? Closing Doors? Alternative Dispute Resolution and Adjudication', *Ohio St. J. on Disp. Resol.*, Vol. 10, 1995, p. 211.

J. Resnik, 'Procedure as Contract', *Notre Dame L. Rev.*, Vol. 80, 2005, p. 593.

J. Resnik & E. Curtis, 'Representing Justice: from Renaissance Iconography to Twenty-First-Century Courthouses', *Proceedings of the American Philosophical Society*, Vol. 151, June 2007, p. 139.

J. Resnik, 'The Rights of Remedies: Collective Accountings for and Insuring Against the Harms of Sexual Harassment', in *Direction in Sexual Harassment Law*, C. MacKinnon & R. B. Siegel (eds.), Yale University Press, 2004, p. 247.

J. Resnik, 'Uncovering, Discovering, and Disclosing How the Public Dimensions of Court-Based Processes Are at Risk', *Chi.-Kent L. Rev.*, Vol. 81, 2006, p. 521.

L Robel, 'The Practice of Precedent: *Anastasoff*, Noncitation Rules, and the Meaning of Precedent in an Interpretive Community', *Ind. L. Rev.*, Vol. 35, 2002, p. 399.

B. Roth-Lochner & L. Fornara, *The Town Hall of Geneva*, J. Gunn trans., Switzerland, Chancellerie d'Etat, 1986.

I Simon, 'Parrhesiastic Accountability: Investigatory Commissions and Executive Power in an Age of Terror', *Yale L.J.*, Vol. 114, 2005, p. 1419.

K. Slanski, 'Mesopotamia: Middle Babylonian Period', in Westbrook, Raymond, *A History of Ancient Near Eastern Law*, Brill, 2003.

J. Stempel, 'Arbitration, Unconscionability, and Equilibrium: The Return of Unconscionability Analysis as a Counterweight to Arbitration Formalism', *Ohio St. J. on Disp. Resol.*, Vol. 19, 2004, p. 757.

R. Wheeler, *A New Judge's Introduction to Federal Judicial Administration*, Washington, D.C., Federal Judicial Center, 2003.

W. Weale, *Gerard David, Painter and Illuminator*, Seeley and Co., 1895.

D. Zaret, *Origins of Democratic Culture: Printing, Petitions, and the Public Sphere in Early-Modern England*, Princeton University Press, 2000.

Representation
of the European Court of Justice
Conscience of the People of Europe or Political Juggernaut?

Claire MICHEAU and Alexander Conrad CULLEY

*Faculty of Law at the University of Luxembourg and Compliance
Officer & Money Laundering Reporting Officer*

I. Introduction

Towards the end of Second World War British Prime Minister
Winston Churchill envisaged the formation of a 'United States of
Europe' on the Continent.[1] Upon the signing of the Treaty of Rome in
1957,[2] establishing the European Economic Community, politicians still
held the momentum in the pursuit of the integrationist agenda. Although
the jurisdiction of the European Court of Justice[3] had been greatly
expanded from adjudicating on disputes within the earlier established
European Coal and Steel Community, few would have expected it to
emerge as the most successful multi-national judicial body in the world
and as the standard bearer for pan-European integration. Today, over
60 years later, the ECJ's prominence within the modern European Union
is almost taken for granted.

As with the other institutions, the Council of Ministers and the
Commission, opinion on the ECJ is polarised. Some view it as a dynamic medium for social change, challenging the outdated status quo –
something made possible by its independence from national interest.
Conversely, others regard the ECJ with disdain, either arguing that it
kowtows to influence of the most powerful Member States or corpora-

---

[1] W. Mauter, 'Churchill and the Unification of Europe', *The Historian*, Vol. 67, 1998,
p. 67-84.
[2] Hereinafter the 'EC Treaty'.
[3] Hereinafter the 'ECJ'.

tions; or that it undermines national sovereignty by acting outside its constitutional limits to pursue a federalist agenda. The aim of this article is to examine these perceptions and assess whether they are justified, focusing on public perception and political utilisation of the ECJ in particular.

II. Public Perception

Few statistical surveys exist charting the awareness, satisfaction or level of support for the ECJ in EU Member States. Only very few studies have analysed the extent to which the ECJ has penetrated the consciousness) of individuals.[4] However, those produced tend to indicate that the ECJ may be one the most recognised institutions in the EU, possibly ahead of its counterparts, the Council of Ministers and the Commission.[5]

Despite its high level of recognition, many European citizens have yet to form a definite view on the ECJ. According to the results of the Eurobarometers surveys canvassing opinion on the ECJ in 1994, 60.8% of respondents in France were undecided or had no opinion on the role the Luxembourg court was performing. It is perhaps unsurprising that views were strongest in the United Kingdom, the most Eurosceptic of the large member states, where only 21.4% of respondents had formed no opinion on the ECJ.[6]

When European citizens do express opinions on the ECJ, whether they are positive or negative is usually determined by what information individuals base their judgment on. Where opinions are expressed, they are generally positive.[7] Surveys point out that opinions are likely to change depending on favourable or critical information is disseminated about the ECJ. It is suggested that opinion towards the ECJ is heavily influenced by the actions of its sister institutions in the EU framework.[8] Indeed, the European Parliament and the Commission conduct extensive

---

[4] According to the ECJ Press and Information Division in 2006, no such survey has been conducted within the last decade.

[5] J. Gibson, G. Caldeira, 'Changes in the Legitimacy of the European Court of Justice: A Post-Maastricht Analysis', *British Journal of Political Science*, Vol. 28, 1998, p. 63.

[6] Eurobarometers No. 38 and 40: 'European Court of Justice', June 1994.

[7] According to Eurobarometers surveys No. 38 and 40 'European Court of Justice', June 1994, the percentage of respondents who are somewhat satisfied with ECJ's decisions presents a range from a low 23% in France to a high of 52.3% in the Netherlands, while the very satisfied respondents varies from a low of 1.2 in Italy to a high of 15.2 in Luxembourg).

[8] J. Gibson, G. Caldeira, *op. cit.*, p. 63.

public relations operations. By contrast, with the exception of 'press release' entries on its section of the Europa web site, an ECJ public relations exercise is virtually non-existant. Instead, the ECJ concentrates on making its decisions more accessible, illustrated by the fact that the majority of its press releases document its handling of significant cases. Therefore, whilst the recognised EU institution and although the number of visitors to the ECJ increases each year,[9] European citizens lack a real understanding of its role and jurisdiction. This situation is not helped by limited participation in events such as political conferences, legal workshops and academic forums by members of the ECJ or Court of First Instance.[10] Likewise, education programmes for universities or schools are non-existent.

The apparent unawareness of European citizens to the role of the ECJ is perhaps paradoxical given the fact that its workload has enormously increased in recent years. While the number of cases brought before the Court of Luxembourg in 1970 was 79, 384 in 1990 and 543 in 1999, 467 have been taken to the Court in 2005.[11] The Court of First Instance, created in 1989 in order to tackle this dramatic increase of cases, has itself to cope with an incredible swelling in its workload. In 1989 the number of cases pending its examination sat at 168. By 2005 this had grown to 1033.[12] Moreover, as Schepel and Blankenburg[13] rightly observed, the ECJ's review function directly involves it in political debates. Tackling sensitive socio-political issues such as rights to minority languages[14] or rights of transsexual is the norm for the ECJ.[15] However, despite this, the ECJ is rarely the subject of the sort of intense debate that often confronts the Commission on the domestic political scene of Member States. It has also avoided featuring prominently in

---

[9]   The percentage of visitors rose 39% in 2005, from 8669 visitors in 2004 to 12049 visitors in 2005 (Data of ECJ Press and Information Division, 2006).

[10]   In 2004, the President of the Court of Justice participated to 22 official events and the President of the Court of First Instance to 17 events according to Annul Reports 2004 of the Court of Justice and the Court of First Instance.

[11]   Annual report, Statistics of judicial activity of the Court of Justice, 2005.

[12]   Annual report, Statistics of judicial activity of the Court of First Instance, 2005.

[13]   H. Schepel, E Blankenburg, 'Mobilizing the European Court of Justice', in G. De Burca, J. Weiler., *The European Court of Justice*, Oxford University Press, 2001.

[14]   ECJ, 28 November 1989, Anita Groener v. Minister for Education and City of Dublin Vocational Education Committee [379/87].

[15]   ECJ, 7th January 2004, K.B. [C-117/01].

heated debates at European level, most notably the explosive exchanges that led to the shelving of the proposed EU Constitution in 2003.[16]

It is certainly unrealistic to expect that the Luxembourg Court will have an influence similar to that of a national constitutional review court at Member State level. Indeed, its decisions pursuant to its enforcement and preliminary ruling procedures are implemented at national level by state legislation and judicial decisions respectively.[17] Therefore, a layperson can be forgiven for being unaware of the ECJ's involvement in national affairs in such circumstances – something which is often cited by Eurosceptics in justifying their allegations that the EU is eroding national sovereignty by stealth (see below).

The cumulative effects of the lack of an orchestrated ECJ public relations campaign and dependence on national legislatures and courts in enforcing its rulings has resulted in a European citizenry ill-informed as to the role of their most prominent judicial institution. However, governments and interest groups are far from ignorant of the ECJ's role and potential.

III. Political Utilisation

Power for and by the people is the principal source of direction and legitimacy in a democratic government. For this reason, the legislative power is always, initially, vested in a representative legislature.[18]

At least this is the theory. The results of the ECJ's interactions with the Commission, governments of Member States and private interest groups has led some to assert that the Court of Luxembourg has breached this fundamental principle, engaging in legislation and becoming a politicised entity.

---

[16] For instance, the ardent debates at the occasion of the approval of the European constitution have shown how the ECJ has been drawn aside. Whereas debates have resulted in calling into question others European institutions, especially the Commission and the Parliament, the Court mainly remained out of the debate. Supporters of the European Constitution have vaguely put forward the element that the Court would exercise a control in the light of the Charter of Fundamental Rights endowed with a binding legal force on EU law. Groups rejecting the European constitution have only pointed out the limits of the ECJ due to the small amount of judges and the lack of counter-power.

[17] Articles 232 and 234 of the EC Treaty respectively.

[18] J. Ferejohn, 'Judicializing Politics, Polticizing Law', *Law & Contemporary Problems*, Vol. 65, 2002, p. 44.

A. Autonomous Actor or Governmental Mouthpiece?

Much debate has considered whether the ECJ is really independent or is merely a subordinate of the most powerful Member States.

Propagators of the subordination theory, led mainly by G. Garrett[19] in the 1990s, argue that the ECJ is viewed by the strongest Member States as a means to pressurise weaker states into accepting and complying with their legislative obligations. This theory is justified by a belief that the ECJ will pre-empt attempts to secure negative treaty or legislative revisions by Member States through their representatives on the Council of Ministers in the event that their wishes are not fulfilled. Moreover Member States may threaten non-compliance with provisions or court decisions considered unfavourable to their interests; risking the unravelling of the EU itself.

Such views are supported by an empirical study conducted by examining the degree of national influence exerted over the decisions of the ECJ in 1989, 1993 and 1997. 615 cases were considered and the results suggest that the Luxembourg court was heavily swayed by key Member States in forming its judgments.[20]

Opponents of the subordination theory, on the other hand, argue that the ECJ is an autonomous entity driving European integration in the absence of the political consensus necessary to achieve it. Indeed, Eurosceptics such as the UK Independence Party assert that: 'The European Court of Justice is not a court of justice, it is an engine of political integration for the European Union.'[21] Such objectors cite attempts to expand EU competency to areas such as criminal justice and taxation as evidence that the ECJ is, with the encouragement of the Commission, working on its own initiative to erode national sovereignty in the absence of enough political support for federalism. H. Rasmussen offers some of the strongest academic criticism in this regard:

> In defiance of much European tradition, the European Court engaged in a teleological, pro-Community crusade, the banner of which featured a deep

---

[19] G. Geoffroy, B. Weingast, 'Ideas, interest and institutions: Constructing the EC's Internal market', in J. Goldstein, R. Keohane, *Ideas and Foreign Policy: an analytical framework*, Cornell University Press, 1993; G. Geoffroy, 'The politics of legal integration in the European Union', *International Organization*, Vol. 49, 1995, p. 171-81.

[20] C. Clifford, G. Matthew, 'Do Governments Sway European Court of Justice Decision-making?: Evidence from Government Court Briefs', *IFIR Working Paper Series 2005-06.*

[21] UK Independence Party, 'Judicial Coup d'Etat – Decision of the European Court of Justice 13th September 2005', speech to the European Parliament, 30th November 2005.

involvement which led it to give primacy to pro-integrationist public policies over competing ones that were often, even outside of the ring of losing
litigants, considered as meriting some protection.[22]

Most academic opponents of the subordination theory, however, do
not go this far. Instead, they argue that the ECJ has shown welcome
initiative in areas that were deadlocked at an intergovernmental level
before the Maastricht Treaty[23] due to the Luxembourg Compromise.[24]
This required that unanimous decisions be reached by Member States in
decision making. For example, Stone Sweet hails the advances in trade,
environmental and social equality by the ECJ's decisions dating back to
the 1960s.[25] In what is commonly coined the 'judicialisation of Europe',
theorists such as M. Pollack,[26] K. Alter[27] or W. Mattli and
A. M. Slaughter;[28] contend that it is unrealistic to assert that the governments of Member States have a stranglehold over the ECJ for a
number of reasons.

Firstly, attempting to avoid compliance with a preliminary ruling of
the ECJ made under Article 234 of the EC Treaty risks violating the
decision of a national court, raising the spectre of a domestic constitutional crisis. Such an undesirable outcome perhaps explains why national governments have deferred to the decisions of the ECJ in even the
most fiercely contested cases, such as *R v Secretary of State for Trans-
port Ex Parte Factortame.*[29] Not even did the fiercely Eurosceptic
Conservative Government led by Margaret Thatcher attempt to challenge the ruling by the British House of Lords, based on a reference to
the ECJ, that the provisions of the Merchant Shipping Act 1988 offensive to EC law be set aside. Doing so would have sparked a crisis in the
Community and within the United Kingdom itself.

Secondly, failing to comply with a ruling of the ECJ following enforcement proceedings brought by the Commission under Article 226
risks severe financial sanctions. As of 1996, the ECJ is now allowed to

[22] H. Rasmussen, 'Between Self-Restraint and Activism: A Judicial Policy for the European Court', *European Law Review*, Vol. 13, 1998, p. 28.
[23] The Maastricht Treaty, Treaty on the European Union, OJ C 191 of 29th July 1992.
[24] The Luxembourg Compromise of 30th January 1966.
[25] A. Stone Sweet, *The Judicial Construction of Europe*, Oxford University Press, 2006.
[26] M. Pollack, 'Delegation, Agency and Agenda Setting in the Treaty of Amsterdam' *European Integration online Papers*, 1999, 3 (6).
[27] K. J. Alter, 'The European Court's political power', *West European Politics*, Vol. 19, 1996, p. 458.
[28] W. Mattli, A. Slaughter, 'Law and politics in the European Union: a reply to Garret' *International Organization 1995*, Vol. 49, p. 183.
[29] ECJ, 19th June 1990, R v. Secretary of State Ex Parte Factortame [C-213/89].

impose financial penalties for non-compliance (Article 228). Penalties take into account not only the extent of the violation, but also the size of the violator's economy. This illustrated by the ECJ's order in 2002 that France pay a lump sum of €20,000,000 plus €57,651,250 for each additional six month period in which it failed to comply with a 1991 judgment for infringing fisheries conservation measures.[30] Although the penalties procedure has been infrequently used, the political conse-quences of such heavy penalties are obvious. As well as discouraging their disobedience, such judgments also serve to seriously undermine arguments that the ECJ is merely a puppet of the most powerful Mem-ber States.

It is at least impossible to deny that the perceptions of the ECJ at a governmental level may be split between those arguing it to be an instrument of Member States and those regarding it as an offensive or desirable autonomous actor. However, such branding is too simplistic without a consideration of influence exerted on the ECJ by third party, non state actors in the Brussels-Luxembourg political process.

B. The ECJ as a pan-European lobbying forum

> Going to court is a classic means by which both individuals and organisa-tional actors can seek policy change. If you are a special interest that fails at or is disadvantaged by lobbying, you can always try to get a law that you like struck down in court.[31]

The ECJ has emboldened private interest groups throughout Europe to seek change previously thought impossible through national legisla-tures. From pharmaceutical firms challenging drugs marketing regula-tions to pressure groups seeking better conditions and equality in the workplace, the ECJ has provided a unique forum for change in a manner and on a scale which its creators probably did not envisage.

The emergence of the ECJ as Europe's most powerful lobbying fo-rum is owed to a combination of its ability to give preliminary rulings under Article 234 of the EC Treaty; and the subsequent development of the doctrine of direct effect whereby individuals can rely on Community legislative provisions that are either incorrectly implemented or not incorporated into national law at all. The interaction of both has contrib-uted to a litigation mechanism central to the theory that Europe has become 'judicialised'. Indeed, case law provides overwhelming evi-

---

[30]   ECJ, 12th July 2005, Commission v. France [C-304/02].

[31]   P. Bouwen, M. McCown, 'Lobbying v. Litigation: Political and Legal Strategies of Interest Representation in the European Union', *University College London School of Public Policy Paper*, January 2006.

dence that interest groups ruthlessly seized the opportunities provided by the preliminary rulings system and direct effect to drive through a reformist, integrationist agenda during periods when national govern-ments were reluctant to pursue this in Brussels.

Amongst the most famous cases instigated by pressure groups are *Defrenne I*[32] and *II*.[33] Here, the litigant challenged her employer, the Belgian national airline Sabena, for discriminating between male and female employees in terms of pay and pension rights contrary to Article 141 of the EC Treaty. Supported by numerous feminist groups, Gabri-elle Defrenne secured a major victory against her employer in that the ECJ ruled that the equality provisions in the Treaty were directly effec-tive against both public and private bodies. This ruling acted as a cata-lyst for a variety of related secondary EU legislation, most notably the Equal Pay Directive,[34] the Equal Treatment of Work Directive[35] and the Working Time Directive.[36] Interest groups encouraged and capitalised on these legislative provisions by supervising their effective implemen-tation in Member States and finding more litigants where conformity was less than satisfactory. For example, in *Boyle v Equal Opportunity Commission*,[37] a case was brought to ensure the maternity rights of pregnant workers conferred by the British Government were compliant with relevant EU legislation.

Whilst it is certainly true that the ECJ has '*opened up a new space for social and political struggles*',[38] any argument that it is deferential to private actors and pressure groups is premature. This is because, whilst the interests of individuals and pressure groups may coincide, it is ultimately up to the individual to assert their rights in EU law. Indeed, the ECJ adopts a restrictive approach to the admissibility criteria for initiating proceedings under Article 230 of the EC Treaty whereby interest groups would not have the *locus standi* necessary to initiate an

---

[32] ECJ, 8th April 1976, Defrenne v Sabena [43/75].

[33] ECJ, 15th June 1978, Defrenne v Sabena [149/77].

[34] Council Directive 75/117/EEC of 10th February 1975 on the approximation of the laws of the Member States relating to the application of the principle of equal pay for men and women.

[35] Council Directive 76/207/EEC of 9th February 1976 on the implementation of the principle of equal treatment for men and women as regards access to employment, vocational training and promotion, and working conditions.

[36] Council Directive 79/7/EEC of 19th December 1978 on the progressive implementa-tion of the principle of equal treatment for men and women in matters of social secu-rity.

[37] ECJ, 27th October 1998, Boyle v Equal Opportunities Commission [C-411/96].

[38] K. A. Armstrong, 'Legal Integration: Theorizing the Legal Dimension of European Integration', *Journal of Common Market Studies*, Vol. 36, No. 2, 1998, p. 155, p. 164.

action themselves. Furthermore, decisions such as that in *Torfaen Borough Council v. B & Q Plc*[39] hardly demonstrate an institutional bias towards private entities. Here, a major British home improvement retailer failed in its attempt to challenge statutory Sunday trading hours under the Shops Act 1950. Rather than holding the statute as an obstacle to the free movement of goods under Article 30 of the EC Treaty, the ECJ held that Member States were free to regulate Sunday trading as a legitimate feature of socio-economic policy.

It appears safe to regard the ECJ as a forum for pan European lobbying, with its processes providing an innovative and powerful new weapon in the arsenal of interest groups. Nonetheless, manipulated it is not and suggestions to the contrary are only credible as a misrepresentation of the Luxembourg Court's relationship with private actors.

Conclusion

> Europe today contends with questions of identity, political imaginations, belonging, loyalty and responsibility, all of them beyond the reach of a legal approach.[40]

In a remarkably short period of time, roughly 40 years, the ECJ has undoubtedly become one of the most prominent judicial institutions in the world. Its high level of recognition amongst European citizens has made it an attractive venue for interest groups to publicly confront Member States, not to mention the prospect of favourable decisions contributing to Europe-wide change as opposed to the narrow focus of domestic litigation. Evidence suggests that the governments of the larger Member States also appreciate the ECJ's wide competency and jurisdictional reach; using it to further national interests through coercion and enforcement actions. In handling the caseload initiated by both of these actors, the ECJ is widely regarded to have pursued its own agenda, or that of the EU, 'tucked away in the fairyland Duchy of Luxembourg':[41] the construction of 'a constitutional framework for a federal-type structure in Europe'.[42] Yet, despite all its involvement in political affairs, any comparison of the ECJ's activities to those of inherently partisan national courts such as the US Supreme Court is short sighted.

The ECJ, whilst certainly a controversial entity, lacks the daily involvement in political life that has long characterised the US judiciary.

---

[39] ECJ, 27th October 1998, Torfaen Borough Council v. B & Q Plc [145/88].

[40] A. Wiener, T. Diez, *European Integration Theory*, Oxford University Press, 2004.

[41] E. Stein, 'Lawyers, Judges and the Making of a Transnational Constitution', *American Journal of International Law*, 1981, p. 75.

[42] *Ibid.*

From the resolution of electoral disputes, such as the now infamous Supreme Court decision in *Bush v. Gore*,[43] to aggressive intervention in campaign finance and the wider organisation of parties and interest groups; the US judiciary demonstrates all the bite of a political animal. Indeed, in some states judges are even elected. All this, together with intensive media coverage of its activities and education, have contributed to a notion amongst most Americans that the Supreme Court and the wider judicial system are the principal guardians of the Constitution. Furthermore, both also make frequent appearances in popular culture. Films such as *Fahrenheit 9/11*[44] certainly help to embed the Supreme Court in the national psyche of the US.

The cultural factor is perhaps more important than it first appears. The ECJ maybe the flagship of EU integration, but it is unlikely to ever capture the imagination of Europeans like the Supreme Court does in the US. An aggressive public relations campaign may raise awareness of the ECJ's roles and responsibilities, but it will struggle to infiltrate the soul of the ancient cultures of Europe with their unique identities and linguistic differences. Add to this the fact that its decisions are often disguised by implementation by national legislatures and courts, European citizens are overwhelmingly unaware of how wide the ECJ's jurisdiction is over socio-political issues and are likely to remain so for the foreseeable future. However, whilst the European public's high recognition of the ECJ appears to be in name only, it has proved beyond doubt that it can serve their conscience. An understanding of its competencies may often be lost in translation. Appreciations of its achievements in those quarters which have benefited from its judgments promoting equality and greater competition in business are not.

References

K. Alter, 'The European Court's political power', *West European Politics*, Vol. 19, 1996, p. 458.

K. Armstrong, 'Legal Integration: Theorizing the Legal Dimension of European Integration', *Journal of Common Market Studies*, Vol. 36 (2), 1998, p. 155.

P. Bouwen, M. McCown, 'Lobbying v Litigation: Political and Legal Strategies of Interest Representation in the European Union', *University College London School of Public Policy Paper*, January 2006.

---

[43] 531 U.S. 98 (2000).

[44] Fahrenheit 9/11, award-winning documentary film by the American filmmaker and political activist Michael Moore, released in the United States and Canada on June 25, 2004.

C. Clifford, G. Matthew, 'Do Governments Sway European Court of Justice Decision-making?: Evidence from Government Court Briefs', *IFIR Working Paper Series 2005-06*.

G. De Burca, J. Weiler, *The European Court of Justice*, Oxford University Press, 2001.

J. Ferejohn, 'Judicializing Politics, Polticizing Law', *Law & Contemporary Problems*, 2002, 65, 44.

G. Geoffroy, B. Weingast, 'Ideas, interest and institutions: Constructing the EC's Internal market', in J. Goldstein, R. Keohane, *Ideas and Foreign Policy: an analytical framework*, Cornell University Press, 1993.

G. Geoffroy, 'The politics of legal integration in the European Union' *International Organization*, Vol. 49, 1995, p. 171-81.

J. Gibson, G. Caldeira, 'Changes in the Legitimacy of the European Court of Justice: A Post-Maastricht Analysis', *British Journal of Political Science*, Vol. 28, 1998, p. 63-91.

C. Harding, 'Who goes to court in Europe? An analysis of litigation against the European Community', *European Law Review*, Vol. 17, 1992, p. 105.

S. Hix, *The political system of the European Union*, Palgrave, 2005.

W. Mattli, A.M. Slaughter, 'Law and politics in the European Union: a reply to Garret', *International Organization 1195*, No. 49, p. 183-190.

W. Mauter, 'Churchill and the Unification of Europe', *The Historian*, Vol. 67, 1998, p. 67-84.

M. Pollack, 'Delegation, Agency and Agenda Setting in the Treaty of Amsterdam', *European Integration online Papers*, 1999, Vol. 3 (6).

H. Rasmussen, 'Between Self-Restraint and Activism: A Judicial Policy for the European Court', *European Law Review*, Vol. 13, 1998, p. 28.

R. Rawlings, *Law and Administration in Europe, Essays in Honour of Carol Harlow*, Oxford University Press, 2003.

E. Stein, 'Lawyers, Judges and the Making of a Transnational Constitution', *American Journal of International Law*,1981, No.75, p. 1-27.

A. Stone Sweet, J. Caporaso, 'La Cour de Justice et l'intégration Européenne', *Revue française de science politique*, Vol. 48, 1998, p. 195-244.

A. Stone Sweet, *The Judicial Construction of Europe*, Oxford University Press, 2006.

UK Independence Party, 'Judicial Coup d'État – Decision of the European Court of Justice 13th September 2005', speech to the European Parliament, 30th November 2005.

J. Weiler, 'A quiet revolution – the European Court of justice and its interlocutors', *Comparative Political Studie*, Vol. 26, 1994, p. 510 531.

A. Wiener, T. Diez, *European Integration Theory*, Oxford University Press, 2004.

Deconstructing 'Justice' and Reconstructing 'Fairness' in a Convergent European Justice System

An Aristotelian Approach to the Question of Representation of Justice in Europe[1]

Theo GAVRIELIDES

Head of Policy of Race on the Agenda
& Director of Independent Academic Research Studies

I. Introduction

In our quest to understand the modern version of the notion of justice, we become acquainted with a feeling that has always accompanied us, but was never easy to pin down. That is the feeling of mistrust and scepticism about the way justice is represented in modern society. John Stuart Mill said that mankind are always predisposed to believe that any subjective feeling, not otherwise accounted for, is a revelation of some objective reality. Our task will be to determine whether the reality, to which the feeling of justice corresponds, is one which needs any such special revelation. For the purpose of this inquiry, 'it is practically important to consider whether the feeling itself, of justice and injustice, is *sui generis* like our sensations of colour and taste, or a derivative feeling, formed by a combination of others'.[2]

---

[1] My contribution would not have been possible without the support of Race on the Agenda (www.rota.org.uk) and Independent Academic Research Studies (www.iars. org.uk). Special thanks to Lewis Parle and Roxani Tsiridou for reading an early draft of this paper, and giving me their expert comments. I also thank them for their love and support.

[2] J. Mill, *Utilitarianism, On Liberty, Considerations on Representative Government*, Everyman, 1993, p. 43.

In other words, if we were to test objectively the image of justice as this is portrayed in modern society, how satisfactory would the outcome be? But what is justice, and how is this deconstructed in contemporary terms? More importantly, against what criteria is this system of representation compared, and what ultimate values are we aiming to attain? It becomes apparent that before we embark on criticising any system of representation of justice, we need to ascertain what the distinguishing character of justice, or of injustice, is. To find the common attributes of a variety of objects, it is vital that we survey the objects themselves in the concrete application of the situation.

Our analysis of justice's norm will need to avoid looking through the tinted glasses of popular culture such as the media, crime fictions, caricatures and films. We need to advert to the various modes of action, and arrangement of human affairs, which are classed by universal or widely spread opinion, as just. This approach will help us go back to basics, breaking free from the 'macdonalised' version of justice. Therefore, our first objective will be to deconstruct the notion of justice using objective tools and principles that are founded in human nature. The founder of Natural Law theory, Aristotle, will be consulted. The teachings of his students Jeremy Bentham and John Stuart Mill will also be discussed.

The second objective will be to use this untainted understanding to compare the norm of justice with its modern representation system. Ultimately, this will allow the identification of any gaps between values of justice and delivery of fairness through its servants: judges, courts, lawyers, the media, policymakers and politicians, government and administrators. Due to the limited space provided for this paper, only the media and the courts will be investigated, using the territory of criminal justice.

The third and final objective will be to drill down to the identified gaps between justice's normative understanding and modern representation system. The distinction between common law and civilian traditions will be examined, testing whether Europe's harmonising legal systems provides the answer that could bridge the gaps that the system of justice's representation allows. This discussion will be developed in the context of a convergent Europe of 25 European Union partners and 46 Council of Europe allies. The trend of a unified, homogenous justice system will be subjected to criticism as equity[3] and various aspects of

---

[3]   The word 'equity' is used in the Aristotelian sense, meaning the correction of the law according to the principles of universal justice in situations for which the law is too abstract or generalised. For Aristotle, equity and justice are closely related. While not absolutely identical, they belong to the same genus and are both morally good. What

normative justice are delivered and represented in common law and civilian legal systems.

II. Justice and Fairness: The Norm and The Real

A. *Methodology & Ground Rules*

The individual man is essentially a member of society, or as Aristotle put it, a 'social animal', whose identity is determined, but not limited, to its membership of different social groups.[4] Our world and realities are often defined by our surroundings, and for those rare thinkers whose views do not conform to what is 'common sense', things become complex, as we tend to ostracize them or label them as 'abnormal'. But justice is hardly a subjective notion. It is made of ingredients that are pure and easy to identify in nature. It is the theories that have been developed to explain these ingredients that are human constructs and hence subjective.

I have presented elsewhere[5] a schema that breaks down the 'world of theories' into three levels. The schema can be illustrated with three circles, the smaller fitting inside the bigger. The larger circle is broad enough to include theories with distinctive accounts of Ethics (how we should lead our lives) and Political Morality (relationship of the individual with the aggregation). According to Aristotle, Ethics is concerned with 'things which are for the most part so [...] things which are capable of being otherwise'.[6] The perfect opposite is mathematics, which is a science that deals with 'things that are of necessity'.[7] Examples of theories fitting in the first circle are the philosophies of liberalism, utilitarianism, communitarianism, republicanism or feminism.

Moving on to the second circle, we find theories for justice systems. These are theories that deal with the justice system in its entirety, and are able to address issues deriving from all stages of the justice process. In other words, theories that belong to the second circle are broad enough to address any justice issues. However, they are not as broad as

---

is equitable is just, in one sense, but in another sense it is higher than what is just since equity is the principle applied to correct justice when it errs.

4   However, as various libertarians would argue, although our membership to different groups (e.g. ethnic, religious, national) is influential, our identity cannot be reduced to membership of a single group. Each one of us is defined by a unique combination of characteristics that make up our personality.

5   T. Gavrielides, 'Some Mete-theoretical Questions for Restorative Justice', *Ratio Juris*, Vol. 18, No. 1, 2005, p. 84-106.

6   Aristotle, *Nicomachean Ethics*, II-27.

7   *Ibid.*

the theories of the first circle, which can take on board issues relating not only to justice, but also to ethics and political morality. Examples include Hart's theory of justice.[8]

Finally, there is the third circle, the smallest one, which includes theories that deal with specific problematic issues of various disciplines, such as criminal justice. Theories that belong to the third circle cannot deal with all problematic issues of justice (like theories of the second circle), and are certainly not interested in questions of ethics or political morality (which are issues that are addressed by the theories of the first circle). Examples include 'just deserts' theories (retributivism) and rehabilitation paradigms.

The delineation of the three levels of theories is important for at least three reasons. Firstly, if we are to analyse the normative concept of justice and compare it with the product of today's system of its representation, then we need to be able to locate ourselves within a certain School of Thought. Our arguments will be relative and will appeal to the followers of that School, but questioned by their opponents. Secondly, in our analysis, we will need to identify the circle within which we will be working, and if it is narrower than the others, then we should avoid making invalid arguments that are too big to fit within our chosen world of theories. Finally, if we are to talk about common law and civilian law systems, then again we will need to move within a certain sphere.

In particular, for the deconstruction of the notion of justice, I will be moving within the first, larger circle, using Aristotle's Natural Law theory and Mill's and Bentham's utilitarian perspectives. This will allow me to paint a picture of justice that is broader than any particular justice system and is detached from modern, limited images of justice as these are represented in today's society. The product will be a normative capture of justice's image which will then be compared to what we witness today as justice. This will allow conclusions to be drawn about the system of representation of justice in modern society. For the comparison between common law and civil law traditions and the way justice is interpreted by these systems, I will be moving within the third circle using a specific area of justice, criminal justice,[9] as this is where the differences between the two traditions are more apparent.

B. The Normative Concept of Justice

Arguably, each legal system is based on the accepted notion of justice by society which then entrusts its application and enforcement to

---

[8]   See H. Hart, *The concept of law*, Oxford University Press, 1961.

[9]   As opposed to other areas of law such as tort, contract law, commercial law etc.

legal practitioners such as judges and lawyers. This statement, by definition, leads us to assume two things; first, that there are different legal
systems and second that there are different types of justice depending on
a local community's understanding. Although this might be true – and
will indeed constitute one of this paper's themes of investigation – what
is undeniable is that justice has a normative concept that is *universal
truth*. Before we move on to any further analysis, this norm has to be
deconstructed and revealed. The chosen School of Thought that will be
used is Aristotle's Natural Law theory.

The starting point for Aristotle's analysis of justice is the individual
as opposed to a state of affairs. Put another way, justice has been
thought to be, primarily, the morally right assignment of good and bad
things (such as punishment, reward, respect, wealth etc). For Aristotle, it
is primarily the virtue of a person who expresses or acts for that right
assignment. In fact, justice is placed at the top of the values' pyramid,
since though other ethical standards (e.g. mercy, compassion, generosity, benevolence) may be valuable, they are supererogatory rather than
required. The man who is not just is the man who takes more than his
share of the things which are good in themselves, but not always good
for a particular person i.e. external goods such as wealth and honour
(particular justice).

But justice, for Aristotle, is not only a value. Justice also means obedience to law. In fact, he thinks that the law should control the whole
range of human life. He proceeds to say that if a particular State[10] does
this only partially that is because it is only a rough and ready adumbra-
tion of what law should be. In his work Nicomahean Ethics, he concludes: 'by 'just' we may mean (i) what is lawful or (ii) what is fair and
equal; these are 'universal' and 'particular' justice respectively'.[11] It is
interesting to note that the Greek equivalent of the word just (from the
Latin word 'jus') is δίκαιος, which meant 'observant of custom or rule'.[12]
In Attic law, αδικείν (to do injustice) was the word used to express any
breach of law. Aristotle says: 'As the defendant in a civil suit is charged
with wronging an individual, the prisoner in a criminal case is thought
of as wronging the city.'[13]

From the above analysis, it becomes apparent that there are two
types of justice. One that is attached to the concept of the law and one
that defines what is fair and equal – we will call it fairness. Although

---

[10] In ancient Greece (Hellas), each city was a separate state (city-state) with its own
sovereignty, army and governance system (see for example Athens vs Sparta).

[11] 1129 & 3-1130.

[12] Cf. Hom. Od. 3, 52.

[13] Aristotle, *Nicomachean Ethics*, II-27.

both should be valued-based, the former is more easily exposed to arbitrariness and human fault. The latter is closer to the ideal, but is abstract.

In our journey to understand the way justice is represented in today's society, we went back to basics looking at what justice is as a normative concept that is detached from reality. To do that we chose Aristotle's teachings, which define justice as part of Natural Law. This School of Thought involves a system of consequences which naturally derives from any action or choice. On this account, justice is a universal and absolute concept, while human constructs such as religions, principles and theories are merely attempts to codify that concept, sometimes with results that entirely contradict the true nature of justice. This analysis is not abstract as it acknowledges the caveat between the normative side of justice and its real dimension which is expressed in the law.

This analysis leads to the question of whether the system of representation refers to justice (the law) or fairness. We would be obtuse to expect from any judge or lawyer to represent the normative concept of justice (fairness). Their job description stops where justice (the law) is done. It is therefore on this type of justice (the law) that we need to focus our analysis, keeping in mind that fairness, being part of nature, always looms to warm up the often cold court rooms and law offices.

III. Mind the Gap between Justice's Norm and Representation System

This part of the paper will aim to address our second objective using the normative understanding we have developed in the previous section. A comparison between justice's norm and representation system will help us test the objectivity of modern legal systems. However, before we move onto this analysis, there is a caveat that needs to be addressed.

This paper has already accepted that although justice is hardly subjective, the various methods of its interpretation are human constructs and hence subjective to fault and relativism. Natural Law theory is no exception; hence our interpretation would have been different, depending on the School of Thought of our choice.

For example, for the advocates of divine command theory, justice is the authoritative command of God. The Pythagoreans had defined justice as reciprocity i.e. that A shall have done to him what he has done to B, or as the Old Testament put it 'An eye for an eye, and a tooth for a tooth' (*Lex Talionis*). Others, such as Plato, have argued that justice is the interest of the strong i.e. a name for whatever the powerful or cunning ruler has managed to impose on the people.[14] For Nietzsche, justice is part of the slave-morality of the weak many, rooted in their resentment of the strong few, and intended to keep the noble man down.[15] Thomas Hobbes sees justice as a collection of enforceable, authoritative rules created by the public and hence injustice is whatever those rules forbid, regardless of their relation to morality.[16] Thinkers belonging to the social contract tradition would argue that justice is derived from the mutual agreement of everyone concerned or from what they would agree to under hypothetical conditions. These examples are only meant to be illustrative of the variations of interpretations of the norm of justice, which we have accepted to be objective, using Natural Law theory.

A. Justice's Modern Representation and Delivery System

To test the objectivity of justice's modern system of representation, we first need to identify the means of its delivery. These can be classified into two general categories. We will refer to the first one as the informal delivery system of justice, encompassing our day-to-day treatment and interaction with others. We have accepted that justice is first and foremost a value that informs our code of interaction and behaviour towards ourselves and others. This is where justice is delivered informally by each one of us in our daily activities. The second system of justice, the formal one, encompasses the justice system that has been constructed to deliver justice through the law and its institutions. For the reasons explained, we will focus on the formal system of justice's delivery though references to the informal one are unavoidable.

To understand the formal delivery system of justice, we only need to follow a law's journey from its conception to its delivery. To deliver justice (the law) formally, first there needs to be an injustice done to society. This needs to be identified and publicly condemned. It also needs to be backed up by a pattern of unjust behaviour. Through this, the need for regulation arises. This requires a mixture of skills and professions including politics, the media, academia, market research, economics, campaigners and so on. Once a law has been produced to regulate this pattern of injustice, then a further series of actors come into play to represent and deliver justice, including lawyers, courts, judges, administrators, the media, film makers, authors, politicians, campaigners and different types of institutions. Once this law is delivered, then a

---

[14] See Plato's *Republic*, esp. Thrasymachus.

[15] Nietzsche said: 'Justice (fairness) originates among those who are approximately equally powerful.' F. Nietzsche, *Human, All Too Human*, CUP, 1986.

[16] See, T. Hobbes, *The Elements of Law, Natural and Politics*, 1889, Ed. F. Tönnies, including 'Short Tract on First Principles', 1889 (written 1630-36).

further chain of maintenance and publicity activity is observed encompassing educational institutions, the media, campaigners, politicians etc.

These agents – whether the media, politicians, judges, lawyers, campaigners, educational institutions – are engaged to contribute to the formal system of justice's delivery and representation. This paper will focus only on a selection of case studies (the media and courts) to test how objective the representation of justice by these agents is.

B. Representation of Justice by the Media: Case Study No. 1

Arguably, the media is one of the most powerful agents in the representation system of justice nowadays. It has a general appeal to the public and can reach almost everyone in their homes, work, schools etc. It is generally accepted that – with exceptions – journalists and media agents in general are committed to a code of ethics that reflects their societies' accepted values. However, on various occasions, the media can misrepresent justice (the law), often creating confusion and hostility that is unjustifiable and unfair (value). To test this claim, we will use human rights legislation and the UK's Human Rights Act in particular as a case study.

Human rights are generally understood as individual entitlements that derive from someone's humanity. They set minimum standards to be respected by States, providing individuals with a mechanism to protect, but also demand, acknowledgment of their basic freedoms and natural rights. In 1998, the British Government passed the Human Rights Act (HRA), incorporating the rights and freedoms protected in the European Convention on Human Rights (ECHR), a regional treaty introduced by the Council of Europe and implemented by the European Court of Human Rights in Strasbourg. It is not within this paper's remit to elaborate on human rights or the ECHR; therefore no critical analysis will be attempted.[17]

As with most common law countries (e.g. Australia, Canada, the USA, South Africa) that have introduced similar Acts, someone would expect that the British public would embrace such major legislation. However, there is evidence to suggest that there is misunderstanding and even hostility towards the HRA and human rights. Unpublished research by the Department for Constitutional Affairs has indicated that this is

---

[17] Further on the concept of human rights in T. Gavrielides, 'Human Rights vs. Political Reality: The case of Europe's harmonising criminal justice systems', *International Journal of Comparative Criminology*, Vol. 5, No. 2, 2005, p. 60-84 and in T. Gavrielides, 'Human Rights and customer satisfaction with public services: a relationship discovered', *International Journal of Human Rights*, Vol 13, No. 1, forthcoming.

mainly due to misleading media coverage particularly by the tabloid press and television.

Some evidence to support this claim can be found in the findings of a 2004 study by the Institute of Public Policy Research (IPPR). Their research was carried out with a sample from the UK's voluntary sector: 'Some sections of the Press have characterised the HRA as a 'criminal charter' and the last refuge for unmeritorious defences.'[18] However, research by the Human Rights Act Research Unit has indicated that the impact of the Act on jurisprudence is minimal, while there is no evidence to suggest that it allows loopholes to be used by criminals.[19]

In 2000, Francesca Klug in 'Target of the Tabloids' went further in analysing the impact of a negative press portrayal of the HRA: 'If the government promote the Act, they risk unleashing 'Eurochaos' scare stories which Ministers fear will provide officials with excuses for not exercising powers that are commonplace in other States which have incorporated the ECHR into local law.'[20] A study carried out by the Telephone Helplines Association supported Klug's comments: 'A large proportion of the general public in the UK is deeply suspicious of anything coming from Europe. It is a shame that useful Directives are rarely shown to come from Europe, whereas anything coming from there which can be described as 'bureaucracy run mad' is splashed all over the red tops.'[21]

Misunderstanding and hostility in relation to the HRA can also be ascribed to campaigning by various political parties. For example, the Conservative Party has recently announced the establishment of a commission to investigate the workings of the Act with a view to reforming or repealing it. The shadow Home Secretary said: 'The HRA has given rise to too many spurious rights. It has fuelled a compensation culture out of all sense of proportion and it is our aim to rebalance the rights culture.'[22] In similar vein, the Spectator wrote: 'considerations of people's supposed rights often paralyse sensible action [and] preclude kindness and common sense...they drive out considerations of... decency, tolerance [and] mutual obligations' (The Spectator, 24th April 2004).

---

[18] Institute of Public Policy Research (IPPR), F. Butler, *Human Rights: Who needs them? Using Human Rights in the Voluntary Sector*, IPPR, 2004.

[19] http://www.doughtystreet.co.uk/hrarp/summary/index.cfm.

[20] F. Klug, 'The Human Rights Act Research Unit. Target of the tabloids', *The Guardian*, 14th July 2000.

[21] Telephone Helplines Association, *THA Bulletin*, October 2003.

[22] D. Davis, 'Victim Nation', *The Spectator*, August 2004, 2005.

However, the media's attack does not only concern human rights leg-islation, but also the meaning and significance of human rights more generally as opposed to the HRA itself. Various studies have suggested that due to bad media coverage, human rights:

- are often conceived by the public to be used only for either ex-treme cases of torture and inhumane treatment[23] – or as a hin-drance in the war against terrorism;
- tend to be seen as luxury entitlements used by celebrities, travel-lers or even convicted criminals who want to avoid punishment or claim compensation for trivial reasons;
- are often associated with political correctness;
- conceived in narrow legalistic terms and largely of interest to lawyers.

It seems that only few people immediately associate human rights with their everyday encounters with public services, while only on rare occasions are civil rights perceived to be about the individual rather than the community.[24]

Human rights are also believed to encourage a 'compensation cul-ture', 'a name, blame, shame and claim culture, the American Model that we all wish to avoid'.[25] The 2004 IPPR study concluded that when people are asked 'what human rights mean to them… the typical re-sponse is: disappearances and torture overseas or protecting the rights of terrorists or people like Myra Hindley. It seems that they have never had anyone raise human rights in any other contexts'. Their report also said: 'Celebrities like Naomi Campbell and Catherine Zeta Jones have used

---

[23] In a live discussion on Radio 5, Late Night Live, 2nd October 2002, an Asian man who fled to Britain 30 years ago phoned in to tell to the radio audience: 'I came here because Britain is a free country. We don't need a Bill of Rights.'

[24] In 2002, in a series of letters to the Lord Chancellor, the Prince of Wales wrote: 'human rights legislation is only about the rights of individuals' (Telegraph, 26th Sep-tember 2002). However, according to the latest report of Mr. Alvaro Gil-Robles, the Council of Europe's Commissioner for Human Rights, the Council was concerned with the frequency with which calls for the need to rebalance rights protection were heard. These calls, the Commissioner said, argue that human rights have shifted too far in favour of the individual to the detriment of the community. However, the Commission said: '…It is perhaps worth emphasising that human rights are not a pick and mix assortment of luxury entitlements, but the very foundation of democ-ratic societies. As such, their violation affects not just the individual concerned, but society as a whole; we exclude one person from their enjoyment at the risk of exclud-ing all of us' in Council of Europe, *Report by Mr. Alvaro Gil-Robles, Commissioner for Human Rights on his visit to the United Kingdom 4th-12th November 2004*, Stras-bourg, Council of Europe, 2005.

[25] HRH The Prince of Wales to the Lord Chancellor, quoted by the *Daily Telegraph* 2002.

human rights arguments to help protect themselves from unwanted media intrusion. Their well-publicised court cases have encouraged a sense that human rights seem to be principally of interest to expensive lawyers.

Francesca Klug argued that:

> Given the absence, to date, of human rights education in schools, most peo-ple glean their understandings of bills of rights from American movies and news reports that gun control cannot be introduced into the US as a result of this albatross. There is confusion between human rights, bills of rights and international or regional human rights treaties. This general lack of clarity tends to result in one of two repeated misconceptions. First, that all bills of rights are presumed to be in the image of the liberal, American model with its Supreme Court that can overturn all legislation. Second, that every time the European Court of Human Rights makes an adverse judgement against the UK, it is assumed that this is part of a plot hatched in Brussels to under-mine British sovereignty. In fact, of course, the ECHR has nothing whatso-ever to do with the European Union...[26]

To sum up, we have used human rights and human rights legislation as a case study to shed some light on the media's contribution to jus-tice's representation system. It becomes apparent that human rights law is not adequately represented by the majority of the media, which in fact have created confusion, misunderstanding and hostility which is not backed up with evidence.

C. Representation of Justice by the Courts: Case Study No. 2

For most lay people, courts are often synonymous with justice (the law). It is interesting to notice that most first year law students are convinced that justice, especially criminal justice, is delivered only in courts. Of course, this is far from true with the majority of cases been resolved at the plea bargaining/ negotiations stage.[27]

For those cases that do end up in court, it is generally accepted that justice (the law) is delivered in a manner that all the participants regard as fair. However, there have been occasions where miscarriages of justice have occurred. Despite their considerable small number, their impact on public confidence is severe, particularly where criminal law cases are involved, as this is where the accused's most basic rights and

---

[26] F. Klug, *Values for a godless age*, Penguin Books, 2000, p. 13.

[27] According to the Lord Chancellor's Department (now Department for Constitutional Affairs), at least 98% of the criminal cases are resolved in Magistrates' court, 82% plea guilty and never go to court while only 2% of cases end up in proper Crown Court trials (see for example LCD 1997 p. 64, 90 and Home Office 1995 p. 31).

liberties are at stake. For this reason, we will focus our analysis on criminal justice.

A fundamental principle in the law of evidence is that its rules and procedures should always be weighted towards acquitting the guilty rather than convicting the innocent. 'Better to let 100 guilty men go free than to wrongly convict one innocent man.' Yet in spite of this, there are no guarantees that innocent people are never convicted. Even the appeal system can often fail, leaving serious question marks about the integrity of the justice process. One example is the 1975 'Birmingham six case', where six men were convicted for their involvement in two serious terrorist bombings in Birmingham, UK. The primary evidence against them were their confessions and forensic evidence. However, they claimed that they were tortured by the police to confess and that they were innocent. Their appeal was dismissed, but in the mid 1980s after a television documentary that covered their case, doubts were created about their guilt. After an MP published a book in which he claimed he had tracked down and interviewed the real bombers, the Home Secretary referred the case back to the Court of Appeal. The appeal was for the second time dismissed. However, in 1990, the case was again referred to the Court of Appeal and on this occasion the appeal was allowed and the defendants' convictions were quashed on the grounds that both the confessions and the scientific evidence were suspect.

The Birmingham six case is only but one example of a number of miscarriages of justice that came to light. Some other examples include: Guildford four 1975-1989, Maguire family 1976-1991, Judith Ward 1974-1992, Cardiff three 1990-1992, Taylor sisters 1992-1993, Bridgewater three 1979-1997. These are examples taken only from one legal system. Things become even more serious if we use jurisdictions that allow capital punishment. For example, in November 2005, Ruben Cantu who in 1984 was found guilty of manslaughter and was sentenced to death being only 17, was finally found innocent after the only eye witness said: 'You've got a 17-year old who went to his grave for something he did not do. Texas murdered an innocent person.'

Finally, miscarriages of justice are also considered by the media to constitute 'juicy stories'. Although, in principle, media coverage is desirable, the way these cases are emphasised often creates further confusion and mistrust in justice (the law). This is a classic example of two justice agents misrepresenting justice (the law) in modern society.

D. Representation of Justice by the Courts & Media: Case Study No. 3

The last case study will elaborate on one of the most apparent failures of both courts and the media to represent justice. This refers to the sexual offending cases that occurred within the Catholic Church and the way both the courts and the media have dealt with them, most of the time misrepresenting justice (the law) so badly that the cost for the victims, their families and society is too considerable to bear.

It all started in the beginning of 2002 in Boston, USA when the Boston Globe acquired documents showing that John Geoghan suspended from priestly ministry in 1994 had been moved from one assignment to another even though it was alleged that he had molested nearly 200 children for more than thirty years. This revelation was followed by an avalanche of hundreds of other similar cases that eventually crashed into court rooms and law offices. I have presented elsewhere a chorology and a detailed analysis of these cases; therefore, I will not elaborate on them further.[28]

The media's criticism does not refer to their whistle blowing; on the contrary, the criticism allowed these cases to come to light and for justice to be sought. In fact, this constitutes an example of the significant role the media can play in representing and assisting justice in bringing balance and restoration to communities and individuals. The criticism refers to the way the trials were covered. The stories that were written, presented in television shows or discussed on radio, in chat rooms, the internet and other sources were primarily interested in the gossipy side of these grievous injustices. As a result, they painted a picture of justice that was far from reality but none the less rather 'attractive' i.e. it sold.

For example, there was tendency for exaggeration including false accusations. One of these cases is the late Cardinal Bernardin of Chicago who was accused by the CNN of committing sexual offences against a minor. This was based on a single testimony which was later withdrawn by the accuser who admitted that his recovered memory was faulty and that the Cardinal was indeed innocent. In their struggle to collect evidence on cases that took places forty or fifty years ago, the media often performed the role of the judge and the jury, the police and the prosecutor, most of the times playing a deaf ear to testimonies that were not that convenient or easy to sell. On the other hand, a number of victims and their families as well as a considerable proportion of society feel disap-

---

[28] T. Gavrielides and D. Coker, 'Restoring Faith: Resolving the Catholic Church's sexual scandals through restorative justice: working paper I', *Contemporary Justice Review*, Vol. 8, No. 4, 2005, p. 345.

pointed with the way the courts and the criminal justice system represented justice. We will focus on one case to understand the reasons for this disappointment.

The first well-known American case in the 1980's was that of Louisiana-based Catholic priest Gilbert Gauthe. Church authorities transferred the priest from parish[29] to parish, where he sexually abused minors repeatedly despite hierarchs' awareness of his reprobate behaviour. Angry parents eventually brought Gauthe and the Church to trial and after tremendous pressure, the Diocese of Lafayette, Louisiana removed Gauthe from his ministry in 1983.

In 1985, local courts sentenced Gauthe to 20 years in prison, but he was released after 10 years. He was later arrested in Texas on charges of fondling a 3-year old boy and was finally re-released from prison again in 2000 (Paulson 6/12/2002). Catholic scholar William Jenkins writes:

> The Gauthe case also established the precedent that such failure to intervene should result in financial penalties, payment for therapy for the victims and compensatory damages for their families. Following Gauthe's conviction in 1985, a group of concerned clergy and laity submitted a confidential report on abuse to the Catholic hierarchy. This document warned of the need to take urgent action in the face of such scandals, and suggested that legal liability payments could run into billions of dollars. It also warned that the Church could no longer rely on the friendship and sympathy of Catholic politicians, judges, and professionals within the criminal justice system...[30]

The Gauthe case put both Catholic clergy and the US judicial system on alert, but the public had only captured a glimpse of the iceberg. News reports coupled with a television drama about Gauthe's molestation of children stirred further concern. But neither the Church ecclesiastical authorities nor the judicial system found an effective, efficient way to resolve the problem. Rather, both moved Gauthe around although the victims' parents certainly favoured incarceration. Loss of faith in the church hierarchy and cynicism about the defrocked cleric's movement through the prison system beleaguered some parents.

---

[29] An administrative part of a diocese that has its own church in Anglican, Roman Catholic, and some other churches.

[30] P. Jenkins, 'Clergy sexual abuse: The symbolic politics of a social problem', in J. Best (ed.), *Images of issues: Typifying contemporary social problems*, Aldine de Gruyter, 1989, p. 105.

IV. Convergent European Justice

It is not the intention of this paper to be dismissive of the media and the courts' role in the representation system of justice. The critical analysis that was attempted focused on a selection of negative cases simply because the working assumption is that the media and the courts as well as the other agents that have been referred to in this paper are overall good representatives of the notion of justice (the law). However, this does not change the fact that they sometimes fail to represent justice. This bears the question of what could be done to move them closer to the normative concept of justice (the law), if this is indeed possible at all. The analysis will focus on Europe and will use criminal justice as its point of reference.

The account is based on a claim that has recently dominated the comparative law literature. This involves the harmonizing trend that seems to exist in Europe's criminal justice systems. It has been a long-standing tradition to think in terms of 'systems' when talking about criminal procedures. According to Davies and Croall, almost all criminal justice systems are divided into four key subsystems: the law enforcement officers, the machinery of the courts, the penal subsystem and the crime prevention machinery.[31] All subsystems are meant to represent the notion of justice (the law) objectively and as close to its normative understanding (the value).

The structure of a criminal justice system is also a reflection of society's attitudes and preferred response to crime. Hence, criminal justice systems tend to vary from nation to nation. However, systems often follow basic principles that are shared by other systems and it is within this understanding that we classify them into legal models. In Europe, the two most prominent models are common law – or the adversarial system as it is otherwise known – and civil law – or inquisitorial system. The former is found in countries such as Ireland, Great Britain and former colonies, while the latter is principally found in the majority of European countries such as France, Germany and Italy.

Although these two systems share a number of similarities – thus it would be a mistake to oversimplify their distinction – they often tend to deliver justice (the law) in different ways. This involves all stages and agents mentioned in the previous section of this paper. This begs the question of whether a different type of justice is delivered.

Over the last fifty years, and especially after the Second World War, Europe has consciously engaged in a regional activity to bring harmony

---

[31] M. Davies and H. Croall, *Criminal justice: an introduction to the criminal justice system in England and Wales*, Longman, 1998.

and unity in the hope of avoiding a similar disaster. This also includes the way justice is delivered in the continent. The literature refers to these changes as 'harmonising factors' and some of them are: EU law, Europol, the introduction of the European warrant, the International Criminal Court and the Rome Statute, a number of multilateral treaties (e.g. against organised crime, money laundering, drugs) and the creation of regional *fora*. One of these is the Council of Europe, comprising 46 member States. One of the Council's most significant achievements is the European Convention on Human Rights (ECHR), which has already been mentioned. The ECHR states in its preamble that the aim of the Council is 'the achievement of a greater unity between its members'. The Convention uses terms such as 'fair trial', 'just society', 'democratic society', 'liberty', 'security' and 'morals' to refer to the whole of Europe, or at least to its 46 signatories. More importantly, through the European Courts' jurisprudence it interprets these abstract words in a concrete manner making them binding for all. This involves an interplay that is taking place between judicial, political and legislative powers and the agents that are set to serve and represent justice in modern society.

We will focus on one Article to test this harmonising trend. This concerns the right not to be tortured or subjected to degrading or inhumane treatment or punishment (Article 3). The terms of this right are absolute and hence where a breach occurs it is not possible to balance it with another individual's or groups' rights. It is interesting to notice how the regional court laid minimum standards to be respected by all signatory States that are bound by their ECHR obligations to represent justice in a uniform manner.

Article 3 has been invoked by members States following both the common law and civil law traditions. Some examples include cases relating to serious assaults in custody (e.g. *Tomasi v. France* A/241-A (1992) 15 EHRR 1), the application of psychological interrogation techniques (e.g. *Ireland v. UK* (1989) 11 EHRR 439), prison conditions (e.g. *McFelley v. UK* (1980) 20 DR 44), suspects in detention, rape while in prison (e.g. *Aksoy v. Turkey* (1996) 23 EHRR 553), and extradition or expulsion where torture or ill treatment might be a consequence (e.g. *Cruz Varas v. Sweeden* (1992) 14 EHRR 1).

For example, in *Ireland v. UK,* the Court defined the meaning of the terms of Article 3, establishing in this way minimum standards to be respected by all members of the Council. After the decision, the UK government compensated the victims and ordered the discontinuance of the techniques used.[32] This was followed by a number of other member

---

[32] Resolution (78) 35 of the Committee of Ministers, acting under A5, adopted on 27th June 1978.

States who saw the decision as laying a principle that was applicable throughout the Council.[33]

Equally important is *Soering v. UK*, which had an impact on how suspect terrorists are treated today. In this case the deportation of a prisoner was found to be in breach of Article 3, as it would lead to the so called 'death row phenomenon'. With its judgement, the regional Court introduced an exception to a rule of public international law, whereby no State could be found responsible for the acts of third States. As noted by the Court, 'this rule cannot exclude State responsibility under the ECHR with respect to events taking place outside their jurisdiction'. As it would be expected, this decision has a major impact not only on the accused State, but also on the criminal justice policies of all the Council's members. For instance, the civil chamber of the Dutch Supreme Court held the surrender of an American soldier would not take place as long as the US government failed to give sufficient assurances that a death sentence imposed by a national court would not be carried out.[34] The decision also affected member States' asylum policies, because, as the Court noted, although States are free to expel foreigners, 'the specific importance of preventing torture justified an exception to that freedom'.[35]

Through the means of a regional treaty that lays standards based on human rights principles, the regional Court aspires to represent justice (the law) in a uniform way across Europe. It is important to note that before any case has reached the Court, it would have exhausted all domestic legal procedures. However, we would be overambitious to think that the referred harmonisation process, particularly the role of the ECHR and the Council, do not face serious obstacles. I have discussed these elsewhere,[36] and it is not the intention of this paper to turn political. Nevertheless, it is important to remember that the referred trend is often overshadowed by political and other factors.

Concluding Remarks

It would be naïve to think that any domestic, regional, national or local justice system can bring uniformity to the way the norm of justice is represented in modern society. Moreover, we would be overambitious to

---

[33] http://www.echr.coe.int/Eng/EDocs/EffectsOfJudgements.html.
[34] HR 30 March 1990 [1991] NJ 249.
[35] *Farrell v. UK* (1982) 30 DR 96.
[36] T. Gavrielides, 'Human rights vs Political reality: The case of Europe's harmonising criminal justice systems', *International Journal of Comparative Criminology*, Vol. 5, No. 2, 2005, p. 60-84.

expect justice's representation system to be a perfect reflection of its norm.

Through the teachings of Aristotle, this paper has deconstructed justice to show that although it is an objective concept, it is split up into the human construct of the *law* and the ethically-based *fairness*. This led us to conclude that any analysis of justice's representation system should focus on its former element and not the latter. The account also helped us to understand that though we can be more demanding in terms of the representation of justice (the law), we have to remain reasonable with our expectations from the agents attempting to represent justice (the value).

A selection of case studies focusing on the agents of the media and courts provided evidence that the system of justice's representation often fails to deliver, and this can have serious repercussions including doing injustice to individuals and the society at large. Criminal justice was selected as the context of our analysis principally because this is where the differences between common law and civil law traditions are set to be more apparent. Subsequently, the examples of the Council of Europe and ECHR were chosen to illustrate the effect of harmonising factors on the understanding and representation of justice at the transnational level. This led us to question whether this type of agency may be more appropriate for a unified representation system of justice that can promote and indeed reconstruct a modern version of justice (fairness).

At the beginning of this paper we asked whether the division between civil law and common law traditions as well as the inconsistency of the system of representation of justice results in justice being distributed unfairly or unevenly. From the evidence presented, the answer should be negative though not definitive. The answer is negative for at least three reasons.

First, the representation system under discussion involves justice (the law), while justice (fairness) is to be found in all good human nature irrespective of the given justice system. We have reconstructed fairness which is primarily a value that is inherent in all individuals. On the other hand, justice (the law) is the object of justice systems which are set up to rectify injustices done to individuals and the society.

Second, when justice (the law) is distributed by the civil law and common law traditions and represented by their respective agents, fairness is always present, being part of nature and a *sine qua non* ingredient of justice (the law) irrespective of the given societal, cultural or political context. This explains why regional courts, such as the European Court of Human Rights, have a moral authority to impose legal standards and represent justice on behalf of national legal systems.

The value of fairness is also present irrespective of the given legal procedures. The distinction between common law and equity is to a large extent derived from Aristotle's recognition of equity as a kind of justice superior to legal justice; it is 'a correction of law where it is defective owing to its generality'.[37] Hence, it is not unattainable and should be pursued.

Finally, although common law and civil law traditions follow different procedures, it would be a mistake to oversimplify their distinction, since most substantive and procedural differences are gradually becoming obsolete.

References

Aristotle, *Nicomachean Ethics*.

Council of Europe, Report by Mr. A. Gil-Robles, Commissioner for Human Rights, on his visit to the United Kingdom 4th-12th November 2004, Strasbourg, Council of Europe, 2005.

M. Davies and H. Croall, *Criminal justice: an introduction to the criminal justice system in England and Wales*, Longman, 1998.

D. Davis, 'Victim Nation', *The Spectator*, August 2004, 2005.

F. Nietzsche, *Human, All Too Human*, Cambridge University Press, 1986.

T. Gavrielides, 'Some Mete-theoretical Questions for Restorative Justice', *Ratio Juris*, Vol. 18, No. 1, 2005, p. 84-106.

T. Gavrielides, 'Human Rights vs. Political Reality: The case of Europe's harmonising criminal justice systems', *International Journal of Comparative Criminology*, Vol. 5, No. 2, 2005, p. 60-84.

T. Gavrielides, 'Human Rights and customer satisfaction with public services: a relationship discovered', *International Journal of Human Rights*, Vol. 13, No. 1, 2009.

T. Gavrielides and D. Coker, 'Restoring Faith: Resolving the Catholic Church's sexual scandals through restorative justice: working paper I', *Contemporary Justice Review*, Vol. 8, No. 4, 2005, p. 345.

T. Gavrielides, 'Human rights vs Political reality: The case of Europe's harmonising criminal justice systems', *International Journal of Comparative Criminology*, Vol. 5, No. 2, 2005, p. 60.

H. Hart, *The concept of law*, Oxford University Press, 1961.

T. Hobbes, *The Elements of Law, Natural and Politics*, 1889, Ed. F. Tönnies, including 'Short Tract on First Principles', 1889 (written 1630-36)

P. Jenkins, 'Clergy sexual abuse: The symbolic politics of a social problem', in J. Best, *Images of issues: Typifying contemporary social problems*, Aldine de Gruyter, 1989, p. 105.

Institute of Public Policy Research (IPPR), F. Butler, *Human Rights: Who needs them? Using Human Rights in the Voluntary Sector*, IPPR, 2004.

---

[37] Aristotle, *Nicomahean Ethics*, 15-1136.

F. Klug, 'The Human Rights Act Research Unit. Target of the tabloids', *The Guardian*, 14th July 2000.

f. Klug, *Value for a godless age*, Penguin Books, 2000, p. 13.

J. Mill, *Utilitarianism, On Liberty, Considerations on Representative Government*, Everyman, 1993.

Plato's *Republic*, esp. Thrasymachus.

Resolution (78) 35 of the Committee of Ministers, acting under A5, adopted on 27 June 1978.

PART III

ECONOMICS PERSPECTIVES
OF REPRESENTATION OF JUSTICE

Representation of Justice
in Law and Economics

Bruno DEFFAINS and Samuel FEREY

BETA, University of Nancy 2 and CNRS

I. Introduction: Justice as a Black Box?

From Smith, writing both the *Wealth of Nations* and the Theory of Moral Sentiments to Walras and the general equilibrium representation of exchange as an impersonal, impartial, and therefore fair, mechanism to determine the prices on the markets; from Rawls and its use of rational action theory in order to solve social contract theory to welfare economics; from libertarian economics to Marxian economics, economics has always been very close to normative considerations about justice. However, mostly, economics deals directly with normative topics as moral, legal or political philosophy and few interests were devoted to positive analysis of justice as a social phenomenon.

Since the 1980s law and economics literature, initially developed in the United States, deals explicitly with the trial process, the organisation of judicial system or the determinants of litigation. Adapting traditional economic tools – rational action theory, optimisation processes and equilibrium – to the study of litigation, law and economics tries to provide a theoretical representation of justice, defined here as the process by which legal conflicts are solved inside the system of courts. Such a representation was needed for at least two main reasons.

First, this approach captures some important determinants of litigation and insists on costs, individual strategies or uses of information by litigants while trial proceeds over time. Economics of litigation highlights a true *economy of trial* which is also a determinant of justice.[1]

---

[1] Obviously, the special features of the American judiciary system have influenced law and economics literature. Some topics such as expenditure and cost of a trial, settlement of cases or bargaining – like the plea bargaining procedure – are clearly impor-

Second, economics of litigation and economics of law complement each other: the latter aims at predicting the effects of legal rules on individual behaviour, the former aims at understanding how rules are applied and interpreted by courts. In other words, the main task of theoretical and empirical law and economics is nowadays to propose a comprehensive view of legal phenomena which could integrate the mechanisms of creation and interpretation of law with the analysis of the consequences of law and the economics and litigation in a coherent framework. Therefore, economics meets legal theory since the role of judges is now considered by legal theory as the heart of legal phenomena. Legal scholarship is particularly concerned itself with how the practices controlling adjudication affect the creation of law by courts. Economics cannot ignore the key role of judge in application, interpretation and creation of laws.

The economics of legal dispute is nowadays a large field of research and the progress on its analysis has been impressive. Even if it would be impossible to take account of each contribution, the economics of litigation share a common representation of justice. The first building block of this representation is to focus on litigants as rational actors taking account of resources needed to succeed. Costs are treated as constraints which influence litigants' choices: asserting a claim, negotiating an agreement with their opponent or expending resources to win their case for example. Yet, summarizing economics of litigation as only a cost saving analysis would be mistaken. Indeed, the second building block of this representation deals with the individual's conduct. The economics of litigation has also enriched our understanding of trials by showing the importance of individual strategies, and the use of available information. The main limit of this representation is to more or less underestimate the role of judges. Justice and the trial are mainly driven by litigants' choices and the judge is still a black box. The main interest of contemporary researches in law and economics is the attempt at opening the black box.

This paper is organized in three parts. First, we present the key elements of the representation of justice in traditional models of litigation. We focus mainly on the constraints litigants face when a legal dispute occurs. Two elements are most important: the costs and the use of information by litigants (I Litigation and surplus). Then, we present how law and economics literature adapts rational action theory to the study of

---

tant in an American context. Yet, such features may also be found in continental judicial systems: the programs of immunity in European antitrust law or the abilities for litigants to make a 'settlement' in civil law in order to save the cost of trials are some obvious examples.

the courts. The litigation process is seen as a sequential decision making process where litigants have several options. Their decision is whether to negotiate an agreement or to go to trial (II. Representing trial as a decision making process). Lastly, we question the representation of the judge and justice in these models. By exclusively focusing on litigants, they tend to underestimate the role played by judges in the resolution of conflict and treat judges as a black box. In our view, providing a theory of the role of judge and opening the black box are the most urgent tasks inside both the theoretical and empirical law and economics field. Analysis is still in progress in relation to these tasks and none of the existing theory fits very well with the importance of the role of the judge in our legal systems. In fact, this conclusion is not pessimistic. It seems that legal theory in general faces the same difficulty: be able to give an all embracing theory of the role of judge (III. Taking judges seriously).

II. Litigation and Surplus

From the economic point of view, the trial is represented as a conflict between litigants. In the paradigmatic case – as in most of civil trial for example – a plaintiff (P) has suffered harm and has a claim against a defendant (D) who is alleged to be liable for the damage. From the underlying event – the accident for example – to final adjudication, the trial is described by law and economics as a complex process of decision-making by litigants. The basic models representing legal disputes consist in systematically studying the determinants of these choices and mainly the two most important ones are the issue of cost and the availability of information for parties to make their decisions.

Representing parties' situations is made by using the rational action theory. Mostly, a Net Expected Value (NEV) is defined for the plaintiff and an Expected Loss (EL) for the defendant. The Net Expected Value equals the awards the plaintiff expects from the trial times the probability he will prevail minus the cost of litigation. Symmetrically, the Expected Loss for the defendant is generally defined as the award the defendant expects to lose times his estimates of the probability to lose the case plus the costs of litigation. In simple models, this probability is given and depends on the merits of the case but it should be noted that this hypothesis is provisional and will be reversed in the researches presented further. Let:

D_p, the monetary value of the damages the plaintiff expects if he wins,

D_d, the monetary value of the damages the defendants expects to pay if he loses,

P_p, the subjective probability of the plaintiff to win,

P_d, the subjective probability of the defendant to lose,

T_p, the costs born by the plaintiff in a court case,

T_d, the costs born by the defendant in a court case,

N_p, the transaction costs of the plaintiff for the negotiation,

N_d, the transaction costs of the defendant for the negotiation,

Negotiation is considered less costly than going to court:

$$(T_p + T_d) - (N_p + N_d) > 0$$

If the parties are risk neutral, the subjective value of the payment hoped for by each of them corresponds to the monetary value of the damages expected, multiplied by the subjective probability of this party of seeing the decision given in favour of the plaintiff.[2] In this way, we obtain an expected gain for the plaintiff ($G_p = P_p\ D_p$) and an expected loss for the defendant ($G_d = P_d.D_d$). In the hypothesis where the parties' expectations coincide ($P_p = P_d$ and $D_p = D_d$), the expected gain for the plaintiff is equal to the loss expected by the defendant. It is thus advisable to include the costs born in both cases in the model, supposing that if it goes to court each party bears their own costs of the proceedings. The overall value of cooperative outcome then corresponds to the net transfer (hypothetically zero) less the transaction costs to be born ($N_p + N_d$). The court ruling value corresponds to the net transfer received ($G_p - G_d$) less the legal costs ($T_p + T_d$).

So, it is easy to show that, under certain circumstances, a surplus exists. The surplus obtained is arrived at simply from the difference between the two values:

$$S = - (N_p + N_d) - [(G_p - G_d) - (T_p + T_d)]$$

that we can write:

$$S = [(T_p + T_d) - (N_p + N_d)] + (G_d - G_p)$$

Basic models require there to be a surplus since this feature of the trial process is essential to explain the choice of the parties during the trial process. It is easy to understand the fact that a surplus occurs has a huge bearing on the decisions taken by parties at the different stages of litigation. We just include some element concerning a surplus before further analysing the behaviour of litigants.

The biggest advantage of the basic model is that it is easily adaptable to a large number of phenomena. Generally speaking, some previous factors, presented as exogenous – costs and probabilities for example –

---

[2]   In fact, in most models, we accept that the amount of damages granted by the court to the victim is known by both parties so that the outcome expected by them only differs by their perception of whether they are likely to win or lose.

may be easily treated as endogenous. Firstly, the outcome of the trial may be determined by the resources that parties expend to win the case and to influence the probability of succeeding. The probability of winning depends on the efforts and expenditures parties put into the trial. In this case, p depends on C_p and C_d and the model may be rewritten with $p(C_p, C_d)$. The Optimisation process indicates that a litigant will invest in his trial until the marginal cost be equal to the marginal benefit, that is to say, when the marginal increase of probability times the amount of the award is equal to the marginal cost.

Secondly, in some cases, the individual costs are influenced by external effects. This may be so when the current litigation has an effect on future litigation for at least one party. In civil law for example, when litigation pits a plaintiff against an insurance company, the insurance company may expect a preclusive effect in case of adjudication in favour of plaintiff. Therefore, the amount of award for the insurance company is stronger that the amount of award for the plaintiff. An external factor creates a discrepancy since the expectation of a loss increases and becomes stronger than the expectation of a gain. Therefore, the bargaining process disappears in this case and explains why cases are not settled. Some procedural rules, like the class action in the United States for example, have an economic rationality and can be understood as legal devices internalizing external costs.

Conclusion: The basic models and its extensions developed by scholars of law and economics insist on the fact a legal dispute is costly and therefore, a surplus may appear to be divided between litigants. We have to notice that a question remains: how such an agreement may be reached by litigants? The fact that a surplus exists is not sufficient to assert that an effective agreement will always be reached. Dealing with this topic, the economics of litigation literature represents a legal dispute as a decision making process by which rational litigants will try to settle the case. As we will show, the cognitive process by which litigation is resolved becomes the core of this representation of justice. This representation adds new essential determinants of litigation to the basic model as expectations, individual strategy or use of information. Therefore, even if within classical models, costs appear as the key elements of a trial, it would be a mistake to consider that it is the only meaning of economics of litigation as a whole when it becomes clear that the heart of legal conflict lies in the informational and cognitive aspect of the interaction between litigants.

III. Representing Trial as a Decision Making Process

Having shown a surplus may exist, one of the main questions of law and economics has long been to study the litigants' decision concerning the process by which an agreement could be reached between them in order to save litigation costs. That is why one of the main topics of the literature is to study whether the parties have an interest in settling the case or to go to court. The question is difficult because the only existence of a surplus is not necessarily the only inducement for the parties to come to an agreement. In order to establish precisely in theory the determinants of an agreement between parties, law and economics uses a representation of justice as a sequential decision making process. At each stage of the litigation process, individuals make choices depending upon the behaviour of the other party and procedural rules: the choice for the plaintiff to assert or not to assert a claim, the choice for both litigants to bargain and settle the case, to expend more or less in order to win, to go to court... As we will show, even if surplus exists and could be divided by settlement, the trial process itself may compel an individual from reaching a satisfactory agreement. In other words, social efficiency (i. e. minimisation of costs) is not always reached by rational players. Strategic behaviour, errors in expectations, optimism or asymmetries of information are key elements to explain such a failure of negotiation. We focus here on the two main reasons identified by literature, optimism of litigants (a. Optimism) and strategic behaviour (b. Bargaining behaviour and asymmetries of information).

A. Optimism

Very simply, the choice between settlement and adjudication may be represented in the basic model by comparing the different cases concerning the surplus. If the expected surplus is negative, the parties will always prefer to resort to a judge. On the other hand, an agreement should arise spontaneously as soon as the surplus shows signs of being positive. Three cases are theoretically possible:

(1) $(G_d - G_p) > - (T_p + T_d) + (N_p + N_d)$: agreement

(2) $(G_d - G_p) = - (T_p + T_d) + (N_p + N_d)$: indifference

(3) $(G_d - G_p) < - (T_p + T_d) + (N_p + N_d)$: court

If the parties' expectations coincide, the left term is cancelled out and the outcome of the conflict becomes transactional as legal costs are seen to exceed negotiation costs.

However, for many commentators, negotiation often fails. This paradox induces them to seek some reasons why rational individuals do not reach an satisfaction agreement. The first explanation comes from the earlier models of litigation in the 1970s[3] and puts the stress on the 'optimism' of litigants. The bargaining process disappears if plaintiff and defendant do not make their choice with the same estimation of the probability of succeeding. For example, if $P_p > P_d$ and/or $D_p > D_d$, both parties can be said to be optimistic because the plaintiff hopes to win an expected amount greater than the defendant's expected loss.[4] By extension, if optimism abounds ($G_d < G_p$), the left term becomes negative and the parties will opt for the intervention of a judge to solve the conflict. Trials can be generated when parties have not the same expectations about the outcome probability.

In non-strategic models, the outcome of conflict depends essentially on the level of optimism or pessimism. It is only when the parties are optimistic that the outcome requires a court to intervene. On this basis, commentators have also endeavoured to anticipate the effect of a change in certain parameters such as the two parties' risk aversion, the amount of damages (i.e. the harshness of the court), the costs of proceedings (lawyer's fees) or the transaction costs. For example, it is shown that the raising of damages granted to the victim increases the probability of a legal outcome by confirming the optimism of the parties.[5]

The main theoretical and empirical problem of this explanation is to explain the reason why litigants are optimistic. It is all the more difficult to explain because many of these commentators consider litigants as rational individuals and the use of an 'optimism assumption' violates the theory of rationality as if the litigant does not use all available information. That is why other explanations are to be found in the literature of law and economics.

B. Bargaining Behaviour and Asymmetries of Information

Since the beginning of the 1980s, a lot of bargaining models have been proposed to explain the failure of negotiation. From the above analysis it appears that where there is a positive surplus there should not be a trial. This conclusion is especially appropriate where both parties have the same perception of the outcome ($G_d = G_p$). The arguments used nevertheless give rise to a problem because prior to the courts' decision

---

[3] W. Landes, 'An Economic Analysis of the Courts', *Journal of Law and Economics*, Vol. 14, 1971, p. 61; J.P. Gould. 'The Economics of Legal Conflicts', *Journal of Legal Studies*, Vol. 2, 1973, p. 279.

[4] The reverse is true f $P_p < P_d$ and $D_p < D_d$. In this case, the amount the plaintiff expects to receive is less than the defendant expects to lose. This shows pessimism on the part of both parties and an agreement is more likely.

[5] R. Cooter and D.L Rubinfeld, 'Economic Analysis of legal Disputes and their Resolution', *Journal of Economic Literature*, Vol. 27, 1989, p. 1067.

the parties are implicitly unaware of the eminently strategic nature of the situation in which they find themselves.

Cooter in particular raises this question when addressing the Coase theory. In fact, Cooter criticizes Coase for being over-optimistic when considering the private transactions which, even supposing rational behaviour and zero transaction costs, do not necessarily lead to efficiency[6]: 'The error in the bargaining version of the Coase Theorem is to suppose that the obstacle to cooperation is the cost of communicating rather than the strategic nature of the situation.'[7]

According to Cooter, the main feature of pretrial bargaining is to reach an agreement on a sharing of the stakes of the negotiation. Moreover, this bargaining is not the equivalent of a zero-sum game, i.e. a game of simple redistribution where nothing is created or destroyed. Quite the contrary, negotiation implies the existence of a surplus in the mind of at least one of the parties. If the outcome is cooperative, the parties agree on a sharing of the stakes including the surplus. However, as with the problem raised concerning the prisoner's dilemma, there is no guarantee that this result will be achieved *a priori*. Over-optimism of the parties in a dispute would thus not be the main reason for a judge to intervene. First and foremost, it is a problem of allocating the surplus within the context of negotiation.

In their article entitled 'Bargaining in the Shadow of the Law', Cooter, Marks et Mnookin[8] apply this idea and develop a non-cooperative game model to cover pretrial negotiation. They analyse the negotiating process as a dynamic game of sharing with simultaneous moves. Each party, in the hope of maximising its expected utility makes an offer to obtain a share of the loot. As in the 'optimistic model', the loot is defined as the sum of the gains obtained by each party when avoiding a solution through the courts. But, negotiation henceforth takes place within a context of uncertainty as to the way in which the players react to the offers made by the other side. The authors do admit that none of the players know the strategy of the opponent at the time the offer is made. They are only aware of their opponents' strategy distribu-

---

[6] R. Cooter, 'The Cost of Coase', *Journal of Legal Studies*, Vol. 11, 1982, p. 1.

[7] Cooter opposes the Coase theorem with what he calls Hobbes theorem (Cooter, 1982). The role of the law would be to reduce inefficiency linked to the nature of the negotiation. In practice, this would mean not allowing the parties to contemplate solutions in which they would all lose out. The Hobbes theorem, by eradicating the possibility of inefficient results, would thus lead to a very nit-picking attitude in the development of contract law.

[8] R. Cooter, S. Marks and R. Mnookin, 'Bargaining in the Shadow of the Law: A Testable Model of Strategic Behavior', *Journal of Legal Studies*, Vol. 11, 1982, p. 225R.

tion, each one believing he has been allocated winning odds not dependant on the context (i.e. without identifying his moment within the negotiation process). The Bayesian equilibrium in this game is attained when the beliefs of each party are consistent with the way in which the opponent behaves in the negotiation process.

The intuition is the following: if one party suddenly increases its claims in the negotiation, this means that not only the coveted share of the loot has increased, but also the chances of going to court. This is because the likelihood of the total amount requested by the two parties being less than the stakes of the negotiation is lower. Conversely, by adopting a 'more accommodating' strategy, a party increases the likelihood of reaching an agreement, but reduces the amount obtained if the deal is indeed made. Theoretically, sequential offers from the parties converge progressively, but as the process is limited in time (trial date) the matter will have to be decided by the court if the offers have not converged enough. In the game of Cooter *et al.*, this result becomes possible when one party makes aggressive or outrageous offers and the opposing party is not willing to sufficiently reduce his claims.[9] The important outcome is that it is not necessary that both parties view a surplus negatively to explain the intervention of a judge in a dispute. As Cooter states,

> bargaining is more likely to break down because miscalculation of an opponent's behaviour is more likely. Players with the same observable traits but different unobservable traits will pursue different strategies. However, the expectations which a player has about his opponent are formed on the basis of observable traits alone.[10]

By looking at the progression of the negotiation, the suggested model already goes one step further than those of Landes and Gould. Henceforth, the beliefs of the parties are consistent in equilibrium in the sense that they commit no systematic errors (subjective probability matches objective frequency) but the likelihood of the negotiation failing is still not zero. This analysis also brings into question some principles which are taken for granted. For example, the 'optimistic model' gave an even greater probability to the coercive outcome because the transaction costs during negotiation were high compared to the cost of proceedings. Indeed, as the parties act in such a way as to minimize their costs, raising transaction costs makes court a more attractive prospect as proceedings costs remain unchanged. The share-out model, however, gives the legal outcome a lower probability when transaction costs increase as this

---

[9] *Ibid.*

[10] *Ibid.*

encourages the parties to become more conciliatory and reduce their claims, thus favouring an agreement.

Compared to the 'optimistic models', strategic models generally offer a richer description of legal process whether or not it arrives at an agreement between the parties. A hypothesis of asymmetrical information is introduced into virtually all models. This is simple and linked to the holding of private information by one of the parties. This type of situation is common in the majority of disputes: the plaintiff may be better informed of the importance of the damage or the defendant may hold further information on the determination of his alleged offence. In the same way, one party may hold an information advantage over his rival about the strict attitude of the court or on the validity of certain proofs. The models may in fact be distinguished according to whether the better informed party plays first or last. If the informed party plays last, confidential information will not be passed on whereas if he plays first, the strategic transmission of confidential information will have to be considered as an indication of how the case will be decided.

Conclusion: Considering trial as a complex decision making process offers a rich description of justice. But we should note that the models are based on the litigants themselves. Very few elements are concerned with judges. In the previous models, the judge's decision is mainly modelled as a probability to win or lose. In fact, the complex reasoning behind a judge's adjudication is made not only by the strict application of law but also by creation of new precedents – in common law – or new interpretations – in statute law – and is summarized as a probability of an uncertain event. This crude representation of the role of judge leads to law and economics dealing directly with modelling judge's conduct in litigation.

IV. Taking Judges Seriously

As Posner asserts 'at the heart of economic analysis of law is a mystery that is also an embarrassment: how to explain judicial behaviour in economic terms.[11] Law and economics has dealt with this puzzle by drawing on two main research programs. The first one, focused on selective mechanisms, attempts to think about justice without the judges. This approach can be said to concentrate exclusively on the 'demand side' of the interaction in litigation. Within this framework, litigants develop the evolution of law through their choice to bring proceedings or not. Yet, this representation of justice cannot be completely relevant

---

[11] R. Posner, 'What do Judges Maximize? (The Same Thing Everybody Else Does)', *Supreme Court Economic Review*, Vol. 3, 1993 p. 2.

since it does not take account of the main feature of justice, namely the judges' behaviour. On the contrary, the second main field of research considers the judge as a utility maximizer. Judges are treated like any other individual seeking their own interests when they decide cases or interpret laws. These models insist on the 'supply side' of litigation interaction and implicitly suppose that judges are free to decide cases as they want. The only constraints they face are the decisions of others judges (and notably superior courts). Even if these two frameworks are fruitful, they appear unable to provide a comprehensive view of justice. The Judge is still a black box (a. Justice without the judge or the judge without justice?). Opening this black box is the main task of contemporary law and economics (b. New approaches: cognitive turn and interpretative turn).

A. Justice without the Judge or the Judge without Justice?

One of the major claims of law and economics literature was that common law – that is to say judge-made law – is efficient. When Posner started to test it on different legal fields in the middle of the 1970s, he was generally concerned with the contrast between statute law and common law. In a sense, the same contrast nowadays still applies in recent *Doing business* reports published by the World Bank.[12] Yet, how do the economics of law represent an efficient lawmaking process? The crucial element to consider is the difficulty of testing such a representation. In Posner's works, for example, tests consist in examining some particular fields of law and estimating the efficiency of rules. But such a method strongly depends on the evaluation of costs – as transaction costs for example – which is a difficult task. Similarly, the recent study made by the World Bank concerning the economic positions in statute law countries and in common law countries may be due to other factors connected with judicial systems without any causative relationship between a judicial system and efficiency.

That is why, within theoretical and empirical law and economics literature, the important point has been to explain how the outcome of a case occurs or does not occur under Common law. In other words, which mechanisms could explain efficient lawmaking? The answer lies in explaining how judges make their decisions, decide cases and also make law by ignoring precedents or changing previous interpretations.

The first set of researches is based on the attempts to represent justice as a selective mechanism of precedents. In common law systems, litigated cases may lead to legal change and judges are the main source

---

[12] The World Bank project can be easily connected to the Law and Finance program developed by La Porta, Lopez de Silanes, Shleifer and Vishny (1998).

of legal change through new precedents. Evolutionary models like those of Rubin[13] and Priest[14] rely on the idea that inefficient rules are more litigated than efficient ones. In the case of inefficient rules, the expected loss by one party is greater than the expected gain for the other because the loss outweighs the gain due precisely to inefficiency. Applying traditional models of litigation, it can be said there is no range of settlement in such a case: going to court is inevitable and rational.

Therefore litigants have incentives to litigate inefficient rules. And as inefficient rules are more litigated than efficient ones, they are more likely to be overturned than efficient ones. The key point is to be aware that it is not necessary for these models to assume that judges consciously aim at efficiency. The process can operate without any courts' preferences on efficiency – at least, judges must not disfavour efficiency too much.[15] Within these frameworks, the lawmaking process has some similarity with the market process since an efficient outcome spontaneously and unconsciously emerges exclusively from rational litigants' behaviour.[16] The evolutionary research program is extremely ambitious since it aims at modelling justice without any action by the judge in the process. But there has been much criticism of it. We may just note that the selective thesis faces the same problem as the basic model. Firstly, as litigation is represented as a game dividing a surplus, litigants may seek to challenge efficient rules in order to obtain a larger share of the surplus. Secondly, interest pressure groups may act on litigation in their own interests which is not necessarily efficient.[17] As such, these models have contributed more to the understanding of the condition under which efficient evolution may occur than they have to demonstrating that such an evolution mechanism towards efficiency actually exists.

At the opposite of these models of 'justice without judges', a second representation of the lawmaking process is developed by law and eco-

---

[13] P. Rubin, 'Why is the Common Law Efficient', *Journal of Legal Studies*, Vol. 6, 1977, p. 51.

[14] G. Priest, 'The Common Law Process and the Selection of Efficient Rules', *Journal of Legal Studies*, Vol. 6, 1997, p. 65.

[15] R. Cooter and D.L Rubinfeld, 'Economic Analysis of legal Disputes and their Resolution', *op. cit.*

[16] This literature is close to Austrian law and economics approach which insists, with Hayek for example, on the evolutionary nature of law. They share the idea that law is a product of a spontaneous order without any plan or purpose. However, this literature is also very different insofar as the analytical tools are still neoclassical (rationality hypothesis for example) while Austrian authors strongly criticize the use of such tools in economics.

[17] J. Hirschleiffer, 'Evolutionary Models in Economics and Law', *Research in Law and Economics*, Vol. 4, 1982.

nomics focused on judges' behaviour. This second research program treats the judge as anyone else in economics that is to say as a utility maximizer. According to this representation, solving litigation and/or creating a precedent is a choice for a judge.[18] Given the constraints and preferences, it is possible for economics to treat this choice like a rational choice.[19] For example, for a judge to ignore or reverse precedents may influence his promotion and thus usefulness. Some tests of this hypothesis have been made in the United States without being completely convincing and no true evidence has been given to validate the influence of judges' individual utility on their decisions.[20] In an important article, Zywicki[21] studies the institutional *prerequisite* for judges to behave efficiently and show how they may be influenced by pressure groups. In any case, it appears difficult to link directly the utility function of judge, to the adjudication and efficiency of decisions.

Yet, representing judges' decisions as choices lead to more interesting results. Indeed, adjudication may be the result from different opinions. This is the case when more than one judge is involved in the decision. The voting paradox – and notably the Condorcet theory about the jury – may apply. This theory shows that irrational collective decisions may occur when aggregating individual preferences. Such results are useful to explain a judges decision when there are more than three judges. But these researches are always specific and may not be considered as a general economic theory of adjudication.

To conclude, these two perspectives – justice without judges and judges without justice – may not be considered as a comprehensive theory of adjudication. If they help to explain some aspects of adjudication and the lawmaking process, they are not able to build a general and comprehensive theory of justice and a lot of studies have got to be undertaken. This is so because the perspectives do not take seriously the fact lawmaking is, above all an interpretative task namely the applica-

---

18   From the legal point of view, this representation is very close to American realist programme in legal theory which insists on the power of the judges when they choose a particular solution. For realists, the one who has the power to interpret law is actually the true creator of the law.

19   See for example, Posner, 1993, It should be noted that this representation appears quite recently. More precisely, an author like Posner uses very often this representation but has waited for a long time (see Posner, 1993) before systematizing it.

20   M. Cohen, 'The Motives of Judges: Empirical Evidence from Antitrust Sentencing', *International Review in Law and Economics*, Vol. 12, 1992; O. Ashenfelter, T. Eisenbert and S. Schwab, 'Politics and the Judiciary: The Influence of Judicial Background on Case Outcomes', *Journal of Legal Studies*, Vol. 24, 1995, p. 257.

21   T. Zywicki, 'The Rise and Fall of Efficiency in the Common Law: A Supply-Side Analysis', *Northwestern University Law Review*, Vol. 97, 2003, p. 1551.

tion of a general rule to a particular case or the attribution of a meaning to a law, a statute or a precedent. They tend to consider adjudication either as a mechanical outcome of the litigation process itself – driven by individual determinants: choices and economic optimisation – or as mechanical outcome of a process of optimisation by judges themselves. None of these two perspectives make it possible to solve the 'mystery'.

In our view, solving this mystery requires that an economic representation of justice be constructed which takes account of the very special attributes of judge and litigation. In these circumstances, is it possible to consider as one the legal aspects of a trial and the economics of trial, interpretative aspects of law and economics ones? For most legal scholars, the only fact that legal adjudication is an interpretative task is sufficient to consider law and economics irrelevant: how a framework based on rationality and optimisation – that is to say on calculus – could take account of 'meaning' and 'interpretation'? Even if the criticism is well thought through, it is not completely convincing. Within law and economics, new researches – theoretical and empirical – take judges and interpretation seriously.

B. New Approaches: Cognitive Turn and Interpretative Turn

New researches focus – from behavioural law and economics to game theory – on the cognitive aspects of litigation. It seems to be a fruitful field within which to analyze litigation from the twofold legal and economics point of view. In insisting on the cognitive aspects of the trial process, a fresh perspective is given on this topic. Behavioural law and economics appears to be one of the most important developments concerning economics of justice and litigation. The aim of behavioural law and economics is to explain the individual misconceptions about judicial decisions. As in the optimistic approach, trial is due to errors made by litigants about their probability to win. But the explanation is not a more or less *ad hoc* one as in the optimistic approach but is deeply rooted in psychology. By assuming – contrary to the standard neoclassical approach – that the individual's abilities for computing information are limited, this approach highlights numerous phenomena which may alter the rational behaviour of people.

The legal side of the problem of litigation is represented as a conflict of interpretation on the meaning of legal norms. The true nature of a legal dispute is above all due to the fact that the parties make some divergent interpretations about what law says. By insisting on this feature, we actually hold the point of view, which fits well with contemporary legal theory that law is considered as mainly an interpretative and hermeneutic practice.[22] There are a lot of reasons why divergent interpretations may arise. This is the case notably because legal rules are never clear by themselves.[23] And contemporary legal theory acknowledges that law is an in depth interpretative process[24]: the topics of the methods of interpretation, the nature of interpretation and the consequences of the judges ability to attribute – or to determine – a specific meaning to a law are now the heart of the legal theory.[25] Economists who are interested in law need to take account of this feature in order to analyze litigation: it is precisely because the meaning of a norm needs always to be reconstructed by the judiciary that conflict may arise. This feature has some huge consequences for the economic analysis of litigation.

From the economic side of the problem, this means that conflict arises notably from the different expectations of individuals on the meaning of the law.[26] As law is always unclear, it is possible for individuals to misconstrue its true meaning (at least, the meaning that the judge will attribute to the norm and the manner by which the judge will apply the law to a particular case). Heuristics may be used to describe some aspects of the cognitive processes by which people will interpret legal norms and by which such a judgment – more or less intuitive – will be the basis for their assessment of the probability of winning or losing the case.

Finally, from a law *and* economics point of view, the two topics (a/ the meaning of law – and conflict about this meaning – and b/ the assessment of probabilities) are the two sides of a same coin: the cognitive mechanisms by which people make judgments about the meaning of

---

[22] See for example: Troper, 2000; Ricoeur, 1995; Frydman, 2005. Actually, the debates concerning the nature of legal interpretation are numerous. However, a lot of legal theory debates deal now with the consequences of the 'interpretative turn' on the nature of the law, the role and the power of judiciary or the methods of legal interpretation.

[23] For example, legal norms are often general and need to be applied to a particular case. The deduction from a general legal statement induces a cognitive process of interpretation to know to what extent the case fits with the law and to determine the meaning of law. The key-feature of this process is obviously the judge insofar as he is the legitimate authority to determine the meaning of law.

[24] B. Frydman, *Le Sens des Lois*, Bruylant, 2005.

[25] M. Troper, 'Une théorie réaliste de l'interprétation', in O. Jouanjan, *Théories réalistes du droit*, Annales de la faculté de droit, Presses universitaires de Strasbourg, Vol. 4, 2000, p. 43.

[26] If laws were completely clear and determined, people would never go to court and a settlement will always be possible.

law and so assess the probabilitiesof winning or losing the case.[27] It is precisely to analyze these two aspects in a unique framework that the concepts developed by behavioral law and economics are useful.

According to this literature, judgments under uncertainty are made thanks to rules of thumb called 'heuristics'. Sometimes, these heuristics may be efficient but sometimes they can lead to systematic errors and some biases can appear. Usually, three heuristics are distinguished: availability heuristic, anchor heuristic and case-based decision. The availability heuristic applies where people 'tend to think that risks is more serious when an incident is readily called to mind'[28]; the anchoring may take place when people use an initial value – whose origin may be irrational – as the basis for their judgments; finally, the case-based decisions may arise when people reason by calling in mind a past case in order to make a judgment about a new case. One of the key-elements of the heuristics literature is to show that the use of such rules of thumb may induce systematic errors on the true probability of an event. More generally, we may consider the classical bias (optimistic bias, hindsight bias and self-serving bias) as such rules of thumb: people tend to be optimistic and an overconfidence in risk judgment may appear. They tend to like the status-quo or they may overestimate the probability of an event simply because this event has occurred.

Each of these biases may have huge consequences on litigation. For example, a famous experiment made by Babcock *et al.* shows that the expectations of litigants concerning their chance to win depends less on the objective merits of the case than on their role in the trial: if they are defendants, they tend to underestimate the probability of losing while if they are plaintiffs, they tend to overestimate the probability of winning. The authors apply here the self-serving bias literature: the individual transforms the objective probabilities and makes a systematic error in the estimation of the occurrence of an uncertain event. This example illustrates very well the fact that attitudes towards risks are essentially a *judgement*: a mix of calculus and interpretation. Litigation – an error in the optimisation process – is due to a bias because 'people interpret

---

[27] More generally, the title of the classical book from Kahneman and Tversky is *Heuristics and Bias: Judgment under uncertainty*. It is very clear that what Kahneman wants to build is a general theory of judgment that is to say a theory of the cognitive mechanisms by which people make some judgments and how these judgments may influence rational behavior.

[28] Ch. Jolls, C. Sunstein and R. Thaler, 'A Behavioral Approach to Law and Economics', in Cass R. Sunstein (ed.), *Behavioral Law and Economics*, Cambridge University Press, 1998, p. 13.

information in a self-serving manner'.[29] Legal rules are signals but like any signals they may be misconceived or misinterpreted and alter rational behaviour. Therefore, a explanation of litigation on economics grounds must take account of the judgements actually exercised by litigants.

Such developments in the economics of the litigation field seem particularly fruitful. Not only because these researches give some foundation for optimistic models but chiefly because they have started to propose a unique framework dealing with rational and interpretative aspects of justice. The cognitive processes that occur during a trial play here the key-role for the explanation. By putting psychology of trial and legal theory together, behavioural law and economics may enrich economics. It also puts together some known results in the game theory as the importance of conventions, fairness or focal points in the solution of some strategic game through litigations. One of the main interests is therefore to design procedural rules which are able to remove bias from individual judgements.

References

O. Ashenfelter, T Eisenbert and S. Schwab, 'Politics and the Judiciary: The Influence of Judicial Background on Case Outcomes', *Journal of Legal Studies*, Vol. 24, 1995, p. 257.

L. Babcock, G. Loewenstein, S. Issacharoff and C. Camerer, 'Biased Judgemnts of fairness in Bargaining', *American Economic Review*, Vol. 85, 1995, p. 1337.

L. Bebchuk, 'Litigation and Settlement under imperfect information', *RAND Journal of Economics*, Vol. 15, 1984, p. 404.

M. Cohen, 'The Motives of Judges: Empirical Evidence from Antitrust Sentencing', *International Review in Law and Economics*, Vol. 12, 1992.

R. Cooter, 'The Cost of Coase', *Journal of Legal Studies*, Vol. 11, 1982, p. 1.

R. Cooter, S. Marks and R. Mnookin, 'Bargaining in the Shadow of the Law: A Testable Model of Strategic Behavior', *Journal of Legal Studies*, Vol. 11, 1982, p. 225R.

R. Cooter and D.L. Rubinfeld, 'Economic Analysis of legal Disputes and their Resolution', *Journal of Economic Literature*, Vol. 27, 1989, p. 1067.

B. Frydman, *Le Sens des Lois*, Bruylant, 2005.

J.P. Gould, 'The Economics of Legal Conflicts', *Journal of Legal Studies*, Vol. 2, 1973, p. 279.

---

[29] L. Babcock, G. Loewenstein, Samuel Issacharoff and Colin Camerer, 'Biased Judgemnts of fairness in Bargaining', *American Economic Review*, Vol. 85, 1995, p. 1337. Another famous example deals with hindsight bias: judges or juries tend to convince defendant since they overestimate the probability of an accident simply because this event has occurred.

J. Hirschleiffer, 'Evolutionary Models in Economics and Law', *Research in Law and Economics*, Vol. 4. 1982.

Ch. Jolls and C. Sunstein, 'Debiasing Through Law', *Journal of Legal Studies*, Vol. 35, 2006, p. 199.

Ch. Jolls, C. Sunstein and R. Thaler. 'A Behavioral Approach to Law and Economics', in Cass R. Sunstein (ed.), *Behavioral Law and Economics*, Cambridge University Press, 1998, p. 13.

D. Kahneman and Sh. Frederick. 'Representativeness Revisited: Attribute Substitution in Intuitive Judgment', in Th. Gilovich, D. Griffin and D. Kahneman, *Heuristics and Biases: The Psychology of Intuitive Judgment*, Cambridge University Press, 2002, p. 49.

J. Kennan and R. Wilson. 'Bargaining with Private Information', *Journal of Economic Literature*, Vol. 3, 1993, p. 45.

B. Kobayashi and J. Parker, 'Civil Procedure', in B. Bouckaert and G. De Geest, *Encyclopaedia of Law and Economics*, Edward Elgar, 2000, p. 1.

W. Landes, 'An Economic Analysis of the Courts', *Journal of Law and Economics*, Vol. 14, 1971, p. 61.

G. Loewenstein, S. Issacharoff, C. Camerer and L. Babcock. 'Self-Serving Assessments of Fairness and Pretrial Bargaining', *Journal of Legal Studies*, Vol. 22, 1993, p. 135.

R. Posner, *Economic Analyis of Law*, Little Brown, 1992.

R. Posner, 'What do Judges Maximize? 'The Same Thing Everybody Else Does'', *Supreme Court Economic Review*, Vol. 3, 1993 p. 1.

G. Priest, 'The Common Law Process and the Selection of Efficient Rules', *Journal of Legal Studies*, Vol. 6, 1997, p. 65.

P. Ricoeur, 'Herméneutique juridique et herméneutique générale', in Paul Amselek *Interprétation et droit*, Bruylant, 1995, p. 175.

P. Rubin, 'Why is the Common Law Efficient', *Journal of Legal Studies*, Vol. 6, 1977, p. 51.

P. Rubin, 'Judge-Made Law', in B. Bouckaert and G. De Geest *Encyclopaedia of Law and Economics*, Edward Elgar, 1999, p. 543.

C. Sunstein, *Behavioral Law and Economics*, Cambridge University Press, 2000.

M. Troper, 'Une théorie réaliste de l'interprétation', in O. Jouanjan, *Théories réalistes du droit*, Annales de la faculté de droit, Presses universitaires de Strasbourg, Vol. 4, 2000, p. 43.

A. Tversky and D. Kahneman, *Heuristics and Biases*, Cambridge University Press, 1982.

A. Tversky, and D. Kahneman, 'Availability: A Heuristic for Judging Frequency and Probability', *Cognitive Psychology Vol.* 5, 1973, p. 207.

T. Zywicki, 'The Rise and Fall of Efficiency in the Common Law: A Supply-Side Analysis', *Northwestern University Law Review*, Vol. 97, 2003, p. 1551.

Representation of Justice and Companies Judicial Strategies in France

Didier DANET

École spéciale militaire de Saint-Cyr
CETIO Université de Rennes 1

I. Introduction

French public opinion has long been disenchanted with its judicial system. One exception to the rule: Louis IX. This king of France (13th century) is known for his image of piety and justice. The popular iconography shows him as an approachable and fair judge, sitting under an oak in front of the royal castle of Vincennes, making equitable and impartial judgements. However, Louis IX is a remarkable but isolated exception to the rule. Throughout history, most of the popular images of Justice have been negative ones. In many famous cases (Joan of Arc, Nicolas Fouquet, Jean Calas or Alfred Dreyfus for example), Justice is shown to be partial, incapable of establishing truth and subject to the most powerful institutions (Church, Government, military hierarchy...) The great French writers are usually severe with judges and the judicial system: La Fontaine, Pascal, Hugo, Zola, etc. all of them protest against the miscarriages of Justice and share the same message: '*Selon que vous serez puissant ou misérables, les jugements de cour vous feront noir ou blanc.*'[1] Not so long ago, the 'judicial disaster' in the so called 'Outreau case' created a general feeling of distrust against judges and obliged the government to reform Justice yet again.[2]

---

[1] 'According to whether you are powerful or poor, the judgments of courts will make you black or white.'

[2] A. Vallini et P. Houillon, Rapport fait au nom de la commission chargée de rechercher les causes des dysfonctionnements dans l'affaire dite d'Outreau et de formuler des propositions pour éviter leur renouvellement, Rapport d'enquête, Assemblée nationale, No. 3125, 6 juin 2006.

Such a negative and constant representation of Justice makes public opinion suspicious or even scared of the judicial system. Most opinion polls confirm this point. Insofar as individuals cannot choose their judges, this distrust is of no great practical consequence. But, in the particular case of commercial litigation, companies have an unquestionable freedom to tailor the legal argument or even to organize their own justice outside of the judicial courts and the rules of procedure. The image of Justice is then of great importance, for it influences, or even determines, the strategic behaviour of these companies as regards the problems all of them face in the business world. The starting point of this paper is the representation of justice in French public opinion, especially, in the opinion of business people. Does public opinion have a positive or negative image of Justice? What are the perceived characteristics of the judicial system? Do judges make good or bad decisions? Within this general image of Justice, the opinion of experts and business people is emphasized. In the second part of this paper, the strategic behaviour of companies *vis-à-vis* Justice is analyzed. Strategies which come into play prior to the lawsuit are distinguished from strategies which tend to manage the lawsuit. Both these strategies are influenced by the representation of Justice.

II. Representation of Justice, Public Opinion and the Opinion of the Business Community in France

Apart from the general feeling referred to the beginning of this paper, what do we know about the representation of Justice according to French public opinion? More precisely, what do business people think of the judicial establishment they are working in?

A. Justice and Public Opinion

Representation of Justice is the subject of many opinion polls. Most of these polls are designed and published on the occasion of crises. The opinion of people is polled when a serious crime is committed and questions are asked such as: Is Justice severe enough with recidivists or when riots occur in the suburbs? Should under age people be jailed as adults are or when an innocent person is sent to prison for many years should judges be responsible in case of miscarriage of justice? The results of such polls can be considered generally biased. But, even if most of the results are distorted, some reliable studies bring to the fore three main conclusions about Justice in France.

1. Justice: an Unknown Institution

According to the CSA Institute, in 2004, only one third of the respondents agree with the following statement: 'I am (well or quite well) aware of the way Justice works.'[3] A further question reveals that people know the main players of the judicial process: judges and barristers especially. But they fail to recognize the technical wheels of Justice: attorneys, clerks or plaintiff.

2. Justice: the Worst Reputation among Public Services

In a recurrent study, 'French people and their public services', the CSA Institute asks respondents to give a good or bad mark to assess public institutions. Justice is awkwardly ranked among services which are in competition. In the years 2000 and 2002, it gets the worst mark of all these services and is still the last but one in 2005. Justice comes far behind city councils or hospitals (which are the usual favourites in the polls); but it is also overtaken by social services and, even, by tax authorities. In 2002, Justice is the only public service whose mark is lower than the average, decreasing from 9.8 to 9.2.[4] In 2005, its mark increased to 10.2 while the one of Employment Agency dramatically fell at the same time. Yet, this relative improvement seems to be very fragile. On the one hand, the unemployment rate has been declining for many months which should improve the image of the Employment Agency. On the other hand, Justice as a whole is involved in the turmoil of the Outreau case in which individual errors and institutional failures followed one another and brought deep discredit on magistrature. Justice will certainly once again rank the lowest in the next poll. According to another poll institute public opinion considers that Justice works worse than before (53%) and that the way it works in 2004 is bad or very bad (70% in 2004, 62% in 2002).[5]

Both polls lead to the same conclusions with regard to the grievances against Justice. Almost all the respondents agree on the statements: 'Lawsuit is an expensive process' (89%) and disagree on these two: 'Justice works quickly' (87%) and 'Justice speaks clearly' (81%).

---

[3] CSA, 'Les Français et la Justice', Sondage CSA Sélection du Reader's Digest, réalisé le 29 juillet 2004.

[4] CSA, 'Les Français et leurs services publics', Sondage CSA Reader's Digest, réalisé le 30 septembre 2002.

[5] TNS Sofres, 'Les Français et la Justice', Sondage TNS Sofres Le Figaro Magazine, réalisé les 13 et 14 octobre 2004.

These conclusions are nothing but astonishing. More interesting is the poll carried out by the CSA Institute[6] which distinguishes two samples: 'ordinary people' and people faced with a problem requiring the intervention of Justice. This second sample forms a kind of 'enlightened opinion' which has been in contact with Justice and directly informed of judicial proceedings. When the results are compared, no significant differences appear in the answers to the two samples. People who experienced judicial procedures are as hard as others on the way Justice works: slow (88% vs. 89%), costly (84% vs. 89%), unclear (88% vs. 89%) The experience unfortunately confirms the prejudice and reinforces the widespread maxim: 'better a bad deal than a good lawsuit.' 80% of 'ordinary people' endorse this view; 69% only among the 'enlightened opinion'. The gap is quite significant and seems to indicate that Justice is more effective than 'ordinary people' believe at first. However, it should be observed that this positive result is very fragile since a wide majority of respondents who have previously been in contact with Justice are inclined to settle, even if it is a bad settlement.

3. Justice: a Trust worthy Institution?

The result of the latest poll proves that French people do not fully trust Justice. Justice is usually considered more reliable than media or politicians who both have lost most of their credibility. But it is by far less trustworthy than armed forces or teachers.[7] In a poll recently published by the CSA Institute, respondents put Justice, banks, companies executives, newspapers in the same category...[8] This intermediate situation is quite stable: about 50% of French people do not have confidence in Justice in 1994[9] as well as in 2004.[10] According to French public opinion, truth does not always become apparent to the judges and they fail in their duty to take into account the position of victims. The image of judges is quite mixed: they are held to be technically skilled but doubts remain as far as their political independence, their fairness or even their honesty is concerned[11] (CSA, 1997; IFOP, 1999). Less than

---

[6] CSA, 'Justice: les Français désenchantés', Sondage CSA L'Express, réalisé le 12/24 juin 1997.

[7] *Ibid.*

[8] CSA 2005b, 'Les personnes inspirant confiance aux Français', Sondage CSA La Vie, No. 0501042, réalisé le 17-19 août 2005.

[9] IFOP, 'La Justice', Sondage IFOP Journal du Dimanche, réalisé les 17 et 18 novembre 1994.

[10] TNS Sofres, 'Les Français et la Justice', Sondage TNS Sofres Le Figaro Magazine, réalisé les 13 et 14 octobre 2004.

[11] CSA, 'Justice: les Français désenchantés', Sondage CSA L'Express, réalisé le 12/24 juin 1997.

half of public opinion agrees with the following sentence: 'an innocent person does not have anything to fear from Justice.' More than 50% would hesitate to sue the person responsible for an offence for damages. They also would fear Justice if they had to deal with it.

B. Justice and Experts

The poor representation of Justice in public opinion is strengthened by assessments of experts such as the World Bank. Its famous 'Doing Business' report answers questions beyond the efficiency of judicial processes: 'Are there significant differences in business regulation from country to country? If so, what explains these differences? What types of regulation lead to improved economic and social outcomes? What are the most successful regulatory models? And, more generally, what is the scope for a government in facilitating business activity?'[12] But, two series of indicators are closely related to the question of efficiency in the administration of Justice: 'Enforcing contracts'[13] and 'Closing A Business'.[14]

Regarding the implementation of contracts, the indicators of 'Doing Business' relate to the number, the duration (days) and the cost (% of debt) of procedures. As far as the two last indicators (duration and cost of the procedures) are concerned, a few countries (Japan, USA, Sweden, Denmark) have an advantage over France: contracts implementation is quicker and less expensive. On the other hand, the French judicial process is more efficient than some others (Greece, Italy Netherlands, Portugal). In some cases, arbitration has to be provided: quicker recovery means higher cost (Ireland, UK); lower cost means longer procedure (Austria, Germany). The comparison leads to mitigate one of the main grievances against Justice. In most countries, the implementation of contracts is not both expensive and slow; neither is it swift and cheaper.

Regarding the administration of bankruptcy, the 'Doing Business 2006' report confirms the calamitous image of French Justice and the obvious failure of the legal rules in that specific part of positive law. With a few exceptions (Greece, Italy, Germany), the position of creditors is far weaker in France than in other countries: the recovery rate is dramatically lower (48% vs. more than 75% everywhere else). The procedures are often longer and more expensive that in other countries (Belgium, Japan, UK, USA) with a few exceptions (Greece, Portugal, Sweden). In short, the judicial system is neither effective nor efficient.

---

[12] World Bank, 2006, 'Doing Business in 2006, Creating Jobs', *World Bank Oxford University Press*, Foreword, p. XIII.

[13] *Ibid.*, p. 61-66.

[14] *Ibid.*, p. 67-71.

For the last two or three decades, the main aim of bankruptcy legislation has been to maintain employment even if it operates to the detriment of creditors (associated with a risk of successive bankruptcies) This obvious failure harbours grievances against commercial Justice. Quite often, courts and judges are blamed for being incompetent and corrupt. In 1998, a report by MPs François Colcombet and Arnaud Montebourg violently criticized commercial courts and, especially, elected judges: 'failing and out of control', 'from neighbourhood to cousinhood', 'emergence and development of corruption in commercial courts'... these are some of the titles of the report[15] A later report by Senator Paul Girod clearly showed that these criticisms were excessive and sectarian.[16] For example, commercial judges cannot be responsible for all companies which go into liquidation and pass away. But because of these criticisms, the image of commercial courts is still worse than the reality described by the World Bank reports.

C. Justice and Business People

The results of the polls make it possible to isolate the opinion of business people on Justice.[17]

The first conclusion is that business people seem to know how Justice works a little better than the other socio-professional groups. Two thirds of them answer that they know little about Justice. This is almost within the average of the population. Beyond that general feeling of shared ignorance, business people know better than others the players of the judicial process. About 80% know what a judge, a barrister or a bailiff is. This last example is quite significant. The gap with other groups almost reaches twenty points. Such a gap could mean that business people are using the services of legal advisers in their current professional environment, especially during the first stages of commercial disputes. For ordinary people, the bailiff is the one who seizes the wealth of those who do not pay their debts. For business people, the bailiff is the one who delivers deeds with solemnity or establishes certified statements. He is part of current business life.

Business people are more severe than other socio-professional groups with regard to the miscarriages of Justice. From 2002 to 2005, even though public opinion is a bit more indulgent to Justice, the mark

---

15 F. Colcombet et A. Montebourg, 1, Rapport sur l'activité et le fonctionnement des tribunaux de commerce, Assemblée nationale, No. 1038, 3 juillet 1998.

16 P. Girod, Projet de loi portant réforme des tribunaux de commerce, Sénat, 23 janvier 2002, No. 178.

17 CSA, 'Les Français et la Justice', Sondage CSA Sélection du Reader's Digest, réalisé le 29 juillet 2004.

given by business people is lowering. Several indicators evince this increasing distrust. More than others, business people assert that Justice treats every citizen equally and that penalties are severe. They obviously reject the common representation of judges favourable to the rich and powerful ones. On the contrary, business people seem to believe that they are targeted by judges, especially when corruption cases are brought to courts. During the 90s, many political parties were sued because of illegal fund raising methods: overbilling, faked bids in public markets, fictitious jobs… Both politicians and executives are responsible for these blameworthy practices. But Justice mainly attacked executives, charging them with misappropriation of corporate funds and changing the corrupter into nothing more than an abettor. Whereas politicians were often leniently treated, judges pronounced many sentences against executives and corporations, some of them based on arguable reasons.[18] Such unfair treatment is likely to have left a deep impression among business people, bitterness against politicians and distrust towards Justice.

III. Representation of Justice and Corporate Judicial Strategies

A company which does not build a judicial strategy is bound to undergo Justice.[19] In some cases, no choice is possible. Public order is at stake and companies are obliged to submit themselves to procedures which are outside their control. For instance, when a commercial court declares a company insolvent, executives are sidelined and they do not really take part in the course of the proceedings. On the contrary, when public order is not at stake, companies can take advantage of implementing strategies which integrate the representation of Justice. Some of these strategies may of course aim at avoiding such a failing and distrustful machine. They are unquestionably the most and best known of all judicial strategies. On the contrary, some strategies rely on the deficiencies of Justice to improve the situation of the company.

---

[18] B. Bouloc, note sous Cass.Com. 27 octobre 1997, Carignon, Dr. Sociétés, p. 869; and L. Saenko, 'La notion de dissimulation en matière d'abus de biens sociaux', *Revue Trimestrielle Droit Commercial*, 2005, p. 671.

[19] C. Champaud et D. Danet, *Stratégies judiciaires des entreprises*, Dalloz, Regards sur la justice, 2006; J. Paillusseau, 'Le droit est aussi une science de l'organisation', *Revue Trimestrielle de Droit Commercial*, 1989, p. 1-57; J. Saporta 'La place de l'environnement stratégique dans la démarche stratégique de l'entreprise', *Petites Affiches*, No. 112, 18 septembre 1987.

A. Avoiding Justice

If Justice is held to be slow and inefficient, or even hostile to business people, the most natural corporate strategy is to avoid public judges every time one can. These avoidance strategies must abide by public order rules but companies have a lot at stake when planning a procedure or choosing the court which will settle their case.

1. Designing the Procedure

Sometimes, public justice cannot be put aside. Thus, the company must seek to consolidate its position. This enforcement strategy consists in organizing litigation beforehand so that it may take place on a favourable basis. The company proposes a legally reasoned argument that Justice will consider without acknowledging that this position often originates from a higher economic power. The weight of inequality is especially obvious when the type of lawsuit arises from contractual provisions. Imbalance is less obvious, even if there are imbalances when the stronger positions derive from established property rights or economic control arrangements.

A contractual arrangement is always ambivalent. It comprises of a fluctuation in convergent and divergent interests. During the negotiations, social environment and future prospect of profit can lead a signatory to underestimate the extent of certain clauses for jurisdictional purpose. Such clauses can aim (or have the effect of claiming) to put the author of the clauses in a situation at the appropriate time of having the advantage in dispute settlement. They can be put into two main categories.

The clauses for jurisdictional purpose make it possible to choose the judge or to oblige him to rule in favour of their author. They withdraw the litigation from its 'natural judge' to submit it to a supposed more favourable one. The shift of the litigation can take place in two different ways: *ratione materiae* and *ratione loci*. In *Ratione materiae*, the clauses of contractual extension transfer the litigation from a public judge to another public judge, of the same status, but of another jurisdictional kind. These rules relating to the jurisdiction of the courts belong to law and order and the extensions are thus confined within narrow limits. But, such clauses are not completely prohibited. Thus a contract can stipulate the jurisdiction of the County Court for litigation involving small amounts. Due to these clauses, most of the potential adversaries will hesitate because of the expenses incurred by the need for a lawyer. It also permits the company to reserve the possibility of lodging an appeal. Even if the validity of the clause is doubtful, it complicates the lawsuit and supports the most powerful party. The same kind of results can be obtained thanks to the clauses of *ratione loci* competence. The author of the clause endeavours to benefit from the differences in litigation settlement which can be related to local characteristics. Thus a company can prefer to stand trial in its 'fief', i.e. a socio-economic environment where its weight will be, at least implicitly, taken into account. It can also ask for the procedure to take place before such Court of Appeal known to allocate more substantial damages than another court.

Contrary to the clauses for jurisdictional purpose, the reservation of rights arises as contractual provisions similar to those which relate to the conditions of the obligation or the conditions of validity of commitments. They do not seem to relate to the procedural rules. But these clauses always reveal a more or less subtle and effective, but deliberate, judicial strategy. They often relate to property rights and the contractual organization of civil liability. In both cases, company strategy consists of reinforcing its position by an *ad hoc* contractual arrangement. For that purpose, the company will insert some clauses into the contract the effect of which is to counter certain fundamental rules of property and contract rights. This modification confers a strong advantage in favour of the author of the clauses.

For example, the company which sells a good can design the mechanism of the transfer of property while inserting a clause of reservation of title. If the buyer does not pay the price, the company will go to court like the owner of the good, not like the creditor of a person who has been adjudicated a bankrupt. The question put to the court will be that of the restitution of a good to its legitimate owner and not that of the forced payment of a due sum. However, it is known that in France the rights of the owner are infinitely stronger than those of the creditor. The claimant avoids costs and delays mentioned by the World Bank even if the debtor is bankrupt.[20]

These strategies are also very important as regard adjustments of contractual liability.[21] The company can avoid many lawsuits by imposing restriction on the other contracting party: shortened time limits on a claim for damages, total or partial exemption, contradictory expertise, various formalities…[22]; Due to these contractual provisions, the action

---

[20] F. Perochon, note sous Cass.Com. 8 juin 1993, Dalloz, 1993, Somm. p. 296.

[21] J.-P. Chazal, 'Théorie de la cause et justice contractuelle, à propos de l'arrêt Chronopost', *JCP*, 1998, I, No. 152; J. Ricatte 'A propos de l'option Effacement jour de pointe dans les contrats', EDF, JCP-E 1988, II, 15247.

[22] P. Malinvaud, 'Pour ou contre la validité de clauses limitatives de la garantie des vices cachés dans la vente', JCP 1975, I, 2690; J. Bigot, *Plaidoyer pour les clauses limitatives entre professionnels*, JCP-G 1976, I, 2755.

of the victim is hampered and made more expensive, which can actually deter many actions when the adversary becomes aware of the brittleness of his position.

2. Avoiding Public Justice

By choosing the arbitration, companies clearly seek to avoid public courts.[23] Arbitration consists in giving individuals the right to settle a dispute.[24] Just like members of the judiciary, arbitrators hold the power of *jurisdictio*. When they pass a sentence, they express a 'social truth' which supersedes the 'factual truth'. Arbitration processes present three fundamental characteristics. First of all, arbitration is entirely rooted in a contractual approach to Justice. The will of parties plays a dominating part until adjudication. In most cases, the commercial contract includes a special clause: the signatories decide to forego recourse to the court in the event of conflict. They agree on the designation procedures of arbitrators. In other cases, arbitration is implemented when conflict arises. A specific agreement is signed which aims at leaving aside the intervention of the judge who would have normally heard the case. In both cases, the arbitration court is composed of arbitrators who are chosen by the contracting parties.

Arbitration may be considered as a response to the bad reputation of the courts. Courts are criticized because the legal proceedings are slow, expensive and quite obscure to the people who have to deal with them. In this respect, the arbitration procedure presents several advantages.[25]

The first of these advantages is discretion. The public does not have access to arbitration audiences and sentences. Arbitrations are confidential. Only the parties can lift the veil of secrecy on the arbitration hearing and the result of the arbitration process. By contrast, any court decision can be freely published, commented on, even circulated to the media and the parties identified. Everyone can discover in the newspapers or in law reviews the names, the circumstances and the terms of the litigation, the industrial, financial or commercial stakes and the sentence passed by the court. This discretion is however lost if one of the parties decides to appeal against the decision.

---

[23] K.-N. Hylton and C.-R. Drahozal, 'The Economics of Litigation and Arbitration: An Application to Franchise Contracts', *Boston Univ. School of Law, Working Paper* No. 01-03, 2001.

[24] J. Robert, *L'arbitrage*, Dalloz Sirey Traités, 1997; E.-L. Rubin, 'The Non Judicial Life of Contract: Beyond the Schadow of the Law', *Northwestern University Law Review*, Vol. 90, 1995, p. 107; S. Shavell, 'Alternative Dispute Resolution: An Economic Analysis', *Journal of Legal Studies*, Vol. 24, 1995, p. 1.

[25] R.-A. Bales, *An Introduction to Arbitration*, Bench & Bar (Kentucky), March 2006.

The arbitration has a second advantage: decisions are quickly made. Except for contrary provision, decision must be made in the six months following the day when the last arbitrator has accepted the case. Many decisions are returned by this deadline of six months. Arbitration seldom lasts more than eighteen months. By comparison, parties can hardly hope for a public judgement in less than twelve months and frequently the procedures stretch over years. *Ceteris paribus*, an arbitration procedure lasts five to ten times less than a judicial one.

From the parties standpoint, one of the most important characteristics of the arbitration procedure is freedom to choose the arbitrators. In most of the cases, the arbitration court is composed of two judges appointed by each party, these two judges choosing then the president of the court by mutual agreement. This faculty of choice is very important since it has as an immediate outcome: the implementation of a competitive process which leads to the 'natural' selection of the arbitrators. Some are accepted and some are rejected.[26]

Last but not least, arbitrators are close to the parties. Unavoidably public court are affected by the distance which they place between the parties and the judge. Legal proceedings appear as well as possibly impartial, but always enigmatic and indifferent. Even the presence of a barrister, who speaks the same esoteric language, takes some part in the reinforcement of the distance between the parties and the judge. On the contrary, in the arbitration procedure, the parties can speak with judges whom they chose because of their competence and who are more accessible than public judges. These arbitrators will pay all the more attention to them as they are in a process of competition.

B. Using the Bad Image of Justice

The bad image of justice cans the companies to be wary of it or to even avoid it. But, on the contrary, the bad image of Justice may appear as a lever in the strategic management of a lawsuit.

1. Taking Advantage of the Fear of Court Proceedings

The fear of recourse to legal proceedings is often used to test the forces of the opposing party and to deter it to begin a long and expensive procedure. Graduated operations tend to intimidate the opposing party.

The most usual tool to threaten an opposing party is giving it notice to pay or to fulfil the terms of a contract. This complaint very often takes the shape of a registered letter with confirmation of receipt. *Per se,*

---

[26]   D.-E. Bloom and C.-L. Cavanagh, 'An analysis of the Selection of Arbitrators', *American Economic Review*, Vol. 76, 1986, p. 408.

resorting to such a letter is common practice and does not really frighten anyone in the world of business. However, this letter exerts some pressure on the recipient because it potentially represents the first step of an escalation which can lead to court. If the recipient does not answer in the desired direction, the sender can renew the procedure by varying measures which become more and more threatening. But, this strategy appears of limited effectiveness because the repetition of the threat which is not effective loses its impact. It is thus necessary to come to a new step in the escalation: the threat in the letter needs to be reinforced by the intervention of a third person.

In the case of an unpaid debt, the creditor can call upon a debt collection agency. Individuals easily get impressed by threatening formulas and quasi-official appearance of the documents. But this tool is far less effective when it is used against companies. It is then necessary to come to a pre-judicial step. A bailiff's intervention may be requested. At that stage of the procedure, the bailiff will only carry out or deliver deeds to which its functions of public officer give much solemnity. The intervention of the bailiff is likely to produce more intimidation if it consists in drawing up a certified statement. The observations drawn up in that statement are of legal effect if the case is referred to the appropriate jurisdiction. It constitutes a more credible threat than an ordinary testimony. Turning to a barrister is the next step in the escalation, the last one before the lawsuit. The deontology rules forbid the lawyer to address a threatening letter to the adversary of its client. He cannot thus answer the grievances raised by the opposing party. But, paradoxically, this compelled laconism reinforces the intimidating impact of the letter in which the barrister requests the recipient to indicate 'the name and the address of the colleague in charge of the defence of his interests'.

Judicial appraisal can be connected with these strategies of pressure. In theory, the appraisal does not intend to intimidate the adversary of the claimant.[27] The procedures are conceived to facilitate the work of the judge by objectively establishing probable but unproven facts or unvouched calculations. However, the judicial appraisal has three hidden effects. First, it enforces the credibility of the previous threats (bailiff, barrister, etc.). The claimant is actually bringing a lawsui t against the opposing party. The action does not get to the bottom of the case. But, for the first time, the case is referred to court. There is no more doubt that the claimant is ready to carry his threats into execution. Second, if an expert is appointed by the judge, the claimant hopes that the discovery application will be a source of annoyance and that the opposing

---

[27] I. Urbain Parléani, 'L'expert de gestion et l'expert *in futurum*', *Revue Sociétés*, 2003, p. 223.

party will negotiate rather than undergo unwanted investigations. Last, the expert's report may reveal pieces of information or facts which the opposing party would like to keep secret and that will be disclosed to all during the judicial lawsuit.[28] The motion for discovery is beyond doubt a tool of intimidation. It is all the more powerful as its capacity as a threat remains largely hidden. A determined claimant will take advantage of justice to put pressure on his adversary and to force him to reach a private agreement. The judges are naturally aware of these strategies. They try to limit their unwanted effects by laying down strict conditions to the action of the claimants. But, in spite of this restrictive jurisprudence, the expertise remains a privileged ground for skilful companies.

One cannot conclude a discussion on the strategies based on the fear of the judge without mentioning the case of penal actions. For many socio-political reasons, the French legislator lets an ill-considered penalization of business affairs occur. Nothing is more frequent than a party who threatens to make a complaint against its adversary. But, if penal law provides many weapons to that purpose, the company wanting to resort to it has to give it second thought. The penal complaint is a powerful threat but it may have a boomerang effect and round on the one who uses it. An improper complaint may entail legal proceedings against the unwise claimant (slanderous denunciation, blackmail…) and significant punitive damages.

2. Taking Advantage of the Slowness and the Cost of Justice

Slowness (and induced costs) is not necessarily the sign of a failing judicial system. To work properly, Justice needs time, weighting, and reflexion. Formalism of procedure is no vain luxury but the origin of fairness. However, a skilful plaintiff can convert these qualities into levers for delaying the normal processing of the case. When the strategic decision to delay the course of Justice is taken, the tactical means are countless.[29]

A first cause of delay, generally unknown to public opinion but widely practised, comes from barristers who do not present their requests and answers within the agreed time. In spite of the reforms requiring judicial deadlines to be observed, it is not rare for a party to obtain multiple adjournments under various pretexts. Sometimes judges pay attention to these dilatory tactics. But, most of the time, permissiveness

---

[28] Champaud C et D. Danet, note sous Cass.Com. 15 juin 1999, Fleury Michon, *Revue Trimestrielle Droit Commercial*, 1999, p. 876.

[29] Ph. Blondel, 'Stratégie judiciaire', in L. Cadiet (ed.), *Dictionnaire de la Justice*, PUF, 2004; L. Cadiet, *Droit judiciaire privé*, Litec, 2004; C. Champaud, 'Stratégie judiciaire' (Droit des affaires), in L. Cadiet (ed.), *Dictionnaire de la justice*, PUF, 2004.

prevails. Where there is a backlog of cases to be heard adjournments lighten the load. As for the barrister of the party who accedes to the adjournment, he may need the understanding of his fellow members in the future. So, if he is not under the pressure of his client, half heartedly opposes delaying tactics.

Another cause of delay lies in matters of procedure. These may occur throughout the proceedings. *In limine litis*, objections come from the defendant. The aim is to halt the action the plaintiff brings against him. The defendant may plead the lack of jurisdiction of the court if the plaintiff has made a mistake or if he has 'forgotten' such a contractual obligation as an arbitration provision[30] In this regard, the arrangements which aim to design the procedure are of great importance. The defendant may also invoke the fact that another case has been referred to another court whose decision will affect the case being heard. The objection will be successful if it appears to the judge that the two proceedings could lead to conflicting decisions.[31] A rare exception may occur where the good administration of Justice is at stake. For example, the defendant may summon a guarantor in the lawsuit. All these exceptions have to be agreed at the beginning of the case, which delays the judgement and discourages the opposing party.

Throughout the lawsuit (even during the appeal) the defendant may ask the judge to dismiss the case on the ground that the claimant is not qualified to act,[32] that he did not take his opponent to court within the legally required time, that he has signed an arbitration clause... These submissions have a doubtful effect as a delaying action. The judge is not compelled to examine them beforehand. He can raise objections to the case and include them in the decision. These exceptions are less effective than exceptions *in limine litis*.

In certain extreme cases, companies deliberately bet on the contrast between the fast tempo of business and the slow tempo of Justice. The case 'Les Trois Suisses vs. La Redoute' is a famous example of this common strategy.[33] In 1995, 'Les Trois Suisses', a mail-order selling company, launches an advertising campaign which is both comparative

---

[30] E. Locquin, 'L'exception d'incompétence du juge étatique tirée de l'existence d'une clause compromissoire', note sous Cass.Civ.2°, 22nd novembre 2001, *Revue Trimestrielle Droit Commercial*, 2001, p. 46; E. Locquin et J.-C. Dubarry, note sous Paris 19 mai 1993, *Revue Trimestrielle Droit Commercial*, 1993, p. 494.

[31] A. Marmisse, 'La litispendance s'apprécie au regard des prétentions des demandeurs', note sous CJCE 8 mai 2003, *Revue Trimestrielle Droit Commercial*, 2003, p. 607.

[32] Y. Chartier, 'L'existence d'une action en justice au nom d'une SARL', note sous Cass.Civ.2°, 22nd octobre 1998, *Revue Sociétés*, 1998, p. 76.

[33] T. Come, *Les stratégies juridiques des entreprises*, Vuibert, Entreprendre, 1998.

and aggressive. The target is the competitor 'La Redoute'. Large notice boards are hung up side by side. The first one reproduces the slogan of the competitor: 'La Redoute delivers orders within 48 hours.' But, the original picture is tarnished by the use of dark and faded colours. In the second poster the sun is illuminating a bright coloured landscape with the following advertisement: 'Les Trois Suisses delivers orders within 24 hours.' There is no doubt that this campaign breaches the provisions of the Neiertz law which regulates comparative advertising in France. La Redoute immediately takes a summary action against its competitor. The judge naturally grants a temporary injunction preventing the continuation of the campaign. In spite of this judgement, the aggressive strategy is completely successful. Thanks to the lawsuit, the media become interested in the case and widely relay the advertisement. 'Les Trois Suisses' do not omit to present their adversary like an wounded competitor, unable to face competition in the market place and obliged to resort to Justice in order to prevent the 'truth' from being brought out into the open. To compound matters further, 'Les Trois Suisses' lodges an appeal and makes statements and gives interviews on classical topics such as virtues of transparency, the defence of consumers' interests and the stifling of innovation... The contrast between the rhythm of Justice and that the commercial world leads to an unexpected result. In taking an action against the aggressor, the victim reinforces the effectiveness of the advertising campaign which deliberately violates the law and it ensures a complete commercial victory to the author of the aggression. It is probably the reason why this strategy is so common in the distribution sector (For instance, Bouzat, 1992).

3. Taking Advantage of the Uncertainty of Justice

In theory, Justice is applied uniformly throughout France. All legal institutions operate to this end. Statute law guarantees the uniformity of the rules; the Supreme Court of Appeal guarantees the uniformity of jurisprudence. Normally, in the same circumstances, the same rule applies in the same way whatever the parties, the judge, the place or the time of the judgement. However, even if authorities strive to standardize judicial decisions, they can not rule out a certain variability of decisions. In some cases, contradictory judgements can occur. According to public opinion, Justice is not free from risks. The polls show that French people are aware of these hazards.

For a few years, powerful parties have developed strategies aimed at using Justice as a tool for managerial or commercial purposes.

A commercial litigant can thus endeavour to initiate favourable legal action. Lawsuits can be instituted to test the reactions of the judges with regard to a new commercial process or innovative contractual clauses which appear to encounter legal or regulatory provisions. ('tests cases') A company may also go to different courts in order to obtain favourable decisions related to a special point. With a bit of luck and skill, the stakeholders (customers, competitors, partners, etc.) will consider that these decisions comprise 'judge-made law' and will take this case law for granted ('matter of principle actions').

These strategies require funds and patience. It is indeed necessary to bring cases to courts when favourable circumstances arise, not when it is known in advance that the case will be lost. These strategies also require financial and technical means, such as a team of lawyers dedicated to the implementation of the strategy. The legal team is devoted to initiation of procedures, trying each time new arguments, producing the pages of legal doctrine... until the team obtains a succession of decisions more or less favourable to its point of view. These decisions are published and widely annotated in law reviews, giving the impression that Justice eventually recognized the merits of the company. This kind of strategy occurred in the sector of selective distribution. One remembers the battle carried out by car producers in order to give rise to a decision refusing any compensation for their agents in the event of non-renewal from the concession at the end of the contractual period.[34]

One could say that these strategies cannot really be effective in a country where statute law is so firmly rooted. The fact that they are usually implemented shows that barriers between statute law and common law are undoubtedly lower than is often said.

IV. Conclusion

The poor image of Justice is not without consequence on actions of business people and corporate strategies. These strategies vary a lot. Some of them are obvious, for example, prioritizing out-of-court settlements to avoid the slowness, the cost and the hazards of going to law. Others are much more subtle and manipulative, such as strategies which take advantage of these actual or perceived defects to deter the opposing party from asserting its rights. In this regard, judges should pay attention to the actions whose genuine goal lies in using public judges and procedures as a tool that can be diverted from its natural purpose in order to require a substantial advantage over other competitors.

---

[34] D. Ferrier, note sous Cass.Com. 9 décembre 1988, Dalloz, Som. p. 19; B. Bouloc, note sous Cass.Com. 6 janvier 1987, *Revue Trimestrielle Droit Commercial*, 1988, p. 122; M. Virassamy, note sous Cass.Com. 4 janvier 1994, Dalloz, 1995, p. 355; L. Malaurie-Vignal, note sous Cass.Com. 9 avril 2002, *Contrat Concurrence Consommation*, 2003, No. 9.

References

R.-A. Bales, *An Introduction to Arbitration*, Bench & Bar (Kentucky), March 2006.

J. Bigot, *Plaidoyer pour les clauses limitatives entre professionnels*, JCP-G 1976, I, 2755.

D.-E. Bloom and C.-L. Cavanagh, 'An analysis of the Selection of Arbitrators', *American Economic Review*, Vol. 76, 1986, p. 408.

Ph. Blondel, 'Stratégie judiciaire', in L. Cadiet (ed.), *Dictionnaire de la Justice*, PUF, 2004.

B. Bouloc, note sous Cass.com. 6 janvier 1987, *Revue Trimestrielle Droit Commercial*, 1988, p. 122.

B. Bouloc, note sous Cass. Com. 27 octobre 1997, Carignon, Dr. Sociétés, p. 869.

P. Bouzat, 1992, note sous TGI Paris 1° Civ. 8 janvier 1992, Leclerc, *Revue Trimestrielle Droit Commercial*, 1992, p. 495.

L. Cadiet, *Droit judiciaire privé*, Litec, 2004.

C. Champaud, 'Stratégie judiciaire' (Droit des affaires) in L. Cadiet (ed.) *Dictionnaire de la justice*, PUF, 2004.

C. Champaud et D. Danet, note sous Cass.Com. 15 juin 1999, Fleury Michon, *Revue Trimestrielle Droit Commercial*, 1999, p. 876.

C. Champaud et D. Danet, *Stratégies judiciaires des entreprises*, Dalloz, Regards sur la justice, 2006.

Y. Chartier, 'L'existence d'une action en justice au nom d'une SARL', note sous Cass.Civ.2°, 22 octobre 1998, *Revue Sociétés*, 1998, p. 76.

J.-P. Chazal, 'Théorie de la cause et justice contractuelle, à propos de l'arrêt Chronopost', *JCP* 1998, I, No. 152.

P. Clément, Projet de loi organique relatif à la formation et à la responsabilité des magistrats, Assemblée Nationale, No. 3391, enregistré le 24 octobre 2006.

F. Colcombet et A. Montebourg, 1, Rapport sur l'activité et le fonctionnement des tribunaux de commerce, Assemblée nationale, No. 1038, 3 juillet 1998.

T. Come, *Les stratégies juridiques des entreprises*, Vuibert, Entreprendre, 1998.

A. Couret et G.-A. de Sentena, 'Le conflit judiciaire comme instrument de communication', *Revue française de gestion*, Vol. 81, novembre-décembre 1990. p. 103.

CSA, 'Justice: les Français désenchantés', Sondage CSA L'Express, réalisé le 12/24 juin 1997.

CSA, 'Les Français et leurs services publics', Sondage CSA Reader's Digest, réalisé le 30 septembre 2002.

CSA, 'Les Français et la Justice', Sondage CSA Sélection du Reader's Digest, réalisé le 29 juillet 2004.

CSA, 'Les Français et leurs services publics', Sondage CSA / France Info / France Europe Express, No. 0501470A, réalisé le 23 novembre 2005.

CSA, 'Les personnes inspirant confiance aux Français', Sondage CSA La Vie, No. 0501042, réalisé le 17-19 août 2005.

D. Ferrier, note sous Cass.Com. 9 décembre 1988, Dalloz, Som. p. 19.

P. Girod, Projet de loi portant réforme des tribunaux de commerce, Sénat, 23 janvier 2002, No. 178.

K.-N. Hylton and C.-R. Drahozal, 'The Economics of Litigation and Arbitration: An Application to Franchise Contracts', *Boston Univ. School of Law, Working Paper* No. 01-03, 2001.

IFOP, 'La Justice', Sondage IFOP Journal du Dimanche, réalisé les 17 et 18 novembre 1994.

E. Locquin, 'L'exception d'incompétence du juge étatique tirée de l'existence d'une clause compromissoire', note sous Cass.Civ.2°, 22 novembre 2001, *Revue Trimestrielle Droit Commercial*, 2001, p. 46.

E. Locquin et J.-C. Dubarry, note sous Paris 19 mai 1993, *Revue Trimestrielle Droit Commercial*, 1993, p. 494.

L. Malaurie-Vignal, note sous Cass. Com. 9 avril 2002, *Contrat Concurrence Consommation*, 2003, No. 9.

P. Malinvaud, 'Pour ou contre la validité de clauses limitatives de la garantie des vices cachés dans la vente', JCP 1975, I, 2690.

A. Marmisse, 'La litispendance s'apprécie au regard des prétentions des demandeurs', note sous CJCE 8 mai 2003, *Revue Trimestrielle Droit Commercial*, 2003, p. 607.

J. Paillusseau, 'Le droit est aussi une science de l'organisation', *Revue Trimestrielle de Droit Commercial*, 1989, p. 1-57.

F. Perochon, note sous Cass. Com. 8 juin 1993, Dalloz, 1993, Somm. p. 296.

J. Ricatte 'À propos de l'option Effacement jour de pointe dans les contrats' EDF, JCP-E 1988, II, 15247.

J. Robert, *L'arbitrage*, Dalloz Sirey Traités, 1997.

E.-L. Rubin, 'The Non Judicial Life of Contract: Beyond the Schadow of the Law', *Northwestern University Law Review*, Vol. 90, 1995, p. 107.

L. Saenko, 'La notiçon de dissimulation en matière d'abus de biens sociaux', *Revue Trimestrielle Droit Commercial*, 2005, p. 671.

J. Saporta 'La place de l'environnement stratégique dans la démarche stratégique de l'entreprise', *Petites Affiches*, No. 112, 18 septembre 1987.

S. Shavell, 'Alternative Dispute Resolution: An Economic Analysis', *Journal of Legal Studies*, Vol. 24, 1995, p. 1.

TNS Sofres, 'Les Français et la Justice', Sondage TNS Sofres Le Figaro Magazine, réalisé les 13 et 14 octobre 2004.

I. Urbain Parléani, 'L'expert de gestion et l'expert *in futurum*', *Revue Sociétés*, 2003, p. 223.

A. Vallini et P. Houillon, Rapport fait au nom de la commission chargée de rechercher les causes des dysfonctionnements dans l'affaire dite d'Outreau et de formuler des propositions pour éviter leur renouvellement, Rapport d'enquête, Assemblée nationale, No. 3125, 6 juin 2006.

M. Virassamy, note sous Cass. Com. 4 janvier 1994, *Dalloz* 1995, p. 355.

World Bank, 'Doing Business in 2004, Understanding Regulation', *World Bank Oxford University Press*, 2004.

World Bank, 'Doing Business in 2006, Creating Jobs', *World Bank Oxford University Press*, 2006.

Representations of Justice in Economic Comparisons of Legal Systems

Thierry KIRAT

C.N.R.S. Research Fellow (IRISES, Université Paris Dauphine)

Economic analysis has been carried out over the past ten years into the quantitative studies of both legal and political institutions. The Rule of Law and the democracy are nowadays the object of analyses which focus on their determinants (economic or non economic) and on their relations with the level of development and wealth of nations (Barro, 2000). In this context of growth of quantitative enquiries into institutions, legal systems in general and judicial systems in particular, became the subjects of economic research that take such a comparative orientation.

Comparative economic analysis has been recently renewed by the works of a group of economists as Djankov, Glaeser, La Porta, Lopez-de-Silanes, and Shleifer[1]; they take as given that the old comparative economics is no longer relevant because of the collapse of centrally planned economic systems in central and Eastern Europe. The comparison of the economic systems (liberal capitalism, State capitalism, collectivism, non planned socialism.) is substituted by a comparison of nations within the market-based economic systems. The capitalist system obviously gained in universality but it did not fully homogeneize national institutional patterns worldwide. Nations still differentiate themselves from the point of view of their institutions and their economic performance in terms of growth, of unemployment, of financing of the economy, etc. This diversity is the foundation of new comparative economies, which attempt henceforth to characterize the existing institutions, to study their determinants, or even their implications in terms of efficiency.

---

[1] S. Djankov, E. Glaeser, R. La Porta, F. Lopez-de-Silanes, A. Shleifer, 'Courts', *Quarterly Journal of Economics*, Vol. 118, No. 3, 2003, p. 453-517 (Henceforth DGLLS).

The progress of comparative economic analysis of institutions was the driving force behind the development of studies dedicated to families of legal systems (Civil Law and Common Law), to judicial systems and to civil procedure. It is concerned with new perspectives, that differentiate between those of the Law and Economics movement which is not generally comparative[2] and focuses on the behaviours of individuals when given a choice between alternative dispute resolution processes, or on recourse to the courts.

It is to these renewed perspectives that this article relates. It will try to shed some lights on the often implicit representations of justice conveyed by the methods of empirical analysis used by academic scholars.[3] Section I will present in more detail the new comparative economics program and the place that justice occupies there. Section II will be dedicated to the status conferred on justice in the studies pertaining to the relationships between the political sphere and the judicial sphere. Section III will focus on the comparisons between judicial systems from a procedural viewpoint and on the basis of numeric indicators.

I. New Comparative Economics: From Institutional Settings to Compared Legal Systems

The method initiated by the proponents of a new comparative economics consists of characterizing in an original manner the reasons for the institutional choices of nations, without assuming *a priori* that they are efficient. It is in this broad context that the study of the legal systems is introduced.

A. Institutional Choices: The Problem Stated

The promoters of the new comparative economics maintain that the emergence of institutions, their development in the course of time and their international diffusion cannot be reduced to a process of selection of efficient institutions. The analyses conducted by DLLS clearly distinguish themselves from new institutional economics (North) as well as Hayek's theory of institutions.

In this regard, the project of Djankov, Glaeser, La Porta, Lopez-de-Silanes, and Shleifer[4] consider that institutions are instruments of social

---

[2]   Some exceptions must be mentioned however: See: U. Mattei, *Comparative Law and Economics*, Ann Harbor, Michigan University Press, 1997.

[3]   And promoters of the Doing Business program of the World Bank, which will not be further mentioned here for the program does not primarily address judicial matters. See World Bank – International Finance Corporation (2006).

[4]   *Ibid.*

control of business which reflect a trade-off between two goals: to provide economic and social order and to prevent the emergence of dictatorial systems of social control. In other words, the institutional choices of a nation inevitably face two constraints: on the one hand to prevent disorder (which, we shall see, needs a strong government) and on the other hand to prevent dictatorship (which need a limitation of State intervention). The balance between these two constraints is supposed to be made along a 'frontier of institutional possibilities' (Figure 1) which illustrate the basic trade-off between disorder and dictatorship in terms of social costs.

Fig. 1: Institutional possibilities

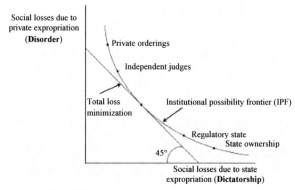

Source: Djankov *et al.* (2003), p. 599.

Four possible institutional mechanisms are listed:

- *Private ordering* is like a market mechanisms, that protects society against the risk of dictatorship insofar as it limits the government's intervention. However, the discipline of the market does not always work; the market doesn't always prevent the formation of monopolies, and in some cases (notably the countries of central and Eastern Europe) it can lead to the emergence of organised crime. While regulation through private ordering controls dictatorship, it doesn't necessarily prevent social disorder.

- *Independent judges:* using an argument *à la* Posner and Hayek DGLLS consider that generally enforcement of good conduct rules in contracts and torts through civil litigation is preferable to governmental regulation. However, DGLLS recognize that judges are not immune to pressures and are susceptible to economic or political influences. Judges cannot always take their decisions in an unbiased or independent manner, since they can be bribed with cash, benefits, and promises of promotion as well as threatened with violence; however, prevention of such risks is done through the framing of judges powers by the government. The assurance of neutrality and impartiality of judges implies a certain lessening of their independence: for example, as judges become employees of the state, they are subject to recruiting and tenure rules, compelled to abide by rules of procedure, etc. In these conditions, the framing of the judicial power is indispensable to guarantee impartiality and neutrality of courts rulings but it implies some risks of 'politicization' of their decisions, therefore of dictatorship.

- *regulatory state* implies government regulation which is legitimate if the risk of disorder cannot be prevented either by the private ordering or by private litigation and independent judges. It offers a certain number of virtues relative to the two previous social control mechanisms: the civil servants and agents of the government have the sense of the public service and the general interest and are generally experts in the areas which are regulated by the government. In counterpoint, the governmental regulation carries a risk of dictatorial drift (by the protection to the highest level of the State of the interests of the controlling class, to the detriment of the other classes). The control of disorder has a high price to pay: that of dictatorship.

- *State ownership* is indispensable in some cases (as in the case of the police or the military). But, if it controls the disorder, it is also amounts to a dictatorial system.

This analytical grid relating to institutional systems, briefly considered here, calls for two comments:

- the position defended by DGLLS is relative which means that one cannot assess institutional choices of nations by confronting them to a single normative model of reference. The issue is instead to assess the choices, or the institutional reforms of a given country, in relation to its own particular national context since some public interventions (for example government regulation) can be efficient in a certain context and very inefficient in others. Thus, in developed and democratic countries, some efficient institutions contribute to review and control the public intervention (by the parliamentary control, by the auditor general's office and through rules of transparency of the public decisions, etc.), whereas in most developing countries such controlling institutions don't exist or function poorly.

- the institutions are, in a certain number of developing countries, a colonial inheritance. More precisely, it is in the domain of legal systems that colonial legacy is most important. The adoption of the French Civil Law system or of the Common Law is not indifferent to the manner of which regulatory and institutional systems are built: the place of the

State, the importance of the public regulation and the bureaucracy, the individual liberties, are especially at stake.

B. Common Law vs. Civil Law

The comparison between Civil Law and Common Law systems has been framed in terms of their relative efficiency initially in the field of finance. Law and Finance specialists argued that common law systems have a better capacity to promote the emergence of an efficient financial market than civilian systems, considering the protection that they assure to the investors and the shareholders. Some went further, arguing that legal system is not only a determinant of the financial market development, but a *cause* of it.

In this respect, Mahoney[5] gave some empirical support to the Hayekian vision: a decentralized legal system such as the Common Law looks like a spontaneous order that guaranties individual liberties and limits more the government than under the rationalistic and constructivist French law. Mahoney argues that 'structural differences' separate the two legal systems: common law countries grant to the courts more independence than civil law countries which are said to be conducive to more governmental interference with property and contractual rights that in common law.[6] Therefore, as the common law countries give more liberty to the citizens, they experience a more vigorous economic growth.

The econometric analysis was carried out by Mahoney from the data of growth of the GDP per capita on 102 countries covered by the Penn World Tables[7] on the period 1960-1992. The analysis attempted to estimate the relationships between legal origins and the growth rate of the GDP per capita with progressively introduced econometric sophistication. The econometric results of Mahoney are clear-cut:

- common law countries experience an annual growth rate on average 0.64% higher than those of civil law,

---

[5]   P. Mahoney, 'The Common Law and Economic Growth: Hayek Might be Right', *Journal of Legal Studies*, Vol. 30, No. 2, 2001, p. 503.

[6]   This rather approximate presentation is probably attributable to the fact that Mahoney only uses two sources of comparative law in support of his analysis: J. M. Merryman, *The Civil Law Tradition: An Introduction of the Legal Systems of Western Europe and Latin America*, Stanford Univ. Press, 1985; T. Reynolds et A. Flores, *Foreign Law: Current Sources of Codes and Basic Legislation in Jurisdictions of the World*, Fred B. Rothman & Co., 1989.

[7]   Data provided by the Center for International Comparisons (Pennsylvania University).

- the average 'contract-intensive money ratio' is higher in common law countries (0.81 against 0.75).[8]

The conclusion of Mahoney is clear and unambiguous: the Common Law is more compatible with economic growth than the Civil Law, for reasons connected with the guarantees granted to the individual liberties and the autonomy of the legal sphere in relation to the governmental institutions. Indeed, Mahoney maintains that if Civil Law countries are oriented toward rent-seeking behaviours and are more susceptible to huge pressures for redistribution than in Common Law countries, it is because the legal system in Civil Law countries is less insulated from the pressures of politicians and administration that in Common law countries. It is worth noting that the merit of Mahoney's analysis is to stress that the law issue can be bound closely to the State, the administration and the public governance.

Thus, the representation of justice revealed by the analysis of Common Law and the Civil Law is marked by two characteristics: on the one hand, it reveals a certain sanctity of the independence of justice as a rule-making institution, because judge made law guarantees both a decentralized regulation and individual freedom; on the other hand, administration of judiciary under Common Law is associated with providing checks and balances *vis-à-vis* the State and its bureaucracy, whereas the administration of the judiciary under the Civil Law system is considered open to political interests. It is this issue that we now consider.

II. Justice, Freedom, and Efficiency: Courts and Control of Government

One strand of economic research on justice attempts to define the effect of independence of the judiciary on economic and political freedom La Porta, Lopez-de-Silanes, Pop-Eleches and Shleifer.[9] This analytical framework may be named a 'politico-constitutional' one: it aims at assessing the effects of the level of independence of the courts and of the constitutional review of laws on the control of the executive, which would not be disposed to individual freedom and the maintenance of

---

[8] Mahoney (Clague, Keefer, Knack et Olson, 1999) made an estimation of the Contract Intensive Money (CIM) defined as the ratio M2-C/M2: (C=currency held outside banks): bank deposits are a measure of the confidence citizens have in the mechanisms that enforce property and contractual rights. A high level of CIM means that individual agents are not reluctant towards long-term contracting.

[9] R. La Porta, F. Lopez-de-Silanes, C. Pop-Eleches, A. Shleifer, 'Judicial Checks and Balances', *Journal of Political Economy*, Vol. 112, No. 2, 2004, p. 445.

property rights. What is then at issue is a representation of the justice as a 'check and balance' institution.

This perspective is influenced distinctly by Friedrich Hayek's philosophy of law, which maintains that judge made law leads to a spontaneous social order; such a non-planned order prevents the extension of the governmental sphere and guarantees the individual's freedom.[10]

In this line of throught, justice is seen as a counterpower. This is apparent in a reconsideration of the two models of judicial systems, the Common Law one and the one of the Civil Law since the 12th and 13th Centuries, by Glaeser and Shleifer.[11] According to these authors, the origin of the legal systems, the emergence of the judges and civil and criminal proceedings are explained by the structures of political power.

A. The Models of Justice: The History of Legal Institutions revisited

The central issue raised by Glaeser and Shleifer (2002) is to know the reasons the Civil Law systems relies on government-employed professional judges, on written records, on the predominance of statute law over judge-made law, whereas common law systems rely on lay judges, juries, oral proceedings, and case-law.

This characterization – very simplified or even caricatural – is linked to the question of the independence of judges. Professional judges are supposed to be controlled directly by the State, whereas lay judges or juries are supposed to be independent from the sovereign. The model of Glaeser and Shleifer is based on the royal judges versus the independent judges who emerged in France and England in the 12th-13th centuries.

Within this framework, the efficiency of the models of justice is assessed in reference to the structure of the political powers and to their relationships with the judges.

The starting point in Glaeser and Shleifer reasoning is the following: basically, one could have expected the following process to happen: In the Middle Ages, the King of England – who had gained autonomy against the nobility – was vested with more of powers over his subjects than the King of France, who was a duke in rivalries with other dukes, and whose military power didn't spread beyond the Ile-de-France area. One could have expected that a system of justice controlled by the sovereign should have appeared where the central political power was

---

10 F. Hayek, *Droit, législation et liberté*, PUF, coll. Libre échange, tome 1 – Règles et ordre [1973 for the original edition in English], 1980.

11 E. Glaeser, A. Shleifer, 'Legal Origins', *Quarterly Journal of Economics*, November 2002, p. 1193.

strongest, namely in England; and that conversely in France – as a country of limited royal control – a system of independent judges should have developed. However, it is precisely the opposite that occurred in fact. It remains to determine why.

The answer of Glaeser and Shleifer is grounded on their specific conception of the interests of local political groups: the ultimate aim of the justice is to protect property rights which pre-suppose that it is insulated from the pressures of interest groups, powerful political figures and corruption. When local pressures on judges are weak, it is possible to rely on independent judges and juries; on the contrary, when local powers are strong, the sovereign has no other choice but to appoint royal judges, under the king's tutelage, to isolate them from the pressures of the local Lords. This is how the 12th century England of Henri II developed the jury system, defined by Pollock and Maitland[12] as 'a body of neighbors summoned by some public officer to give upon oath a true answer to some question'. The jury was an assembly of local notables that informed itinerant royal judges on the local facts. It was a means to collect some information. Thereafter, with the *Magna Carta*, the power of juries grew insofar as the decision of the judges was held to be accepted by the jury. The jury became then an institution limiting the discretion of the royal judges.

Thus, the English and French models of justice illustrate a basic trade-off: either a royal judge who receives the sovereign's incentives (through the grant of a judicial office or earnings) and is less exposed to the local pressures; or a jury who doesn't receive any incentives but is an institution whose preferences are close to those of the community in which the judge exercises his jurisdiction.[13] In this regard, the formal model proposed by Glaeser and Shleifer makes a crucial assumption according to which the utility function of the jury is identical to the preferences of the community.

The assumption that 'the tastes of the jury mirror those of the community, in part because the jurors come from among them'[14] clearly reveals the author's representation of justice (see III of this paper). This representation – which is far from being exempt of normative content and gives a picture of what an efficient justice system looks like – is one of a justice of laymen, decentralized, loosely organized and predominantly oral proceedings. In short, it refers to – in Max Weber's words – a *qâdi* justice, in which each case is considered on its individual merits without reference to abstract principles, on the basis of concrete ethical

---

[12]   1898, quoted by Glaeser, Shleifer (2002), *op. cit.*, p. 1198.

[13]   Glaeser, Shleifer (2002), *op. cit.*, p. 1202.

[14]   *Ibid.*, p. 1204.

or other practical value judgments, and with no formalism in proceedings.[15]

B. Economic and Political Freedom

La Porta, Lopez-de-Silanes, and Shleifer[16] offer a 'constitutional' approach of institutions. It focuses on the degree of independence of judicial power and the level of constitutional review. The framework of analysis is based on the search of a relation between these institutional features and economic and political freedom, in several dozen of countries. The virtues of the independence of courts can be found both in the relationship between citizens and the State, and in private litigation. In the first case, a judicial system, independent *vis-à-vis* the government, guarantees the judges impartiality in conflicts between the citizens in the State. In the second case, independence of judges prevents the government from putting pressure on the courts in order to unduly favour a political ally. In any case, the Justice is considered as an institution protecting property rights and the individual freedom against State interference and limitation.

The constitutional review is a mechanism different from that of Civil Law: it can counter promulgation of laws or regulations by the legislature or the executive that are oriented toward the satisfaction of interests groups' politically connected power, or even the electoral majority.

The results are in conformity with the theory of Hayek:

Consistent with the theory of Hayek and others, we find that both judicial independence and constitutional review are strong indicators of freedom. We find that judicial independence is important for both kinds of freedom [i.e. economic and political, TK], whereas constitutional review provisions are prerequisites for political freedom.[17]

However, the independence of the courts is empirically greatly associated as a feature of Common law.

After all, in Common law systems there is a representation of justice which is seen as opposing the excesses of the state: the independent judges are anxious to slow down the excessive political interventions in the economy.[18] The Common Law would be then much more a guarantor the liberties and for property rights than Civil law systems, where justice is less powerful, less independent and where the State may be bound by particular interests.

---

[15] The *qâdi* justice was seen by Weber as 'substantively irrational'.

[16] R. La Porta, F. Lopez-de-Silanes, C. Pop-Eleches, A. Shleifer (2004), *op. cit.*, p. 445.

[17] *Ibid.*, p. 448.

[18] *Ibid.*, p. 449.

C. Legal Origins: Institutions Are Not (Necessarily) Efficient

The basic dilemma concerning justice in the perspectives of the new comparative economics is clearly stated: the independence of judges exposes them to the risk of corruption, whereas the absence of independence exposes them to the absolute submissiveness to the political power.[19] But this first dilemma doesn't exhaust the question of influences on judges insofar as it is necessary to distinguish between private influences and political influences.

On the one hand a system of decentralized justice in which the judges are safe from State interference exposes them to the risk of corruption or influence through bribery; on the other hand, a judicial system which is centralized, under narrow control of the government, guarantees the judges against the influences of private interest groups but puts them under the control of the State.

Glaeser and Shleifer argue that the models of justice adopted by England and France during their history are efficient solutions to the specific features of their political structures. However, a number of countries formerly under former colonial domination were not able, during their history, to design judicial institutions fitting their own context; these transplanted institutions are not without their problems. However, analysts rather correlate them with the inheritance of French law. Thus, Glaeser and Shleifer argued, via a mathematical model destined to show the implications of the model of the jury and the one of the royal judge on social welfare, that a Civil Law system functions rather well, from this point of view, when the sovereign's preferences are close to those of the community. If such a system was to be transplanted in a context where the king's preferences and those of the community differ, it is more that likely that the sovereign uses his power on the judges to 'politicize' the courts rulings. According to Glaeser and Shleifer, it is quite obvious that 'The transplantation of common law does not suffer from this problem to the same extent, since enforcement is relatively depolitized – juries (and judges) are independent'.[20]

D. Independence?

The conception of the independence of the judicial system *vis-à-vis* the political power is not limited to France and England of the 12th and 13th Centuries; it has a more general scope and concerns the current judicial systems as well. It sums up, *in fine*, to an opposition between lay judges and professional magistrates, the first being considered as

---

[19] E. Glaeser, A. Shleifer (2002), 'Legal Origins', *op. cit.*
[20] *Ibid.*, p. 1221.

independent when local powers are weak, and the second put under the control of the government. This way to formulate the problem of the independence of justice is quite disconcerting, for it's true that all democratic States constitutionally guarantee the independence of courts in ways that do not depend on the manner in which those jurisdictions are composed. In Europe, the European Convention of the Human Rights constitutes a supplementary guarantee to the citizens in terms of access to justice and equitable lawsuit as well as dealing with cases without undue delay.

In this regard, it is interesting that both Common Law (United Kingdom) and Civil Law countries are concerned by rulings of the European Convention on Human Rights and the decisions of the European Court of Human's Rights.

In La Porta *et al.*,[21] the analysis of judicial checks and balances rests on empirical data designed to capture, under the form of a specific variable, the degree of the independence of the judiciary. This variable is constructed from other variables that relate to the length of tenure of both judges of the Supreme Court and of administrative courts judges (life-long tenure, tenure exceeding six years, tenure less than six years) and to the contribution of case-law to the creation of law (dummy variable: 1 if yes, 0 if no). The 'independence of justice' variable is calculated as the sum of the variables 'judges' tenure' and the variable 'case law'. The procedural rules which guarantee impartiality and fairness don't seem to be captured by the variable of La Porta *et al.* Finally, it seems, at the very least, questionable to summarize in a numeric value choice (0 or 1) the role of case law in a legal system. Even France admits that courts rulings are a source of law. This fact should result in treating France in the same way as the United Kingdom, the United States or Australia.

Finally, the representation of the independence of justice revealed in La Porta *et al.*[22] associates it almost exclusively to the length of judges' tenure. The relationships between tenure and independence is *a priori* indeterminate: a judge with life-long tenure can equally well be considered a civil servant whose progress in career advancement can depend on his own propensity to be well considered by Attorney General or like a person endowed with the spirit of public interest and attentive to impartiality and fairness. In the same way, a 'temporary' judge can be seen as a person deciding cases in the way pleasing to his tutelage in order to reach a life-long tenure, or like a judge of which the briefness of tenure is a guarantee against his exposure to local pressures or political

---

[21] R. La Porta, F. Lopez-de-Silanes, C. Pop-Eleches, A. Shleifer (2004), *op. cit.*
[22] *Ibid.*

of influence... The position of La Porta *et al.* is to consider that 'When judges have long-life tenure, they are both less susceptible to direct political pressure and less likely to have been selected by the government currently in office'.[23] This concept is unconvincing. But, to conclude for the moment on this point, it is quite obvious that this concept of the independence can only affect the sensitivity of jurists, political scientists and philosophers who think that the relationships of justice and the political sphere cannot extend beyond the procedural and institutional mechanisms by which the justice operates.[24]

III. Justice from a Procedural Viewpoint

Efficiency of the court system as an institution for the processing of dispute resolution is certainly an important issue, but it is rather complex if one considers the several layers of criteria whereby matters are decided.[25] In this regard, one cannot ignore the contribution of Djankov, La Porta, Lopez-de-Silanes and Shleifer.[26]

A. Renewed Look on the Courts

These authors have proceeded to an econometric analysis of 109 countries from the viewpoint of the efficiency of their judicial systems. The starting point of their analysis is that if the economists[27] were generally optimistic on the notion of courts as institutions guaranteeing property rights and contracts, they devoted little attention to the limitations of judicial systems.

According to DLLS, two competing claims are generally made on this subject:

- the 'development theory' predicts that courts, like other institutions, are more efficient in rich countries than poor countries (Demsetz, North): the reason is that as creation of institutions implies high fixed

---

[23] *Ibid.*, p. 453.

[24] The story of the threat of reform of the Supreme Court of the United States by President Roosevelt in the beginning of his mandate is likely to contradict the positive and meaningful interrelationship between the independence of the justice and the adherence to the Common Law group. The same applies when one recognises that the nomination of the judges of the Supreme Court is a political act. See Schwartz (1993).

[25] E. Breen (ed.), *Évaluer la justice*, PUF, coll. Droit et Justice, 2002, 301 p.

[26] S. Djankov., R. La Porta, F. Lopez-de-Silanes, A. Shleifer, 'Courts', *Quarterly Journal of Economics*, Vol. 118, No. 3, 2003, p. 453 (herein 'DLLS').

[27] See for example R. Coase, 'The Problem of Social Cost', *Journal of Law and Economics*, 3, 1960, p. 1.

costs, they are only socially beneficial when the demand for institutions is sufficiently strong to justify these costs;

- the 'incentives theory' maintains that the quality of justice is influenced strongly by the incentives on participants (justiciables, judges, attorneys); courts in poor countries would be inefficient because they deliver bad incentives: the judges are not concerned with delay, it is in the interest of attorneys to prolong the legal proceedings unnecessarily.

In this regard, the analysis of DLLS is truly original insofar as it constitutes the first attempt by economists in measuring the length of civil proceedings (at least since Bentham's *'Introduction to the Principles of Morals and Legislation'*).

B. The Measure of 'Procedural Formalism'

The empirical method of DLLS consists in constructing an indicator of 'procedural formalism' for dispute resolution on the basis of about fifty institutional variables whose table 1 (hereinafter) gives some examples.

Table 1

Variables	
Professional versus laymen	Court: general or limited (i.e. specialized) jurisdiction
	Professional or nonprofessional judge
	Legal representation mandatory or optional
Written versus oral	Filing: written form or oral complaint
	Evidence: written or oral
	Judgment: written form or orally pronounced
Legal justification	Complaint: legally justified or not
	Judgment: legally justified or not
	Judgment: grounded on law or on equity
Incentives of parties	Mandatory time limit for notification of judgment
	Quota litis or contingent fees prohibited or not
	Loser pays rule or not

Source: adapted from Djankov *et al.* (2004, p. 463-473).

The procedural formalism index is constructed on the basis of an inquiry in courts of first instance. Data collection has been achieved in about one hundred countries by law office affiliated with the international associations *Lex Mundi* and *Lex Africa*. The inquiry is conducted from two standard cases: the eviction of a tenant debtor of rents and the recovery of an unpaid cheque. The collection of qualitative data has been completed by other sources, notably the data of the World Business Environment Survey on quality of justice by small enterprises.

The DLLS's analysis lead them to conclude that procedural formalism is very more accentuated in the civil law world that in common law countries; it is associated, in the first place, with lengthier court procedures, rather than consistency, honesty, fairness in judicial decisions, to higher levels of corruption and to a weaker level of the quality of justice.

C. Point of Reference Revealing an Ideal of Justice

To understand the representation of justice which the analysis of DLLS reveals, it is important to emphasise that the procedural formalism index is interpreted from a point of reference.

This point of reference has the characteristic to be a case of efficient dispute resolution with no procedural formalism i.e. an out-of-court settlement of disputes between neighbors: 'In a theoretical model of an ideal court, a dispute between neighbors can be resolved by a third party on fairness grounds, with little knowledge or use of law, no lawyers, no written submissions, no procedural constraints on how evidence, witnesses, and arguments are presented, and no appeal.'[28]

However, the data on existing procedural formalism are used to construct measures 'defined as the extent to which regulation causes dispute resolution to deviate from the neighbor model'.[29] In other words, the method consists in constructing indicators of procedural complexity that measure the extent of the deviation in relation to an ideal situation of dispute resolution. This point of reference is not exempt from normative value, since it is associated with an 'ideal'.

However, this point of reference is close, or even similar, to the model of settlement of disputes between neighbors of Ronald Coase where transaction costs are nil. In his famous article from which the famous 'Coase theorem' has been deduced, Coase[30] argued that the negative externalities between individuals using their own property rights resulting in mutual harms, can find an efficient solution through a bilateral bargaining process. Such a bargain can correct a prior inefficient allocation of the rights by a court. When the private bargain is not hindered by positive transaction costs, it constitutes a process of re-arrangement by the market of rights granted by the judge: the argument made in 'The Problem of Social Cost' is that, 'in an ideal world in which the costs of a settlement would be nil, that allocation of the rights... must be determined not by either a government... or a court..., but by

---

[28] S. Djankov., R. La Porta, F. Lopez-de-Silanes, A. Shleifer (2003), *op. cit.*, p. 455.

[29] *Ibid.*, p. 456.

[30] R. Coase, *op. cit.*

the market'.[31] However, when such a private rearrangement is impossible, 'courts proceedings become a necessary evil'.[32] The judges are invited then, by Coase and by Posner, to take into account the economic consequences of their decisions, in other terms to decide in ways that contribute to the maximization of production (Coase) or of the wealth (Posner).

D. English Magistrates' Courts as a Model?

One can wonder about the innocence of the method of 'standardization' of judicial systems of DLLS, but what matters more is from the fact that the normative preconceptions of the authors prevent them from taking into account of the effects of the formalisation of the proceedings on the expectations of individuals and to a certain extent, on legal certainty. This certainly supposes a rigorous procedural framework, written proceedings and legally grounded judgments. Nothing ensures that the model of judicial proceedings is compatible with legal certainty, far from it.

In this regard, the works of Bell and Dadomo[33] on the magistrates' courts in England are of a considerable interest, insofar as these jurisdictions return a quasi profane kind of justice: as the courts are not compelled to state the legal grounds of their decisions, and conditions of appeal are narrow, the English magistrates' courts prove to be close to the ideal of justice argued by DLLS. Bell and Dadomo paint a very negative picture of these courts and caution the French authorities against the dangers of the administration of a similar model of judicial action. A few of the critiques raised by these two English jurists are worth repeating:

- the judgments pronounced by the magistrates's courts are never motivated,

- in the rulings on minors in criminal cases, the judges show evidence of a striking amateurism and have more resort to detention that the judges of the Crown Courts,

- because of (their) approximate knowledge of the law, the magistrates' courts are susceptible to pronounce their judgements on the basis of presentiments rather than of proofs. (Bell and Dadomo, 1996, p. 614).

---

[31] E. Serverin, 'The Negotiation of Disputed Rights, or How The Law Comes to Economics', in B. Deffains, T. Kirat (eds.), *Law and Economics in Civil Law Countries*, The Economics of Legal Relationships, Vol. 6 (series editor N. Mercuro), Amsterdam, JAI Press-Elsevier, 2001, p. 46.

[32] *Ibid.*, p. 47.

[33] B. Bell, J.-L. Dadomo, 'Les Magistrates' Courts: un modèle de justice de proximité pour la France?', *Rev. Sc. Crim.*, No. 3, 1996, p. 607.

Conclusion

Several ideas are clearly set out in the literature on economic comparative analysis of legal systems.

Firstly, the literature maintains that the Common Law system, marked by a weak codification of law and an important contribution of the courts to making law, would tend to guarantee economic liberties and to sustain the more important economic growth than the civil law systems, which are on their part characterized by a legislative and regulatory origin of law and a secondary place granted to the courts. The Civil Law systems would tend to the hypertrophy of government regulation, whereas those that belong to the world of the Anglo-American law are characterized by less legislative control and a higher level of political and economic freedom of the citizens.

Secondly, the representation of an ideal model of justice is the one of a justice without magistrates, or even without courts. It is like layman's justice or, at best, justice provided by non professional conciliators.

Thirdly, procedural formalism of the courts is associated, unambiguously, to a damaging excessively exacting regulation of economic activity. It must be underscored that, in all the studies reported in this article, the procedural formalism issue is never linked to the constraints of impartiality and fairness in the jurisdictional proceedings in democratic states. Besides, nothing permits the affirmation that an oral proceeding is less formal than a written proceeding, or that the former is less costly in terms of transaction costs than the latter.

It would be tempting to conclude that economists don't like judges and institutional justice or, even less, don't understand them in a suitable manner. This pessimistic statement is reinforced, in France, by works of labour economists who think that the judge's control on the causes of layoffs is an economic absurdity that could be replaced usefully by a taxation of the layoffs.[34]

References

R. Barro, 'Rule of Law, Democracy, and Economic Performance', in *2000 Index of Economic Freedom*, Heritage Foundation, 2000.

O. Blanchard, J. Tirole, *Protection de l'emploi et procédures de licenciement*, Rapport du Centre d'Analyse Économique, Paris, La Documentation française, 2003.

---

[34] O. Blanchard, J. Tirole, *Protection de l'emploi et procédures de licenciement*, Rapport du Centre d'analyse économique, Paris, La Documentation française, 2003.

J. Bentham, (1824), 'An Introduction to the Principles of Morals and Legislation', partially reprinted in: A. Ryan (ed.), *Utilitarism and Other Essays. J.S. Mill and Jeremy Bentham*, London, Penguin Books, 1987.

B. Bell, J.-L. Dadomo, 'Les Magistrates' Courts: un modèle de justice de proximité pour la France?', *Rev. Sc. Crim.*, No. 3, 1996, p. 607-618.

J. Botero, S. Djankov, R. La Porta, F. Lopez-de-Silanes, A. Shleifer, 'The Regulation of Labor', *Quarterly Journal of Economics*, Vol. 119, No. 4, 2004, p. 1339-1382.

E. Breen (ed.), *Évaluer la justice*, PUF, coll. Droit et Justice, 2002, p. 301.

P. Cahuc, F. Kramarz, *De la précarité à la mobilité: vers une sécurité sociale professionnelle*, rapport au Ministre de l'économie et des finances et au Ministre de l'emploi, Paris, 2004.

C. Clague, P. Keefer, S. Knack, M. Olson, 'Contract-Intensive Money: Contract Enforcement, Property Rights, and Economic Performance', *Journal of Economic Growth*, Vol. 4, No. 2, 1999, p. 185-211.

R. Coase, 'The Problem of Social Cost', *Journal of Law and Economics*, No. 3, 1960, p. 1-44.

K. Davis, M. Trebilcock, 'Legal reforms and development', *Third World Quarterly*, Vol. 22, No. 1, 2001, p. 21-36.

B. Deffains, 'Competition Between Legal Systems: A Comparative Law and Economics Perspective', in B. Deffains, T. Kirat (eds.), *Law and Economics in Civil Law Countries*, The Economics of Legal Relationships, Vol. 6 (series editor N. Mercuro), JAI Press-Elsevier, 2001, p. 9-21.

S. Djankov, E. Glaeser, R. La Porta, F. Lopez-de-Silanes, A. Shleifer, 'Courts', *Quarterly Journal of Economics*, Vol. 118, No. 3, 2003, p. 453-517.

S. Djankov, E. Glaeser, R. La Porta, F. Lopez-de-Silanes, A. Shleifer, 'The new comparative economics', *Journal of Comparative Economics*, No. 31, 2003, p. 595-619.

E. Glaeser, A. Shleifer, 'Legal Origins', *Quarterly Journal of Economics*, Novrember 2002, p. 1193-1229.

F. Hayek, *Droit, législation et liberté*, Paris, Presses Universitaires de France, coll. Libre échange, tome 1 – Règles et ordre [1973 for the original edition in english], 1980.

R. La Porta, F. Lopez-de-Silanes, C. Pop-Eleches, A. Shleifer, 'Judicial Checks and Balances', *Journal of Political Economy*, Vol. 112, No. 2, 2004, p. 445-470.

R. La Porta, F. Lopez-de-Silanes, A. Shleifer, R. Vishny, 'Legal Determinants of External Finance', *Journal of Finance*, vol 52, No. 3, 1997, p. 1131-1150.

R. Levine, 'Law, Finance, and Economic Growth', *Journal of Financial Intermediation*, No. 8, 1999, p. 8-35.

P. Mahoney, 'The Common Law and Economic Growth: Hayek Might be Right', *Journal of Legal Studies*, Vol. 30, No. 2, 2001, p. 503-525.

U. Mattei, *Comparative Law and Economics*, Ann Harbor, Michigan University Press, 1997.

B. Schwartz, *A History of the Supreme Court*, Oxford University Press, 1993.

E. Serverin, *Sociologie du droit*, La Découverte, coll. Repères, 2000, p. 128.

E. Serverin, 'The Negotiation of Disputed Rights, or How The Law Comes to Economics', in B. Deffains, T. Kirat (eds.), *Law and Economics in Civil Law Countries*, The Economics of Legal Relationships, Vol. 6 (series editor N. Mercuro), JAI Press-Elsevier, 2001, p. 43-60.

World Bank – International Finance Corporation, *Doing Business in 2006: Creating Jobs*, Washington D.C, 2006.

Cross Representations of Law and Economics in Corporate Governance

Tristan BOYER

Luxembourg School of Finance and Centre de Philosophie de Droit of the Université catholique de Louvain

I. Introduction

The object of this contribution is to address as an illustration the potential of relying on cross representations to improve economic theory, analysis and descriptions. Both law and economics shape representations of the world: law focuses on rules and justice; economics focuses on efficiency and allocation. They describe common situations and 'objects' such as firms and their functioning, both with positive (analytical) and normative perspectives. However, their descriptions and remedies for the issues which they tackle are very different due to the differences in their philosophical and sociological goals.

The Law & Economics perspective can be described as the use of the economics theoretical framework upon issues of law. In this perspective, law issues are addressed as any other economic phenomenon through the prism of efficiency. From this perspective, law is contingent upon normative conditions of economic theory and the best solution arises after a standard process of optimisation. This paper will set out a reversal of that epistemological position: instead of using economic representations to improve the state of law, representations of law will be aimed at testing and improving the economic analytical framework. Since corporate governance issues are structured by domestic laws as well as by economic regulations, legal representations will be discussed in light of economic corporate governance analysis.

Corporate governance is a subject upon which economists and lawyers seem to share the same object (the firm) and to have a common perspective. Most of the literature defines corporate governance as the answer to 'what means are open to assist shareholder in controlling the managers?' This perspective can be considered as a narrow one (still it is the most widespread perspective among economists and lawyers), but it can be extended with a 'stakeholder' approach that relies on a broaden definition of corporation. In this extended perspective, the question of corporate governance can still be put in terms of control: what are the possible ways that would enable stakeholders (including shareholders, employees, creditors and sometimes also customers, suppliers, local communities, environment, etc.) to take part in the corporation's decisions?

The narrow (but dominant) economic perspective about corporate governance carries out its reflexions within the framework of agency theory that considers the firm as a nexus of contracts where shareholders try to align the board of directors' members interests with their own. The parallel jurists' perspective on corporate governance focuses on the same issues: both American and European practices are focused on the same set of legal mechanisms described by national legal frameworks (and sometimes also by international bodies as the OECD[1] or institutional investors as CalPERS[2]) about control and transparency in the corporations.

Despite an unquestionable relevance in their questioning (information and disclosure are linked to the enhancement of the financial market's efficiency), the relevance of their normative responses is questionable from both the theoretical and the practical points of view. The aporia of the agency theory lies in its incapacity to conceive the firm as anything else than an nexus of contracts: this definition excludes everything except bilateral bargaining and consequently neglects the existence of social constraints and of any form of collective action.[3]

The solutions to the issue of reliability of information, which is the paradigmatic issue of agency theory, are only described and conceived in terms of incentives meant for the agent to act solely in the interest of the principal. According to this theoretical framework, decisions are taken through the mechanical framework of an optimisation program. This perspective denies the existence of any social and/or collective phenomenon. This is the reason why we reject the agency theory theoretical framework as an adequate framework for solving corporate

---

[1] OECD, 2004, Principles of Corporate Governance, Paris.

[2] CalPERS, 'Corporate Governance principles & guidelines', 2007, http://www. calpers-governance.org/principles/

[3] J. Lenoble, 'From an incentive to a reflexive approach to Corporate Governance', in Cobbaut and Lenoble, Corporate Governance: an institutionallst approach, Kluwer Law International, 2003.

governance issues: in our opinion, it is disconnected from the concrete reality of the firm's situation.

II. Firm's Representations in Economics and in Law: a Cross Fertilization

The search for a more accurate theoretical and practical framework for corporate governance issues than that of the agency theory requires an understanding of the nature of the firm and of its interest. The nature of the firm is a subject upon which the lawyers' representations about economy cross those of economists and managers about law. In order to reconstruct a theory of corporate governance, we will first consider these representations separately and then cross them.

From an epistemological point of view, our approach distinguishes itself from the posnerian approach of 'law and economics' issues. This approach is a typically economist approach: it focuses on law with a normative objective. The main question of posnerian law and economics is the question of efficient allocation: judges (as law makers) are not supposed to make their judgements with an objective of justice but with the only objective of efficient allocation.[4] In this normative theory, judges have to respect only one rule, derived from the paradigmatic economic 'law' of optimization.

Our approach is different in its foundations and is closer to Williamson's. His heuristic perspective develops the idea that the law is one of the foundations of any economic action.[5] Then the objective is not to define what kind of rule must be applied to optimize the well being of the economic agents, but how law, *via* its representations in economic agent's minds, influences the economic actions of people. We must emphasize that this is not the same as looking, as most economists do, at the legal framework as an exogenous constraint because it allows to endogeneise the influences of laws and rules and by extension, to consider the possibility of improving the set of rules implemented.

Aligning managers' interests with the shareholders' interests is pertinent only when the analysis is focused on contractual relations and excludes any other relation: because contracts are considered as complying with the rule of equivalence and would not be accepted by one of the parties if it was not so, they are also supposed to protect both of the contracting parties. Workers, managers, consumers, suppliers have one or more contract(s) with the firm. For this reason, they are considered as

---

[4]   T. Kirat, *Economie du droit*, La Découverte, Repères, 1999.

[5]   O. Williamson, *The Economic Institutions of Capitalism*, The Free Press/Macmillan, 1985.

protected by their contract and also subject to asymmetrical information problems, while the shareholder, whose stakes are not protected by a contract, appears then as the weakest stakeholder of the firm and also the one who the best embodies its interests. This analytical perspective,[6] which is the mainstream one, considers the firm as the shareholders' property. It is considered as an object whose property rights belong to the shareholders. Thus, the interest of the shareholders and the interest of the firm are the same.

The confusion of the shareholders' and the firm's interests is not a scientific assertion: it is the common representation of a majority of researchers in corporate governance. This point can be addressed by the civil law analysis of the firm in a way that can reveal the weak points of this standard perspective and overcome its aporia. Crossing the representations of law with the economic ones, in this case where lawyers and economists share the same 'object', contributes to the emergence of a new framework in corporate governance analysis. By revealing the underlying beliefs of the mainstream corporate governance theory, both lawyers and economists can improve the efficiency of their normative propositions.

The first point with this crossing of representations of law and economics is that, historically, the enterprise does not exist in either of these disciplines.[7] The closest concept in economics is the concept of entrepreneur whose aim is to optimise (as a price taker) the production.[8] From the juridical point of view, the firm is reduced to the concept of company which is considered as an autonomous person.[9] In both cases, the question of governance cannot be considered as a question solved by those perspectives: the firm is represented as an autonomous person, with a personal and clearly defined interest.

If we assume that these descriptions are the accurate framework for analyzing corporate governance issues, we must agree with Kreps' foreword[10] on his seminal article about corporate culture: we don't have anything to say, nor as an economist nor as a lawyer upon this subject.

---

[6] For further development and precisions see S. Grossman, O. Hart, 'The Costs and Benefits of Ownership: A Theory of Vertical and Lateral Integration', *Journal of Political Economy*, Vol. 94, 1986, p. 691.

[7] T. Boyer, 'Gouvernement d'entreprise et décisions d'emploi', Thèse de doctorat en économie soutenue à l'Université Paris X, 2002.

[8] This neo-classical description of the firm is based on L. Walras, *Éléments d'économie politique pure*, LGDJ, 1874, french re-ed. 1976.

[9] J.-P., Robé, 'Enterprises and the Constitution of World Economy', *International Corporate Law*, Vol. II, 2003.

[10] D. Kreps, 'Corporate culture and economic theory', *Perspectives on positive political economy*, Cambridge University Press, 1990.

As provocative as it may seem, this point is to state that these representations lead to an impossibility of conceiving the firm as a place governed by people with different interests which must be considered in order to succeed. As a consequence, corporate governance cannot be an issue within this theoretical framework.

However, if the crossing of representations between classical standard economics and standard positive theory of law does not open any fruitful perspective, this crossing is much more promising when we look at the ways lawyers and economists cope with this aporia. In order to analyse questions of governance within the firm, both economists and lawyers have to pass through the representation of the firm as a black box. The first way we will explore is linked to the question of rights of property.

The property rights theory is the economic theory that arises as the foundation of any corporate governance issue with the question of 'ownership and control' over the firm.[11] It is the basis upon which mainstream analysis is built. As the subject of this work is to analyse the value of considering the representations of law in order to improve our understanding of corporate governance, the property rights theory can be interestingly re-interpreted in accordance with the juridical perspective. Actually, property rights are a well-known legal category and we will question the accuracy of applying this category to the firm and the shareholders.

III. The Legal Representation of Property

In the ancient roman law (and also in civil law), the bundle of rights that together constitutes full ownership of property comprises three separate sub-bundles: (1) *usus* the right to use or possess, i.e., hold, occupy, and utilize the property; (2) *abusus* the right to abuse or alienate, i.e., transfer, or even destroy the property, and (3) *fructus* the right to the fruits, i.e., to receive and enjoy the earnings, profits, rents, and revenues produced by or derived from the property. Ownership may be allocated in various combinations among different persons, with each having less than full ownership. For example, the owner of a legal usufruct ('*usufructuary*') has the right to use the property burdened with the usufruct (*usus*) and to enjoy the fruits of that property (*fructus*), but does not have the right to alienate the property (*abusus*); that right belongs to the naked owner, albeit subject to the usufruct. The owner of the *abusus* cannot sell the property: he or she can only sell its part of the

---

[11] A. Berle, G. Means, *The modern corporation and private property*, MacMillan, 1932.

property (the *abusus*) and this cannot deter the *usufructuary* from his or her prerogatives.

The notion of incomplete ownership is particularly accurate for this critic, because in our opinion, shareholders cannot be described as the sole owners of the firm. The property rights theory assumes that because shareholders are the residual claimants of the firm, they are the owners of it. Our aim is to show that their ownership is incomplete and depends of their situation. As a consequence, other stakeholders must be considered also as incomplete owners of the firm and should then be able to exercise the associated rights.

What could be the ownership of a firm? From a juridical point of view, this question would be considered as a non-sense: the company[12] is a legal person and the shareholders do own shares, they do not own the company because it is a person (nobody can own a person, even if it is a legal person). But in our critical perspective, the legal representation of property will still be applied in order to challenge the property rights approach.

What could be the *usus*, the *fructus* and the *abusus* of a firm? As the *usus* is about the control of the use, we can assume that the control of the firm by the manager is the closest approximation. The *fructus* should be considered as the profit of the firm (in technical terms: Net Operating Profits After Taxes a.k.a. NOPAT) and not only as the dividend which is the share's *fructus*. The *abusus* can obviously be defined as the right to end or sell the firm. With this framework we can now test the accuracy of the property right theory.

Individually, a minority shareholder cannot make use of his right of *abusus*: the decision of ending a company can only be made by a majority of the shareholders or, in some countries by a majority of 2/3 of the shareholders. Shall we then consider that a minority shareholder is an *usufructuary* of the firm? Actually, as the *usus* must be delegated to a director (shareholders elect among themselves the board whose mission is to control the management of the company), we can assume that a minority shareholder cannot be considered as having the *usus* of the

---

[12] The question of the status of the company (e.g. is the company the same thing as the firm?) is particularly discussed among the lawyers community (see M. Despax, 1956, *L'entreprise et le droit*, thèse pour le doctorat en droit, publiée dans la collection 'bibliothèque de droit privé', LGDJ, 1957; J. Paillusseau, 'Les fondements du droit moderne des sociétés', JCP, I, 3148, 1984 or G. Teubner, *Le droit, un système autopoïétique*, collection les voies du droit, PUF, 1993), but won't be taken into account in this development at this moment: we will consider, in the first instance that 'company' and 'firm' are synonyms. The translation of an economic category to a juridical category is tricky and causes difficulties that go far beyond the scope of this text.

firm. For the same reason, he or she will not be considered as having the *fructus* of the company.

Collectively, the property of the firm must be differently considered. Even if the *usus* and the *fructus* are delegated, the community of shareholders owns these rights. The *abusus* is also owned by the community of shareholders. For these reasons, the shareholders *as a community* can be considered, *at first sight*, as owners of the firm as they seem to have the full set of rights that characterised ownership.

From this point of view, the property rights theory can be considered as solidly confirmed in its construction of 'the shareholders as the owners of the firm'. Meanwhile, does the property of the firm belong only to the shareholders? As creditors can demand (only in some cases of financial distress) the liquidation of the company, which is the prerogative of the owner's *abusus*, we must recognise that shareholders do not have the complete *abusus* of the firm. Moreover, in some cases of severe fraud or misconduct, the State can require, in some countries, the winding-up of a company. In certain countries, a part of the profit is compulsorily dedicated to employees by a legal mechanism of 'participation', which lessens the *usus* of the shareholders.

As we have demonstrated that shareholders do not completely have the full set of property rights, we must then consider that shareholders are not *at all times* the only residual claimants of the firm. Thus we have now to find out in what circumstances other stakeholders are involved because of their part of the property rights. The answer is found through an analysis of the firm's interest.

IV. The Question of Firm's Interest

In capitalist countries, free entrepreneurship has been the key element of development during the industrial revolution of the 19th century. The industrial development tended to increase the need for big companies, big enough to be able to raise enormous amounts of capital (e.g. railroads). At this time, the general rule for firms was unlimited liability: the associates were liable on their own patrimony for all the obligations of the firm and the consequences in case of bankruptcy were financially disastrous for the associate(s) sued by the creditor(s) (in addition to the penal sanctions).[13] Financing such projects needed huge amounts of finance capital that consequently needed large numbers of small savings in addition to the other significant blocks of capital. In order to attract

---

[13] R. Szramkiewicz, *Histoire du droit des affaires*, Montchrestien, Domat droit privé, 1989.

these small savings, the status of these companies should be a status of limited liability.

In the first half of the 19th century in Europe and in USA, that kind of company (with limited liability) had to be founded by a State Charter (royal or from a national body) because limited liability was derogatory. This process was cumbersome and too heavy in a period of fast economic development. If, at the beginning of the industrial revolution, the involvement of the public interest was the only acceptable justification for allowing the limited liability of a firm, limited liability became, in a few years during this period of history, the common status of entrepreneurial activities.

As from this time (mid and late 19th century), the promotion of the public interest was no longer a requirement for a company to formed. Still, the possible impact of bankruptcy on the economy was a matter of concern for the legislators who decided that the State and the creditors (e.g. suppliers, bankers, employees, etc.) should be able to ask for the dissolution of a company in case of unpaid debt. This shows that, from a legal point of view, the firm's stakeholders are not only the shareholders. As a consequence, the firm's interest, even if it is no longer directly bounded by the public interest, is still linked, for example, to the creditors interest when the existence of the company is at risk (especially through insolvency, but also when public order is jeopardized).

In civil law, the interest of the firm is considered different from the shareholder's interest[14] and is described as the interest of all its co-contractants. This means that the firm's interest is the superior interest of its stakeholders: an interest common to the shareholders, the employees, the providers of finance, services or goods, the customers, and the State.

Despite the fact that shareholders (mostly pension funds) tend to stay for shorter periods in companies' capital, it has been argued that all these stakeholders have the same interest in the long run and that shareholders, as they are less protected than other stakeholders (as they are not 'protected' by a contract, they have the fewest incentives to act in a different interest from the company's one), are the best representatives of the firm's interest. As obvious as it may seem (the survival and, if possible, the development of the firm is the common goal), the civil law recognises that a decision taken in the sole interest of the shareholders and different from the company's interest can legally be cancelled.

---

[14] The idea of a single and homogeneous interest is flawed: shareholders have individually different time horizons and different risk to different opinion.

These arguments show that shareholders cannot, in any situation, be considered as the only residual claimants of the firm. The fiduciary duties of the managers do not go to the shareholders: they must also take into account other stakeholders' interests because they are part of the company's interest. However, these arguments about the company's property do not lead to the conclusion that shareholders are not legitimate owners of the firm: they only state that they are not the only owners of the firm and that in certain cases, legitimate owners of the firm can also be other stakeholders. Depending on such cases, the stakeholders that should be involved are not always the same: this has to be defined by a contextualised approach.[15]

Conclusion

In conclusion, we consider that the theoretical mainstream framework of corporate governance (the agency theory and the property rights approach) must take into account that shareholders are not the only residual claimants of the firm and that the other residual claimants must be defined after an analysis of the situation. In this perspective, employees are not always residual claimants of the firm, but may be considered so, for example, in case of financial distress. Moreover, one must point that stakeholders do not have equivalent stakes in the firm and that this should also be taken into account. Our aim was not to destroy the foundations of the theory of corporate governance but to point out its limitations in order to improve the incentives it can produce.

The use of law's representations in order to test the assumption of the economic property rights approach can be regarded as successful. Applying the legal framework leads to an enhancement of the basis of the property rights theory. Instead of using philosophical and political objectives of law or economics to evaluate respectively economics or law, theoretical representations of both economics and law are crossed with respect to corporate governance. Within the framework of the introduction of law's representations in an economic theory (the property rights theory), perspective regarding governance issues (especially in this matter of corporate governance) has changed from a comprehensive approach based on aligning interests toward a new coherent framework relying on ethics and contextualisation.

---

[15] For further developments on this point see J. Lenoble, M. Maesschalk, *Toward a Theory of Governance: The Action of Norms*, Kluwer Law International, 2003.

References

A. Berle, G. Means, *The modern corporation and private property*, MacMillan, 1932.

T. Boyer, 'Gouvernement d'entreprise et décisions d'emploi', Thèse de doctorat en économie soutenue à l'Université Paris X, 2002.

CalPERS, 'Corporate Governance principles and guidelines', 2007, http://www.calpers-governance.org/principles/.

M. Despax, 1956, *L'entreprise et le droit*, thèse pour le doctorat en droit, publiée dans la collection 'bibliothèque de droit privé', LGDJ, 1957,

S. Grossman, O. Hart, 'The Costs and Benefits of Ownership: A Theory of Vertical and Lateral Integration', *Journal of Political Economy*, Vol. 94, 1986, p. 691.

J. Lenoble, 'From an incentive to a reflexive approach to Corporate Governance', in Cobbaut and J. Lenoble, *Corporate Governance: an institutionalist approach*, Kluwer Law International, 2003.

OECD, *Principles of Corporate Governance*, Paris, 2004.

J. Lenoble, M. Maesschalk, *Toward a Theory of Governance: The Action of Norms*, Kluwer Law International, 2003.

J. Paillusseau, 'Les fondements du droit moderne des sociétés', JCP, I, 3148, 1984.

T. Kirat, *Economie du droit*, La Découverte, Repères, 1999.

D. Kreps, 'Corporate culture and economic theory', Perspectives on positive political economy, Cambridge University Press, 1990.

J.-P Robé, 'Enterprises and the Constitution of World Economy', *International Corporate Law*, Vol. II, 2003.

R. Szramkiewicz, *Histoire du droit des affaires*, Montchrestien, Domat droit privé, 1989.

G. Teubner, *Le droit, un système autopoïétique*, PUF, collection les voies du droit, 1993.

L. Walras, *Éléments d'économie politique pure*, LGDJ, 1874, french re-ed. 1976.

O. Williamson, *The economic institutions of capitalism*, The free press /Macmillan, 1985.

Index

A

Accusation, 51, 66, 70, 109, 140
Activism, 16
Adjudication, 195, 204, 210, 215,
    219, 228, 272, 280–84
Advocating, 66
Agency theory, 326, 333
Allegory of Justice, 28
American culture, 29, 36, 87, 119,
    131, 155–57, 176–78, 188, 210,
    258
Amsterdam, 13, 198–203, 242, 321
Anonymity, 101, 104, 119, 150
Appeal, 112, 133, 150, 163, 260,
    297, 321
Arbitrary power, 175
Arbitration, 220, 293, 298
Architecture, 19, 118, 123

B

Bargain, 169, 222, 225, 259, 275,
    320, 326
Bayesian equilibrium, 279
Behavior (Impact of representation
    of Justice on —), 27, 158, 176,
    228, 290
Blogs, 226
Bourgeois idealism, 142
Bribery, 200, 316
Bureaucracy, 30, 36, 148, 185, 257,
    311, 312
Business Community, 290

C

Career (Law —), 9, 161, 317
Caricaturists, 39
Catholic Church, 261

Clothing, 49, 52, 118–24, 191
Colonies, 36, 55, 60, 66, 263, 310
Comic elements, 85
Commercial constraint, 117, 120,
    123
Commercial court, 49, 294
Common law, 99, 156, 164–66, 280
Country, 256
Court, 119, 203
Compensation culture, 257
Complexity of Law, 166–69, 320
Compliance, 189, 193, 198, 241
Confidentiality, 169, 223, 224
Conflict (political and social), 195
Consciousness (legal —), 25, 75, 89,
    176, 188, 238
Conspiracy, 44, 65, 83, 181–84, 198
Constitutional crisis, 242
Corporate governance, 325
Corruption, 31, 71, 112, 200, 294,
    314, 316, 320
Cost of Justice, 46, 213, 272, 293
Court room, 16, 52, 117, 254, 261
Courthouse, 123, 140, 158, 161, 204,
    212, 222
Criminal sanctions, 227
Criticism of Justice, 25, 29, 39, 68,
    250, 261

D

Damages, 53, 106, 180, 227, 262,
    273, 274, 277, 293, 297, 301
Databases, 208, 217
Defamation, 98, 103
Delaying tactics, 302
Democracy, 307
Detective, 23, 80, 126
Diegetic Justice, 28, 35, 140
Dignity, 49, 96, 118, 127, 161, 196,
    209, 228

Dilemma, 155, 161, 278
Discourse, 68, 228
  Colonial discourse, 61
  Discourse of law, 192
  Discourse of victimisation, 72
  Discourse on Law, 25, 61
  Intellectual discourse, 59
  Legal discourse, 33
Discretion, 298, 314
Dispute resolution, 197, 220, 232,
  308, 314–19
Documentary, 27, 75, 80, 84, 88,
  116–29, 131–51, 151, 160, 166,
  246, 260
Drama, 9, 79, 80, 84, 85, 117, 122,
  131, 140, 143, 147, 155, 165, 197,
  262
Dreyfus affair, 40, 60, 62, 71, 289
Due process, 33, 35, 176, 212, 215

E

Education (Legal —), 75, 163
Efficiency, 46, 276, 278, 281–84,
  293, 307, 311, 313, 318, 325–28
  Efficiency of the Justice system,
  34, 112, 318
Emotion, 120, 127, 140, 143, 161,
  177, 213, 223
Enforcement authorities, 33
Engagement, 16, 62, 66, 71, 75–78,
  175, 186–88, 193
England, 98, 163, 197, 206, 226,
  263, 313–16, 321
Epistemology, 131–33, 141, 148,
  325–27
Equity, 15, 250, 267, 319
Ethics, 18, 79, 155–57, 157, 159–64,
  168, 170, 251–56, 267, 333
Ethnocentrism, 68
European Court of Human Rights,
  107
European Union, 17, 19, 237, 239–
  45, 250, 259, 264
  European Court of Justice, 16–19,
  237–41

Evidence, 102, 115, 124, 133, 140,
  159–62, 169, 211, 216, 261, 266,
  320
Execution, 53, 63, 196, 209
Expectation, 15–19, 24, 90, 128,
  146, 149–57, 164, 167–90, 266,
  274–80, 285, 321
Expensive procedure, 299

F

Fair trial, 99, 100, 104–8, 264
Fairness, 15–18, 42, 101, 209, 230,
  250–55, 266, 287, 292, 301, 317,
  320–22
Female lawyer, 51, 160
Feminism, 182, 251
Fiction, 226, 250
Financial penalties, 243, 262
Firm's interests, 328
Formalism, 221, 301, 319
Forum, 63, 88, 99, 100, 193, 243,
  245
France, 23–39, 59–93, 95–114, 119,
  134, 145, 156–60, 166, 169, 200,
  238, 243, 263, 264, 289–303, 313,
  316, 321, 322
  French administration, 31, 64
  French law, 96, 113, 311, 316
  French revolution, 59
  French television, 88, 157, 158,
  160, 165–70

G

Game theory, 284, 287
Geneva, 17, 61, 200
Germany, 87–89, 108, 115–29, 141,
  226, 263, 293
  German Expressionism, 142
  German law, 36, 116, 119
  German occupation, 63
  German television, 115–26
Globalization, 119
Guilt, 34, 56, 85, 97, 109, 115, 140,
  162, 169, 198, 213

H

Habits, 112, 176, 190
Harmonisation, 104, 109, 113, 265
Hazard, 303
Hearings, 9, 10, 52, 56, 100–121,
   189, 203–18, 219, 224–27, 231,
   298
Hegemony, 177, 188, 191
Hermeneutics, 25, 132, 151
Hero, 50, 83–86, 126, 142–51
   Heroic lawyer, 84, 86, 145
Honesty, 161, 292, 320
Human Rights, 17, 95, 104, 108,
   206, 255–58, 264, 317
   European Court of Human Rights,
   104–8, 113, 256, 259, 266
Humour, 52–56, 78, 159

I

Ideology, 60, 66, 70, 73, 132, 134,
   142, 146–49, 175–78
Illusion, 42, 46, 132, 137, 142, 146–
   51
Imagery, 16, 157, 209, 231
Impartiality, 97, 105, 310
Independence of Justice, 292, 309–
   17
Information (asymmetrical —), 280,
   328
Injustice, 32, 47, 55, 63, 67, 70, 73,
   85, 150, 228, 249–55, 266
Innocence, 46, 47, 85, 97, 102, 108,
   133, 321
Inquisitorial procedure, 166, 263
Instrument of Justice, 70
Intellectuals, 61–66, 72
Interest pressure groups, 243, 282
Internet, 17, 209–12, 226, 239
Interpretation of Law, 272, 280, 284
Interviews, 121, 125, 166, 183, 230,
   303
Intimidation, 46, 300
Investigation, 30, 66, 69, 102, 107,
   126, 253, 301
Ireland, 23, 29, 59, 95–114, 263, 293

J

Journalist, 40, 66, 97–101, 106–23,
   256
Judicial disciplinary, 159
Judicial obligation, 163
Judicial process, 81, 95, 113, 291–94
Judicialisation of human relations,
   27, 242
Juge d'instruction, 41, 112, 157
Jurisprudence, 190, 257, 264, 301,
   303
Jury, 18, 44, 47, 51, 77, 81, 101, 119,
   140, 142, 145, 165, 261, 283, 314,
   316
Justice
   Blind Justice, 35
   Notion of —, 59, 60–63, 69, 249–
   52, 263
   Quality of —, 319, 320
Justification, 15, 61, 137, 193, 203,
   207, 210, 228, 231, 319, 332
Juvenile legal system, 80, 103

K

Kuleshov experiments, 139

L

Language, 29, 33, 109, 118–22, 132–
   35, 142, 147, 168, 181, 205, 208,
   219, 299
Law and popular culture, 134
Law firm, 168
Law in action, 16, 25, 27
Lawsuit, 210, 224, 290, 292, 296,
   303, 317
Lawyer, 9, 10, 15–19, 39–57, 75–90,
   103, 109, 115–28, 133–74, 185,
   189, 192, 209, 213, 219–22, 230,
   250, 253–59, 277, 296, 300, 304,
   320, 325–30
   Corporate lawyer, 83, 161
   Entrepreneurial lawyer, 224
Legitimacy, 16, 32, 66, 71, 118, 121,
   140, 188, 231, 240

Literature, 23–29, 33, 75–79, 86, 90, 197, 263, 271, 275, 276, 281, 286, 322, 325
Litigation, 18, 95, 99, 109–11, 186, 189, 220, 224, 227, 243, 245, 271–90, 295–98, 310, 315
Lobbying, 243, 245, *See* Interest pressure groups

M

Malagasy Revolt, 63
Marxian economics, 271
Marxist rhetoric, 70
Meaning of Law, 175, 285, 286
Media, 9, 10, 15, 35, 95–114, 117–29, 157, 169–70, 173–89, 205–9, 205, 224–27, 246, 250, 254–66, 292, 298, 303
  Broadcasting decisions, 103
  Collusion between media and politicians, 128
  Court reporting, 123, 128
  Film audience, 132, 140–46, 150
  Film industry, 88, 142, 148
  Filmic persuasiveness, 142
Miscarriage of justice, 47, 164, 290
Mission civilisatrice, 66, 73
Mistrust, 249, 260
Morality, 251, 271
Movie, 36, 77, 135, 160, 166, 184, 191
Murder, 53, 55, 109, 116, 123, 127, 140, 145, 162

N

Natural Law theory, 250–55
Neutrality, 35, 310
Norms, 18, 26, 28, 53, 161, 164, 176, 197, 205, 211, 215, 220, 226, 231, 284
  Production of norms, 196
  Professionnal norms, 161
Notables, 49, 314

O

Obedience, 195–97, 253
Objectivity, 254
Open court, 102, 113, 204, 216
Opinion polls, 290
Oppression, 33, 60, 71
Optimism, 72, 276–87, 318
Outsourcing, 215, 220, 225
Overconfidence, 286

P

Parliament, 40, 226, 310
Partners, 126, 156, 250, 304
Perception, 16, 26, 128–32, 140–43, 238, 274, 277
Photography, 150, 208
Police, 29, 33, 35, 53, 64, 67, 79, 83, 115, 166–69, 184, 227, 260, 310
Politics, 16, 30, 40, 57, 72, 82, 85, 120, 128, 134, 147, 182, 196–97, 212, 240–42, 255, 262, 283
  Political commitments, 197
  Political consciousness, 55
  Political correctness, 182, 258
  Political independence, 292
  Political lawyer, 16
Politician, 45, 57, 111, 127, 237, 250, 255, 262, 292, 295, 312
Popular culture, 134, 150, 175, 184, 246, 250
Press, 40, 89, 95–114, 122–24, 159, 178, 193, 206–27, 239, 257, 327
Private ordering, 310
Procedure, 16, 103, 110, 116–22, 176, 198, 203, 210, 212, 221–26, 243, 271, 290, 293, 296–310
Prosecutor, 47, 52, 53, 83, 93
Public
  Attendance, 216
  Exposure, 118
  Interest, 104–7, 122, 124, 317, 332
  Opinion, 16, 205, 289–95, 301, 303
  Service, 80, 161, 256, 258, 291, 310

Space, 193
Publication of decisions, 207
Punishment, 23, 33, 196, 228
Punitive damages, 301

R

Rational choice theory, 283
Redistribution, 278, 312
Regulation, 191, 210, 217, 255, 293, 308–12, 320, 322
Regulatory models, 293
Reporter, 116, 122–24, 159, 179, 204, 224
Reporting, 35, 99, 101–6, 106, 108–14, 122–24, 128, 174, 178, 183
Republican justice, 60–63, 69–73
Reputation, 42, 56, 63, 99, 105, 108, 112, 118, 122, 161, 187, 298
Revolution
    Industrial revolution, 331
    Revolutions in film, 143
Rhetoric, 28, 67, 139
Rights of audience, 198
Ritual (court —), 32, 118, 121, 195, 204
Robes *See* Clothing
Rules of law, 197
Rumour, 110

S

Sanction, 18, 97, 99, 106, 161
Scandalous cases, 124
Scene, 17, 41, 57, 83, 108, 123, 125, 136, 159, 162, 167, 169, 198, 200, 239
    Crime scene, 140
Scepticism, 41, 44, 57, 249
School, 87, 103, 110, 115, 123, 164, 173–93, 207, 212, 239, 256, 259
    Law School, 76, 78, 131, 195
Secrecy, 44, 102, 110, 113, 117, 223, 232, 298
Sedimentation, 190
Sensationalism, 112, 122

Sentence, 55, 65, 97, 103, 110–18, 123, 198, 209, 213, 227, 265, 293–98
Series, 9, 17, 31, 34, 39, 79–90, 79, 116–27, 155–70, 155, 180, 255, 258, 293, 321
Sexual connotation, 126, 179
Sexual harassment, 173–93, 227
Simplification, 16, 123
Sketch, 40, 45, 56
Social cultural context, 75
Social functions, 117
Social Justice, 27, 70
Social organization, 188
Social prestige, 49
Social problem, 179–84
South Africa, 226, 256
Sovereignty, 64, 205, 238, 241, 253, 259
Spectator, 52, 133, 137, 197, 204, 210, 217, 228, 231
State power, 121, 203, 229
Stereotype, 41
Stigmatization, 185
Storytelling, 133, 137, 139–43
Strategies, 134, 149, 164, 188, 215, 271–80, 290, 294–97, 300–304, 304
Subjective and objective perceptions, 141
Symbols, 19, 51, 118, 123
System of representation, 15, 16, 250, 251–54, 266

T

Tabloid, 257
Television, 9, 10, 18, 77–82, 86, 87–90, 104, 115–29, 155–58, 160–70, 184, 191, 257, 260–62
Tenure, 310, 317
Testimony, 115, 162, 165, 204, 216, 261, 300
Tests cases, 304
Torture, 64–71, 71, 102, 258, 264
Town Hall, 13, 198, 204
Traditions, 36, 95, 104, 112, 124, 196, 207, 210, 250, 252, 264–67

Trust, 83, 93, 167, 169, 292
Truth, 9, 15, 32, 57, 81, 115, 118,
    122, 125, 133, 135, 139–51, 165,
    190, 193, 204, 253, 289, 292, 298,
    303
TV programme, 88, 106

U

Understanding
    Normative —, 250, 254, 263
United Kingdom, 80, 88, 105, 123,
    238, 242, 258, 263, 317
United States, 60, 79, 81, 84, 88,
    142, 144, 156, 164, 168, 175, 195,
    206–15, 206, 220, 222, 225–29,
    230, 237, 246, 271, 275, 283, 317,
    318
Urban legend, 34
Utility function, 283, 314

V

Vengeance, 63, 210
Verdicts, 150

Violence, 33, 180, 196, 227, 309

W

Warrant, 162, 163, 185, 264
Witness, 9, 39, 41, 44, 46, 51, 53, 62,
    65, 82, 99, 103, 107, 115–20, 125,
    126, 132–35, 146–51, 155, 159,
    161–65, 204, 208, 209, 213, 228,
    231, 252, 260, 320
World Bank, 281, 293, 294, 297, 308

Y

Yugoslavia (International Criminal
    Tribunal for the Former—), 208

Z

Zeitgeist, 77, 90

Personalia

Mairead ni Bhriain is an IRCHSS Government of Ireland Scholar based in the Department of French at the National University of Ireland, Galway. Her current research interests include French intellectual and colonial history and representations of France and the french way of life.

Tristan Boyer has a PhD in Economics and a LLM in Corporate Law. He is the head of the Corporate Governance Unit in the Luxembourg School of Finance (part of the Université du Luxembourg). He is also associate researcher in the Centre de Philosophie de Droit of the Université Catholique de Louvain).

Alexander Conrad Culley, BSc (Hons) (Plym), LL.M. (Dub) is currently employed as the Compliance and Money Laundering Reporting Officer to Computershare Investor Services (Ireland) Limited. His research interests include international law, financial services law and banking law.

Dennis E. Curtis is Clinical Professor Emeritus of Law and Professorial Lecturer in Law at Yale Law School. His subjects include professional responsibility, legal profession, campaign financing, sentencing, and parole and post-conviction remedies. Professor Curtis received his B.S. from the US Naval Academy and his LL.B. from Yale.

Didier Danet is an Associate Professor at 'Ecole Spéciale Militaire de Saint-Cyr and Rennes University where he teaches Law and Management. His current research interests are in public and private governance, business law and competitive intelligence.

Bruno Deffains is Professor in Economics at University Nancy 2, where he teaches Law and Economics, Microeconomics and Public Economics. He is vice-director of the Bureau d'Economie Théorique et Appliquée (CNRS Unit) His current research interests concern the interaction between Law and Economics and more specifically the comparison between legal systems, liability law and conflict resolution.

Pascale Duparc Portier is a Lecturer in Law (Legal French) at the National University of Ireland, Galway. She holds a Doctorate in Law from the University of Montpellier, Masters in private Law and in Applied Languages from the University of Paris-X, France. Her main areas of interest are comparative law and linguistic rights as well as legal terminology.

Samuel Ferey is Assistant Professor in Economics at University Nancy 2, where he teaches competition policy, economic history and economic policy. He is member of the 'Bureau d'Économie Théorique et Appliquée'. His research field mainly concerns the history of ideas in Law and Economics and economic analysis of labor law.

Dominique Jeannerod is Lecturer at Queen's University Belfast. His current research interests are in detective novel, intertextuality and image theory, representations of power and history of ideas.

Dr. Theo Gavrielides is the Director of Independent Academic Research Studies (IARS) and the Head of Policy of Race on the Agenda (ROTA), a UK based policy think-tank. Dr. Gavrielides is a restorative justice and human rights expert with particular interest in issues of public & social policy, strategy and service delivery.

Dr. jur. **Ruth Herz** has been a Judge at the court of Cologne, Germany since 1974. She has taught Criminology at the University of Toronto, Toronto, Canada and at the Hebrew University Jerusalem, Israel. She introduced the 'victim offender mediation and reparation' as an alternative sanction for juvenile offenders to the German legal system for which she received the Medal of Merit of the State in 1998. From 2001-2005 she played the part of the judge in a daily court series on German television. She is currently Associate Researcher at the Centre for Criminology of the University of Oxford working on the portrayal of justice on television.

Thierry Kirat is CNRS Research Fellow at the Institut Interdisciplinaire de Recherche en Sociologie, économie et Science politique at the Université Paris-Dauphine. He teaches legal theory and Law and Economics in several universities in Paris. His current research interests are in socio-economics studies of law in the fields of labour law, public procurement law, and land-use conflicts.

Antoine Masson is currently working at the University of Luxembourg and collaborating to the CEPRISCA at the University of Picardie (France). He has been part-time lecturer at Trinity College and researcher at HEC-Paris. His topics of interest are in jurisprudence history of law, law and linguistic, European law, legal activism and legal strategies.

Claire Micheau is Researcher at the University of Luxembourg where she lectures European Law. After completing her law degree at the University of Cologne and University Paris 1 Sorbonne, she graduated with a Master's Degree in Global Business Law and Tax Law at Paris 1 Sorbonne and HEC, as well as an LL.M. at Trinity College (Dublin). As lawyer qualified for the Paris Bar, she also has a teaching background, having taught at the law schools of the University of Paris 1

Sorbonne and Trinity College. Her current research areas are European law and international economic law.

Kevin O'Connor is a qualified solicitor currently practising as an in-house counsel with a bank and is based in Dublin. He obtained the degree of Bachelor of Civil Law from University College Dublin in 1975 and was admitted to the Roll of Solicitors of the Law Society of Ireland in 1977. He also obtained a Diplôme en français juridique through the Law Society of Ireland.

Laurent Pech is Jean Monnet Lecturer in EU Public Law at the National University of Ireland, Galway. His research interests include the constitutional law of the EU and the protection of fundamental rights in the EU legal order.

Judith Resnik is the Arthur Liman Professor of Law at Yale Law School, where she teaches about federalism, adjudication, equality, sovereignty, and citizenship. Along with Dennis E. Curtis, she is writing a book, Representing Justice: From Renaissance Iconography to 21st Century Courthouses, which is under contract with Yale Press.

Peter Robson is Professor of Law in the University of Strathclyde where he teaches Law, Film and Popular Culture. His research interests include the impact of film and television images on legal culture and he is currently working on the link between the attitude of the jury and popular culture.

Jessica Silbey is Professor at Suffolk University Law School in Boston, Massachusetts where she teaches constitutional law and intellectual property. In addition to her law degree, Jessica Silbey has a PhD in comparative literature and film. Her research interests include cultural analysis of law, including intellectual property law, and the intersection of law and film (legal practice and the art of film making).

Susan Silbey is Professor of Sociology and Department Head of Anthropology at the Massachusetts Institute of Technology where she does research on the role of law in scientific laboratories, comparing the place of law in expert communities and popular culture. She is supervising research on the development of new safety regimes in research labs, the effects of laboratory organization on gender hierarchies in science, and variations in engineering education.

Solange Vernois is Senior Lecturer at Poitiers University where she teaches contempory art history. She is a member of the Gerhico research team. Her research interests include caricature, illustration, cartoon and relations between the arts.

Barbara Villez is Professor at the Department of English Studies, which she chaired from 2004-2006, at the University of Paris 8. She teaches legal language and culture in the law faculty of Paris 8. Her area of research is Justice and Image and has specialized in the analysis of the representation of Justice in television legal dramas and has published a book and numerous articles on this subject. She currently chairs the international network, Images of Justice.